上帝有形為喻無形乃實論　　艾約瑟敬撰

有形者必受統於無形故身為使而心為主無形尊而有形卑有

能造一切物而一切受造之物總以無造者為根無造者生一切有

造者不能有形者拙滯無形者精靈萬彙中之最精靈者為

一切物之根源即上帝是已有形之物耳得而聞其聲目得而觀其狀口鼻

得而知其氣味無形者則超於耳目口鼻之外有形者不能無所不在不能同

時而在各處上帝則無所不在烏得於形像中求之耶約翰福音一章云未

有人見上帝惟子在父懷者彰明之是上帝無形基督即其形上帝

無像基督即其像五章云基督謂門徒曰爾未聞其聲未見其形提

摩太前書六章云彼使永生處於光明衆不能至人所未見亦不得見願以

尊榮權力稱之永世靡暨此言無形之實證也其於默示錄中則言目見

上帝四章云我即感於聖神見在天有位亦有坐之者貌如碧玉瑪瑙有

意珩環繞其位是皆喻言也其五章所云執冊緘七印焉啟七緘亦

言也蓋聖言書於他處言及基督顯現終以人身而此忽以羔為言者

God's Chinese Son

GOD'S

The Taiping

太平天父上帝

天王洪日

天兄基督

CHINESE SON

Heavenly Kingdom of Hong Xiuquan

JONATHAN D. SPENCE

W. W · NORTON & COMPANY · NEW YORK · LONDON

The author gratefully acknowledges the following for their generous permission to reprint copyright materials: Australian National University Press, Canberra, for excerpts from Prescott Clarke and J. S. Gregory, *Western Reports on the Taiping: A Selection of Documents* (1982), permission applied for; Cambridge University Press for excerpts from C. A. Curwen, *Taiping Rebel: The Deposition of Li Hsiu-ch'eng* (1977); Stanford University Press for an excerpt from Dian Murray and Qin Baoqi, *The Origins of the Tiandihui* (1994); University of Washington Press for excerpts from *The Taiping Rebellion: History and Documents,* volumes 2 and 3, by Franz Michael, in collaboration with Chung-li Chang (1971); and Yale University Press for excerpts from Jen Yu-wen, *The Taiping Revolutionary Movement* (1973), and from Norman Cohn, *Cosmos, Chaos, and the World to Come: The Ancient Roots of Apocalyptic Faith* (1993).

The text of this book is composed in Granjon
with the display set in Arcadia
Composition and manufacturing by Maple-Vail Book Manufacturing Group.
Book design by Antonina Krass
Cartography by David Lindroth

Library of Congress Cataloging-in-Publication Data

Spence, Jonathan D.
God's Chinese son : the Taiping Heavenly Kingdom of Hong Xiuquan /Jonathan D. Spence.
   p. cm.
Includes bibliographical references and index.
ISBN 0-393-03844-0
1. Hung, Hsiu-ch'üan, 1814–1864. 2. China—History—Taiping Rebellion, 1850–1864.
I. Title.
DS758.23.H85S64   1996
951′.034′092—dc20   95-17245   CIP

ISBN 0-393-03844-0

W. W. Norton & Company, Inc., 500 Fifth Avenue, New York, N.Y. 10110
W. W. Norton & Company Ltd., 10 Coptic Street, London WC1A 1PU

1 2 3 4 5 6 7 8 9 0

For Chin Annping,
and to the memory of
Chin Yü-fu

Hong Xiuquan's hand-written response to Joseph Edkins.

This only surviving example of Hong Xiuquan's theological thinking in his own handwriting dates from the spring of 1861. The writing in black ink is by the Rev. Joseph Edkins, who visited Nanjing at that time, and constitutes an argument for the incorporeality of God. Edkins argues that all references to God's form, as they can be found in John's Gospel, the epistle to Timothy, the Book of Revelation, Isaiah, and Exodus, must not be taken literally but must all be read as figurative (yu).

Hong's comments are written across the same sheets in red ink. His displeasure can be seen at the very start, as he scores out Edkins' title and suggests his own version. In the seventh line of the essay, seven characters down, Hong erases the reference to Jesus being God's "only" son, and substitutes the word for "elder brother" (xiong). If Jesus were God's only son, then clearly Hong could not be Jesus' younger brother, and the change takes care of that. In the middle of line twelve, Hong erases the word "figurative" (yu) in relation to God's form, and writes in the word for "real" (shi). He makes the same change at the top of lines thirteen and sixteen. The heavy red scoring in the middle of the essay shows Hong's displeasure with Edkins' reading of Revelation.

At the end of Edkins' essay (see back endpaper) Hong scores out the last line which reaffirms the incorporeality of God, and writes out a poem of his own to clarify his theological points to Edkins. (The poem is translated below, p. 289.) On the back of the sheet on which he wrote the poem can be seen the imprint, also in red, of the massive Taiping state seal. Some of this red ink has bled through the paper and marked the top center of the poem. The scattered blobs of red ink across the poem reflect, perhaps, the agitation of the Heavenly King as he wrote out his response.

This document is printed here by courtesy of the British Library, Oriental and India Office Collections.

. . . and there shall be
Beautiful things made new, for the surprise
Of the sky-children.
                    —John Keats, "Hyperion"

Contents

List of Illustrations

List of Maps

Acknowledgments

In my struggle to understand the multileveled worlds of Hong Xiuquan, I have been helped by many friends and scholars. They need feel no responsibility for the way this book is shaped, nor for the errors of fact or fancy that it may contain, but I trust they will accept my gratitude. During two visits I made to Beijing in 1991 and 1993, and subsequently on his own visits to the United States, Wang Qingcheng was a particularly generous guide, sharing his own voluminous Taiping works, answering my endless questions, and introducing me to his former dissertation student Xia Chuntao, whose own knowledge and generosity thenceforth were equally boundless. It was thanks to Wang Qingcheng also that my wife, Chin Annping, and I were able to meet several of her grandfather Chin Yü-fu's former colleagues and students, giving us a sense of the powerful impressions that great scholar left behind him. Wang also introduced me to another leading Taiping scholar, Zhong Wendian, who looked after me in Guilin, and taught me much of the Hakka point of view. It was Zhong Wendian who in turn eased my route toward Guiping, and introduced me to my Jintian guide Huang Weilin. And it was thanks to Huang that for the first (and last) time I was able to sample the odorous Guiping lizard wine, and in his company in the mud and sultry heat of a Guangxi summer day that I saw the ribbon waterfalls flickering through the dense foliage in the foothills of Thistle Mountain. In Nanjing, it was Mao Jiaqi and Zhu Qingbao who served as my guiding spirits as I searched in the sprawling, smog-filled, broiling Yangzi city for echoes of the vanished New Jerusalem. And as if to round off all those quests, it was Willie Ruff in his flame-red Porsche who blared me into Shelbyville, Tennessee, on another summer's day, to show me where the Baptist preacher Issachar

Jacox Roberts stretched his spiritual muscles in the 1830s, before he heeded the call to China, and received his chance to teach the Bible to the future Taiping Heavenly King.

My special thanks also to Judy Chiu-ti Liu, whose combination of knowledge in Chinese Christian sources and classical Chinese made her an invaluable guide both to the newly discovered Taiping prophetic books and to the tracts of the early Protestant convert Liang Afa; to Laura McDaniel, for exploring the Baptist archives in search of Roberts, and the National Archives in search of renegades and diplomats; and to Min Ye, Richard Menard, Hong Xiang and her husband, Che Wei, Liang Kan, Wen-wen Liu, Yar and Mei Woo, Nicholas Spence, and others who helped with leads and translation. The staffs of many institutions and libraries were constantly helpful, not only in the various Yale collections, but in Harvard, New York, and Washington, D.C., and overseas, especially at the Oriental and India Office collections of the British Library in London (where Frances Wood, Linda Raymond, and Graham Hutt all went out of their way to help), at the British Library newspaper depository in Colindale, at the School of Oriental and African Studies in the University of London, at the Public Record Office in Kew Gardens, and in the Department of Prints and Drawings in the Victoria and Albert Museum. In Taiwan, I benefited from exploring holdings at the Academia Sinica and at the Palace Museum, and received much help from Chuang Chi-fa, Ch'en Kuo-tung, and Wang Ai-ling. At various lectures too, in Academia Sinica as at Bryn Mawr, Harvard, Washington University in St. Louis, and McGill, scholarly questions or follow-up correspondence gave me new ideas or corrected old errors.

Among experts on the Taiping period or religious fundamentalism who answered my letters of inquiry or shared their own riches of information were Stephen Averill, Richard Bohr, Ralph Covell, Joseph Davis, William Doezema, Linda Gerstein, Norman Girardot, Steven Leibo, Jessie Lutz, Susan Naquin, Eileen Scully, Audrey Spiro, J. Barton Starr, Barend ter Haar, and Yu Chun-fang. In Melbourne, Jack Gregory shared his thoughts and also gave me a precious copy of the invaluable book he and Prescott Clarke compiled on Western reports on the Taiping; in London, R. G. Tiedemann shared information from his ever-growing and long-awaited bibliography of Western-language materials on the Taiping; and on various occasions Rudolf Wagner shared his great knowledge of esoteric sources and unexplored archival treasures (which were sometimes in one's own backyard).

Some of the research, and much of the traveling and thinking that led at last to this book, were conducted while I was on a MacArthur fellowship. The parts that I wrote then I have now abandoned, but false starts are part of most absorbing ventures, and I am grateful to that free-fall fellowship for making such a period of experimentation possible. The chaos of my longhand drafts was reduced to order by the calm intelligence of my typist Peggy Ryan. Betsy McCaulley kept the world at bay when it had to be so. At Norton, both Donald Lamm and Steven Forman encouraged this project from its inception, and managed to keep me hard at work by the level of their excitement rather than by invocation of deadlines. And Chin Annping, through her love, energy, and unflagging common sense, ensured that I could be totally absorbed by Hong Xiuquan but not ensnared.

Foreword

The story of Hong Xiuquan and his Taiping Heavenly Kingdom is as strange as any to be found in Chinese history. Born early in the nineteenth century to a South China farming family of modest means, and for a time employed as a village schoolteacher, Hong soon found himself caught up in the turbulent crosscurrents of Western ideas that were being introduced to China during his youth. Of these, the most important to his fate were certain strands of Christian doctrine that had been translated into Chinese—along with the Bible—by a dedicated group of Protestant missionaries and their local converts. Some intersection of Hong's own mind and the pulse of the times led him to a literal understanding of elements of this newly encountered religion, so that the Christian texts he read convinced him that he was the younger brother of Jesus, imbued by his Father God with a special destiny to rid China of the conquering Manchu demon race, and to lead his chosen people to their own Earthly Paradise.

Borne aloft on the wings of such millenarian belief, Hong began late in the 1840s to assemble an army of the "God-worshiping" faithful, who by 1850 had coalesced into the Taiping Heavenly Army. It was at the head of this army that Hong fought his destructive yet triumphant way through southern and central China, until in 1853 his combined forces seized the mighty Yangzi River city of Nanjing. Here, in a community that was at once scriptural, imagined, and rooted in the soil, they created their Taiping New Jerusalem, which remained their base for eleven years until in 1864—after twenty million people or more in the regions under their sway had lost their lives in battle or from starvation—Hong and the remnants of his army perished in their turn from famine, fire, and sword.[1]

The roots of the apocalyptic visions that led Hong and his followers to this passionate catastrophe go back to the second millennium B.C. Before their emergence in that time period a different pattern of belief had prevailed in many cultures—most prominently the Egyptian, the Mesopotamian, and the Indo-Iranian. According to this prior understanding, the universe displayed a delicate but sustainable balance between the forces of order and prosperity on the one hand and the forces of darkness, chaos, and destruction on the other. In the words of *The Prophecies of Nefertiti,* the fluctuations of the river Nile were themselves proof of such a continuing pattern:

> Dry is the River of Egypt,
> One crosses the water on foot;
> One seeks water for ships to sail on,
> Its course having turned to shoreland.
> Shoreland will turn into water,
> Watercourse back into shoreland.[2]

In those days, death was seen as a silence and a perpetual waiting, without hope of an awakening. Though there might be various forms of solace brought by burial with precious possessions, and from the attention of those who survived one, there was no way back to life. In the words of the Sumerian *Epic of Gilgamesh,* death took one to the terminus:

> To the house from which he who enters never goes forth;
> To the road whose path does not lead back;
> To the house in which he who enters is bereft of light.[3]

But starting perhaps as early as 1500 B.C. the Persian seer known as Zoroaster or Zarathustra gave rise to a pattern of belief we have come to call millenarian, in that it promised the possibility of a final world in which there would be "cosmos without chaos," a world of "making wonderful," without imperfections, an eternal peace beyond history, a changeless realm ruled by an unchallenged god.[4] Resonant and immensely powerful, these beliefs entered the thinking of many peoples, not least those of Syro-Palestine, through whom they inspired the biblical prophetic visions of Jeremiah, Daniel, and Ezekiel, and through them came down to Jesus of Nazareth and his later follower the author of the Book of Revelation. These teachers and prophets foresaw that before this new world was attained there would be a final, apocalyptic battle between the two forces, a battle in which, after much agony, the good would triumph and the evil be driven from the earth.

Quite independently as far as we know, and somewhat later, a similar shift occurred in China. The elements of both balance and closure had been long accepted by the Chinese, finding their most famous expression in the *Book of Changes* during the first millennium B.C. According to this text, the creative forces are at best a "wavering flight over the depths." In cases of conflict, "a cautious halt halfway brings good fortune," and each earthly attachment, like fire, "flames up, dies down, is thrown away."[5] In the fifth century B.C. work the *Lao Tzu,* which so influenced later generations in China, paradox, balance, and the absence of dogmatism were essential to each other. "Turning back is how the way moves," the author wrote. "Weakness is the means the way employs." In all our varied existences, "the myriad creatures carry on their backs the *yin* and embrace in their arms the *yang* and are the blending of the generative forces of the two."[6]

But these apparently established certainties eroded in China also, just as they had in other civilizations. Linked often to a transformation of that same *Lao Tzu* text whose message had once seemed to be so different, by the second century A.D. in China the idea of a "Way of Great Peace"—a "Taiping Tao"—had begun to take hold, along with a "Way of the Celestial Masters." These movements had messianic elements, in that they looked to a supreme deliverer who would force the human race from the miseries of its current state, and end history as it had been known by instituting the period of Great Peace. "Come quickly, join with me!" ran one of these second-century texts. "My followers are numerous. . . . I will not suddenly abandon you. . . . I myself will change destiny. In this present age I will choose the good people. You must not select yourself; by [your] upright behavior and self control I will recognize you."[7]

Between the third and sixth centuries these apocalyptic visions grew in sharpness and intensity, as different strands within Taoism and Chinese Buddhism complemented and reinforced each other. Now the coming period of destruction—marked by sickness, famine, the tyranny of cruel and arbitrary rulers, and often accompanied by a great and terrible deluge—was given a specific time in the near future. Only a handful of the human race, guided by a celestial savior and his representatives on earth, would survive this terrible period. When it was over, the faithful would draw together into their own ideal community, in which they would live at last in peace and harmony.[8]

From that time forward, both in China and in Europe, the millenarian and apocalyptic strains of belief stayed vigorously alive. And in both China and Europe, the proponents of these beliefs came to link them to radical political and egalitarian programs that brought numerous new followers from among the poor, and also led them at intervals into violent conflicts with the state. In China, across the whole span of time from the tenth to the nineteenth century, the state often blamed such uprisings on the followers of the "White Lotus Teachings," but in fact there was no one central teaching, rather a host of conflicting and competing centers of revelation and resistance.[9]

In Europe, too, the many strands of millenarian belief that had so challenged the Catholic church continued—with renewed intensity—after the Protestant Reformation. Transposed to the soil of colonial North America, the Puritan visionaries found what at first seemed the perfect setting for their various New Jerusalems and "praying towns." And though that vision faded in the face of eighteenth-century realities, even those who now attacked excessive liberty and equality still created their timetables for the end of the world and kept the worlds of Daniel and Revelation alive through their "federalist millennialism."[10] Especially through American Baptist missionaries, these impulses were carried back to China in the early nineteenth century, where they reinforced the message being brought by evangelical Protestant missionaries from the British Isles and central Europe. By the early 1830s these new forces were institutionally established in South China, ready to compete with indigenous Chinese elements for the loyalties of the youthful Hong Xiuquan. It is the outcome of that conjunction that is the subject of our story.

I feel fortunate that I was introduced to the many levels of Taiping history by Jen Yu-wen, one of the greatest scholars of that strange upheaval, whom my teacher Mary Wright invited to Yale in the late 1960s, so that he could complete an English-language digest of his imposing three-volume work on the Taiping Heavenly Kingdom.[11] But though I was fascinated by the Taiping, nothing then, or in the two decades following, led me to think that I would ever write on the Taiping myself. Not only Jen Yu-wen but literally hundreds of historians and editors in the People's Republic of China were at work on the Taiping, since the Communist authorities chose to view the Taipings as proto-socialists from whose experiences much could be learned concerning revolution, not least the fact that without the vanguard leadership provided by a disciplined Marxist-Leninist party, such peasant uprisings could never succeed. In addition, virtually all the known surviving Taiping documents had been translated into English in accessible editions, and it seemed to me that everything that could be known about the Taiping had been fully aired.

In the late-1980s, however, I became aware of two Taiping texts—printed in Nanjing in three volumes during the early 1860s—that had been found in the British Library in London. These texts recorded a protracted series of heavenly visions said to have been relayed through Jesus and his Father to their faithful Taiping followers on earth. Through the courtesy of the British Library, I was able to consult the new texts in the original and to make my own copy; and on a later visit to Peking I met their discoverer, Wang Qingcheng, and had a full discussion of their significance.[12] I came to realize that the discovery of these texts made it possible after all to take a fresh look at the Taiping.

One could of course argue that heavenly visions of the kind recorded in these newly found texts are not historical sources in any precise sense of the term. And yet the visions are fixed in space and time with such precision, and describe the behavior of specific Taiping leaders and their followers in such detail, that it seems to me they do illuminate the uprising in central ways. Furthermore they are so bunched as to offer us insight into two key Taiping periods: one group (those said to be from Jesus) being concentrated in the early years of the formation of the Taiping movement in the mountains of Guangxi province, and the other group (those said to be from God the Father) being focused on the early years of the Taiping rule in their New Jerusalem of Nanjing. The visions also relate to numerous other events in Taiping history: in the case of the two volumes dealing with Jesus' descents to earth, they give us much completely new information about the rural society of the time; and in the case of the visions of God the Father they give essential information on the interconnection of events in Taiping history with the visits of Westerners to the Heavenly Capital. Though to me the main interest of the new texts lies in the light they shed on Hong Xiuquan himself, they also help us understand the audience he attracted, and the way he and his followers responded to that audience. Such questions are of central importance as we try to grasp how millenarian leaders create a practical base from which to operate.[13]

Writing about Hong, I learned almost immediately, was writing about texts as much as about a man, and most especially about what many see as the text of texts, the Bible. Since I am no Bible scholar, and make no claims to be, this was a daunting prospect. But I was raised for over a decade in schools where the Bible was read daily, and I could see that there was no denying the strength, the inspiration, and the sense of purpose that Hong derived from the Bible, even though his response was intensely personal. Partly this was because the Bible was mediated for him in the

Chinese language, either through Chinese converts to Christianity or through Western Protestant missionaries with some knowledge of Chinese who had settled in China's southeast coastal towns. The fact that it was these random acts of translation, with all their ambiguities, errors, and unexpected ironies, that brought him to his faith and his sense of destiny, rather than any formal religious instruction, was doubly intriguing to me.[14] It not only reasserted the extraordinary dangers that may flow from the unguided transmission of a book so volatile, and thus highlighted the central importance of the West to Hong's story; it also helped me understand how Hong, when he at last acquired the Bible, made it so peculiarly his own. And because it was his own, after a period of reflection, he felt free to alter it, so that he could pass God's message on to his followers in an even "purer" form.

This book does not attempt to give a total picture of the Taiping movement, its formation, maturation, expansion, suppression, and effects on China as a whole. Many fine scholars have written on some or all of these aspects of the story, and I am happy to build on their work rather than attempt to duplicate it.[15] Instead, I focus on the mind of Hong Xiuquan and seek to understand—as far as I am able—how it could be that this particular man had such an astounding impact on his country for so many years. It is my belief that Hong's visions were shaped in some fashion by the overlapping layers of change that the Westerners were bringing to China along with their Christianity; these constituted an aura perhaps, as much as an influence, but an aura that was dense enough to give Hong a range of new feelings about the religious and social beliefs that he had absorbed at home as a child. When context is combined with vision in such a way, it seems to me, we can get at least an inkling of the logic that lay behind Hong's actions. This is not to deny that Hong's attempts at the social and religious transformation of China were often both muddled and inept. But it should help us to understand why he pursued the dreams he did, and why so many were willing to follow and die for him as he sought to make the dreams reality.

Many questions remain unanswerable, perhaps most crucially those linking Hong's own character to the Apocalypse he helped to cause. Did he have the faintest inkling, as he began during the 1840s to preach to small groups of farmers and migrant workers in the hills of Guangxi province, that the trail of events set in motion by his visions would lead to the deaths of millions of people, and would require a decade of the concentrated military and fiscal energies of some of China's greatest statesmen to suppress? It seems unlikely, for by identifying himself with the heavenly forces, Hong came to believe he removed himself from the ordinary judgments of humankind. But if he *had* reflected on it, the Book of Revelation, which he studied with great care, would have told him that such catastrophes had been long foretold, and that the chaos and horror were just a part of the glory and peace to come. I cannot find it in me to wish that Hong had succeeded in his goals, but neither can I entirely deny that there was true passion in his quest. As the epigraph to this book suggests, in the words of Keats, which themselves build on those of the Book of Revelation, Hong was one of those people who believe it is their mission to make all things "new, for the surprise of the sky-children." It is a central agony of history that those who embark on such missions so rarely care to calculate the cost.

West Haven, Connecticut
May 15, 1995

The great seal of the Taiping. This version of the Taiping state seal, measuring 20.5 centimeters square, was probably made in 1860 or 1861 during the last years of Taiping rule over their Heavenly Kingdom. The seal is in the form of an acrostic, and Chinese scholars have long debated the exact order in which the characters on the seal were meant to be read and interpreted. The most definitive recent interpretation, offered by Wang Qingcheng, suggests starting with the central characters at the top of seal, proceeding with alternating lines in the bottom half of the seal (fanning out from the center and reading from right to left) before concluding with the smaller outside characters in the top half. This yields the following reading:

The Taiping state seal:
[Of] God the Father,
The Heavenly Elder Brother Christ,
The Heavenly King Hong, the sun, ruler of the bountiful earth,
[And] the Savior and Young Monarch, the True King, Guifu.
Exalted for a myriad years, eternally granting Heaven's favor,
Eternally maintaining Heaven and earth in gracious harmony and convivial
   peace.

God's Chinese Son

1

W A L L S

 It's hard to be always on the outside, looking in, but these foreigners have no choice. They live crammed together by the water's edge, two hundred yards or so beyond the southwest corner of Canton's crumbling but still imposing walls. They climb often to the roofs of their rented residences, and gaze from there across the walls to the close-packed streets and spacious landscaped residences of the Chinese city that lie beyond. They are allowed to stroll along the west wall's outer edge and peer, past clustered Chinese guards, through the long dark tunnels that form the city's major gates. If times are peaceful, a group of foreign men by prearrangement meet at dawn and walk the city's whole outside perimeter, a walk that takes two hours or so if no one blocks the way. During the fire that raged all night near the end of 1835, and destroyed more than a thousand city homes, one Westerner clambered onto the walls to watch the flames; initially turned away by Chinese guards, he was allowed to return the next afternoon, and walk along the walls at leisure. But this was exceptional grace, and not repeated. Some, with permission, visit rural temples in the hills, which from their upper stories give a different angle to the view across the dis-

tant walls. Others scan old Chinese maps that let them place the city's
major landmarks in the context of the unwalked streets.[1]

In their frustration, the foreigners pace out the dimensions of their
allotted territory. It takes them 270 steps to cross the land from east to
west, and fewer still from north to south. Along the southern edge of their
domain, where the Pearl River flows, there is a patch of open ground, and
this the Westerners call their "square" or "esplanade." But 50 paces from
the shore rise the solid fronts of the buildings where they live, and these
fill almost all the space remaining, save for three narrow streets that intersect them from north to south, closed at night by gates. Here, in 1836, live
307 men—British and Americans, in the main, but also Parsees and Indi-
ans, Dutch and Portuguese, Prussians, French, and Danes. No women are
allowed to be with them, and the 24 married men must leave their wives
in Macao, one hundred miles away, three days by sampan on the inland
waterways where travel is the safest. Twice, in 1830, defiant husbands
brought their wives and female relatives to visit them. But even though
the women came dressed in velvet caps and cloaks to hide their sex, and
stayed indoors all day, when they went out at night (a time chosen because
the shops were closed and the streets seemed empty) to see the sights,
excited shouts at once announced the arrival of the "foreign devil women."
The local Chinese lit their lanterns, and blocked the roads till all the
foreigners retreated back to their homes. And the authorities, threatening
to cancel all foreign trade unless the women returned to Macao, won their
point.[2]

Not that the life lacks compensations. There is money to be made, by
old and young alike, two thousand dollars in a few minutes if one deals
in opium and a buyer is in urgent need, smaller but still steady sums from
trade in tea and silk, furs and medicines, watches and porcelain and fine
furniture. The foreign community publishes two weekly newspapers,
printed on their own presses, which cover local news and feud and bicker
over trade and national policy. There is a fledgling chamber of commerce,
and two hotels where one can stay, for a dollar a night, in a four-poster
bed, with hot water for shaving, but no mirror. There is fresh milk to
drink every day, from the small herd of cows that the foreigners keep
always nearby, either in local pasturage or aboard specially adapted boats
that moor in the River. There is a small chapel that seats a hundred, a
dispensary, and a branch of the Society for the Diffusion of Useful Knowledge. There is even a new mail service, between the factories in Canton
and the city of Macao, collected Wednesdays and Saturdays, five cents a
letter and twenty cents a parcel, to replace the old letter boats, whose

volatile crews sometimes tossed the mailbags overboard, and left them bobbing in the water until they were rescued (if they had not sunk).[3]

The thirteen rows of buildings, known as "hongs," or "factories," rented from the small circle of Chinese merchants licensed by the state to deal with the foreigners, are spacious and airy. Many of them were destroyed by the great fire of 1822, but they have been well rebuilt, of granite and local stone and brick, two stories high near the waterfront, rising to three stories in the rear, and are better protected from fire than before, with well-designed fire pumps ready in the yards. Arched passageways give access and privacy within each of the thirteen lengthy structures, which are divided into contiguous apartments, storerooms, and offices, and shaded from hot summer sun by long verandas and venetian blinds; the men sleep well, despite the heat, on clean, hard rattan mats, or mattresses filled with bamboo shavings, unnostalgic for the feather comforters of home.

Each building is named for the foreign nation that rents most of the space within it. So one finds the Spanish and the Dutch, the Danish and the Swedish hongs, the English, the Austrian Empire's hong, and, most recently, the American. But these national labels are not exclusive, and the small community is interlayered among the thirteen hongs. Some of the buildings have billiard rooms and libraries, spacious terraces jutting out toward the river to catch the evening breeze, and grand dining rooms with gleaming chandeliers and candelabra shining on the silverplate and spotless table settings. Meals can be sumptuous, with solemn Chinese servants in formal hats and robes, silent behind every chair.[4] The inventory of one young American's personal possessions, as tabulated by watchful Chinese clerks, shows glimpses of this life: thirty knives and thirty forks, thirty glasses and decanters, one trunk of woolen clothes, shaving kit and mixed colognes, mirror, soap and candles, hat and spyglass, framed pictures, a gun and sword, fifty pounds of cheroots and 542 bottles of "foreign wine."[5]

There is friendship among the foreigners, and sometimes music. A red-coated band from a visiting ship plays in the square, to the delight of the Westerners, but to the astonishment and tonal anguish of the listening Chinese.[6] Or—a novelty first seen in 1835 at Canton—a steam-driven pleasure boat with band aboard takes parties down the river and into the beautiful, isle-filled sea.[7] And out beyond the harbor one can scramble up the narrow track to the top of Lintin Mountain, aided by fifteen bearers, and picnic there on a large flat rock, laid with a repast of poultry, fish, pastry, ham, and wine, while again a band that accompanied the climbers plays. Replete and rested, one can, if one chooses, slide back down the

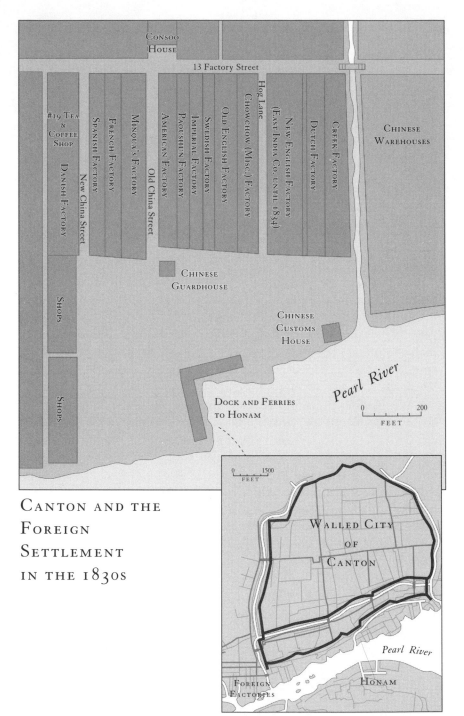

CONSOO
HOUSE

13 Factory Street

#19 TEA
&
COFFEE
SHOP

DANISH FACTORY

New China Street

SHOPS

SHOPS

SPANISH FACTORY

FRENCH FACTORY

MINQUA'S FACTORY

Old China Street

AMERICAN FACTORY

PAOUSHUN FACTORY

IMPERIAL FACTORY

SWEDISH FACTORY

OLD ENGLISH FACTORY

Hog Lane

CHOWCHOW (MISC.) FACTORY

NEW ENGLISH FACTORY
(EAST INDIA CO. UNTIL 1834)

DUTCH FACTORY

CREEK FACTORY

CHINESE
WAREHOUSES

CHINESE
GUARDHOUSE

CHINESE
CUSTOMS
HOUSE

Pearl River

DOCK AND FERRIES
TO HONAM

0   200
FEET

CANTON AND THE
FOREIGN
SETTLEMENT
IN THE 1830s

0   1500
FEET

WALLED CITY
OF
CANTON

Pearl River

FOREIGN
FACTORIES

HONAM

hillside on one's bottom through the long dry grass.[8]

Language might seem a problem, since in all of Canton and the foreign hongs there is no Chinese who can read or write in English or other European languages, and only a few Westerners who know enough Chinese to write with even partial elegance. This has not always been the case. In the 1810s and 1820s, when the East India Company was at its peak of power, there were a dozen or more young men from England studying Chinese in the Canton factories. They translated Chinese novels and plays, and even the Chinese legal code, so they could assess the equity of the government's rules more carefully. Though the local officials on occasion imprisoned Chinese for teaching their own language to foreigners, and even executed one, and Chinese teachers often had to shelter privately in their pupils' lodgings, the East India Company representatives fought back. By tenacity, they won the right to submit commercial documents in Chinese translation, rather than in English, and to hire Chinese teachers, for study of classical texts as well as Cantonese colloquial dialect. And though the company directors never won official acknowledgment of their right to hire Chinese wood-carvers, they went ahead anyway and block printed an Anglo-Chinese dictionary using Chinese characters; in addition, they managed to accumulate a substantial library of four thousand books, many of them in Chinese, which they housed in their splendidly appointed hong, with the company's senior physician doubling as the librarian.[9]

With the termination by the British government in 1834 of the company's monopoly of China trade, these glory days were over. Most of the language students and experts were reassigned to other countries; their finest teacher, Robert Morrison, died the same year; and the great library was scattered. Only three young men, who had been classified on the company's roster as "proficient" enough to receive an annual student's allowance, are left in Canton by 1836, and their main role is to be caretakers of the company's former buildings and oversee their closing down.[10] Nor are there any established bookshops to be found in the foreigners' restricted zone of residence, for specific laws forbid the sale of Chinese books to foreigners, and even make it a crime to show them one of China's local histories or regional gazettes. Those who wish to search out books must walk some distance to the west, where two bookshops on a side street (a street with gates locked and barred at night) will break the law to the extent of selling novels, romances, and "marvellous stories" to the foreigners, and sometimes arrange for purchases of other titles from the larger stores within the city.[11]

But years of experience have led to the growth of a language shared by nearly all who live among the foreign hongs, a language known as "Canton Jargon" or "Pidgin English." This serves to keep the differing communities in touch, by mixing words from Portuguese, Indian, English, and various Chinese dialects, and spelling them according to Chinese syntax, with *r* transformed to *l*, and *b* to *p*. "Pidgin" itself comes from the word "business," via its intermediate mispronunciation "pidginess"; gods are *joss* from Deos; and a religious service is thus a "joss pidgin." Sex is "lof-pidgin." Thieves become *la-de-loons* from ladrao, ships become *junks*, markets *bazaars*, lunch *tiffin*, a letter a *chit*, one who commands (mandar) a *man-ta-le* or *mandarin*, a document a *chop*, an urgent document *chop-chop*, one hundred thousand of anything a *lac*, a laborer a *coolie*, a conference a *chin-chin*, one's good acquaintance *number one olo flen*.[12] Double *ee* is added after dental consonants, so want becomes *wantee*, catch *catchee*. Chinese shopkeepers have at hand little books of terms compiled locally as guides to business, guides in which the Chinese characters for a given object are also glossed below, with other characters suggesting—in Cantonese dialect—the way to say the English. Scales are rendered *sze-kay-le-sze*, January *che-na-li-le*, west wind *wi-sze-wun*, and one-two-three *wun, too, te-le*.[13] Thus can the wealthy merchant Howqua, forewarned that a senior Chinese official is coming to demand a massive bribe, say with resignation to a young American trader "Man-ta-le sendee one piece chop. He come tomollo, wantee too-lac dollar," and everyone knows what he means.[14]

Even though the city of Canton is closed to Westerners, Chinese life enfolds them in their little enclave. The riverbank is lined with boats of every size and shape, so that one can barely see the water. There are cargo boats from up-country, passenger craft, floating homes and floating brothels, drifting fortune-tellers, government patrol ships, barbers' boats, boats selling food, or toys, or clothes, or household notions.[15] And mixed with these amid the din are the ferryboats that run from the jutting pier at Jackass Point across the river to Honam Island, with its tea plantations, ornamental gardens, and temples where the Westerners are—at intervals—permitted to take the air.[16] There are eighty of these little ferry craft, each holding eight passengers, and charging a standard fee of two copper cents a passenger, or sixteen for the whole boat, if one wishes to travel alone. And there are the larger floating theater boats, where the actors rehearse their plays as they travel from location to location between engagements, and where opium is provided to all visitors with the ability to pay.[17]

If the owners of such floating pleasure palaces by smile and gesture invite the foreigner aboard in hopes of financial gain, the same commercial motive is not present in all those one meets, and genuine hospitality or warmth is by no means lacking. The workers from a wheat-grinding mill, washing their bodies after a day of work, and munching their meal of rice and vegetables, welcome a visitor to view their eleven huge grinding wheels, and the oxen who drive them. A noisy group of carpenters and masons, gathering at sunset to eat and drink beneath an awning spread across an angle of the street for shade and shelter, beckon a passing Westerner to join them. Gangs of tough, barefoot or grass-sandaled, almost naked coolies, after waiting patiently for hours in the sun for casual work, squatting or standing amidst the stalls and markets, each with his bamboo pole with ropes dangling empty, still greet one cheerfully and show nothing but good will.[18]

The foreigners know some of the Chinese they deal with by name, or at least by Western variants of their Chinese names. Among these are the hong merchants, thirteen in all, who have the formal monopoly on foreign trade, own the buildings in which the Westerners live, and filter all their petitions and complaints to the higher authorities, and whose own huge homes and warehouses flank the thirteen factories to west and east along the Pearl River: Howqua, Kingqua, Pwankhequa, and the rest. The official "linguists," five in 1836, who travel door to door with crucial messages, which they deliver in their hybrid Pidgin English—Atom, Atung, "Young Tom," Alantsei, and Aheen—are known to all.[19]

Others have become known in their role as patients, carefully recorded in the registers of Dr. Parker's dispensary and hospital, opened in late 1835 on the second floor of number 7, Hog Lane, rented for $500 a year from Howqua. Atso, the rice merchant, the girl Akae, Matszeah, the scribe in the governor's office, Changshan, the soldier, Pang she, the seamstress, 925 of them in all, just between November 4, 1835, and February 4, 1836, with cataracts, tumors, abscesses, deafness, partial paralysis, and a score of other woes.[20]

At first glance, Hog Lane is an unlikely site for such benevolent work, but number 7 is at the north end of the narrow street, away from the river, near the busy Chinese thoroughfare that marks the northern boundary of the foreigners' domain. As Parker explains his choice, his "patients could come and go without annoying foreigners by passing through their hongs, or excite the observation of natives by being seen to resort to a foreigner's house." Bamboo strips, numbered in Chinese and English, are issued by the porter downstairs to each patient who comes to seek treatment (some

The Canton Factories. The world that the Western merchants created for themselves in the restricted area of residence that the Chinese allowed them southwest of Canton found its greatest chronicler in the British painter George Chinnery (1774–1852). Chinnery settled in Macao in 1825, and made this drawing of the Canton American factory in 1826 (below). Chinnery also liked to sketch the Western residents of Canton, and it was in 1832 that he made this drawing of the protestant missionary Karl Gutzlaff dressed in the garb of a Fujian fisherman. A brilliant linguist, Gutzlaff often travelled the coast of South China in such clothes, preaching in various Chinese dialects, and distributing Christian tracts in Chinese translation. On one of these trips, in 1835, Gutzlaff took along the American missionary Edwin

Stevens; in 1836 Stevens gave a set of Christian tracts to the young Hong Xiuquan, later to be the self-styled Taiping Heavenly King.

Chinnery also trained a number of Chinese painters, one of whom made this panoramic view of the factory area in the later 1830s (above). The American factory had been partly rebuilt since Chinnery's earlier sketch, and we can see that some of the other factories had fenced in several areas of the once open esplanade to make private gardens. The entire factory area as depicted here was looted by the Chinese during the warfare of 1841, and burnt to the ground the following year.

have been waiting outside all night), and they are received in turn on the upper floor, where Parker deals with all he can manage. Their ages range from six to seventy-eight, and there are women as well as men, and in large numbers, to his surprise: "Difficulty was anticipated in receiving females as house patients, it being regarded [as] illegal for a female to enter the foreign factories," as Parker put it, but with male relatives usually in attendance, to watch over them and prevent any whispers of impropriety, "the difficulty has proved more imaginary than real," and female patients number around one-third of the total.[21]

Others, nameless to the observers, give a fuller sense of Chinese life. Two blind girls, nine years old at most, walk to the esplanade, holding on to each other and clutching their wooden begging bowls, laughing and chatting despite their rags, bare feet, and lice.[22] A traveling librarian, banging his rattle, his current stock of popular novels packed into boxes dangling from a bamboo pole across his shoulder, evades the rules that apply to bookshops by walking from door to door in search of customers among the Chinese clerks and coolies. He shows his wares to foreign questioners, and tells them he has no complaints. The three hundred volumes he is carrying—small, light, paperbound—are but those remaining from over a thousand he currently has out on loan.[23]

On the esplanade are rows of stands, whose owners—each with a distinctive cry—sell fruit and cakes, sweets and soup, dogs, cats, and fowl, slabs of horsemeat with the hooves still attached and strings of dried duck tongues, shaped like awls and hard as iron to the touch.[24] Others lure viewers to their peephole boxes, decorated brilliantly in red, or erect a tiny stage on which to mount their puppet shows. Old women sit on the ground, with needle and thread, to mend your clothes, or play a game of chance together, the prize a pair of shoes; a healer presses bamboo cups to men's naked backs, to draw the blood; tinkers at their stalls mend locks and pipes, drill broken glass and porcelain and mend the shards with finest wire, sharpen razors, fill cracks in metal pots. Bird fanciers squat in solemn circles, some with their precious birds in cages, others with birds perched on sticks, or cradled in their hands.[25]

Three streets cut through the foreigners' businesses and residences, dividing them into four blocks of unequal width. All are densely packed with shops. Old China Street, the widest, is twelve feet broad, New China Street and Hog Lane a little less. The streets in general are so narrow that it's almost impossible to move, and one is jostled by the crowds, or bumped harshly by the coolies carrying palanquins with passengers, or massive loads.[26] Buddhist nuns with shaven heads, Taoist and Buddhist priests, ratcatchers with a dozen or more of their captured prey dangling in rows from bamboo poles, fortune-tellers, itinerant doctors, money changers, sellers of the finest fighting crickets that have been collected from the hills outside the town—all join the throng.[27] The shops that sell expensive goods the foreigners might like to buy have signs in Roman letters to render the owners' names and English descriptions of their treasures: carvings of ivory, turtle shell and mother-of-pearl, silks of all kinds, lacquer ware, and paintings of insects and fruits, or of famous battles, where red-coated Englishmen in cocked hats sit rigidly in rows under the relentless fire of Chinese guns. For every item purchased you must get the shopkeeper's chop or seal on your invoice, else it will be confiscated as you leave Canton.[28]

One June evening in 1835, at the entrance to a side street leading to the more affluent Canton suburbs, a dead baby lies in a basket among the rubbish, its body doubled up and its head, slightly swollen, dangling over the basket's edge. So narrow is the way, at this spot, that a Westerner, returning from a stroll in the countryside, has to step over the basket, noticing the contents only when his foot is in midair. As he stares in shock and bewilderment at the baby's face, a group of Chinese bystanders gaze, in equal bewilderment, at him.[29]

THE WORD

The Reverend Edwin Stevens has been in Canton since October 1832. His sights are set on higher things, for in Yale College he was caught up in the great religious "awakening" that swirled through New England, was ordained a minister after study in the New Haven Theological Seminary, and accepted a posting to Canton as the chaplain of the American Seaman's Friend Society. Living in the American hong, he has followed a rigorous schedule of study, preaching, and tract distribution, commuting on Saturdays down the Pearl River on whatever foreign longboat can offer him a ride to the main anchorage for ocean vessels at Whampoa, and returning thence each Monday. When Stevens cannot find a foreign boat, he must hire the local Chinese boatmen to take him to his duties. It is four Spanish dollars for the twelve-mile passage, and about three and a half hours rowing and sailing time when against the tide, with mandatory checks at every customs station. Even this short trip has its dangers. Foreign officers and sailors, traveling the same route, have been waylaid by Chinese ruffians, and robbed or held to ransom. Stevens sometimes finds it hard to persuade ship's captains to let him use their decks or cabins for his services, for some find him "austere and unsocial," since he shuns everything "vain or sportive," and devotes his energies to combating the evils of strong drink, visiting the sick and dying, and giving the dead a Christian burial.[1]

The seamen to whom he preaches are often in desperate enough straits after long months at sea packed ten or more in cabins twenty feet long and half as wide, driven wild by the excitement of three days' shore leave granted after their long voyage from Philadelphia or from Liverpool. The Chinese compound the turmoil by selling to the thirsty sailors the local brand of drink they call "firewater," a blend of raw alcohol, tobacco juice, sugar, and arsenic, which causes, writes Stevens, "a degree of inebriety more ferocious than that occasioned by any other spirit." Inside Hog Lane, where the establishments that cater to the foreign seamen have their own alluring signs spelled out in Roman letters, "Old Jemmy Apoo," "Old Good Tom, old house," and "Young Tom, seller of wines of all kinds and prices,"[2] this firewater can "destroy the reason and the senses" of its drinkers, oftentimes leading the sailors from their initial euphoria into "riotous scenes of the greatest enormity." Despite the fact that the drunken sailors are often robbed and even stripped by Chinese toughs, and that the government issues constant edicts against the sale of liquor to foreigners, the sailors always return for more, preferring the risks of Hog Lane to the more sheltered tea and coffee shop at number 19, New China Street, which worried Christian philanthropists have set up for them.[3]

Other temptations abound. Those Westerners who like to chart such things believe there are eight thousand prostitutes or more in the Canton area. Some are unreachable behind the city walls, but many others can be found in the enclave of Honam Island that the sailors have affectionately named Portsmouth Point, where the coolies employed by foreigners also congregate. And every sailor or preacher rowing up the river has seen other women preening themselves on the decks of their "flower boats," small feet or large, red jackets or green, butterfly shoes and silver anklets, rising and falling at their pilings with the tides.[4]

To add to the lures, small and nimble "wash boats," paddled by three or four women, dressed in the dark and faded trousers and jacket of the locals, but with brightly colored head scarves over their hair—a fashion garnered from the Portuguese—will pull alongside the foreign vessels as soon as they moor, offering a wealth of promise besides the laundry in their cheerful greetings: "Ah, you missee chiefee matee, how you dooa? I saavez you long tim, when you catchee Whampoa last tim."[5] The banter ought to lead no further, since nominally each foreign boat has two Chinese officials on board for the duration of its harbor stay, but such rules are laxly followed. Nominally, too, no liquor that might loosen the rules is ever brought on board, but sailors smuggle drink onto their ships in every way, from waterproof containers tied to their waists to entire ballast casks from their longboats filled with firewater.[6] No wonder the congregations are sometimes muted of a Sunday. "Preached this day in the *Splendid*," Stevens notes in his journal, "to an audience of some 80 or 100 hearers, from the text, 'Fools make a mock at sin.' I enjoyed considerable freedom and there was the best attention; but I saw no apparent conviction of sin, or sorrow for it." A week later, preaching to the officers and crew of the *Otters Pool,* with the Bible's soothing words "Come unto me all ye that labor and are heavy laden, and I will give you rest," Stevens finds that "no one seemed deeply affected."[7]

But Stevens accepts such apparent setbacks as part of a wider plan, as he tells his congregation in a Sunday sermon: "The word of the Lord has been thoroughly tried in all ways. It has been tried by history, and not found wanting. It has been tried by astronomy, by geology, by argument, and by ridicule. It has been tried during thousands of years by every man who pleased, in every way he chose; by all the learning which could be brought against it, by the conceited and the ignorant; by friends and foes, by him that believed and him that believed not. It has stood all trials."[8]

To deepen his understanding of Christian missionary work in China, Stevens has talked at length with a Chinese Christian from Canton, Liang Afa. Born in 1789 to a poor family, Liang received only four years of schooling before he had to find work, first as a maker of writing brushes, and then as a carver of the wooden blocks used in book printing. Liang was plying this trade near Canton when in 1815 the Scottish Protestant missionary William Milne hired him—even though Liang was at this time a devout Buddhist—to work on the blocks of a series of religious tracts and sections of the Bible that Milne and his Protestant co-missionaries were currently translating. Among Liang's first tasks in this new employment were the printing of Chinese versions of Deuteronomy and Joshua, by means of which he learned something of the Bible's content and structure.[9] This knowledge was soon deepened, for Milne was an exacting master who insisted that all those in his employ attend his daily Christian services, whether they believed in Christianity or not. Even though among the Chinese listeners "some would be talking, some would be laughing at the novelty of the doctrines preached, and some smoking their pipes," Milne was undismayed. Preaching in Chinese, he challenged his congregation to see the falsity of the Buddhist ways to salvation, and to choose the harder yet truer roads of Jehovah and Jesus. After much internal struggle,

Liang was won over, and on a November Sunday in 1816 he received baptism from Milne's hands.[10]

Believing, Liang began to write. He called his first Chinese tract "An Annotated Reader for Saving the World." In thirty-seven pages he told of God's power as creator, and of His Ten Commandments, and used a variety of Paul's epistles to describe God's anger and His mercy. Carving the wooden blocks himself, Liang printed two hundred copies, and had just begun distributing them in and around Canton during the spring of 1819 when he was arrested by the Chinese authorities, imprisoned, fined, and savagely beaten. The officials also confiscated Liang's house and burned all the wooden printing blocks that he had made. Undeterred, over the ensuing months he converted his wife to Christianity and baptized her in person. Shortly thereafter, the couple prevailed on Robert Morrison to baptize their son.[11]

After Milne's death in 1822, Liang worked for the London Missionary Society as an evangelist and Chinese-language teacher, and was himself ordained as a preacher in 1827. During these years he struggled to compose a longer work in Chinese that would fully develop his ideas on Christianity and serve as an introduction to the full range of his newfound faith, and in 1832 he was done. He titled his book *Quanshi liangyan*— "Good Words for Exhorting the Age"—and after asking the Chinese-speaking Western missionaries to check it over for theological faults, Liang printed the book in Canton the same year.

In the nine chapters of this book, Liang tried to encapsulate all he had learned from his fifteen years with the Westerners. He quoted passages, both long and short, from the Old and the New Testament, transcribing the strange-sounding biblical names into Chinese characters by sound rather than sense, just as his missionary teachers had. He told of the fruit the serpent led Eve and Adam to eat and of their expulsion from the garden of Eden. He told of Noah's Ark and the great flood that destroyed almost everything on the earth. He told of the destruction of Sodom and Gomorrah. He warned his people with the words of Isaiah and Jeremiah, and encouraged them with chants of Psalms 19 and 33. He recorded all of Jesus' Sermon on the Mount from Matthew's Gospel; and gave the last chapter of the Revelation of John the Divine, which sealed the book for all time with the terrible oath of the Lord. Liang commented on those passages, sometimes briefly, other times at length, as he explored the mysteries of God's grace and the range of human failings; he offered his own ruminations on fate and faith; and, in chapter 6, wrote out his own spiritual autobiography for all to see.[12]

Liang Afa was an expert at the printing and distribution of tracts. He traveled constantly by boat and on foot among the villages around Canton, choosing the perfect blocks, hiring extra carvers when he could find them (bargaining with them for the best price), then collating their labors while another Christian Chinese friend, named Agong, stitched the works into neat volumes. The two men also learned to use the new lithographic press that the missionaries made available to them, and were soon able to produce single broadsheets with an illustration on one side and a short text on the other, or lengthy and complex evangelical works.[13]

By the time Edwin Stevens met him, in 1832, Liang had begun a program of roaming the countryside around Canton, traveling as much as 250 miles and handing out as many as seven thousand Christian tracts on a single journey. Protestant missionaries had already begun illegally to prowl China's coast by sea, dropping off Bibles or tracts wherever they could go ashore. Now Liang developed a new strategy: together with Agong, he began to follow the itinerary of the Qing dynasty officials who went from town to town to administer the local Confucian examinations, hoping thus that his tracts would reach the hands of the examination candidates, an influential audience—if not necessarily a sympathetic one.[14] By the mid-1830s Liang had refined this strategy further, and began to hand out his tracts near the examination hall in Canton city, where those who had proved successful at the local towns' qualifying examinations met to be tested for the second time. In no other place in southeast China could one find a larger gathering of Chinese of proven education and of potential influence in their country's life.[15]

Stevens quickly saw the benefits of spreading the Christian message by means of the printed word:

> To have any sort of access to ten or twenty millions, and to leave there the Christian Scriptures and books, which may preach during the necessary absence of the living herald, is very different from entire exclusion. Nay, who will believe that of the many thousand volumes circulated there during the last three years, all are forgotten before God, and will "return void?" May we not rather indulge the hope, that at this very time these tracts are giving instruction to the inmates of some humble Chinese dwelling on the coast; yea, even carrying the true light from heaven into some heart that was lost in the darkness of paganism?[16]

One need expect no political revolution in China, thought Stevens, "we do not speak of a growing public sentiment in China, as in other countries, which is soon to burst forth in a universal call for rational liberty and the natural rights of man." But the Chinese were "as intelligent and as wronged as the lamented Poles," and had a natural openness that—were their government leaders absent—led them to see the foreigners as their friends, and to be potentially open to the Christian message.[17]

That being so, how close could a Westerner in this environment come to emulating Liang? In two lengthy and adventurous expeditions with Chinese-speaking Western missionaries, one in the spring and one in the autumn of 1835, Stevens put one side of these dreams of wider tract distribution into effect. Taking temporary leave from his Whampoa ministry, he shipped out of Canton on an American brig, cruising along the coast of China, as far north as the mountainous inlets of Shandong, exploring the narrow waterways and mudflats of the river Min in Fujian, negotiating the wide stretches of the Woosung River that led him at last to see the serried masts of the Chinese vessels in Shanghai. The trips elated Stevens, both for the number of tracts distributed and for the beauty of China, especially the coastal reaches of Fujian, which few Westerners had ever seen before. And as the foreigners sailed back, out of the local residents' lives, Stevens could reflect how he had left behind him several hundred "volumes of books, which may teach the way of salvation," books that would remind the Chinese "of the kindness of foreigners, long after the noise of the present events had died away."[18]

In the brigs' longboats, with a mixed crew of Lascars and Malays, lying under a tarpaulin slung aft among the piled supplies of rice, oil, vegetables, and meat, or else hiking on foot among the fields and villages of the busy countryside, Stevens traveled with his boxes of Chinese Christian books, prepared so laboriously by Milne, Liang, Morrison, and others: translated lives of Christ, commentaries on the Ten Commandments, collections of homilies, Gospel elucidations, hymns. He and his companions distributed several thousand copies on the first voyage, more than twenty thousand on the second. Chinese government war junks, full of troops, often shadowed the brigs, and Chinese patrol boats glided along behind Stevens' longboat as he probed the inner waterways. Once a cannonade was fired at his boat, and two crewmen wounded. Mounted Chinese military officers sometimes warned back the Chinese villagers, plainclothes policemen mingled with the crowds, students from local schools cried out in protest against the anti-Confucian Christians, and one grim day the local officials shredded an entire consignment of his books in front of his eyes, dropped the pieces in a basket of loose-packed straw, and set them afire.

But despite such interdictions the books left Stevens' hands as fast as they could be unloaded and carried ashore. On some days the crowds were eager and smiling, neat and courteous, as the decorous distribution proceeded; on others, they pressed around with such uncontrollable force that Stevens clambered up on walls to escape the grasping hands, or flung the books and tracts at random up into the air above the waving arms of the potential converts. Sometimes, in lonely villages, he laid a copy on the stoop of every home. Once a huge crowd stood sodden and motionless in the driving rain as—equally soaked—Stevens shared the word. Once the Chinese onlookers stood around him with fingers on their lips, showing him they had been forbidden by their officials to speak aloud to foreigners. Yet still they took the books, as did priests in Buddhist temples, and scholars in their homes. Sometimes, as if in anticipation of baptismal rites, the Chinese waded out through the water to his boat before he could go ashore, and asked him for their copies.[19]

With these exemplars and experiences to draw on, Stevens by 1836 has other thoughts to ponder. As one spreads God's word in China, how much should one try to be, or act, Chinese? Stevens knows something of the different adaptive skills shown by different missionaries at different times. He has been privileged by two years' friendship with Robert Morrison, and has heard how that distinguished scholar-missionary, on first arriving in China, dined with his Chinese-language teachers, ate with chopsticks, "imitated the native dress also, let his nails grow long, cultivated a queue, and walked about the Hong in a Chinese frock and thick shoes," and even said his good-night prayers "in broken Chinese."[20]

Although Morrison's "Chinese habits were soon laid aside," that was not true for Karl Gutzlaff, a missionary from Pomerania with whom Stevens traveled up the coast in 1835. Gutzlaff loved to dress in the Chinese garb of a Fujian sailor when he traveled, or in other variants of Chinese clothes. Thus arrayed, he looked to some Chinese so like themselves that they thought he was a foreign-born Chinese. The confusion was compounded by Gutzlaff's uncanny skill at Chinese language: he could pick up the nuances of each local dialect after only a short period of fierce concentration. Hearing Gutzlaff speak their dialect, baffled Chinese would peer under his hat, to see if he did not have concealed there the long queue of hair that all Chinese wore.[21] Such ambiguity bore advantages and dangers. "If the Chinese costume were adopted," wrote Stevens after one of his trips, "this might prolong the time of detection, but would much more diminish personal safety"—for discovery was inevitable, and heavy punishment would follow.[22] News of the illegal coastal journeyings had swiftly reached the emperor, who issued a strict denunciation of those who sought "to distribute foreign books, designing to seduce men with lies,—a most strange and astonishing proceeding!" and likened their actions to those who earlier "clandestinely brought foreign females to Canton."[23]

Suppose, whether in disguise or not, one were to penetrate the walls of Canton? There were some Chinese inside who would be sympathetic— that was certain—though it was hard to tell how many. The English-language newspaper *Canton Register* in the spring of 1834 had noted in detail how Gutzlaff's continuation of the *Chinese Monthly Magazine,* a journal first conceived and written in Chinese by Milne and Liang Afa almost twenty years before, was flourishing still. Each new issue of this journal, "written in the Chinese language by a foreigner" and "printed withinside the city walls," was "delivered from the Chinese press to the agent of the editor; sent by him to the subscribers; and by them distributed gratuitously" to the Chinese, thus "making its way among the native pop-ulation of Canton." Private initiative then took over and speeded circula-tion, for "portions of their contents have been copied, and hawked about the streets for sale. Parties of Chinese have been observed clubbed together reading and explaining them." The *Canton Register* editor focused on the scientific and commercial information that the Chinese were thus acquir-ing, and speculated that by such means the West could "get a hold of the Chinese mind." How could the missionary not reflect that by such means one might also get a hold of the Chinese soul?[24]

By 1836 the pressures are mounting along with the sense of growing opportunities. Partly because of the emperor's edict attacking the illegal voyages, and also because of new activities by Catholic missionaries operating out of Macao, the local Canton officials have felt the need to act. In early 1836 their staff raid the workshop of a leading printer in Macao, and seize there "eight kinds of foreign books." The printer has been thrown in jail, his stock confiscated. The Chinese residents of the Macao and Canton region have been given six months in which to hand over to the magistrates all foreign books that teach the religion of "Yasoo" (Jesus) or of the Lord of Heaven. If they meet this deadline, they will not be punished, but after the deadline punishment will be severe.[25]

And there is a final factor. Even if one enters the city and hands out religious books, the motives of the Chinese accepting the books will be mixed; that much Stevens knows. For there is always idle curiosity and greed along with good will, as he has noted on his two coastal journeys. As if to balance those Chinese with open countenance, who seemed to understand the purpose of the books and offered little presents in return— white grapes, for instance, or pears, a pinch of tobacco, a handful of millet or a little mound of salt-fish roe—others fought among themselves to add a red-jacketed book to a brown-bound one, though each was otherwise the same, or offered the books they had just received for sale in the village streets before Stevens had even left; some pressed around, wheedling, begging for opium (which the brigs indeed had carried), or for medicines from the supplies the missionaries had with them, showing that desire for cash or fear of potential sickness might be their motive more than any spiritual need.[26]

But in summation, reflecting on the opportunities and challenges that tract distribution in such a land offers, Stevens acknowledges no limits to his rights or to his goals:

> We have a more sure mandate to preach the gospel *in all the world,* than the monarch of China can plead for his title to the throne. By what right are the millions of China excluded from the knowledge of Christianity? They are most unjustly deprived of even an opportunity to make themselves happy for time and for eternity, by an authority which is usurped, but which they cannot resist; and there they have been from age to age idolaters, and are so still, cut off without their own consent from that which makes life a blessing. Against such spiritual tyranny over men's conscience, and rebellion against high Heaven, I protest; and if we take upon ourselves the consequences of governmental vengeance, who will say that we do wrong to any man?[27]

HOME
GROUND

 Hong Huoxiu, the future Heavenly King, comes to Canton for the Confucian state examinations in the early spring of 1836. It is a month since he passed the qualifying examinations in the small rural township of Hua county, near which he dwells. Now he must compete with the brightest scholars from the whole of Canton prefecture, which embraces fourteen counties. As always, there are thousands of candidates assembling in the huge examination compound in the eastern part of the old city, and rigorous quotas ensure that only a tiny fraction will pass. There is a portent this year: snow has fallen, the first snow in Canton in forty-six years according to older residents, two full inches, which for a startling while bedecked the rooftops and foliage in shimmering white. Such portents can be read in many ways.[1]

In the years that he has been preparing for the examinations, Hong has lived surrounded by his family—his father, who has remarried after Hong's mother's death, though there are no children by this second union; two elder brothers and their wives; and one older sister. Hong also has his own new bride, named Lai, whom he married after the first young woman his parents arranged for him to marry died at an early age. Hong is the scholar of the family, and his relatives all wish him well, even though there is too little income from the family farming to keep him as a full-time student. Hong teaches in the village school—where as well as small sums in cash the payment is in food, lamp oil, salt, and tea—to earn the extra that he needs.[2]

Local practice gives to those who succeed in the examinations at Canton an accolade that reminds one of those reserved for the gods at their solemn festivals. Although tiers of other examinations still lie ahead, the country people see passing the licentiate's exams in Canton as the mental and social triumph that it is, the due reward for years of sacrifice and patient study. All those who pass the final rounds for this degree, once the awards are posted, assemble dressed in red caps, blue outer garments, and black satin boots, and proceed together in sedan chairs to the Confucian temple of Canton, to pay their homage to the sage. Thence they process to the offices of the educational director to express their thanks and receive their investitures: two gold flowers for their red hats, a red wreath, and a cup of celebratory wine. Leaving the hall one by one, with their relatives and friends crowded around them, they are escorted home "with drums, music and streamers," to worship their ancestors and pay homage to their parents. The next day, with presents all prepared, they pay formal visits to their tutors, who made the successes possible.[3] Any young man can nurture dreams like these.

The Hongs live in Hua county, thirty miles north of Canton by land, forty miles by river. Hua is a new county by the region's standards, created in 1685. Originally, this area was known as the Hua Mountains, a wild and rugged belt of forested highland that was subdivided between five separate counties. This made it a natural base for bandits and marauding gangs, for by moving only a few miles they could slip easily from jurisdiction to jurisdiction without ever leaving their mountain fastness, and the chances of five separate county magistrates coordinating an attack on bandits all at once were slim indeed.

The chaos of the period from the collapse of the Ming dynasty in the 1630s through the civil wars that marked the Manchu conquest of the south from 1645 to 1680 made this situation bleaker than ever, and the area became a no-man's land. Representatives of local scholarly families petitioned the government for redress and, after being once rebuffed, were finally rewarded by the creation of a newly named Hua county, a block of land about forty miles by thirty, carved out of the northern sections of the two large and populous counties between which Canton was subdivided. Hua received its own magistrate and staff, its county school, its clerks and tax inspectors, its grain storehouse and orphanage, a wall with four gates, and a force of four hundred men, half of them to guard the county seat and half scattered in garrisons among the surrounding villages. Thus reassigned were a total of 5,223 households, comprising 7,743 men and 6,775 women, working between them taxable farmland of around forty thousand acres.[4]

Hong's ancestors migrated here from the northeastern part of Guangdong province in the 1680s, just as the new county was being formed. They settled and farmed in Guanlubu, to the west of the county town, on a stretch of well-watered level land, with mountains rising at their backs as they faced the sun. Guanlubu had been nothing but a couple of shops on the road when they first arrived, but by the time Hong Huoxiu was preparing for the exams a century and a half later, it was a good-sized village, dominated by people of the Hong lineage, with at least three streets of homes and a large pond in the front.[5]

The Hongs are Hakkas—"guest people"—as they are called in the local dialect of Canton, or "Nyin-hak," as they call themselves in their own dialect. To be a Hakka is to be not quite a local, and Hakka are granted two special slots in the local examinations, to help in their assimilation. The Cantonese whose ancestors settled in the area earlier emphasize their own priority by calling themselves the "original inhabitants."[6] But to be a Hakka is not to be purely an outsider. It is not to be like the Miao tribesmen from Guangxi province to the west, who sometimes travel in their boats down the West River to Canton, to sell their oils and trade for city goods. These are truly strange-looking men, their religions all their own, their language unintelligible to Hakka and Cantonese alike, their hair not neatly shaved in front and braided at the back, in obedience to the style imposed on all Chinese by their Manchu conquerors in 1645, but piled in wild profusion upon their heads.[7] Nor is it to be socially inferior, forbidden to take the examinations and kept out of prosperous marriage ties. Such stigmas are reserved for the actors, or barbers, or the restless Tanka boat people, so named from the rounded twelve-foot boats like severed eggs in which they live, who pass their whole lives on the water and are forbidden—even if they had the means—to buy land and build a home on shore, or marry there. The greatest difference between Hakkas and other Chinese families in the region is that by Hakka custom their women do not bind their feet to make them small. Thus Hakka women can walk freely, and work in the fields with their men; they will also always marry Hakka men, since the other Chinese will find them unattractive.[8]

The Hakkas as a people place their origins in the central China plains to the south of the Yellow River, below the former capital of Kaifeng, and through their oral histories and their written genealogies trace their successive movements south across the centuries, in response to outside invasions, civil wars, and economic deprivation. The language they speak—"foreign" to many around Canton—is seen by themselves as in direct descent from the purest language of ancient Chinese civilization. Indeed, not long before Hong's birth Chinese scholars of linguistics have begun diligently tracing Hakka words and diction to illuminate their own historical past.[9]

Hong's lineage traces its roots back through scholars and ministers of the Song dynasty, in the twelfth century, to more shadowy figures in the Tang dynasty, and, even earlier, to the period of the later Han dynasty in the second century, when the Hong name can first be found. Across the centuries, too, they could point to members of the Hong line who passed the higher examinations, and in one case even the highest of all, which led to appointment first in the Hanlin Academy of Confucian scholars in Peking and later, after a successful bureaucratic career, to promotion to vice-president of the Board of War.[10] The branch of the family from which the Guanlubu Hongs trace descent had moved to northeast Guangdong province near the Fujian border during the Song dynasty, and were based mainly in Meixian—the greatest center for Hakka people then and now—though other members of the lineage had scattered far and wide across the country.[11]

The move to the hitherto unknown region of Hua by Hong Huoxiu's great-great-great-grandfather was a bold one, for Hua was not the center of Hakka life and language that Meixian had been. And though the region of Hua was prosperous, with plentiful crops of rice and wheat, hemp and beans, cabbages and greens, peaches, peas, melons, oranges and dates, as well as liquor and honey and edible oils, fish and shrimp, chickens, ducks and dogs,[12] it is unlikely that the Hongs were able to get prime land to farm, even though they saw themselves as pioneers, and they had to move in isolated family groups rather than as a whole lineage. For the land was settled already by the original inhabitants, and as in many other parts of South China the Hakkas were different enough not to be fully welcome. But even when isolated, they kept their numbers up and their solidarity intact through their dialect and language ties; and a bride from outside the village, even if speaking other dialects, would be compelled to learn that of her husband's family, and their children of course would do the same.[13]

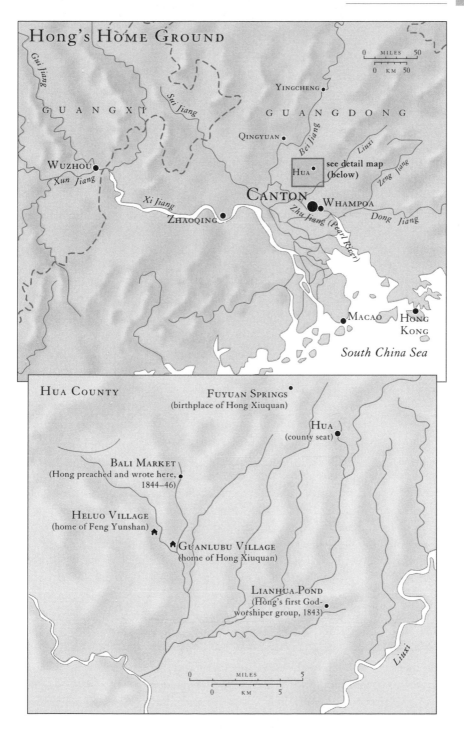

Hong's Home Ground

Gui Jiang

GUANGXI

Sui Jiang

WUZHOU

Xun Jiang

Xi Jiang

ZHAOQING

YINGCHENG

GUANGDONG

QINGYUAN

Bei Jiang

Liuxi

Hua — see detail map (below)

Zeng Jiang

CANTON

WHAMPOA

Zhu Jiang (Pearl River)

Dong Jiang

0 MILES 50
0 KM 50

MACAO

HONG KONG

South China Sea

Hua County

FUYUAN SPRINGS
(birthplace of Hong Xiuquan)

HUA
(county seat)

BALI MARKET
(Hong preached and wrote here,
1844–46)

HELUO VILLAGE
(home of Feng Yunshan)

GUANLUBU VILLAGE
(home of Hong Xiuquan)

LIANHUA POND
(Hong's first God-
worshiper group, 1843)

Liuxi

0 MILES 5
0 KM 5

From the seventeenth-century period of the family's move down to Hong Huoxiu's own time of schooling, none of the Hongs in Hua county are recorded as having passed the state examinations, even at the local level. And though Hong Huoxiu's father was described in the family genealogy as well respected, a leader and mediator of disputes in the village of Guanlubu, the house in which he raised his family was simplicity itself: it was on the western end of the third row of houses, set back from the pond, with a small courtyard dominated at the back by a largish family meeting room, quite open to the air, flanked by small rooms for the family members, the whole one story high, with floors of beaten sand and lime, walls of clay and lime, and a roof of laths laid with interlocking tiles.[14]

It is the magistrate of Hua who leads his county residents to the rhythm of the rituals dictated by the state. The opening and closing of the year, the changing of the seasons, all have their solemn ceremonies in the county temple, as do the founding teacher—so they call Confucius—and the emperor, empress dowager, and heir-apparent, duly honored in far-away Peking. The emperor's "Sixteen Instructions" on virtuous behavior must be both venerated and read aloud, and for such events the successful degree candidates gather with the local officials to offer ritual sacrifices and hear the ritual music.[15] As written by the emperor, these sixteen maxims—later amplified by the commentaries of other emperors and distinguished scholars—summarize the behavior expected in each town and neighborhood. They extol respect and obedience to the state and one's senior relatives, harmony in each community, thrift and industry, scholarship and education, good manners, prompt payment of taxes, and mutual security. A few hold warnings—to reject strange and heterodox religions, to avoid all false accusations, and not to hide fugitives from justice.[16]

Three other gods receive the assembled dignitaries' worship in spring and autumn, and their prayers for Hua's protection: the god "of clouds and rain, wind and thunder"; the god of the district's mountains and rivers; and the city god of Hua. For each the offerings are calibrated, to show their ranking: four ritual vessels of wine and four bolts of white silk for the four forces of the weather; three vessels and two bolts for the gods of space; three vessels and one bolt for the god of the city, even though it is to him that the most urgent prayers for rain in time of dearth are first addressed, and it is he who controls the routes to the lands of the dead.[17]

These are the gods and spirits that have force for all the community, so it is meet to sacrifice to them with bureaucratic style. As for the middle range of human families, the magistrate is content to let them worship their own past ancestors in their burial grounds, with their own assembled relatives. But below these departed shades, who have families to honor them, are those who have been lost to sight and history, and here the state asserts itself again. For these are "orphan ghosts" who have no one to pray for their spirits after death. Individuals of compassion often remember them collectively at the All Souls' festival, where they burn paper clothes for the spirits, and make them offerings of wine, fruit, and rice in the ceremony called "burning the street clothes." Still, their ability to harm the community remains disquieting, and therefore the magistrate holds ceremonies on their behalf at a specially erected altar in the north of the county town. The litany of the fates of these orphan ghosts, written by a local scholar long before, remains an echo of the present world in Hua:

> These are those who died for reasons that we can no longer know: Amongst them are those who died from cruel wounds in battle, those who died from flood and fire and bandits, those who saw their property seized and so took their own lives, married women and young girls seized by force and killed, those who while being punished died unjustly, those who fled from natural calamities and died from illness on the road, those destroyed by wild animals or poisonous snakes, those who died from famine or exposure, those who were caught up in wars and lost their lives, those who killed themselves because of danger, those crushed to death when walls or houses collapsed on them, or those who after their deaths left no sons or grandsons.[18]

For such souls, and all others gone before and still to come, the founding magistrate of Hua in 1686 had carved this prayer in stone: "Let cruel animals stay away, the nests of robbers never more be formed, the people henceforth live decent lives, the tax quotas to the state be always met, and people's spirits all be good. From this will come our happiness, a golden age in heaven and earth."[19]

Even these solemn ceremonies can be slighted by exaggeration, or disjointed into carnivals. During the protracted drought of 1835, the governor abandoned the regular sacrifices to the city god, and offered vast rewards to any "extraordinary man" or "wonderful scholar," no matter from what district or believing in what faith, who could use his arts "to drive away the dragon" that was blocking off the clouds, and thus cause the rain to fall. The citizens mocked him publicly, with poems written in bold characters and posted on the walls. Yet they gathered in great crowds when a volunteer came forward to drive away the dragon. He was a man claiming to be a monk from Sichuan province and he stood three days before the altar in the governor's yamen, three days under the burning sun, an upright staff pushed into the ground by his side, with no sign of

weakness, no sign of perspiration on his face, with candles burning steadily on the altar, next to a bowl of pure clear water. Again the people
mocked, until suddenly the rains came, and they were silenced. Only to
mock again when the governor, to thank the gods, ordered ten married
women to sacrifice a sow at the south gate of the city, and burn off its
tail.[20] Less than a month later, as epidemics followed the drought and the
sudden rains, the people brought the image of the famous second-century
god Yingtuo out from his shrine inside the Great South Gate of Canton
city, and paraded it through the street, escorted by drummers and by
crowds of young girls chosen especially for their looks.[21]

Predators often prowl at such scenes of petitioning or rejoicing, encouraged by the expensive preparations and the flocks of people, and attempts
to keep decorum sometimes fail in curious ways. At the autumn festival
of All Souls, allegedly the most solemn ceremony of the ritual year, held
in 1836 at a village in the western suburbs outside Canton, the bamboo
structures, the booths, the glittering displays in the temple ground were
so astonishing, funded by subscriptions from local merchants and worthies
totaling seven thousand ounces or so of silver, that the magistrate ordered
two parallel roads built out to the temple grounds, one to be used only by
men and one by women. But this prompted two young men to dress as
women, so they could join the women on their walk, and rob them there
at leisure. At last their looks betrayed them, and they were arrested and
"made a show to the assembled multitude."[22]

Hong Huoxiu is twenty-two years old in 1836. As he mingles with the
crowds of fellow students on the road outside the lieutenant governor's
official residence near the examination halls, two men catch his attention.
One of them is a Cantonese, and acts as interpreter for the second, a
foreign-looking man who does not speak good Chinese. This second man
is strangely dressed: as Hong later remembers him, he has a "coat with
wide sleeves" in what appears to be the style of the former Ming dynasty,
and his hair is "tied in a knot upon his head." Through his interpreter,
this second man tells the bystanders "the fulfillment of their wishes," even
if they have not yet questioned him. To Hong he says, "You will attain
the highest rank, but do not be grieved, for grief will make you sick."[23]

The next day Hong sees the same two men again, standing on Longcang
Jie, the "Street where the dragon hides," or "Street of potential wisdom,"
some way south of where they were the day before, but still near the examination halls. This time no words are uttered, but one of the men reaches
out to Hong with a book in his hand. Hong takes the book. It is Liang
Afa's collection of religious tracts, "Good Words for Exhorting the Age."[24]

Hong's description of the foreign man is vague, and the words he ascribes to him elusive. But everything about this stranger points to Edwin Stevens, returned a few months before from the longest of his coastal trips. In the early spring of 1836 Stevens has taken on a new calling in addition to his formal title of chaplain for the Seaman's Friend Society—that of "missionary to the Chinese"—and a friend lists "distributing Bibles and tracts" as now foremost among Stevens' interests.[25] And yet despite his several years in China, Stevens still needs an interpreter, for he finds the language vexingly hard. There are two views on learning Chinese, he has written recently, "One, that the attainment of the language was next to impossible; and the other more modern, that its acquisition is as facile as the Latin or Greek. While we subscribe to neither of these extremes, we confess ourselves inclined more towards the former than the latter opinion."[26] As one who knew him well in Canton was to write after his death, though Stevens "made considerable proficiency in the study of the Chinese language," it was always true that "accuracy rather than rapidity characterized his progress." And only the pure language will do in this context. One can hardly use the merchants' and sailors' Pidgin English to spread the word of God.[27]

Certainly Stevens has lived long enough on the edge of Canton to know that the guards at those imposing city gates—despite the brave show that they make, in their red-and-yellow jackets with the character for "courage" writ large on front and back—are often lazy, and that bribing them is common.[28] Furthermore, he has recently gained the experience, from his shoreline journeys, to compare the Chinese of the north—"suspicious and reserved"—with those among whom he lives in the south, who manifest what he now perceives by contrast to be a "ready cordiality" and a "roguish" wit.[29]

Hong's description of the Cantonese interpreter is as vague as his description of the foreigner. We know that it cannot be Liang Afa, for Liang left Canton the previous year, after being arrested once again by the Chinese authorities, on charges of illegally distributing Christian tracts. Though bailed out by the Westerners in Canton, he felt he could no longer endure the risks to himself and his growing family, and retreated to the safer realms of Malacca. Nor is it Liang's friend Agong, the one who earlier on distributed tracts with Liang to the examination candidates. Agong has also left the city, forced to flee after local enemies denounced him to the authorities for dealing too closely with the foreigners.[30] Nor is it either of those two men's sons, for Liang Afa's son has fled to Singapore, and Agong's son is held in jail in the place of his fugitive father. The closest we can come to his identity is through a letter written that same spring by a British resident of Canton, in which he states that all the Chinese Christians who once consorted with Liang Afa are scattered "except one, a man of some literary acquirements, who corrects many of our tracts for the press, improving a little the style, etc."[31] But if this Chinese man does pluck up the courage to go and spread God's word with a Westerner inside Canton's walls, he is unlikely to write about it publicly. Nor does Stevens reminisce about the moment, or share his thoughts on it with others. For at the end of 1836, while on a trip to Singapore, Stevens is struck by blinding headaches and by a raging fever that the doctors cannot reach. Within three weeks, aged thirty-four, he is dead.[32]

As Hong remembers it, he does not read Liang's set of tracts carefully, but gives "a superficial glance at their contents."[33] What exactly does Hong see? He does not say. But there, in the table of contents, is the Chinese character for Hong's own name. The character is sharp and clear, as the fourth item in the fourth tract. The literal meaning of Hong's name is "flood," and the heading says that the waters of a Hong have destroyed every living thing upon the earth. The passage in the tract itself repeats this startling news, and states that this destruction was ordered by Ye-huo-hua, the god who created all living creatures. The Chinese transliteration for this god's name is Ye-huo-hua, the middle syllable of which— "Huo," or "fire"—is the same as the first syllable of Hong's given name, Huoxiu. So Hong shares this god's name. There is flood, there is fire. And Hong Huoxiu, in some fashion, for some reason, partakes of both.[34]

How enraged this god has been, Liang's book tells Hong, enraged at the sins of those he has created. Only one man, named Noah, found favor in this god's eyes, for Noah alone of all those on earth followed the true path of righteousness. Noah was already six hundred years old when this god told him to build a boat, and though so old, he obeyed at once. His three sons helped him. The boat was huge, three stories high, three hundred feet long and fifty broad. There was a window in the boat, and a great door, and all the animals came in, seven by seven or two by two, and all the birds, and pairs of all the creeping things. And Noah joined them, with his wife, and his three sons, and his three sons' wives. The god's flood covered the whole earth. Except for those inside the boat, the god killed everyone. The god's flood killed the giants, who lived on the earth in those days, killed all the other animals and birds and creeping things. Only in their boat, above the mountaintops, eight people floated free, just eight in one family, they and the creatures they brought with them.[35]

Hong's second name is there in other places too, for another god—described as "the highest Lord of all"—sent fire to destroy two cities with curious names, just as Ye-huo-hua had sent the flood to destroy the people of the earth. Like the first, this god was angry, for the people of these two cities gave themselves to lust and wildness, leaving no depravity unexplored; with his fire the god destroyed them, every trace, every person, every house, and finally the very soil itself, converting the land into a monstrous lake. But once again the god chose one family to be saved, that of a man named Lot. Lot had a wife, and two daughters, and god saved all four; till Lot's wife looked back at the blazing cities and was turned to salt. So only three remained.[36]

Liang's book does not say what happened at the end of either story. What of that family of eight? What of the animals and birds crowded in around them? Did they float thus through all eternity? Did they ride the waves in their enormous boat, beneath the rain-sodden sky, forever and a day, skin and fur and feathers, until they became one with the water, the wood, and the wind?

And why salt?

Hong fails the examinations. He keeps the book.

4

SKY WAR

 Hong has grown up in Guanlubu with many different gods, and paid homage to them in a host of ways. First in each year come the series of celebrations to honor the new year and the first full moon of spring, followed by the Qing-Ming festival in memory of the dead, and the Dragon Boat festival of five-five (the fifth day of the fifth lunar month). This festival, at which boats from different villages race each other on the rivers, honors the loyal but disgraced minister of a ruling house two thousand years before, who committed suicide in a southern stream after writing China's most celebrated lament. At the Dragon Boat festivals around Canton the people hang rushes and artemisia outside their doors, and offer horn-shaped cakes of sweet and sticky rice to their ancestors before sharing them among themselves, and with family and neighbors, while the children hang amulets and seals on colored threads around their waists. Despite the glory of their boats and their colorful costumes, the men competing for the prizes often erupt in fights, fed by the tension of the times and by old, still smoldering, feuds. Violence has grown so bad that in 1835 the governor from his office in Canton forbids the races to be held, an order that is observed by few, if any, villages.[1]

After the celebration of the summer solstice, the year starts to turn toward its end. On the sixth day of the seventh month, so it is said, Heaven's daughter sends down her seven sisters, and so do the women in Hua county prepare festoons of colored silk and gather, in their best clothes, between noon and early afternoon, to worship the visitors and beg their help for skill in needlework. They hire blind singing boys and girls to chant their ballads and on their tables lay out fruit and flowers and pretty ornaments. The next day is double-seven, the festival of the herdboy and the weaving maid, who meet on that day only, using the Milky Way as their bridge. That festival overlaps with the early autumn feast of All Souls, when hungry ghosts are delivered from their anguish by the intercession of the Buddha, in rites first practiced eleven hundred years before. These ceremonies are hardly over when bowls of rice are prepared for all the Buddhist and Taoist monks and nuns and for any beggars in the town, who on seven-ten shall not go hungry.[2]

At the double-nine, all worship again at ancestral graves, and picnic— if they can—in the hills, to remember the reclusive sage Fei Changfang, who once saved a disciple's life by urging him to flee to the hills with his young family since death was coming to his home. The disciple followed his advice, keeping his spirits up with chrysanthemum wine, and upon return found all his chickens and farm animals dead in the yard—taken as substitutes, said Fei, since death could not find the humans he was seeking.

A few days later, as the ninth month ends, the Fire God has his festival: for three full days, street by street, people implore his protection, for fire is the worst enemy, one that has leveled towns and villages so many times. For three days lamps blaze all night in streets festooned with streamers, and the residents and shop owners in the wealthier roads stage plays to serve as the "Fire God's Requiem." Sometimes of course, as happened in the Dragon Boat races, such ceremonies reverse themselves—in one village near Canton, which celebrated the festival in 1835 with five days and night of plays accompanied by fireworks, the flaming devices set the tents and chests of theatrical clothes on fire, forcing the terrified audience to run for their lives, trampling ten or more in the melée. Just one year later, in a village outside Canton, another crowded theater caught on fire, and this time two hundred men and women were killed in the terrified stampede.[3] The festival year ends with the celebration of the winter solstice and its promise of lengthening days, and the visit of the kitchen god, who must be fed and welcomed if his favors are to be granted in the new year.[4]

In Hua, where heat and hunger, dampness and diseases are never far away, these festivals take on a special urgency. The people of Hua, according to their own early historian, are the kind who will summon a doctor if they have a slight illness, but if their sickness is severe they turn to the spirits. At New Year's time, before the dawn, they bathe in scented water as the festival begins, and amidst the sound of firecrackers and the drinking of spring wine they weigh the rainfall day by day for twelve days straight, to gauge the coming year's prospects. Similarly, they chart the wind's direction, wishing for a cold north wind that will reverse itself and lead to a warm spring, and praying to avoid a southern wind that brings bad luck. Men and women crowd together as they pray before clay figures of water buffalo and their celestial drover; they stage plays in the street to entertain the spirits, scatter pulse and grain on the ground to bring a fertile year, and eat cakes of plain flour and vegetables to keep them free of smallpox. After the first full moon, they welcome the Yellow Emperor by hanging chains of garlic on their doors to ward off evil forces, and cook large round pancakes of sticky rice on which they place a needle and thread, which they say will help them patch the heavens.[5]

In the fourth month, too, they gather to share a ritual meal, in this case the flavored liquid in which the Buddha's image has been washed outside the temple gate, and then eat sweet rice cakes cooked with a hundred herbs. Some say this will cure delirium.[6] At the summer solstice, they cook and eat dog meat, to keep away malaria, and at the coming of winter they share a broth of meat, peaches, and mustard greens, to keep any other sicknesses away. Even more careful than the procedure followed in the first month is the charting of the rains and wind at the end of the sixth month, on the day they call the Dragon's Measure. "Heavy rain on this day," goes the local saying, "means that one will plow the mountaintops; no rain, that one will have to plow the bottoms of the ponds." But there are other signals from the heavens that must be watched with equal care: a squall that doesn't last, despite its initial fury; a sudden violent cloudburst, with heavy wind and thunder; or a severed rainbow after rain, known as the Mother of Typhoons, that presages the rage and roar of the fiercest storms that knock down homes and trees, and make travel on the waterways impossible. These are called warnings from Pengzu himself, China's longest-living patriarch.[7]

In Hua, the people are told that to avoid poverty they must light huge fires in the street to greet the Yellow Emperor's arrival, and placate the grain spirits by offering them boiled suckling pig and wine. To further assure good fortune, they should eat dried fish in bulk at the moment of the winter solstice. To place themselves under the Jade Emperor's protection at year's end, they burn model houses of bamboo and stay awake all night, hang strings of oranges before their doors, and carve peachwood charms for the gods of the gate. To keep cold winds away, they eat boiled noodles cooked in ritual vessels. To greet the moon in the middle of the autumn, they prepare three separate types of mooncakes, called "goosefat," "hardskin," and "soft skin" cakes, ranging in weight from an ounce or two to several pounds, some sweet, some salt, their surfaces decorated with multicolored pictures of humans and animals. Eaten as the lanterns are hoisted high to greet the moon, these cakes bring promise of early marriage and plenteous children.[8]

Animals and birds, mythical or real, are an inextricable part of these relations with the spirit worlds. Dragons are linked through ceremonies to certain days of the year, when the way they are propitiated can determine the force of the sun or prevent the rain clouds from forming and releasing their bounty; at the winter solstice, for instance, "the hidden dragon represents the Celestial Breath which returns to the point of its departure." In this role, the dragon stands for the *yang* force of the east, the strength of sun and light.[9]

The tiger and the cock each features prominently in many ways and guises, also linked to the changing cycles of the seasons, especially the passage from winter into spring. Because of stories from antiquity, the tiger is often associated with a giant peach tree, under which he stands at the eastern corner of the world waiting to eat the spectral victims bound and passed on to him by two divine protectors of the human race. By association of ideas—and lacking real tigers—the magistrates often place peachwood images of human guardians outside their formal office entrances, and painted tigers on the lintels, from which also dangle the ropes of reed or rush in which the specters had once been bound. The specters entering the tiger's maw had approached the peach tree from the northeast, and thus the tiger came to represent the *yang* force vanquishing the powers of winter, cold, and *yin* (the north).[10]

The red color of peach can counteract evil. Strips of red paper on a house door are effective substitutes for peachwood images, just as peach twigs can serve in exorcism, and even the roughest picture of a tiger guard a house from harm, as infants might also be protected by wearing a simple "tiger hat."[11] A white tiger, however, represents different kinds of danger—it is linked to the stratagems and the violence of war, the thirst for blood, and also can bring mortal danger to infants and to pregnant women. With its name linked to certain so-called baleful stars, the white tiger figures centrally in astrologers' calculations of avoiding disaster.

Thus can a spirit considered the protector become, in altered guise, a force of death and destruction.[12]

The cock looms large in local consciousness as well. Sometimes it is sacrificed, its blood smeared over door lintels to give protection, the very lintels on which the tiger images are hanging. In early tales, the cock presided in the tree under which the tiger ate his victims. "In the mountain or land of the peach capital is a big peach tree with a foliage extending over three thousand miles. A gold cock is perched upon it, and crows at dawn."[13] Even though the blood of freshly killed cocks can help exorcise demons, they must not be slain on the first days of the year, when only their presence can provide the force to counteract the demons escaping the tiger's jaws. At other times, cocks—especially those of reddish color—would be sacrificed to the sun, a practice some ascribed to the ancient state of Lu, where Confucius was born and where he taught, "because its voice in the morning and its red feathers drove evil from the rulers of that state." Like the peach, it was observed, "the cock dispels disease on account of its solar propensities, and moreover confers on man the vitality bestowed by the universal source of life, of which it is the symbol."[14]

The category of religious books known as the *Jade Record* also chart the course of every year, although in harsher ways, as they present the march of souls through hell. The prologues to the *Jade Record* state that the central holy text was sent down to earth by the being termed the Highest God, after being submitted to him by Yan Luo, the king of hell, and by Pusa, the compassionate Bodhisattva. The purpose of the text is to clarify for all human beings the relationship between bad deeds on earth and suffering in hell after death, and to show how suffering can be averted by good actions on earth. In dealing thus with the world of hell, and with the souls of the dead, the text deliberately reverses the well-known words of Confucius, who had always said to his disciples that since we cannot even fully understand life on earth, how can we presume to discuss the gods or the afterlife?[15]

In line with these principles, tradition says that the text of the *Jade Record* was initially given not to a Confucian worthy but to a Buddhist priest, and by him passed on to a wandering Taoist. As stated in the book itself, this was in the reign period of Taiping, or "Great Peace," a title adopted by both the Chinese Song emperors and the barbarian Liao invaders, a dual coincidence that allowed ingenious scholars to place the heavenly transmissions with precision to the years of 982 and 1030. All who read and absorb the message of the *Jade Record,* and print extra copies so that others too may read and learn, will not only escape the worst torments of hell, and bring prosperity to their families and descendants, but in the transmigration of their souls may be reborn as human beings, or even move to higher stages of life—men to the happy lands, and women to the life of men. Those who ignore, deface, or mock the tracts will find no such mercy, but be condemned at death to descend to the lower layers of hell and, according to their crimes on earth, move through each of the ten hellish palaces in turn.[16]

Pictures in the *Jade Record* show, for those who cannot read, how the judged souls are transformed. Only a few return as happy, healthy humans. Of the others, some are allowed to stay human, yes, but condemned to be ugly, misshapen, poor, and ill; while many, according to their sins, return as horses, dogs, birds, fish, or creeping things.[17] Copies of the *Jade Record* are everywhere as Hong Huoxiu is growing up, since editions begin to proliferate just in the years when he is preparing for his exams, even though the sixteen maxims that the scholars read aloud to educate the people include a ringing condemnation of the Jade Emperor and the books issued in his name.[18]

The calendar printed in each *Jade Record* devotes the first day of the first lunar month to the Maitreya Buddha, the Buddha of the future, whose plump, smiling presence can be found in many a temple, and whose protection can be sought by prayer and intercession, and by taking on this day a vow to respect heaven. The eighth day, in contrast, belongs to Yan Luo, known to all as the king of hell. Strangely, though, the *Jade Record* notes that Yan Luo has lost his former proud position as lord of the first of the hellish palaces. In that role, long ago, he proved too compassionate to those who had been unjustly killed, and allowed them simply to return to earth again to lead new lives. For this error of compassion the Highest God demoted him to the fifth palace, where he now presides, though it is his name above all others that still stands for hell itself. In the sixteen dungeons of his hell, his minion devils tear out the hearts of those who committed any one of a varied group of crimes: whose faith in the Buddha is weak, who while on earth did not believe in retribution, who killed live creatures, or who broke their word, used magic arts, wished death to others, forcibly or guilefully seduced the innocent, cheated in business, let their neighbors die, spread discord, or nursed their rancorous hearts in other ways.

Outside his dungeons Yan Luo has built a tower, which he calls his "Tower to View the World," a tower shaped like a bow, eighty-one units of distance around, the back like a taut string facing toward the north, the curved front spanning east and south and west. Sixty-three steps lead

The sixth court of hell, as portrayed in a nineteenth-century edition of the Jade Record. These tracts, representing the teachings of moralistic forms of folk-Buddhism, circulated widely in South China during Hong Xiuquan's youth. After his conversion to Christianity, Hong argued that all such tracts should be destroyed. The illustration above shows the underworld king Biancheng sitting at his desk as he presides over the sixth court of hell. He is flanked by his two assistants, one in scholar's garb to summarize the dead person's record on earth, and one in demon form to supervise the appropriate punishments. The accompanying illustration shows four of the sixteen torments that are imposed on sinners by King Biancheng: hammering metal spikes into the body, flaying alive, sawing the body in half vertically, and kneeling on heaps of metal filings.

After passing through all the ten levels of
hell, the dead proceed to the palace of the
goddess Meng, where they receive a potion
of forgetfulness before their souls transmi-
grate back to earth for a new cycle of life, as
insect, bird, animal, poor human, or rich,
according to their deserts. This process is
presided over by the two demon-spirits
shown here. Though the exact details vary
in different texts, "Life-is-short" (top) usually wears dark clothes, is armed, and
laughs uproariously. "Death-has-gradations"
(bottom, sometimes rendered as "Death-
comes-swiftly") is always dressed in white,
wears a conical white hat, wails continu-
ously, and carries an abacus to tally the
exact amount of each person's sins. *Courtesy
of Yale University Library.*

to its summit, forty-nine measures above the ground of hell, and to this lofty eminence the tormented souls are led by their demon guardians, so that, all unseen, they can gaze upon the earthly families they have been forced by death to leave.* And with the wisdom of death and Yan Luo's help they see how their dear children and closest relatives, heads bent over the departed one's coffin in apparent mourning, in fact are cursing the dead one's memory, defying his instructions, selling off the goods and property he so painfully acquired, and battling through lawsuits for what is left.[19] Tormented by these visions of life on earth, they are assigned by Yan Luo to his sixteen separate dungeons, where they join the bandits and prostitutes on whom Yan Luo did not waste the subtler sorrows of the tower. Here, the guilty souls are seated on iron blocks and tied to metal pillars with copper chains. With small, sharp knives the demons slice their chests and bellies, and tug the hearts out with a hook. As the souls look on in agony, the hearts are sliced in pieces and fed to a crowd of waiting wolves and serpents.[20]

Only one day after King Yan Luo's feast, on the ninth day of the first month, comes the day of the Highest God, also called the Jade Emperor, or, in combination, "Jade Emperor the Highest God." For him, the vows that must be made are those of loyalty and filial devotion, for his power exceeds that of all the others, though his exact origins are vague. According to common tradition, the future Jade Emperor was conceived by his royal mother after a dream, in which she was visited by Lao Zi, Confucius' contemporary, and the earliest great philosopher of the religion later known as Taoism. The babe was born on the ninth day of the first month, at noon, and at the moment of his birth the splendor from his body filled the whole land. During his princely childhood, he was endowed with sublime intelligence, and showed himself at all times loving and compassionate, distributing his goods and the surplus of the treasury to the poor, the sick, the widows, and the orphans. Called to ascend the throne after the death of the king, his "father," he handed over the government to his ministers, and withdrew to the mountains to a life of religious contemplation. Achieving a state of perfection, he attained immortal life in heaven, but chose to revisit earth in three protracted cycles of eight hundred visits each; during these forays back to earth, he preached his doctrine of compassion and salvation, healed the sick, and taught the people. By a series of imperial decrees issued between the years 1015 and 1017

---

*As with many other numbers in these texts, we are here being presented with mystical multiplications of the numbers seven and nine.

by the Song dynasty emperor Zhenzong, this figure was officially deified as the Celestial Jade Great Ruler of Heaven.[21]

Under the Highest God's general supervision, each of the other nine gods of hell—just like Yan Luo—has his holy day, and an invocation that, if correctly and respectfully uttered, may ward off his rage. Cumulatively, among themselves, they judge every foible of which humans are capable, and few will escape being punished by them. The role of the god who rules the first hell is preliminary scrutiny of the newly dead, prior to passing them on to others: in his palace hangs a mirror, called the Mirror of Reflection, where all must see their own sins through their own eyes. Most are pushed on at once to the other palaces of hell, where their specific sins are dealt with, but two groups are kept for further suffering through thought: the first is composed of those who killed themselves without good reason, out of petty spite or sputtering anger, not because of unbearable hardship or humiliation. In taking their lives for inadequate reasons, such people betrayed both the gods of the land who gave them existence and the parents who spawned and raised them; for this ingratitude, they must, once in every twelve-day cycle, endlessly relive the exact suffering that led them to the act of suicide itself. Those in the other group are Buddhist and Taoist priests who were careless in their chanting of holy texts, or took money for their services, or deceived the gullible; each is enclosed in a narrow cell lit only by a guttering lamp with an endless line of wick and a hundred pints of lamp oil, until every word of the sacred books has been read aloud correctly.[22]

As for the other palaces of hell, all those who have not lived purely and thus could not avoid the mirror's judgments, must face their suffering in turn. Thither go the quack doctors who in search of profit harm their patients, the priests who deceive children of either sex to be their acolytes, people who sequester others' scrolls or pictures, marriage go-betweens who lie about their clients' charms.[23] Hither come shop clerks who deceive their customers, prisoners rightfully condemned who escape from jail or exile, grave robbers, tax evaders, posters of abusive bills, and negotiators of divorce.[24] Hither come those who won't yield the right-of-way to those who are crippled, who steal flagstones from the road and tiles from public buildings, who refuse to help the sick, who sell fake medicines or debase the quality of silver, who foul the streets with filth. The rich who forcibly build on the land of the poor, the careless or mischievous who set fire to hillsides or to property, the killers of birds, the poisoners of water, the destroyers of religious images, the defacers of books, the writers and readers of obscene literature, the hoarders of grain, the heavy drinkers, spendthrifts, thieves, bullies, the drowners of baby girls, the killers of slaves, gamblers, lazy teachers, neglectors of parents—all, all, all shall suffer the penalties due them. The *Jade Record* lists every punishment for every category, the suffocating and the lacerating, the slicing and the burning, the breaking of bones and the yanking of teeth, snakes in the nostrils and worms in the brain, severing the penis, smashing the knees, pulling the tongue, tearing out nails, scratching out eyes—until the mind staggers under the horror of it all.[25]

Yet it is a melancholy truth that the world in and around Canton provides violent deaths enough to test the mettle of all ten kings of hell and to wear the treads on the stairs of King Yan Luo's Tower to View the World. The Canton authorities execute hundreds of their people for violent crimes each year, and both these killers and their victims must face judgment once again in the courts below the earth.[26] Often there has been both public spectacle and retribution, as with the Canton wife condemned to death by slicing because she killed her husband. Huge crowds assembled to watch her death, drawn, it is said, by her pride and fierceness, her amazing beauty, and the tiny size of her feet.[27] Crowds gather too to see a woman who murdered her mother-in-law executed in her husband's presence, and to watch as a member of the pirate gang that killed twelve innocent foreign seamen is executed by being nailed to a giant cross.[28]

Others around Canton have committed crimes for which punishment both on earth and in the realms of hell seems justified to their contemporaries. The men who pose as regular sedan chair carriers, using their disguise to kidnap and sell blind singing girls; the Buddhist priest who runs a den of thieves from his temple outside the city's eastern gate; those who rob the local graves not only of the ritual objects that might be buried there but of parts of bodies, to practice their "murdering, diabolical and magical arts."[29]

Other gods and spirits have their places and their days in the *Jade Record:* Guanyin, the compassionate Bodhisattva of mercy, and the Buddha Sakyamuni have two days each, one for the day of their earthly birth and one for the day on which they achieved enlightenment; the kitchen god has two as well, once for his birthdate and once for the day at the end of the year when he reports back to heaven what he has seen down here on earth. The city god has his day in the middle of summer, as do the local gods of the soil, in the middle of spring. The goddess Meng has her day on the thirteenth of the ninth month. Her role is a central one, for in the ten reaches of hell where the dead souls wander and suffer, the focus of the other gods is on judgment and remembrance, so that all human souls can be punished until the record is clear. But Meng's role is to induce forgetfulness, so that those born again to various forms of life on earth will not be burdened—or overgifted—with earlier memories.

Goddess Meng's Tower of Forgetting, subdivided into 108 chambers, lies just beyond the tenth palace of hell, where all souls have received their final decisions on reincarnation. In every chamber of her domain her demons lay out cups of the "wine that is not wine," and every soul that enters is forced to drink. As they drink, their past lives vanish from their senses, they are stripped clear of memory, and tossed into the red waters of hell's last river. Borne by the current, they are washed ashore at the foot of a red wall, on which a message four columns long is hung: "To be a human is easy, to live a human life is hard; to desire to be human a second time, we fear is even harder. If you wish to be born into the Happy Lands, there is one easy way—say what is really in your heart, then you'll reach your goal." Two demons then haul them ashore, to send them on to their newly allotted spans. One demon is tall, round-eyed and laughs uproariously; he is in a fine robe, with a black scholar's hat on his head, writing brush and paper in his hands, a sword on his back. His name is Life-is-short. The other is dressed in soiled cotton clothes, blood flows from his head, he furrows his brows and loudly sighs, carries an abacus for calculations, and has an old rice bag slung around his shoulders in which he stuffs scrap paper. His name is Death-has-gradations.[30]

There is one group of souls, the *Jade Record* tells us, who after they have passed through all the trials, and been prepared for their return to earth, petition the demons to stay as ghostly souls a while longer, before regaining their corporeal forms, and sometimes their petition is granted. These are women who have been so badly treated by men in their former lives that they wish to return as ghosts to get revenge. Some were falsely promised marriage then betrayed, some were seduced, some were promised they would be the principal wife and found other consorts already in the home. Some were widows, promised shelter for their aged parents, or succor for their children from a former marriage, and for these or other reasons, when humiliated or betrayed, took their own lives. If the men who wronged them so on earth are about to sit for the examinations, and the women succeed in getting the demon's permission to delay return in bodily form, as soon as the evildoers congregate in the examination halls the women will hasten thither. Then in their formless state they will enter the halls and approach their abusers, now their victims, and addle their minds and misguide their writing brushes, so that they have no chance of passing. The men faced with this disaster have one way out: on the seventeenth day of the fourth month, on the holy day for the king of the tenth and last palace in hell, if they worship him sincerely, and promise to reform themselves and live by the precepts of the *Jade Record,* then they can pass their examinations and be safe at once from the women's shades, the exactions of the Mandarins, and the dangers of flood and fire.[31]

* * *

Once the New Year's festivities of 1837 are over, Hong Huoxiu yet again takes the qualifying examinations in Hua county. He passes this early round and, as he did in 1836, takes leave of his family, and travels to Canton for the second stage. This time, the pressures in the city are even higher than the year before. The literary director of Canton has warned of the prevalence of dishonesty among the licentiates in his region, and announced that any candidates offering bribes to have their papers given special commendation will be strictly punished. Mockingly, he records the euphemisms given by the candidates as they seek his special favor: "conveying expenses," "book gold," or "small expenses for opening the door."[32] In contrast to the previous year, no foreign tracts are being distributed, and so many Canton printers have been rounded up that it is hard for publishers to meet their deadlines. Yet the *Jade Record* still circulates, assuring the hopeful that one sure way to attain examination success is to follow its admonitions for a virtuous life, and giving numerous examples from previous reigns to ram the moral point home.[33]

Late in the second lunar month of 1837, Hong learns that despite his success in Hua he has yet again failed the round of examinations in Canton. Feeling too ill to make the long walk home, he hires a sedan chair with two bearers, reaching Guanlubu on the first day of the third month, the birthdate of the king of the second hell, who punishes the purveyors of false hopes. Now too weak to move, Hong goes to bed.[34] A great crowd gathers around his bed, summoning him to visit King Yan Luo in hell. It is a dream, but Hong sees it as the warning of the end. He calls his family to him, and his two elder brothers hold him half upright in the bed. Hong's parting words, as remembered by his cousin, are these: "My days are counted, and my life will soon be closed. O my parents! How badly have I returned the favour of your love to me! I shall never attain a name that may reflect its lustre upon you."[35] Hong's wife, too, is weeping by the bed, and to her Hong says, "You are my wife. You must not remarry. You are now pregnant and we do not know whether you will bear a son or daughter. If it is a son, let my elder brothers look after you, and do not remarry. If it is a daughter, do likewise."[36]

Hong lies back on the bed, too weak to say more, and the family realize that he is about to die. His body is still, his eyes are closed. In his crowded brain, another throng assembles. There are men playing music. There are children in yellow robes. There is a cock. There is a tiger. There is a dragon. Attendants bring a sedan chair, in which Hong takes his seat. Borne aloft on their shoulders, accompanied by his varied retinue, Hong is carried away toward the east.[37]

Inside his sedan chair, Hong stirs in fear. But when the procession halts at the great gates, the crowd is bathed in light, and welcoming. The attendants who greet him wear dragon robes and horn-brimmed hats, not the martial dress of Life-is-short, or the soiled motley of Death-has-gradations. Though they slit him open, like the fiends in hell, it is not to torment him but only to remove the soiled mass within, which they at once replace with new organs, sealing the wound as though it had never been. The texts they unroll slowly from a scroll before his eyes are clear to read, not distorted by a sputtering wick, and he absorbs them fully, one by one.

His reading finished, a woman comes to greet him. She is not the goddess Meng, forcing him to drink beakers of forgetfulness on the edge of a blood-colored stream. For this woman calls him "son," and herself his mother. "Your body is soiled from your descent into the world," she tells him. "Let your mother cleanse you in the river, after which you can go to see your father."[38]

Hong sees that his father is tall, and sits erect, his hands upon his knees. He wears a black dragon robe and high-brimmed hat. His mouth is almost hidden by his luxuriant golden beard, which reaches down to his belly. There are tears of anger and of sorrow in his eyes as he addresses Hong, who prostrates himself before him, then stands to one side in reverent attention.[39]

"So you have come back up?" says his father. "Pay close attention to what I say. Many of those on earth have lost their original natures. Which of those people on earth did I not give life to, and succor? Which of them did not eat my food and wear my clothing? Which of them has not received my blessing?" Again he asks, "Have they no scrap of respect or fear of me?" Hong stands attentively. "It is the demon devils who have led them astray," says his father. "The people dissipate in offerings to the demon devils things that I have bestowed on them, as if it was the demon devils that had given life to them and nourished them. People have no inkling as to how these demon devils will snare and destroy them, nor can they understand the extent of my anger and my pity."[40]

Moved to outrage by his father's grief, Hong offers to start at once arousing and enlightening people to the demon devils' evil ways, but his father checks him saying, "That will be hard indeed." He shows his son the myriad ways the devil demons harm the people on the earth. The son sees how the father, unable to bear looking any more, turns his head away from the sight in sorrow.[41]

Angered also by the tragic sight, Hong asks his father, "Father, if they are as bad as this, why don't you destroy them?" Because, comes the reply, the devil demons not only fill the world; they have forced their way even into the thirty-three layers of heaven itself. "But father," Hong asks again, "your power is so vast that you can give life to those you want to have life, and death to those you think should die. Why then allow them to force their way in here?" "Wait," says the father. "Let them do their evil a little longer. They shall not escape my wrath." But, says Hong, if they keep on waiting, those he loves on earth are only going to suffer more. If you find the evil intolerable, replies his father, then you may act.[42]

Hong watches the demons carefully, and sees that the leader is Yan Luo, the king of hell, whom people on earth call also the Dragon Demon of the Eastern Sea. Again, he begs his father for permission to do battle, and this time it is granted. To help him in the struggle, his father gives him two gifts, a golden seal and a great sword called Snow-in-the-clouds. With the sword and seal, Hong goes to war on his father's behalf. Up they fight, through the thirty-three levels of Heaven; he wields the sword; his elder brother stands behind him, holding the golden seal, the blazing light from which dazzles the demons and forces them into flight. When Hong's arms grow weary, and he has to rest, the women of Heaven surround him and protect him, reviving his strength with gifts of yellow fruits. When he is rested, they return to battle together, and fight on side by side. Devious is King Yan Luo, and capable of endless transformations—now he appears as a great serpent, now as a flea on the back of a dog, now as a flock of birds, and now as a lion. Forced slowly down through the many levels of Heaven, at last the demons are driven down to earth itself, and there Hong and his celestial army behead them in great numbers. At one moment, Yan Luo himself is in Hong's grasp, but Hong's father orders his son to let the demon go, for such a captive would pollute the very heavens, and in his guise as serpent might mislead people still, and eat their souls. Protesting but obedient, Hong spares the devil king. As to Yan Luo's minions, all those that Hong can find in the world below, his father lets him slay.[43]

With the great battle over, although the final outcome still is unresolved, Hong rests in Heaven. He lives in his palace in Heaven's eastern reaches, with his wife, the First Chief Moon. She tends him lovingly, and bears him a son, whom they have yet to name. Their Heaven is full of music, and Hong finds it easy to forget the world from which he came. Patiently, his father guides him through another group of moral texts, awaiting his transformation. When Hong remains unchanged, his father guides him word by word, till understanding comes. His elder brother is less patient, and grows furious at his obtuseness. At such times Hong's elder brother's wife acts as mediator, placating her husband and reassuring Hong. Hong comes, in time, to see this elder sister-in-law as his second mother.[44]

Despite these joys and studies, Hong's father will not let his son forget the world below. Hong must return to earth, his father says, the demons still are strong, and the people there debauched. Without Hong, how will they be transformed? Before he goes back to earth, Hong's father adds, he must change his name. The name of Hong Huoxiu is no longer fitting; it violates taboos. Instead of the *Huo*, or "fire," in Hong Huoxiu, the father orders him to use the name "completeness," *quan*. Hong himself can choose any one of three ways to use this name, his father tells him. He can keep the new name secret from the world, and style himself Hong Xiu. He can jettison both his earlier given names, and style himself Hong Quan. Or he can keep the non-tabooed given name, and call himself Hong Xiuquan. To prepare for the return to earth, his father combines Hong's new name with a formal title, reflecting his newfound power and dignity: "Heavenly King, Lord of the Kingly Way, Quan."[45] And as another parting gift, the father chants two poems that he has composed for his son, to take with him on his journey back below. Their meaning now seems shrouded in mystery, he says, but one day they will become clear.

Hong takes the gifts and says farewell to his wife and son, who cannot accompany him on the long journey to earth. They must stay in Heaven with Hong's parents, and Hong's elder brother, wife and children. There will they find comfort and safety till Hong returns from earth in glory. In final benediction, Hong's father reassures his son, "Fear not, and act bravely. In times of trouble, I will be your protector, whether they assail you from the left side or the right. What need you fear?"[46]

Hong's earthly family have watched over him day and night as he sleeps and wakes and sleeps again. Now he is deadly quiet; now he shouts out excitedly, "Slash the demons. Slash the demons," pointing to "one here, one there," as they wing their way past him, and crying out that none of them can resist the blows of his sword. Now he leaps from his bed and runs around his room, shouting battle cries and moving his arms as if in combat; now he falls back again, silent and exhausted. Repeatedly, he sings the same two lines from a popular local song: "The victorious swain travels over rivers and seas /He saves his friends and kills his enemies."[47] Sometimes he addresses himself as Emperor of China, and is delighted when others do the same. He writes out in red ink the words of his new title, "Heavenly King, Lord of the Kingly Way, Quan," and posts it on his door. For his older sister, Hong Xinying, he writes the four characters of an alternate title he has adopted, "Son of Heaven in the Period of Great Peace." To other visitors he sings aloud what he has learned to be "the sounds of high heaven." He openly contradicts his own father, and denies that he is his father's son. He argues with his older brothers. Father, sister, brothers, visitors, all feel the bite of his tongue, and hear his assertions of his duty to judge the world, to separate out the demons from the virtuous. He remembers and writes down poems that he composed during those sky-war days and nights. One goes:

> My hand grasps the killing power in Heaven and earth;
> To behead the evil ones, spare the just, and ease the people's sorrow.
> My eyes roam north and west, beyond the rivers and mountains,
> My voice booms east and south, to the edge of the sun and moon.[48]

Another has these lines:

With the three-foot blade in my hand I bring peace to the mountains and rivers,
All peoples living as one, united in kindness.
Seizing the evil demons I send them back to earth,
And scoop up the last of the evildoers in a heavenly net.[49]

His own closest relatives and the people in Guanlubu village murmur that Hong Xiuquan may be mad. His brothers take turns to see that the door to his room is kept shut, and that he does not escape from the house. Such precautions are essential. Chinese law holds all family members responsible for any acts of violence committed by an insane person. If a madman kills, all his family members will pay the penalty.[50]

Yet slowly Hong Xiuquan calms down. Family and friends grow used to his new name. His wife, Lai, bears him a baby girl. He returns to his Confucian texts, and begins to prepare yet again for the examinations. He resumes his teaching duties at a nearby village. The dream is beyond interpretation, and therefore by common consent it can have no meaning.[51]

5

THE KEY

 It is in 1843, in the summer, that Hong Xiuquan realizes he has the key in his own hand; it has been there all the time for seven years. Enmeshed as he has been in the rhythms of state-sponsored ceremonial, examinations, and family, his dream has stayed fastened in his mind in all its detail, but still without clear explanation. A friend and distant relative named Li Jingfang, in whose family Hong has been teaching, drops by Hong's house, sees an odd-looking book, and asks for the loan of it, which Hong as casually grants. The book is Liang Afa's set of nine tracts, "Good Words for Exhorting the Age," brought home by Hong in 1836, and since then neither read nor thrown away. Li Jingfang reads the tracts with rapt attention. Returning to Hong's home, he urges that he read it too. Hong does.[1]

Liang's tracts fit the lock of Hong's mind in many ways, for they focus on the source of evil, and the meaning of the good.[2] In their strange complexity, they talk to the world within his head and to the world of war that has been swirling around Canton from 1839 to 1842.

It has been a strange and episodic war, fought over trade and money and prestige and opium, a war of threats and counterthreats, of bluster and evasion. The world of the foreign factories by the waterfront has been transformed and the British, driven from the city, have seized Hong Kong in recompense. At first in 1839 the Chinese seemed to have the upper hand. Exasperated by the ever-rising shipments of opium, grown in India under British supervision, they made the British give up all their stockpiles of the drug—20,283 chests in all—each chest containing forty balls of opium, each ball composed of three pounds of the refined opium extract, wrapped in heavy coverings of poppy leaves.[3] The Chinese forced this surrender by blockading the foreigners in the thirteen factories on the Canton waterfront, cutting off all river contact with the outside world. Chinese troops lined the streets behind the factories, placed guards in the esplanade, and stationed three cordons of boats on the river, all the way from the Creek to the Danish hong. Every Chinese servant and cook, linguist and comprador, coolie and water carrier—some eight hundred men in all—was ordered to leave his job with the foreigners, or be beheaded. A great silence fell over the normally lively area, as the isolated Western men tried to clean their rooms and sweep the floors, fill their own lamps with oil, polish their silverware, wash their plates, and cook in whatever way they could their stockpiled food, their diet determined by their skills: boiled eggs and potatoes, toasted bread, and rice.[4] As for the opium, the Chinese officials spent days disposing of it, mixing it in pots with lime and—after first apologizing to the spirits of the waters—flushing it out to sea. When all the opium was handed over, the British were allowed to leave Canton, and most other foreigners did the same.

But British merchants were affronted, London roused. A fleet and troops were sent, Chinese forts and ships destroyed, treaties agreed at gunpoint, only to be broken, the factories reoccupied by British traders and again abandoned in the face of Chinese rage, and fears of massacre. By May of 1841 the shifting tides of war had sent Chinese crowds surging through the abandoned foreign factories, gutting all that lay between Hog Lane and the Creek, smashing or stealing the mirrors, chandeliers, and marble statues, the weather vanes and clocks, and burning what remained.[5] Yet at the self-same moment the war, for the first time in China's history, brings British troops to the hills above Canton's walls—not now as isolated strollers or viewers of the fire, but fully armed and uniformed, backed by armored vessels in the river.

The British fleet—led by the British ironclad steamboat *Nemesis*—sinks over seventy Chinese junks and fireboats, and their guns raze much of the waterfront that has not already been fired by the Chinese themselves. British and Indian sepoy troops, in a daring amphibious maneuver, land from the river north of Canton, march around the city, and seize from the rear the four mountain forts that were meant to guard the city from all assaults. In a triumphant gesture of disdain, the British sailors cut the queues of hair off their Chinese captives, and take the clothes of several. Thus bedecked, in Mandarin robes, Chinese hats on heads, and dangling down their backs the severed queues of jet-black hair, they receive the plaudits of their countrymen.[6]

As negotiations on the city's fate continue through sweltering days in May, British and Indian troops patrol the area of Sanyuanli, north of their encampment, on the road that leads to Hua county. There are incidents, clashes: troops march across the paddies full of ripening rice; gates are broken, food is stolen, clothes vanish. There is "foraging" for animals without due payment. Chinese women are accosted, raped. Graves are violated in the name of scientific curiosity—to see whether or how the Chinese embalm their dead. The small bound foot of a woman's corpse is taken from her coffin. The villagers of Sanyuanli bang gongs, assemble their irregular militiamen, most armed initially with little more than hoes, though some have spears. Other villagers join them from the northwest, and some of these have simple guns. More Chinese villagers come from the north, ten miles nearer Hua, some of them trained for water combat.[7]

It is scorching hot, the numbers grow: five thousand, seven thousand, seven thousand five hundred. Combat, when it is joined, is chaos, in a sudden swirling rainstorm that ends all visibility, makes swamps of paths and lakes of paddies, soaks muskets so they will not fire, leaves commanders helplessly looking for their troops. The British lines hold firm, although some of their men are literally hooked out of the rain-soaked ranks by Chinese wielding weapons like enormous shepherd's crooks attached to bamboo poles, and badly wounded. The sepoys dry their sodden muskets with the linings of their turbans, or are issued new muskets with percussion caps, less sensitive to moisture, that let the fire resume. The scattered troops are rounded up and reunited: the toll for the British, one dead and fifteen wounded. Deaths to the Chinese, many but unknown.[8]

By the end of May 1841, each side feels poised for victory: the British, with their discipline and heavy guns, could blitz or occupy the city; the village militiamen, grown now to almost twenty thousand, from 103 different villages, could overwhelm the British with their numbers and their righteous wrath. Above the heads of both, a deal is struck by diplomatic means: the city will be saved, but pay six million taels in indemnity; the militias will disperse; the British will leave the hills. The prefect of Canton, She Baoshun, makes sure the terms are met. Grudgingly, the Chinese irregulars disperse. But, as they see the British also file away, the city spared, the ill-armed villagers claim a total victory.[9]

After this settlement, in the examination halls of Canton, the staid environment is filled for a moment in 1841 with flying ink stones, hurled by the enraged scholars at officials they have come to fear and hate. This too is an aspect of the war, one that begins to divide the Chinese against themselves. For as a result of the fighting the belief is growing that the country is full of traitors, Chinese traitors to their race. New kinds of angers flare as the blame for humiliation and defeat is parceled out among the vanquished. To the examination candidates in Canton, as they shout their anger and hurl their only available projectiles, the carved ink stones, often of great beauty and antiquity, that constitute one of the scholars' "four treasures"—the others being the brushes, brush holders, and the ink itself—the enemy is their chief examiner, the prefect She Baoshun. For in persuading the militiamen at Sanyuanli to disperse, even though he doubtless also saved the city from destruction, he seems to the educated candidates to have gone too far in appeasing the voracious foreigners. When he retreats, mortified, before the barrage, other emboldened students try to smash the sedan chair in which he flees.[10]

At other times it is the officials themselves who spur the local Canton hunts for traitors, seeking out those who trade with foreigners, translate or teach Chinese, row or sail their boats, or—most heinous crime of all—guide the British officers and their vessels through the ill-charted and shifting mud flats of the creeks along the Pearl River. Some of those accused of such collaboration are punished by means of sharpened wooden sticks thrust through their ears, the ends sticking straight up above their heads and topped with tiny flags, as they are hustled through the streets.[11] The militiamen of Sanyuanli and elsewhere kill more than a thousand of their own countrymen as they seek out anyone who collaborated with the British; and the Banner troops of the Qing state, the "regular army" that was of little service in the fray, now roam across the countryside accusing of treason those whose property they covet.[12]

As the British fleet moves northward, massing by the Yangzi River delta, probing Hangzhou Bay, attacking Shanghai, and finally laying siege to Nanjing, a new element enters the story. For now it is the Manchu officers of the ruling dynasty, fearing subversion from the Chinese in the very cities they seek to defend against the British, who launch preemptive strikes against their own people, killing Chinese on vague treason charges just at the news of the imminent arrival of the British forces. British troops see Chinese people fleeing from their "protectors" in the Manchu Banner armies, and if they force an entry find the streets within filled with Chinese dead. Not surprisingly, as they so swiftly learned to do in Hong Kong when the British seized it as a spoil of war in 1841, these Chinese survivors seem eager to work with the British and thus fan the very basis of suspicion about their loyalties.

The self-reinforcing cycle of myth and fear increases as members of secret societies, bonded by blood oaths and secret passwords, and pledged to eventual overthrow of the alien Manchus and restoration of the long-defeated house of Ming, also flock to areas where the British have control. Though some are double agents, reporting back their findings to the Qing officials, many use the war and its dislocations to engage in piracy, continued opium running, or other rackets under protection of the Union Jack. In other cities it is the Manchus who destroy their own women and children first, before taking their own lives by fire or sword or drowning.[13]

No Confucian texts, no local histories, no *Jade Record,* can quite define these strange catastrophes. But in Liang's first tract, near the middle, a new voice calls out to Hong Xiuquan. It is the voice of a foreign sage or scholar named Isaiah, and this is how Liang records Isaiah's words:

> Why should ye be stricken any more? ye will revolt more and more: the whole heart is sick, and the whole heart faint. From the sole of the foot even unto the head there is no soundness in it; but wounds, and bruises, and putrifying sores: they have not been closed, neither bound up, neither mollified with ointment. Your country is desolate, your cities are burned with fire: your land, strangers devour it in your presence, and it is desolate, as overthrown by strangers.[14]

The fire that Isaiah cites has not only scourged the Canton waterfront but has consumed the Chinese warriors in new and terrifying ways. Some have been blown through the air in balls of fire when the rockets of the British ironclad paddle steamers hit the stores of gunpowder in the war junks' holds, their bodies tumbling back to earth in shattered fragments.[15] Wounded Chinese troops have been scorched to death or blown apart as they fall on the gunpowder pouches slung around their waists, ignited by the slow matches for their newly issued matchlocks that they clutch in their inexperienced hands. Others have staggered naked out of their burning clothes as the houses where they were sheltering caught fire or clung to the stern chains or rudders of their burning boats until the ships blew up or the intense heat forced their grip to loosen and they sank beneath the surface of the water.[16] Never in the Canton Delta has there been heard a sound like that of February 27, 1841, when the British captured and set fire to the 900-ton ship *Chesapeake,* just below Whampoa. The Chinese had bought the ship the previous year from the Americans and tried to convert it into a man-of-war, hoisting the red flag of the commanding admiral on its mainmast, decorating the poop and taffrail with colored streamers, and filling it with gunpowder and munitions. When the flames reached the magazine and the ship exploded, the sound could be heard for thirty miles. The ship split through as though severed by a giant saw, the flaming fragments were hurled high into the heavens, and set fire to houses far away.[17]

Once again, speaking through Liang's translation, it is the man Isaiah who seems to have foreseen the nightmare, and to have given it his words:

> And the destruction of the transgressors and of the sinners shall be together, and they that forsake the LORD shall be consumed. For they shall be ashamed of the oaks which ye have desired, and ye shall be confounded for the gardens that ye have chosen. For ye shall be as an oak whose leaf fadeth, and as a garden that hath no water. And the strong shall be as fibers of hemp, and the maker of it as a spark, and they shall both burn together, and none shall quench them.[18]

It is on the very first page of his first tract that Liang introduces evil and its begetter. There is a god whose name is Ye-huo-hua, writes Liang, who created earth and all the living things. But of all the things created, the serpent is the most devious, for this serpent is none other than the god of evil, who has transformed himself into a serpent demon. This serpent demon lures a woman into eating a fruit that gives knowledge of evil ways; she in turn feeds it to her husband, for which both are cursed by the god and banished from the garden where they had lived. On the eastern edge of the garden, God places a being called a Cherubim, constantly watchful and grasping a blazing sword, to preserve the source of life and to stop the couple from ever returning to that land of happiness. Liang gives a source for this story, as a scholar should. It is the third chapter of a book he identifies as a "Sacred Text" *(shengjing),* entitled "The Book of Creation," chapter 3.[19] This is what Liang writes and Hong reads. There is no way for Hong to tell that Liang has added to the Book of Genesis his own explanation that the serpent in Eden is the god of evil, the serpent demon.

Liang repeats the story in the third tract, though this time in a different context. The serpent demon is still defined as being the evil god, but now the god Ye-huo-hua is called "the Highest God of Heaven." In the second tract, where the serpent demon's wiles are again discussed, God has yet another name, "Great Ruler of things created on heaven and earth." It is not until the beginning of the sixth tract that Liang removes what may be lingering doubt by explaining that all these names refer to the same true God.[20] But whatever name for God one uses, the extent of the serpent demon's damage can now be seen in full. For when the first couple lived in their garden there was neither excessive heat nor excessive cold, no need for men to till the soil or women to spin, no floods or droughts, no sicknesses or death. In the beginning, human nature was good, and evil thoughts did not arise. But once the serpent demon spun his plans, evil entered the world, and now the nature of men holds more bad than good, and the numbers of the righteous and the pure of spirit are few indeed.[21]

On the question of evil, Liang in his second tract thinks aloud an elusive and difficult problem. Since the Lord of Heaven clearly has the power to create all the myriad beings on this earth out of a state of nothingness, if he had wanted to he could have created a different set of beings with living souls. But because he loved his creatures as parents love their children, he sent his only and beloved son down to earth, to meet his death and thus expiate people's sins. God did not *have* to do this, Liang emphasizes, it was something that he chose to do.[22] So evil remains for now, and God's goodness with it.

Liang tells how this Highest God of Heaven sent his own holy son down from the heavens to earth, placing the child's spirit in the body of a young pure woman, so that she would be pregnant and bring his body out into the world, even though untouched by man. She gave birth to the boy in a rustic hut, giving him the name Jesus, which translates as Savior of the World and Lord. At the time of his birth, an emissary from God appeared in the sky, calling out that no one needed to fear, for he brought good and joyful news, of the birth of a savior. And as he spoke, suddenly, from out of the clouds came a great celestial army of the emissaries of God, crying out, "Glory to God in the Highest, and on earth Taiping, Great Peace and good will toward men."[23] Since this took place on the same continent as China, adds Liang, one might expect some traces of it to be found in China's own early classics. But that would be an erroneous expectation, for these events happened in the time of Emperor Ai of the Western Han dynasty, and the classics had been written long before. So though in China's earliest books there can be found hints of the actions of the Highest God of Heaven, one cannot expect to find in them similar traces of his son.[24]

Liang's text, too, provides a key to the linked significance of age and action. Liang describes how Jesus was a studious and hardworking child, who already showed his intelligence by the age of twelve. But he took his time to find his calling, only slowly developing his mission as a teacher. It was not until the age of thirty, the age that Hong is now as he reads the tract, that Jesus cast aside his old life and began to preach openly, explaining how his holy father had sent him down to earth with specific orders, to exhort the people of the earth to repent of their lascivious and their evil ways, to get rid of all their idols and images of false and Buddhist gods, and to follow only the way of the One True God.[25]

So Jesus taught, and gathered his disciples around him, till at the age of thirty-three he had completed his allotted span on earth and was vilified, tormented, and nailed to a cross, on which he seemed to die. At that time the sun and the moon lost their luster, and terrible earthquakes split apart the earth. But after three days and nights Jesus reasserted the divine nature with which he had originally been endowed, a nature that let him attain everything, "attain completeness," and though lying in his tomb he brought himself back to life from his state of death. And in forty final days of preaching, he showed his followers how to spread his words, how those who believed God's teachings would attain an everlasting happiness, while those ignoring them, or refusing to believe, would suffer for all eternity. His mission done, Jesus returned to Heaven, being greeted there by countless numbers of his father's host.[26]

The reference to the era of Great Peace, Taiping, in the angel's mouth at the time of Jesus' birth, fits with another passage in which Liang explains the phrase "Tianguo," Kingdom of Heaven. Liang shows that it can be used in two ways: one is the eternal happiness in Paradise, which will be enjoyed by the souls of all the righteous people when their physical bodies have died; the other is a community within *this* world, formed by congregations who believe in Jesus and worship the Lord of Heaven.[27]

The words of Jesus are like nothing Hong has heard before, although Confucian virtue has been the object of his studies for two decades. Liang gives a transcript of a speech Jesus made while seated on a mountaintop, as the words have been preserved in another sacred book, this one called "Madou" (Matthew), chapters 5 to 7. In one section Jesus tells his people to rejoice, not grieve, over their misfortunes:

> Blessed are they which are persecuted for righteousness' sake: for theirs is the kingdom of heaven. Blessed are ye, when men shall revile you, and persecute you, and shall say all manner of evil against you falsely, for my

sake. Rejoice, and be exceeding glad: for great is your reward in heaven: for so persecuted they the prophets which were before you.[28]

Jesus also tells his followers how to pray to their God, with these words:

> After this manner therefore pray ye: Our Father which art in heaven, Hallowed be thy name. Thy kingdom come. Thy will be done in earth, as it is in heaven. Give us this day our daily bread. And forgive us our trespasses, as we forgive those who trespass against us. And lead us not into temptation, but deliver us from evil: For thine is the kingdom, and the power, and the glory, for ever. Amen.[29]

And Jesus issues warnings that evil is pervasive and perhaps innate:

> Beware of false prophets, which come to you in sheep's clothing, but inwardly they are ravening wolves. Ye shall know them by their fruits. Do men gather grapes of thorns, or figs of thistles? Even so every good tree bringeth forth good fruit; but a corrupt tree bringeth forth evil fruit. A good tree cannot bring forth evil fruit, neither can a corrupt tree bring forth good fruit. Every tree that bringeth not forth good fruit is hewn down, and cast into the fire. Wherefore by their fruits ye shall know them.[30]

Though Hong was not at the examination hall in 1841, when flying ink stones filled the air, in 1843, before reading the tracts, Hong Xiuquan has sat for the examinations a fourth time in Canton, and for the fourth time he has failed. In a passage in the first tract, Liang's words affirm to Hong that taking the examinations is a senseless and self-defeating pastime.

> This practice of Confucian teaching often is full of vanity or absurdity. The scholars pay reverence to the idols of Wenchang and Kuixing* and implore their protection, in order to broaden their knowledge and quicken their intellectual skills, so that they will pass at the head of the examination lists. Most Chinese who study the Confucian texts feel they must pay obeisance to these two idols; they beg these idols' help in passing the provincial level examinations and then the national examinations, so they can be members of the capital's Hanlin Academy and receive official posts to rule the people. How is it possible that everyone always worships these two idols, and yet there are many people who have been studying and taking the exams since their childhood, and reach the age of seventy or eighty without even passing

---

*Respectively named for the constellations Ursa Major and the Big Dipper, both worshiped as the God of Literature.

the very lowest levels of the exams and becoming licentiates, let alone passing
at the higher levels? Haven't these men prayed to these idols every year?
Why didn't they win the idols' protection, and pass successfully? From this
we can see that these Confucian scholars are bewildered and obsessed by
their ambitions, so they cling to their delusions and worship these idols
instead of with a humble mind worshiping the Ruler of Heaven and Earth,
the God who rules the entire world and all its wealth and glory, and thus
being in accordance with the sacred principles of the Great Way.[31]

As Liang says elsewhere in the tracts, our lives are fleeting—which of us
can be sure he will live to be fifty or sixty, let alone eighty or a hundred?[32]
Hong absorbs this message too. He never sits for the exams again.

To an extent, of course, as Liang's words tell Hong, the Confucian
scholars and their idols are no more misled than other people. Buddhists
and Taoists, and the gullible and careless from all walks of life, get caught
up in the same frenzied search for security and reassurance. In olden days,
people limited their worship to the spirits of mountains and of rivers, or
to the images of loyal officials and worthy scholars. But now people of all
walks of life—scholars, farmers, artisans, merchants—worship every kind
of image: those painted on paper, invoked in calligraphy or woodblock
prints, fashioned out of polished stone, carved wood, modeled in clay, in
colored porcelain, squared stones, or pyramids and cones.[33]

Wherever you look in China today, writes Liang, you find examples of
this folly. Rich merchants and other wealthy families have the altars in
their homes, to Guanyin, the Bodhisattva of Mercy, to the gods of wealth,
of childbirth, of the well, of the kitchen, of the locality—their incense and
lanterns, their offerings of wine, follow in endless succession.[34] The farmers pray to their gods of crops and grains, begging their help in matters of
wind and rain, redoubling their prayers when blight or mice or insects
strike their fields. Never do they invoke the true Lord of All, creator of
everything that grows.[35]

Similarly, the tailors say that Xianyuan, the Yellow Emperor, was the
first to make humans clothes, so they worship him to gain the skills to
prosper in their trade. The carpenters claim that Luban was the first to
invent the art of exact measurement, so they erect their shrines to him,
and greet his birthday with ritual plays, in order that they may prosper in
their business.[36] Sailors who roam the seas believe their fates are in the
hands of the North Emperor, or the Heavenly Empress. They write their
prayers out to these spirits and display them on their vessels, to keep them
safe from storms and bring calm waters in every season, so that they too

can profit from their ventures.[37] As for the women and unmarried girls, for them it is any one of three spirits who gives protection, either Guanyin, or Madam Golden Flower, or the Minister of Births. They say that Guanyin is a woman, and thus she understands their hopes and pains and the hardship of their lot, and brings them special solace. As for Madam Golden Flower, she as a woman bore many sons, so she will help them do the same. Those who are childless, especially, invoke her aid. The Minister of Births can bring to them a quick delivery, if he so chooses, and save them from the worst of pains.[38]

If the Confucians are thus deluded, the craftsmen, and the women, one can expect no better from the Buddhist and the Taoist priests and nuns. The Taoists claim to know the triune secrets and forces of the universe, but which of us has ever seen them become immortal spirits and rise to Heaven? Humiliation is more commonly their lot.[39] Chanting their sutras every day, yearning for the joys of the Western Paradise, what do the Buddhists pray to but a long dead man? He is unable to affect their fate, as some "dress beautifully in the very finest clothes, gorge themselves with food, indulge in lust and vice," while others lie ravaged with sickness in the beds of hospitals, beg in the streets, or "die of starvation on some mountain road, their putrid carcasses a breeding ground for maggots."[40]

Liang puts the lessons of these stories and the story of man's disobedience both in the distant past and in the present. In ancient times, he writes, there was a sage named Moses, who led his people out of a foreign country into a desert. There, on a mountain with the name of Sinai, the Lord of Heaven gave him, in person, ten prohibitions that all his people should observe. Yet though Moses diligently tried to teach his people these divine instructions, they would not listen, and slowly, one by one, they died in the desert, often with the greatest suffering.[41] So it is with those today who will not listen to Jesus' teachings. The factors of time and distance play a part, writes Liang; everyone cannot receive the message all at once. But as the rising sun sends out its first reflections, and later its full blazing light, the news will slowly spread. Now the truth has come to Canton city, brought by foreign people on their ships. To achieve this task, they do not grudge a cost of tens of thousands in cash and gold, and even learn the Chinese language no matter how much toil it takes so they can translate the sacred books, and bring the message to the Chinese people. Now that task is done, the translation is completed, so all can get the full impact of the holy text's complete decrees.[42]

This theme of Liang's, though written years before, fits well with the realities around Canton, as the treaty settlement that ends the Opium War in 1842 is negotiated by the Manchus and the representatives of the British crown. The treaty ends forever the system of the thirteen hongs and foreign factories crowded on the Canton shore, and opens instead five ports—Canton being one—to foreign residence and trade. In 1843, additional treaties guarantee the rights of foreign Christian missionaries, both Protestant and Catholic, to build their churches in these cities, and freely to preach their faith. Buoyed by this concession, missionaries who had been sheltering in Hong Kong until the war was over, now move back to Canton. Gutzlaff is active once again, though busy translating for the British and even administering captured territories for them; and so is his good friend Issachar Roberts, who came from the Tennessee town of Shelbyville in 1837 at the age of thirty-five to work at Gutzlaff's side. Roberts, a self-educated preacher, raised in the passionate religious world of tent revivals and covered-wagon services, independent-minded, free of supervision and bored with rules, is first to return, renting a little house just outside Canton's walls. Despite the treaty provisions the virulence of anti-foreign feeling still makes it impossible to reside within. Dressing in Chinese clothes, working with a local convert tied by loyalty to him in person as well as to his redeemer, Jesus Christ, Roberts restlessly prowls the countryside, preaching in the Hakka dialect he has been studying, and distributing religious tracts.[43]

Liang does not say what ten prohibitions God issued to his servant Moses on the Mount of Sinai, and thus it is unclear what exactly Moses' followers did or failed to do before they died their desert deaths. But in two of the other tracts Liang outlines six groups of acts that the highest God considers as the worst of evils: in one the list consists of murder, rebellion, stealing and swindling, adulterous lust, magical arts, and disobedience to one's parents.[44] In the other, Liang gives Jesus' own list, as he told it to a rich young man who sought to enter the Kingdom of Heaven: Not to kill; not to commit adultery; not to steal; not to bear false witness; to honor your parents, and to love your neighbor as you love yourself. And Liang adds one new prohibition of his own: not to smoke opium, a vice as bad as any of the others.[45]

All human beings can recognize these actions to be evil, writes Liang. Why then, when all can see the harm, do people persevere in doing wrong? Partly because of human stubbornness, he answers, and partly because of ignorance of history, disregard of sacred truth, and obedience to social conventions that give the highest praise to those constructing temples and making precious offerings to the idols.[46] But booksellers are to blame as well, for along with their Confucian classics and their books of morals they sell all kinds of lascivious short stories, novels, and plays, leading people into evil ways as directly as if they had openly preached evil to them. It is a melancholy fact that however many exhortations to virtue one might publish, most people prefer to read tales of sex and sin.[47] There are two categories of human actions that are not so different as they sound: some people spend money to do evil, whereas others do evil to earn money.[48] As for the Buddhist priests with their deceitful teaching of reincarnation, and the Taoists with their "Great Jade Emperor" and "Old Master of Transcendence Lao Zi," they mislead the people even more than the pornographers do.[49]

How does one show that one believes, and that what one believes is right? Liang tells the story of one man, Paul (who like Hong had changed his name). This Paul persuaded people to give up their books of magical arts, preached so well against the idols that the makers of silver images feared they would lose their livelihoods, and exorcised the evil spirits from a madman, when all the other magic makers had failed. Paul tells the faithful in a foreign land that they need to receive the Holy Spirit, and that to do that they must be washed or purified not just in the name of John but in the name of Jesus Christ, for John had said he bathed them in repentance until Jesus would be with them. And when Paul purified them with the water, they received the Holy Spirit, and not only that, they could all speak different languages, and make prophecies.[50]

The passage is hard for Hong to understand, and nowhere in the tracts does Liang say exactly what was done with water, or when, or how, while Jesus lived. But in the sixth tract, talking of his own life with Milne, Liang reports the definition that Milne gave to him: "In the ritual of purification by water, one takes some clear water, and sprinkles it on the person's head, or on his body. The inner meaning of this is to wash away the filth of the person's sins, and allow the Holy Spirit to transform his heart. After one has received this ritual of purification by water, one comes to love goodness and hate evil, and sloughing off the old nature one becomes a new being."[51] On the next holy day, when Liang expressed his deep repentance and love of Jesus, Milne scattered clear water on his head, and he was purified. Sometime thereafter, Liang purified his wife with water by himself, and got Morrison to purify his son.[52]

The moral of this whole tragic yet joyful story rests on two different levels, Liang suggests. Long ago, God chose one country to be his own, the land that he named Israel. There he gave his prohibitions, and there he sent his son to save all human souls from sin. But just as in the time of Moses the prohibitions and God's words were ignored, so was Jesus killed upon the cross and all his followers scattered. And God's vengeance was terrible, for the evildoers in that land not only met their individual fates, but the whole country of Israel was itself subjugated, and "up to the present time this country is no more, and its people scattered among all the other nations."[53]

Such a fate is also the final, absolute, and universal one for all unbelievers, Liang concludes, as the ninth tract ends. All the world must expect a Last Judgment, which will sweep upon all people as surely as the pains of a woman in labor, yet as furtively and unseen as a thief in the night. God's retainers will unroll the scrolls on which all our sins are listed; all people of all nations shall be judged, as surely as the shepherd separates out his sheep from the mountain goats. To those who believed in Jesus, and sheltered the believers in his name, will come the blessings of almighty God. But for the others, there will be only eternal torment in the eternal fire, with the demons as their guardians.[54]

The throne of the Savior, at that final hour, will be like blazing wheels of fire, and the Savior will order his millions of attendants to burn all creatures to ashes in the flame of his father's anger. As the Judgment ends, the Savior will descend in a cloud amidst the shouts of angels, blowing the trumpets of God his father, and all who believed early on in Jesus' name and died for him shall be resurrected, followed by those who were slower to see the light, but did so before it was too late. And all those saved shall be raised in the cloud, and welcomed by the Savior in the heavens, and their bodies will be restrengthened and purified, and no one will be bride or groom, but all shall live like angels of the lord in Heaven.[55]

The collection of tracts is long, full of strange terms and stranger names, and there are many things that Liang does not explain. But Hong feels the key has opened up his head and heart. The man with the golden beard of whom he dreamed, and for whom he fought the demons, is God the Father, the Lord Ye-huo-hua, who created Heaven and earth. The elder brother who shone the golden seal upon the demons, fought at Hong's side, yet scolded him severely is Jesus the Savior, son of God, killed on the cross and returned again to Heaven. The retainers who welcomed Hong and helped him in his heavenly battles are the angels who live with God. The texts unrolled before his eyes or explained to him point by point are the words of Liang's, or the words of other sacred texts that Liang transcribed or summarized. The evil one, Yan Luo, is the demon devil serpent who ruined the happy life of man and woman in their first idyllic garden. The sword with which Hong fought the demons is like the sword that guarded the eastern gate of Paradise. God does speak directly to mankind, as he did to Moses on Mount Sinai, and as he has to Hong. Jesus too has lived and toiled upon the earth. The raging flood that almost swept away all living things is a sign of Hong's own destiny. His name Huo, or fire, was tabooed because it was the middle name of God the Father. His new name Quan—"complete" or "whole"—begins, closes, and reverberates throughout the sacred texts. The Confucian examinations are worthless vanities, spreading false hopes, engendering false procedures. The foreigners, despite the opium and the wrath of some of their number, have good intentions, and perhaps will save the land from death. Idols are evil, and the festival days that mark the working Chinese year do not reflect the rhythms of worship due the highest God. Sin ravages the world, encouraged by false priests, the lustful, the pornographers. The cleansing rituals that Hong went through in Heaven were foretellers of his baptism. There are legions of demons still to slay on earth, for evil has infiltrated all the human race. And since Jesus is the son of God, and also Hong's elder brother, then Hong is literally God's Chinese son.

6

WANDERING

 One is what one believes. Hong starts to preach. The man he reaches first is Li Jingfang, with whom he read the text. Piecing the baptismal ritual together from the scattered bits of information left by Liang—who in his tracts chose not to present any of the four Gospels' accounts of Jesus' baptism by John, or Jesus' baptism of others—Hong and Li baptize each other, in a private ritual, as Liang had baptized his wife. Liang has written that only those who believe in Jesus and receive baptism shall receive everlasting life, while those rejecting Jesus will receive everlasting pain. So as the two men sprinkle water on each other's heads they pray to their new True God, promise to follow His commandments, and to keep away from idols, evil, and the evil spirits. Together they chant their own new invocation: "Purification from all former sins, putting off the old, rebirth." His heart filled with happiness, Hong writes his first poem using his new Savior's name:

> Sure is it that our sins surge up to heaven;
> How good to know that Jesus bears them all on our behalf.
> No longer trusting in the demon devils we obey the holy word
> Worshipping the One True Lord to cultivate our hearts.[1]

The two men discuss Hong's dream, and feel that some of it, at least, can be understood literally. So together they order a local craftsman to forge two double-edged swords—each sword nine pounds in weight, and three feet in length—with three characters carved upon each blade, "Sword for exterminating demons." They celebrate the moment in a poem:

> Grasping our three-foot swords we bring order to the mountains and valleys,
> All within the four seas will be one family, living in kindly union. . . .
> Tigers roar and dragons call. Light fills the earth;
> Great will be our joy as the Great Peace reigns.[2]

The words seem now to pour out of Hong, and spread beyond his village. As at the time of his dream, some think him mad; but when anxious friends post a man to watch him, Hong converts the watcher to the logic of his views. Hong talks often, too, with two of his relatives, who listen with particular attention to his words. One, Hong Rengan, lives in Guanlubu, and is a cousin on his father's side; the other, Feng Yunshan, is related to Hong's stepmother (Hong's father's second wife), and lives in a village less than a mile away. Like Hong, they have education but have not succeeded in their examinations, and serve as village teachers. In the summer of 1843 Hong converts them both. The three men celebrate with a double ceremony—first Hong administers the baptism privately, in the school where the elder cousin works; but then, spurning privacy, they go to a stream that runs nearby and immerse themselves completely. From this time onward, it is Feng and Hong Rengan who share Hong Xiuquan's innermost councils—and despite his sword Li Jingfang drifts out of the inner circle of believers.[3]

Rereading Liang's text with his two new converts, Hong Xiuquan comes to a realization he has not had before. As Hong Rengan later remembers it, Hong phrased it thus: "If I had received the books without having gone through the sickness, I should not have dared to believe in them, and on my own account to oppose the customs of the whole world; if I had merely been sick but not also received the books, I should have had no further evidence as to the truth of my visions. . . . I have received the immediate command from God in his presence; the will of Heaven rests with me."[4] The words cannot be changed, says Hong, and God's commands cannot be disobeyed, for "the word of the Lord Jehovah is right." The proof lies in Psalms 19 and 33, each of which is translated in Liang's tract. The psalms—Liang translates no others, so Hong cannot know the rest—are full of Hong's own name, they reverberate with

"Quan," and Hong chants the words aloud: "There is no speech or language, where their voice is not heard. Their sound is gone out to the *whole* earth—to the earth that is Quan's—and their words to the ends of the world."[5] "The Judgements of the Lord Jehovah are true, and righteous *altogether*—Quan is righteous—more to be desired than gold, yea than much fine gold, sweeter also than honey and the honeycomb."[6] "Who can *fully* understand—understand like Quan—his errors? Cleanse thou me from my secret faults."[7]

For the next few months, they pore over Liang's text, exploring, preaching, trying to see which pronouns fit with which being, earthly or divine. Slowly the three men convert members of their own and each other's families. And two distant cousins of Hong Xiuquan from the western province of Guangxi, who come to Guanlubu on family business (or other business of which we have no record), are moved by his words, baptized by him, and later take the message home with them.[8]

To strike at the idols, as God has ordered them, the three move first against the ones they know best and face the most often, the tablets to Confucius that stand in the place of honor in each of the schools where they teach. One by one they remove the tablets, purging their schoolrooms of the heathen icons. This is not a simple task, for there are many varieties of tablets, in many styles and sizes. In Hua county, as elsewhere in China, the centerpiece of homage to Confucius is, by law, a replica of the four characters of calligraphy written in 1686 by Emperor Kangxi to honor the Sage: "Model Teacher of a Myriad Generations." Each wooden board on which these characters are written, specifies the government's decree, is to be 2.37 feet in height, four inches wide, and seven-tenths of an inch in thickness; while the base on which it rests must be four inches high, seven inches broad, and three inches thick. The background must be in bright vermilion, the lettering in gold.[9] Then, depending on the grandeur of the shrine or center of display, tablets of sizes graded somewhat smaller are arranged symetrically around the main Confucian tablet. These are all in black lettering on backgrounds of less fiery red, and list one by one the names of Confucius' four favorite and most talented disciples, his other early followers, and all those across the next two thousand years whom various emperors have acknowledged as worthy to be added to the list of great Confucian activists or thinkers. By the time of Hong Xiuquan this list had swelled to over one hundred names, all of whom he could be expected to recognize, and many of whose texts or commentaries he read intensively in school while preparing for the state examinations.[10]

Slowly, as the parents of their pupils hear that the Confucian tablets are coming down, the pupils are withdrawn. The incomes of the schools decrease. Some men near Guanlubu who have attained the licentiate's degree that Hong has sought so long chide him for his conduct, and for spreading his new beliefs. One, recognizing Hong as a serious scholar, with a lively mind, even offers to read all Liang's texts, and refute the errors in them one by one. Affronted, Hong breaks off their relationship.[11] In the first month of 1844, the local village worthies still reach out to Hong, for they respect his education and his versifying skills. When he refuses their request that he write an ode in honor of that year's lantern festival—for he sees, now that his eyes are opened, that such a poem would be "to praise the merits of the idols"—they chide him with a verse:

> We unskillful old folk hoped for help from the young,
> Little imagining you would have nothing to do with us.
> You are crammed with learning, and could have used it—
> But convinced by slanderous words, you cling just to them.[12]

Hong Xiuquan responds in verse, matching the local scholars' rhyme scheme and reversing the argument of their final line in his opening one:

Not because we were convinced by slanderous words did we turn down your
    request,
But because we only follow the True God's commandments.
Sharp must be the line between the roads to Heaven and hell—
How can we with muddled-heads traverse this earthly life?[13]

The clash seems elegant, for these are cultured men, even if living in the villages rather than the more sophisticated county town. But anger is there not far below the surface. Before the spring is over, Hong and his cousins lose their jobs.[14]

What should they do? Hong and his friends decide, as they phrase it, "to travel throughout the world, and teach to all the people the doctrine of repentance."[15] They have little money, and Hong Xiuquan's wife, Lai, has just borne her second child, another girl. Their hope is that they can sell ink and writing brushes as they go, to pay their way. Five of them plan to go together, but before they leave, Hong Rengan is forced to abandon the group. His parents and elder brother forbid him absolutely to make the journey. Although his age is already over twenty, they have not hesitated to beat him severely and tear his clothes to punish him for defacing Confucian tablets, and he knows their words have to be taken seriously. So it is Hong Xiuquan, Feng Yunshan, and two of Feng's relatives who take their leave of Guanlubu in early April 1844.[16]

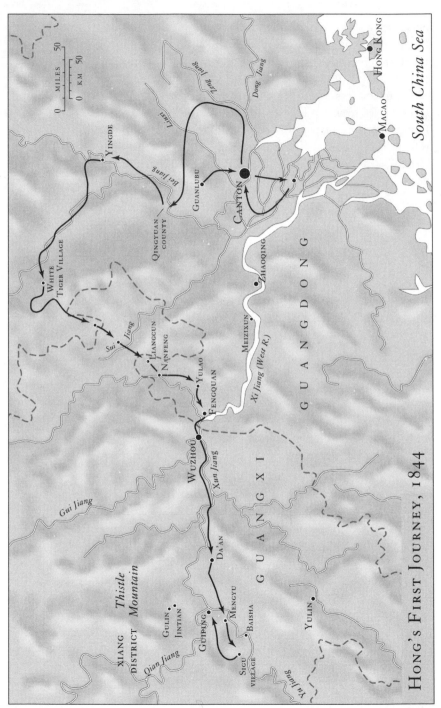

South China Sea

HONG'S FIRST JOURNEY, 1844

Is their plan somehow to emulate the restless traveling of Jesus, or the far-flung journeying of his Apostles? Or is it mere survival? They do not say, but their initial route betrays their indecision, as if they want to travel far and yet not get too far away from home. First they go to Canton city, re-traveling, for Hong, the route of four examination trips; the open fighting there is over, the cannon stilled, but still the city seethes with bitterness, of Chinese against the Manchus, and of the populace against the British, whom they will not allow to enter within their walls, despite the specific treaty provisions. Unwilling to provoke another war, the British continue to negotiate, and build their Hong Kong base. From Canton the four men travel down into the delta region, then curve northwest, reentering the city via the western gate, exiting through the eastern gate, marching and preaching in a semicircle through the eastern hills until they rest for a while in Qingyuan county, some forty miles north of Guanlubu. Here they are welcomed by the locals, and baptize many in the clan of the Li—relatives perhaps of Hong's first convert—who remain thereafter steadfast in the faith. Heading farther north, then west again, they pause at White Tiger village in early May. They have tramped around their province for thirty-four days, and have ended up a little over a hundred miles from where they started.[17]

Here, at Hong Xiuquan's own urgings, the little group breaks up. According to Hong's later recollections, he wished to travel on alone, but Feng Yunshan insisted on accompanying him, while Feng's two relations chose to return to their homes and families.[18] The plan that Hong Xiuquan and Feng devise is bold and potentially dangerous. They will walk all the way to Guangxi province in the west, to the village of Sigu ,in Guiping county. They choose this destination because it is the home, among others, of that same Hakka family named Huang, distant relatives of Hong Xiuquan's, two of whose members had visited him the previous year, and been converted and baptized by him before returning home. Hong and Feng know little of the geography of the region, nor even the best route to follow for this journey of 250 miles or more across rather than along the major river routes, and through mountainous regions, many sparsely settled, or inhabited mainly by native Miao or Yao tribesmen with little knowledge of or interest in Chinese government and culture.[19]

But as it happens, the journey is peaceful. People along the way reach out to help them, especially a Chinese teacher who has made his home among the hills, and runs a school there for the children of the Miao. He entertains them, and believes their message, and they entrust him with spreading their message among the Miao, for neither Hong nor Feng can understand a word of the Miao people's dialect. As they leave, they write out their doctrine for the teacher, and he in turn gives them a little traveling money. Often they walk all day with only occasional cups of tea and snacks they buy at roadside village stalls. Despite these hazards, and their shortage of funds, they know that they "travel under the One True God's protection," and reach the Guangxi town of Mengyu on May 21, 1844, after seventeen days of travel, averaging over fourteen miles a day. From there they travel another fifteen miles farther west, till they reach the Huang family home in Sigu village, where they are welcomed by their host, the two men previously baptized in Guanlubu, and five other branches of the Huang and Hong clans, with whom they are able to stay in turns.[20]

To reach out effectively to potential converts, and speed the holy work, Hong knows—it is Liang Afa who taught him—that one needs tracts describing the One True God's religion. So while staying either in or near Sigu village, Hong starts to write his own "Exhortations to Worship the One True God," echoing the title of Liang Afa's tracts. These "Exhortations" are Hong Xiuquan's first substantial pieces of writing, except for short poems and examination essays. As the months glide by he continues to write, in paired verse couplets of seven characters each, which will make the message easier to remember for those who cannot read.[21]

Almost certainly Hong's "Exhortations" are built from material in Hong's head, as he and Feng can have carried few books with them on their two months of marching, and a nonscholar family in rural Guangxi probably had scant library resources. For a man trained for the Confucian examinations for twenty years or more, China's basic Confucian texts are firmly lodged, as are the basic outline and major figures in China's long recorded history. In any case, Hong keeps most of the allusions simple.[22] And though we cannot tell if he has taken Liang Afa's text with him on his journey, with his mental training he will have committed all the major parts to memory, and recall them at his own volition.

Hong may have written several "Exhortations," but only one complete example has come down to us, the "Ode on the Origin of the Way and Our Salvation." As Hong explains in his preamble to this ode, China has fallen away from a basic belief that once was shared by all:

> God the Father and Lord of All belongs to all people.
> The idea that the world is one dates from long ago.
> From the time of Pan Gu* through the first three dynasties
> Rulers and subjects alike revered the Lord of Heaven.[23]

*In Chinese mythology, Pan Gu was the embryonic being who first brought order to the universe, and from whom the human race sprang.

In that ancient time, such faith and belief were automatic: Heaven and humans, in those earlier days, saw as one. So how could God then have needed anyone to supplement Him? Certainly not the Buddha, who did not even exist in those far-off days. Our central task is to shun the evil spirits, and cleave to the way of moral rightness—those who cleave to such rightness will be embraced by Heaven—those who do not will be abhorred by Heaven. And so, writes Hong, we must follow six commandments that will keep us on the path of righteousness: The first of these is never to follow the path of lust. The second is always to obey our parents. The third is never to kill people. The fourth is not to steal. The fifth is to stay away from all witchcraft and magical arts. The sixth is never to gamble.[24]

In glossing each of these, Hong uses his years of reading to emphasize the moral point. Lust changes us to demons and thus enrages Heaven, he argues in explaining the first commandment. Debauching others and debauching ourselves are equally outrageous. How much better it would be to chant the poem in the Confucian *Odes* about the footprints of the Lin. Hong is confident that anyone of any education knows this poem from China's earliest anthology:

> The feet of the Lin—
> The noble sons of our Prince,
> Ah, they are the Lin.
>
> The forehead of the Lin—
> The noble grandsons of our Prince,
> Ah, they are the Lin.
>
> The horn of the Lin—
> The noble kindred of our Prince,
> Ah, they are the Lin.

Hong and his readers know the "Lin" is a fabulous female creature, symbol of the good, made up of parts from other creatures of good omen: she has the body of a deer, an ox's tail, a single horn, a horse's hooves, a fish's scales. Confucius told us to remember the footprints of the Lin because the Lin can move so lightly that it harms no living thing by its tread, not even the grass. Similarly her horn is tipped with flesh, showing that though she stands ready to fight with it if necessary, she much prefers the path of peace.[25]

We can see a similar point being made, writes Hong, in the answers that Confucius gave to one of his sincerest disciples, Yen Hui, who asked about the attainment of perfect virtue. Such virtue, said Confucius, lies in restraining the self by means of ritualized propriety. The steps on this path to virtue must be fourfold: by controlling vision, hearing, speech, and actions.[26]

The second commandment, always to obey one's parents, is self-evident and barely needs illustration, writes Hong. Even the animals and birds intuitively understand it, as the lamb kneels down to suck its mother's milk, or the fledgling crow returns to its parents their proffered food. The great sage ruler Shun wept and cried aloud as he worked in the fields at the foot of Li Mountain, because he could not understand why his parents should hate him when he sought only to serve them dutifully. Twice, indeed, they sought to kill him, to get his property, his wives, his flocks and land. Once they fired the storehouse when he was working on the roof, and he would have perished in the flames had he not swiftly extemporized a pair of wings and glided down to safety. And once, when he was working at the bottom of a well, they filled it with stones to crush him, but he escaped through a transverse tunnel he had cunningly prepared. But despite this vivid evidence of their hostility to him, he never wavered in his affectionate regard for them.[27]

The third commandment, not to kill, is also self-evident in various ways: since in this world all are brothers, killing anyone of our own species must be wrong; since all of us are God's children, to destroy others is to strike at Him. Thus in ancient China people never killed wantonly, and the early rulers wept when they had to punish people and even gave up territory rather than fight. Those who kill are no better than bandits, and those who take up arms to kill those in authority will either end up being driven to take their own lives or will vanish as though they had never been—this is as true for those who sought to destroy the Ming dynasty as for those, long before, who fought against the rulers of the Qin or Tang.[28]

The fourth commandment, not to steal, is for Hong not a question of social order but one of internal moral stance. It is true that Heaven will withdraw its protection from all who form gangs for the purposes of robbing others, but at the same time the man of moral principle will not dream of taking another's property even if he has the opportunity. He will turn away from those who distress him by their moral failings, just as the old histories show Yang Zhen and Guan Ning took their stance. When Yang Zhen was a senior official, one of his subordinates, in a private meeting at night, offered him ten ounces of gold. Yang Zhen refused it. Angered, the man said, "Twilight has fallen, no one will ever know about it!" To which Yang Zhen replied, "Heaven will know, the spirits will know, I will know, you will know—how can you say no one will know about it!"[29] The scholar Guan Ning was at home reading when an official of the highest rank, in fancy carriage and hat of state, rode past his door. Guan Ning never even looked up from his book. When his closest friend, with whom he was sitting on the same mat, did look up, Guan sliced the mat in two, saying, "You're no friend of mine."[30]

To reinforce these first four commandments, Hong has used mainly classical and historical allusions. For the fifth, "not to practice witchcraft," he gives no Chinese examples, but simply invokes the language used by Liang Afa in his tracts—though Hong does not acknowledge Liang by name. Witches and magicians, practitioners of heterodox arts, all work against Heaven, for it is Heaven that decides the rhythms of our life, and when and how death comes. Incantations, processions, fasting, worship of demons have no effect, and one can see all too easily how those who claim to master magical arts themselves live in poverty:

> The demons' agents serve the demons and end up possessed by them.
> The gates of hell are always open to receive the followers of sin.[31]

With the sixth commandment, "not to gamble," Hong returns to his Confucian texts and histories. Though he has tried to take Confucian tablets out of the schools in which he and his fellow believers were teaching, he still does not reject the sage himself. Twice, in listing the reasons against gambling, he praises Confucius and his followers for their patient acceptance of hardship, their simple life, and their upright natures. Whereas gambling represents a "hidden blade" that seeks to cut against the will of Heaven, which distributes wealth and poverty according to God's rules, not man's; it keeps us from being diligent and accepting adequate recompense for our work. In this, continues Hong, gambling is like both the drinking of wine and the smoking of opium. Wine wipes out families and has destroyed the strongest of rulers: "With iron they bound rivers and hills; because of wine they perished." Opium smoking makes some men mad and weakens others beyond recourse: "In the present times how many spirited Chinese have ruined themselves by their constant use of the opium pipe!"[32]

Hong makes no attempt to list any more of the wrongs that afflict the world:

It is hard to list all the other wrongful acts one by one:
Each individual must differentiate between the minute and the vast.

For if they do not think through each specific action, their virtue will be compromised.
Before the solid ice has formed, tread lightly on the frost.[33]

Some time during his first months of living in Sigu village, Hong hears of a local place of worship, the Shrine of the Six Caverns, which seems to draw together all his worst fears and warnings about the society's loss of moral order. When he asks who is venerated in the shrine, he is informed that it is built to the departed spirits of a man and a woman. Hong asks if they were married or not. The reply given by the locals horrifies him: "No, they were not. Long ago those two sang together on this mountain, made love, and died. Later, people believed the couple became immortals, so they erected their images here and sacrificed to them." How could they possibly become immortals, Hong asks, after illicitly running away and living together? Heaven would punish such a couple, not confer immortality upon them, and their so-called shrine must be nothing more than a lair of demons.[34] So again, Hong turns to verse to express his feelings:

I take up my writing brush and compose a poem, condemning this "Six Cavern Shrine."
Those two demon devils should be killed, exterminated.
The mountain people here have reverted to being animals—
Wherever you go the men sing their songs and the women respond in kind.
Sinners end up with the reputation of achieving immortality,
And wildly promiscuous women become the village wives!
One day from the midst of the storm clouds the thunder will strike them
When Heaven can bear no more, what will become of them?[35]

Reading, writing, teaching, moving from house to house among his hospitable Hakka relatives, Hong spreads his message of sin, redemption, and remorse. Again and again, he tells of his dream and its significance. The simple religious service he has improvised back home in Guanlubu is formalized now, in the western mountain setting, and some of the elements first used are gone. No longer, for example, is God's name written on a tablet or golden paper, and displayed with burning incense on the altar. Instead, during services, two burning lamps are placed upon the table, and three cups of tea to make a simple offering. The congregation grows and the Hakka women join their menfolk, though men and women sit in separate rows. Hymns are sung to God, for the people here are full of song, but these hymns speak of God's grace, and Hong's sermons underline the message with warnings against idolatry, and emphasis on Jesus as redeemer. When praying, all kneel together facing the light, which pours into the room, for in these mountain dwellings the walls are often open to attract the breeze. They keep their eyes closed, and one person in turn speaks their prayers aloud.[36]

> I, Your unworthy son / daughter [here each person utters his or her own name] kneeling on the ground, with true heart repent my sins. I pray to the Heavenly Father and Great God, of extraordinary goodness and mercy, to forgive my former ignorance and frequent transgressions of the Heavenly Commandments. I earnestly beseech the Heavenly Father and Great God, to extend His grace and pardon all my former sins, and permit me to reform my faults and renew myself, so that my soul may ascend to heaven. May I henceforth sincerely repent and reform, not worshipping false spirits nor practicing perverse things, but obeying the Heavenly Commandments. I also earnestly pray to the Heavenly Father and Great God, to bestow on me constantly His Holy Spirit, to change my wicked heart and never to allow the devilish demons to deceive me. Constantly look after me, and never permit the devilish demons to harm me. I am blessed that every day there is food and clothing, and neither calamity nor hardship. In this world may I enjoy peace, and in ascending to heaven, may I enjoy eternal bliss. Blessed by the merits of the Saviour and Heavenly Elder Brother, Jesus, who has redeemed us from sin, we pray through him to our Heavenly Father, the Great God, who is in Heaven, that His will be done on earth as it is in heaven. Look down and grant my request. Amen.[37]

Within a few months, Hong has converted around a hundred people in the mountain area of Sigu. Those desiring to receive baptism first make a written confession of their sins, which they then read aloud; or they can offer an oral confession if they do not write. The written confessions are burned at the altar, the smoke rising up to God the Father.[38] They then pledge themselves "not to worship evil spirits, not to practice evil things, and to keep the heavenly commandments." Water is poured over their heads, and Hong cleanses them of their past lives with these words: "We wash away all your former sins, slough off the old and give birth to the new." Those who have received their baptism then bathe their bodies in the river, drink the tea that has been standing on the altar, and wash their chest around the area of their heart, to signify that their inner and outer cleansing is completed. Henceforth at every meal they will offer up this simple prayer: "We humbly give thanks to the Heavenly Father and Great God, for His many blessings, for each day's clothing and food, for sparing us calamity and hardship, and helping our souls rise up to Heaven."[39]

Learning can be used in many ways. Although Hong has never received his licentiate's degree, and has resolved never to try for it again, he knows the language of the bureaucracy, and the forms that need to be observed. Thus when the son of his host and convert Huang Shengjun is arrested on a charge brought against him by a neighboring clan, Huang and his family turn to Hong for help. At first he urges them to pray to God for the young man's release, and this they do. But Hong reinforces these pleas for divine assistance with a polished petition to the local magistrate who oversees the case. The petition is effective and within a few weeks the prisoner is released and back at home. Shortly after his return, he too is converted to Hong's new faith.[40]

Everything does not always go so smoothly for Hong Xiuquan in Sigu. There are some kinds of "serious family troubles" at the Huangs, perhaps involving something more than the charges brought against their young son and his subsequent incarceration. Hong leaves the Huang's home for a period, and goes with his close friend Feng Yunshan to stay in a hut in the mountains. In that rural retreat he is insulted in some way by people's remarks about him—perhaps resenting his religion, his moralism, or his verbal attack on the Six Caverns Shrine. Not long after this, though Hong returns to the Huangs, Feng goes off to live in the larger town of Guiping, the county seat, where he has made new friends—the Zhangs, who are supervisors of the city's water ponds and dikes—and in six or seven days Feng spends much of his (and Hong's?) remaining funds.[41]

It is in November 1844 that Hong decides at last to leave. He has been in Guangxi for more than five months, and it is close to eight months since he first left home to tour the world and preach God's word. Even though he has managed to send one letter home, by the hands of relatives traveling to Canton, his family must be worried. There is another factor. Hong has been preaching that not to be a filial son is one of the six main sins against Heaven's True God. But as the basic Confucian texts on filial piety state, in volumes that every student reads as he begins his education, of all unfilial acts not to have a son to carry on the family line ranks highest. And as of now, Hong has only daughters.

Huang Shengjun, so long the sheltering host, sees Hong Xiuquan safely to Guiping township. They search for Feng at Zhang's home, but do not find him. Zhang tells them he has heard that Feng has already left for Guanlubu, and Hong accepts this as accurate, making no further attempt to track down Feng. Hong says farewell to Huang Shengjun and travels back to Guanlubu alone. This time he goes by boat, presumably paying for his fare and food with money given by the faithful of Guangxi. The voyage—downstream along the Xun River till it flows into the West River, which in turn leads straight to Canton—is fast and uneventful. In twelve days Hong is home, with his parents, wife, and daughters.[42]

7

THE BASE

 When Hong gets back home the first thing he asks everyone is "Where is Feng Yunshan?" And they all say, "We thought he was with you." There has been a muddle, one which can be explained if not condoned. In Guiping town ship, when Hong went to the house of pond and irrigation supervisor Zhang to ask him where Feng was, Zhang replied that Feng and one of Zhang's nephews had announced they were returning to Canton and Guanlubu. Without checking further, Hong took the story at face value, and returned, to be scolded by Feng's family for abandoning the son he had first converted and then persuaded to accompany him on his far-flung travels.[1]

There is little that Hong Xiuquan can do about it. He has neither the funds nor perhaps the energy or will to make the trip all the way back to Guangxi again. Besides, local village leaders in Guanlubu once more offer him back his old teaching job. He accepts, and supports his family by his teaching while he continues to develop the range of religious tracts that he first began in Sigu village with the Huangs of Guangxi.[2]

In his absence, it is Feng Yunshan who makes the moves that will most deeply color his and Hong's own future lives. Feng was in fact in Guiping township all the time that Hong Xiuquan was there asking for him in November 1844, but staying with another member of the Zhang family, Zhang Yongxiu. A month or so after Hong left, Feng and Zhang decide to leave Guiping but not to return east, down the river, to Canton. Instead, they move due north, to the lower foothills of the mountain ranges that dominate this part of northern Guangxi province. First they stay in the village of Gulin, where the Zhangs have property. Early in 1845 they push northwest, along the valleys of the rivers that flow down there from the Thistle Mountain region, to a deeply secluded village where the Zhangs also have some land.[3]

All this time, Feng makes no attempt—perhaps he has no opportunity—to communicate with his family or with Hong Xiuquan back in Guanlubu. Instead, he preaches constantly the message of redemption that he has learned from Hong, and describes Hong's dream in ever-growing detail, as he seeks to spread Hong's personal encounters with his older brother Jesus, and with their Father, the One True God. As Feng makes fresh converts, and baptizes them in the way that he has also learned from Hong, the nucleus of a religious group is formed. He christens it the "Bai Shangdi Hui," "God-worshiping Society." A local family, the Zengs, come to believe his message with exemplary fervor. In 1846 Feng moves into the Zeng's home, even farther north, in the heart of the Thistle Mountain area. Feng stays there into 1847.[4]

What is going on? In moving ever deeper into the mountains, Feng is moving ever farther away from the state, from the centers of Confucian education and influence, from the cosmopolitan urban markets, from the richest farmland and the powerfully connected landowners, and from the descendants of the Chinese families who first opened up the area and now call themselves the "original inhabitants." Like Hong, Feng is a Hakka, and he mingles easily with the other Hakkas in the hills and mountains, and even with the mountain tribesmen among whom they dwell. Their beliefs may be "idolatrous," but they are shifting, flexible. Their songs, their stories, their mountain love games, like those of the couple in the Six Caverns, may cry out for censure and reform; but many of these people are, if not literally the dispossessed, those exercising simple crafts or performing backbreaking tasks on the very edge of subsistence, just like those to whom Jesus seemed to be talking in his sermon on the mountaintop, in the words so faithfully transcribed by Liang Afa.

Among these earliest God-worshipers are miners who work either in the silver lodes that can still be found in Thistle Mountain, or in the coal mines that dot the region; there are carpenters, blacksmiths, and rice flour grinders, itinerant barbers and fortune-tellers, sellers of medicines, salt, opium, or bean curd, boatmen, fuel gatherers, charcoal burners, herdsmen, peddlers, as well as those casual laborers who get by from day to day as best they can.[5] "My family was destitute and had not enough to eat," one early God-worshiper later said of his upbringing in this region. "We lived by tilling the land, cultivating mountain slopes and hiring out as laborers, keeping to our station and accepting our poverty. At the age of eight, nine and ten I studied with my uncle, but my family was poor and I could not study longer. But I worked as a laborer in many schools and knew them well." In such an existence, as the same man noted, "it was difficult to make ends meet each day; to get enough a month was even more diffi-cult."[6] For this part of Guangxi was by reputation poor, and suffered extra blows from droughts at this same period, which brought famine condi-tions to many areas, leading some miners—desperate to appease their hun-ger by any means—to eat their own coal.[7]

Banditry made the hard life worse. Such areas as Thistle Mountain in Guangxi—Hua county, when Hong's family first moved there in the seventeenth century, had been similar—were natural shelters for those outside the law, providing safe havens from which they could descend to rob the richer farmers or townsmen in the valleys below, before returning to their mountain fastnesses if the state responded by sending troops against them. But at the time when Hong first preaches in Sigu village, and Feng continues with his work in Thistle Mountain, the problems of lawlessness have been compounded by a new influx of bandits into the rivers and valleys of southern and eastern Guangxi.

Strangely, it is the British who largely lie behind this latest scourge. Having fought their brief but bitter war against the Chinese government to end the restrictive Canton system, open five new treaty ports, and gain independence for their missionaries to establish churches and spread the word of God, they now proceed to use the power of their steamships and their disciplined armored fleets to start ridding the South China Sea of the pirates who have preyed there for generations.[8] Since 1805 when seven of the most powerful pirate leaders met to form a federation, the pirates have carved up the water world of the South China coast between them-selves, with their own secret registration systems, signals, rules of conduct, and zones of operation. Within the pirates' federation, the leaders strengthen their base of operations by marrying off their sisters, daughters, or captured women to other pirates, or create "fictive lineages" through adoptions that bond potential leaders to their own ranks through "family loyalties." Bonds are forged, too, by the male leaders' homosexual relationships with certain captives, who if the liaison blossoms might be promoted to their own commands.[9]

For many years the pirate confederation was led and held together by a woman, Shi Yang, a former prostitute from near Canton who became wife of one of the main pirate leaders, bore him two sons, and after her husband's death married her former husband's male lover, bearing a child to him also. Though she more or less retired from the pirates' world after her second husband's death in 1843, aged sixty-eight, she is still living as a wealthy widow near Canton, and runs a successful gambling house inside the city.[10]

Hong Kong, expanding rapidly as the base of British power, is after 1842 the center of this endeavor to clear the way for British trade, whether that trade be legal, in tea and silk, or illegal, in the ever-expanding sales of opium. Working sometimes independently, sometimes in uneasy conjunction with the Chinese authorities in Canton, the British seek to utilize the anti-piracy provisions of the law of the sea, and establish a pirate-free cordon around Hong Kong itself. Pirates caught within three miles of Hong Kong are tried in the British colonial court, and sentenced to death or transportation. Those caught outside those limits are either tried by the British or handed over to the Chinese for punishment.[11] The appointment of a new assistant superintendent of the Hong Kong police in 1843, an Englishman who has served for years as a Chinese interpreter, brings a whole new range of British options, for he knows how to use local informers skillfully, and questions captured crewmen on the junks that cruise the Hong Kong waters for news of the pirates' movements. The colonial government also institutes new registration laws for Chinese residing in Hong Kong, as well as for the crews and their womenfolk on all the lighters and ferryboats that cruise the harbor, and orders registry numbers clearly painted on their craft. With dubious justification under international law, the British authorities assume sweeping powers to enter any house or boat within the colony or nearby waters if it is "wholly or partly inhabited or manned by Chinese."[12]

But as the British slowly begin to drive the pirates from the seas, the pirates take shelter inland along China's rivers, especially the West River, which leads from Canton city to the heart of Guangxi province. Here, by the provisions of the treaties, the British cannot follow them. Nor can the scattered groups of ill-trained and ill-equipped river police of the Qing or provincial governments do anything to check them. There are only four largish government patrol boats, each carrying fourteen troops and sailors, for all the eastern Guangxi rivers, backed by eighteen other small boats, each with two sailors and two soldiers.[13]

Such puny forces can do nothing against well-armed, experienced sea-farers, and they are frightened, too. The pirates are famous for their relentless cruelty to captured troops, for mutilating ransom victims in their friends' presence to pressure their families into redeeming them, for seizing the bones from lineage burial grounds and holding the bones until the clan buys them back, and for slicing off the ears or setting afire the Qing dynasty patrol officers who fall into their hands.[14] If cornered, the pirates have proved that their ferocity is only deepened. They have been known to grab a lighted fuse and race to the gunpowder magazines of their vessels if boarded by patrols or British sailors, blowing themselves and their assailants to eternity rather than face capture. And if, driven from their boats and floating in the sea after a fierce engagement, they find a Qing or foreign sailor in the water, they will smash their skulls against their attackers' in a final attempt to kill them, or else lock their legs around them in a fierce embrace, so that both sink together thus entwined, to die upon the ocean floor.[15]

Hong Kong provides a haven of sorts, and source of fresh supplies and arms for such men, despite the British efforts to suppress them. Many pirates, disguised as ordinary merchants and fishermen, use the well-equipped Hong Kong docks to refurbish their vessels. Men like Chui-a-poo, working as a barber in Hong Kong, and used on occasion as a special agent by the British in their anti-pirate ventures, obtains from the British authorities a license to make gunpowder, which he then sells secretly to his pirate contacts.[16] Among Chui-a-poo's confederates are men like the Muslim soldier and deserter Yow-a-he, a half-breed born in Malaya to a Chinese migrant and a Malay mother, recruited and trained by the Ceylon Rifles, who deserts his regiment in Hong Kong, goes into hiding in a village, and sells his expertise and the names of his contacts along with the rifle issued to him in the name of her Britannic Majesty, Queen Victoria.[17] In Macao, mixed marriages or liaisons between the Portuguese and the Chinese are common, and their offspring can swell the pirates' ranks, none better known than "Big-head" Yang, born of a Chinese father and Western mother, whose forces later move inland and terrorize the region near Guiping.[18]

Even more complex are the dealings of the Chinese woman called Akeu, who not only conducts a successful trade in sugar, cooking oil, and cotton on ships she rents or buys outright from Chinese and from Western brokers, but also sells both opium and gunpowder to many of the major pirate gangs, commodities she obtains in volume from her lover Captain J. B. Endicott, owner of the United States opium-receiving ship the *Ruparell*.[19] In the 1840s, as she raises her and Endicott's children in a house she rents in Macao for $150 a year from a Portuguese landlord, she buys six-pounder guns from British master mariners on credit (at $130 for a pair), and obtains sea-spoiled opium at a discount from shipwrecked vessels. Akeu speaks some English, and has among her treasures a telescope by Cox of London, a silver watch by Guinaud Brenet, two sets of calibrated money-weighing scales, and a single-barreled English fowling piece.[20] Confronted by a British patrol in Hong Kong harbor, and threatened with arrest for smuggling and abetting piracy, she jumps from the vessel to a waiting sampan and is poled to safety. But if a Chinese tries to double-cross her—as one does, by seizing two vessels of her fleet—she blackmails him with threats of vengeance from her "foreign friends" until he makes good her loss.[21]

The Anglo-Chinese Nanjing treaty settlement of 1842 has left the status of the opium trade unresolved. Allegedly illegal still, the sales of the drug expand, and move along the waterways beyond Canton. Probably by the time of Hong's first preaching in Guangxi in 1844, and certainly by the time that Feng has reached the heart of the Thistle Mountain region in 1846, the first of the former pirate groups, now river bandits, are entering the region around Guiping, as "protectors" of the opium runners. This area of the country is new to most of them, and so they use local bandits from the hills, or local villagers bought or coerced into service, to be their guides.[22]

Guiping township is a natural center of such activity, for it is situated at a junction of two rivers, the Yu and the Qian, which flow in turn into the larger river Xun, the one that Hong, like thousands of other passengers each year, traveled along to go back home. Upstream from Guiping there are rocks and rapids and a maze of smaller tributaries. Downstream, prosperous commerce, and good passage for the larger vessels. The constant loading and unloading of the vessels makes it a natural focus for bandits' attention, and the scores of little islands and inlets along the main stream's course provide natural hideaways and shelters for water-borne plunderers. Shrewdly aware of the amounts of money to be made from drugs and ransoms and the protection rackets, Guangxi men and women provide food and shelter to the river bandits. By the middle 1840s some of these "Rice Hosts," as they call themselves, have formed joint stock companies to invest in the rackets, drawing back a percentage of the profits in return.[23]

Many of the river bandits, too, were members of secret societies or brotherhoods during their seafaring days, and they bring their old allegiances with them to their new river domains. Strongest of the groups—

really a loose confederation—are the so-called Triads, or Heaven-and-Earth Society. The initial formation of this brotherhood dated to the 1760s, when a group of restless, disaffected men—among them itinerant monks, teachers of Chinese boxing techniques, gamblers, candy makers, traveling doctors—who grew up in the southeastern provinces of Fujian and Guangdong, bonded together. They signed a blood covenant, adopted one of their number as their "teacher," arranged themselves in a numero-logical hierarchy of "brothers," and drank together a mixture of wine and the ash from burning incense to "unify their hearts." Their plans were fluid, but included the recruitment of new members by the founding group, and the robbery of wealthy homes, storehouses, and county treasur-ies so as to amass the funds to "commence their great undertaking."[24]

The spread of the Heaven-and-Earth Society was hard for the Qing state to stop with force because it was not simply either a rebellious or a religious grouping. It was, much more, a broad-based "brotherhood" that promised local people protection and support in harsh and troubled times. As one arrested member explained to the authorities:

> The name Tiandihui [Heaven-and-Earth Society] comes from the fact that Heaven and Earth are the source of being for mankind. The only meaning is respect for Heaven and Earth. Originally, the reason for people's willing-ness to enter the society was that if you had a wedding or funeral, you could get financial help from the other society members; if you came to blows with someone, there were people who would help you. If you encountered rob-bers, as soon as they heard the secret code of their own society, they would then bother you no further; if you were to transmit the sect to other people, you would also receive their payments of "gratitude." Therefore, those who want to enter the society are many in number.[25]

Such mutual aid and "protective" activities slid easily into "protection rackets," as the testimony of a local man named Xu in Guangdong prov-ince clearly showed. His business was peddling brewer's yeast, which he bought from a store owner called Lai in Fujian, and carried back for resale in his hometown. Robbed one day by five men of all the silver he possessed, Xu hurried in desperation to Lai's shop. Lai's response was direct: "If you join the Tiandihui you can avoid being robbed on the road in the future, and I can also get back the silver that was robbed from you." Xu agreed to be initiated into the Heaven-and-Earth Society, his money was soon returned, and most importantly he was told what to do when he traveled the region in the future. If approached by robbers again, he should at once hold up his thumb—code signal for the word for "heaven." The robbers would respond by raising their little finger, to signify "earth," and he would pass on his way, unmolested.[26]

Such quietly effective and inconspicuous identification signs were common throughout southeast China, though other variants were also used. Society brothers in teahouses would hold three fingers together when drinking tea or smoking their tobacco pipes. Or they would leave the second button of their outer garments unfastened, or coil their queues of hair up on their heads with the end sticking up through the center of the coil.[27] They also used a choice of standard identifying phrases, unobtrusive to the uninitiated but immediately recognizable to brotherhood members: "We never met before, but from today we are mutually acquainted." If asked, by robbers or strangers, where they were going, they were to say, "I've come from the east and am going to the west," but if asked whence they came, then they were to say, "I have passed under the bridge," in reference to their passage under the line of knives or swords held over their bodies as they passed through their initiations.[28] Shared by members in all the southern provinces was a rhyming jingle they were also told at their initiations, so that they would never forget it: "Kaikou buliben / chushou bulisan"—"When speaking, never leave out the basic [word]; when extending your hand, never forget the three [fingers together]."[29]

The "basic word" they had never to forget was "Hong," meaning vast or flood. This was the same character used as the family name of Hong Xiuquan, and though Hong's family had used the name long before there was a Heaven-and-Earth Society, for the tens of thousands of initiated brotherhood members the character had a special aura as an invocation. This aura grew in power as the brotherhood expanded in extent and influence between the 1760s and the 1840s, and created and refined its own foundation myths; that same character "Hong" had in fact been one of the many names or pseudonyms of the brotherhood's founder in the 1760s. It was also the first character of the imperial reign name of the founder of the Ming dynasty in 1368, Hong-wu, a symbol of great force and power that the brothers invoked as they spread their goal of "restoring the Ming by overthrowing the Qing" and created a fictional and patriotic lineage for their own organization that ran back into the seventeenth-century period of the Qing conquest of the Ming. Besides that, the character appeared in earlier Chinese Buddhist and messianic texts foretelling apocalyptic disasters, where it was often linked to a counter-vision of an age of "great equity" or "great peace"—Taiping.[30]

But never forgetting the "basic word" was not to mean that one should utter it out loud: rather the brotherhood members broke the character "Hong" into component parts, each of which could be represented by a Chinese number. Thus since "Hong" had three dots on the left-hand side, a two-dot form similar to the Chinese number "8" at its base, the form for "one" at its center, and a shorthand form of "20" at the top, brotherhood members would use the phrase "3-8-21" when speaking or introducing each other, or could combine the three dots and the two dots into the word "five" and identify themselves by saying "five and twenty-one."[31]

By the time that Hong Xiuquan and Feng Yunshan are preaching in Guangxi, the Heaven-and-Earth Society has spread there both among the Hakkas and the original inhabitants. Just as the society brothers once did in the Canton delta region, they swell their numbers in Guangxi by forcing local farmers—with threats, or murders of those who show reluctance—to join them, and few dare refuse.[32] Through their own contacts in Hong Kong and elsewhere, they too have access to Western weapons, which they ship inland by boat. It was a head of the local Heaven-and-Earth Society in Hong Kong, for instance, who bought the rifle off the deserter from the Ceylon Rifles, and other brothers used a house owned by a society member next to the schoolhouse outside the east gate of Canton city as the base for their communications with dealers in Hong Kong.[33] On both the main rivers of Guangxi, and the smaller tributaries, they often set up "toll stations" to take their dues from those moving river goods and passengers. Others shift their major gambling operations, once flourishing in the area around Canton, to the towns around Guiping, openly flaunting their control.[34] Perhaps it is the brazenness of this conduct that prompts Hong Xiuquan to list gambling as the sixth of his commandments, and to link it to both wine and opium, and Feng to find a ready audience when he repeats the same message.

For those Chinese who bitterly resent the river bandits' power and choose not to join them, one alternative is to form their own militia groups, as local communities have for centuries past, not only in such famous gatherings as the righteous hosts of gentry and farmers assembled against the British troops on the hills above Canton at Sanyuanli, but in countless other regions and communities as well. By 1846 such militias are growing numerous, controlled by Chinese landlords, recruited at the village level from local residents paid in grain, often with village tax money, some of which was also paid by Hakkas.[35]

The migration of Hakka people to the Guiping region from the area north and east of Canton city has been a steady one for fifty years or more, long antedating the problems with the displaced pirates. But the movement continues as the social order cracks apart, so that in some areas, especially in the hills, the Hakkas now outnumber the original inhabitants. Since these Hakkas are often members of the Heaven-and-Earth Society, feuds become a feature of eastern Guangxi life in the 1840s, as the various groups clash over areas of residence and land use rights, "Revenge against those who speak the Hakka tongue" becomes a popular slogan among the local Chinese families.[36] Hakka farmers—both men and women—in their hillside plots take weapons to their work, and rally in groups a hundred strong with hoes or spears if the alarm is given. The local tribal leaders, dispossessed by both groups, and themselves often corrupt or heavily in debt, watch from the sidelines but take no action.[37]

For beleaguered Hakkas in this tense environment, Hong's message of salvation has a special resonance, and Feng Yunshan's Society of God-Worshipers draws eager converts not only for its religious message but because its numbers and organization give promise of solidarity against threatening forces all around.[38] As a poverty-stricken God-worshiper describes this chaotic process of divided and uncertain loyalties: "Bandit raids continued year after year, with unending robbing of pawnshops and attacks on towns. The country people were used to seeing [armed] bands and ceased to be afraid; so when they saw the troops of the God-worshippers arrive ... they did not flee elsewhere. Because of this, they were oppressed by the militia and therefore joined us in bewilderment."[39]

If the Hakkas of the Guiping region begin to flock in growing numbers to Feng's God-Worshipers, it may also be because the ground for Christian faith there has been prepared by Karl Gutzlaff, the German missionary who cruised the Chinese coast in 1836, handing out his tracts with Edwin Stevens. Since that time, Gutzlaff has not only been developing a new technique for spreading his Redeemer's words; he has also been serving as the interpreter and Chinese-language secretary to the newly appointed British superintendent of trade, and so is in an excellent position to know the state of anti-pirate campaigns and the social conditions of the Chinese countryside.[40]

Gutzlaff, unlike the more cautious missionaries in China, continues to think that one should do everything possible to understand the Chinese, in order to convert them: to "learn from their own mouth their prejudices, witness their vices, and hear their defence, in order to meet them effectually. . . . In *style* we ought to conform entirely to the *Chinese taste*."[41] Gutzlaff also believes that "the converts ought themselves to contribute towards the advancement of the blessed work, and the congregations formed become missionary societies to all around them," so he creates in 1844 an organization of Chinese to work with him to achieve their common Christian goals, the "Chinese Union." Claiming 37 members in that first year of operation, by late 1845 he reports the membership has jumped to 210. The following year, as numbers continue to rise, subsidiary posts of the union are formed in Guangxi province, among them one in Guiping county itself, whither Chinese preachers from the union travel in some numbers to spread the word, and report that "lots of people" in Guangxi are becoming "worshippers of Yesu" (that is, of Jesus), among them even converted pirates.[42]

Gutzlaff himself, as a member of the "Moravian Brethren" of Christians, has a profoundly open view of missionary endeavor. He believes that the Chinese Union, even if composed of largely untrained Chinese converts, can still spread the ideas of a shared spiritual brotherhood and the values of communal life, and that the central goal of conversion to Christ far outweighs any scruples about the specificities of particular denominations or churches, or whether the Chinese Christians still practice ancestor worship or make offerings to God the Father.[43]

Already in the 1830s, before the Opium War began, Gutzlaff had been publishing pamphlets in Chinese on religious, educational, and scientific subjects, and circulating them both in Canton city and along the coasts as he explored them on his illegal journeys. In the 1840s, as the Chinese Union grows and spreads, he immeasurably increases this production, and uses the considerable cash contributions that flow in to him from European supporters of his missionary endeavors to pay his union members to spread the tracts to inland China, especially Guangxi. These tracts are far smaller and hence easier to carry and distribute than the bulkier version of Liang Afa, even though Liang's nine-chapter text was not always circulated as one volume, but sometimes as four or five bound clusters of two or three chapters, or even as nine separate stitched volumes of single chapters, which would have made them lighter but even harder to follow.[44]

Each of the more than fifty tracts that Gutzlaff or his Chinese Union members write or circulate in the 1840s has a simple theme. Some cite passages from the New Testament and elaborate briefly on them: "Blessed are the Poor in Spirit," "Blessed are those who suffer for Righteousness' sake," "They that are in the flesh cannot please God," "Love Thy Neighbor as Thyself." Some are on specific elements within the Christian faith: on repentance, prayer, Jesus' love, the resurrection, everlasting life, God's forgiveness of our sins. Some deal with specific verses or chapters from the Bible, such as Genesis, chapter 3, on the fall and expulsion of Adam and Eve, or the First Epistle of John, chapter 1, on the light and joy brought by Jesus to our lives:

> That which we have seen and heard declare we unto you, that ye also may have fellowship with us: and truly our fellowship is with the Father, and with His Son Jesus Christ. And these things write we unto you, that your joy may be full. This then is the message which we have heard of Him, and declare unto you, that God is light, and in Him is no darkness at all. (1 John 1:3–5)

Other passages are chosen by Gutzlaff with special artfulness and pertinence, such as the opening of Paul's Epistle to the Romans, with its message of travel and expansion of the faith: "I am debtor both to the Greeks, and to the Barbarians; both to the wise, and to the unwise. So, as much as in me is, I am ready to preach the gospel to you that are in Rome also."[45]

While Feng Yunshan moves slowly deeper into the mountains of Guangxi, Hong resumes his life at Guanlubu. Tired of wandering, Hong earns his keep by teaching once again, and continues to work on his own tracts, two of which he finishes in 1845 or 1846. In the first, Hong draws on Chinese classical writings such as the *Book of Rituals* and the *Book of Changes* to explore how China once shared a vision with the rest of the world that was both compassionate and without local hostilities and divisions. In the time of China's early sage rulers, "those who had and those who had not were mutually compassionate." No one needed to bar their doors, and the world maintained a natural virtue as "men and women walked on different paths." Human love for others extended far beyond the confines of the family: all the young were given the resources they needed to grow, all able-bodied adults received employment, all those disabled by disease were nourished, all the aged were cared for until their deaths.[46]

One of the human tragedies that broke this harmony was the spread of localism and special interests. Hong Xiuquan uses two lines from the thirteenth hexagram of the *Book of Changes*, "Human Fellowship," to illustrate this point concisely: "Fellowship with people in the open, success. Fellowship with people in the clan, humiliation."[47] The language in which Hong expands on this idea seems full of his experiences both with his own family and community in Guanlubu and with the problems of the Huangs and Zhangs in Sigu village and Guiping on his Guangxi visit. Our lives and ways have become "intolerant and shallow," writes Hong, and we have come to be ruled by selfishness:

Hence, there are cases where this country resents that country, and that country resents this country. Worse than that, there are cases within one country when this province, this prefecture, or this district resents that province, that prefecture, or that district; and that province, that prefecture, or that district resents this province, this prefecture, or this district. And beyond that again, there are even cases within one province, prefecture, or district where this village, this hamlet, or this clan resents that village, that hamlet, or that clan; and that village, that hamlet, or that clan resents this village, this hamlet, or this clan. The ways of the world and the minds of men having come to this, how can they do otherwise than to insult each other, to wrest things from each other, to battle with each other, and to kill one another, and thus perish altogether?[48]

Since all of us, in all countries and all clans, share the same Great God and Universal Father, why do we keep on with these absurd distinctions and conflicts?

How can it be that this perverse and unfeeling world cannot in a day be transformed into an honest and upright world? How can it be that this age so full of insults and violations, fighting and killing, cannot in a day be changed into a world where the strong no more oppress the weak, the many overwhelm the few, the wise delude the simple, or the bold annoy the fearful?[49]

In the second, and much longer, tract Hong pursues the same ideas of fractured harmony, but now he concentrates his energies on exploring the reasons that can be gleaned from China's own history for the falling from a grace that all had once shared. Hong's quest is for a continuity between past and present, for all interpretations that deny such continuity must, in their essence, be false. If we are told that something "is applicable to modern times and not applicable to antiquity," then we can be sure that it represents "the false way, the evil way, and the small way."[50] The powers of the demon devil king Yan Luo are a case in point. People ascribe the power over life and death to this spirit, but he is only the same old "serpent devil" who deceived Adam and Eve, as he deceives us now by his endless transformations, but his power has never been anything compared to that of God.

The growth of superstitious beliefs of this kind can be traced epoch by epoch, ruler by ruler, says Hong, and he proceeds to draw on his earlier historical studies to do just that. First to slide away from worshiping the One True God were tribes on the periphery of China proper, like the Li and Miao, who began to venerate the demons. Then came early rulers of the founding Qin dynasty, who searched for secrets of immortality among the islands of the Eastern Sea. After them, the rulers of the early Han dynasty sought by sacrificing to the Kitchen God to transmute cinnabar to gold and managed to draw a throng of charlatans to their court; their successors of the later Han, and rulers of the Liang and Tang, sent their magic specialists to India in search of the Buddha and his bones. Most damaging was the ruler of the Song, who changed the name of the True God of All to the "Great Jade Emperor," this being to Hong "the worst kind of blasphemy" of them all. Such absurdities have since been spread and elaborated through such books as the *Jade Record*.[51]

In contrast, writes Hong, the books brought by the foreigners to China show clearly enough how God's plan really was conceived, and how erroneous these Chinese aberrations must be seen to be. The vast waters of Noah's flood, proof of God's wrath and spreading over the world for forty days and nights, show clearly enough that it cannot be the dragon devil of the Eastern Sea who brings rain to China, despite the sacrifices so many people make to him. When God called Moses to Mount Sinai, He warned him clearly not to let the people of the world set up any kinds of images, or worship them. The "real nature" of the demon devil evaporates on close inspection, in just the same way as bean curd turns out to be full of water. How ever could such a demon devil as Yan Luo be called divine? Even Jesus himself, our Savior and the Son of God, may be called our Lord *(zhu)* but not our God *(di),* even though except for Jesus' Father none are as great as he is. How could one, knowing this, rebel against God's commands and "join with the evil demons in rebelling against Heaven"? Nothing could be more pitiable, more sad, than that![52]

While Hong Xiuquan writes and teaches, others are talking about him. It is known to some in Canton city that he has read and believed the tracts of Liang Afa, that he preaches, that he has friends who do the same. These men in turn tell members of the Chinese Union, who work with Issachar Roberts. Roberts came to China from Tennessee at the invitation and under the inspiration of Karl Gutzlaff, and was the first to return to Canton from Hong Kong after the Opium War of 1839–42: living in the suburbs of the city, dressing in Chinese clothes, erecting a small chapel with a bell tower, learning Hakka dialect, and gathering a small group of Chinese converts around him.[53] A maverick whose affiliations with mission groups in the United States are often temporary and stormy, Roberts joins up with Gutzlaff's Chinese Union in the mid-1840s, and gratefully accepts the small payments that Gutzlaff makes to him. For Roberts, the heart of Christian conversion and devotion lies in the act of baptism, and his own most lyrical writings describe the joys of thus greeting new Christians in the rolling surf off the shores of Hong Kong or in the flowing rivers of China. For choice, in the hot seasons of the south, Roberts takes the baptismal candidates out into the water at nighttime, when the moon is full and bright, immersing each one completely "in the spacious deep in imitation of the death and burial of his Lord," before raising them once again "in imitation of the resurrection of Jesus."[54]

A Christian convert from Canton visits Hua county in 1846, and urges both Hong and his cousin Hong Rengan to visit Roberts at his chapel and hear his preaching. Both Hongs are too busy with their own teaching to accept. But early in 1847 Roberts' senior assistant, a convert and member of the Chinese Union, writes formally to Hong Xiuquan and urges him to visit. This time Hong accepts, and persuades Hong Rengan to accompany him. Roberts receives them cordially, and under his general supervision the two cousins read the Bible, in Gutzlaff's translation, both the Old Testament and the New. Though Hong Rengan does not stay long, Hong Xiuquan perseveres, and asks Roberts (as Liang Afa some thirty years before asked Milne) to prepare him formally for the rites of baptism. Roberts agrees to take him in his care, and sends two of his Chinese converts to Guanlubu, to see what sort of reputation Hong Xiuquan has at home.[55]

As has happened before in Hong's life, suddenly and without clear explanation something goes wrong. Just a few days before, baptism seemed assured. Hong had written out his statement of faith and purpose for Roberts, as baptists must, to prove the sincerity of their religious call, and Roberts found it satisfactory. Nothing untoward was said about him to the investigators in Guanlubu. Some contemporaries say that Hong falls into a trap, a trap laid by other jealous Chinese converts who work for Roberts. Knowing that Roberts hates those who claim they seek baptism only in order to gain employment or a stipend from the Christian missionaries, and fearing that Hong might be hired by Roberts and thus cost one of them his job, they tell Hong to ask Roberts for financial reassurance about the future. Guilelessly, Hong does just that, forfeiting Roberts' trust and support. It sounds far-fetched, but times are hard for those with or without education living around Canton, and Roberts is famous for his sudden tantrums and zealous adherence—when it suits him—to the articles of his baptist faith. Roberts' only comment on the matter is that Hong chose to leave before Roberts was "fully satisfied of his fitness."[56]

Whatever did happen between Hong and Roberts, on July 12, 1847, Hong goes on the road again, without receiving the promised baptism.

But he does not turn north for home and family in Guanlubu, as one would expect. Instead, almost penniless except for some borrowed copper cash, with his few possessions on his back, and his cherished demon-killing sword in a scabbard he has had specially made, marked with the single character of his dream-state name of Quan, he turns his steps once more toward the west, in search of Feng Yunshan, asking his newfound Chinese Union friends to tell his family where he has gone.[57]

Hong walks westward along the river, too poor to pay the boat fare, feeding as best he may. He has got as far as the river town of Meizixun, more than halfway to the Guangxi border, when ten or so men, dressed as an anti-smuggling patrol, block his way. When Hong has relaxed his guard, they draw out guns and knives, demand his money and his bundle of possessions. Such acts of impersonating government personnel have been growing in numbers, though certainly they are not new. When Hong was first an examination candidate, a gang killed a magistrate and his staff and then took over their office and their duties along with their insignia, and ran the county for several months before anyone arrested them. On other occasions, gang members rode in official sedan chairs and claimed to be functionaries, ending by ransacking people's homes and assaulting their women.[58] While Hong was living in Guanlubu, a hundred or more bandits just north of Canton city set up road and river barriers, apparently immune to government reprisal, demanding money from all travelers, and causing such disruptions to trade that honest merchants and opium smugglers alike have to reroute their goods due west.[59] Qing government embassies to Annam can get to that neighboring kingdom only by paying "protection" to the local river bandits; and students from West Guangdong, however well prepared, cannot even get to Canton city to take the examinations.[60]

Perhaps if Hong had raised his thumb to represent the Heavens, worn the second button of his summer robe undone, stretched out three fingers together in a greeting, said truthfully that he was traveling from the east towards the west, or even murmured a coded version of his own name, then they would have let him be. But he has not been made privy to these mysteries, and the ten men rob him of his borrowed money, his sword and scabbard, and everything else he carries, leaving him only a single change of clothes.[61]

Despite this added blow Hong does not turn back. Instead he petitions the Qing prefect of the nearest city for aid. The prefect points out that Meizixun is not in fact within his jurisdiction, and thus he need bear no responsibility for Hong's losses; but sympathizing with him nevertheless, he gives Hong a string of copper coins worth close to half an ounce of silver. With this assistance, as long as he contents himself with a single meal each day, Hong can afford to take a boat once more, at least for a few stages; and the enigmatic remark of a bystander who notes his dejected countenance strengthens his resolve: "A broken cord of course is mended with a line, and when the boat comes to the bank, the way opens again."[62]

Once on the boat for Guangxi, Hong has a chance to meet more scholars. They pity his plight, admire his erudition, and listen with interest to his teachings on the One True God. Sometimes these scholars feed him, sometimes they give him tea, sometimes they give him cash, or persuade the boats' captains to let him off his fare. Thus it is that, within a month, he reaches Sigu village and the Huangs. When they tell him Feng Yunshan, who visited them the year before to give them his new location, is now in Thistle Mountain, Hong at once turns his steps northwards, to the hills, accompanied by the young son of the Huang family he helped to spring from prison in 1844.[63]

It seems that Hong, far from being dejected or exhausted by his journey and his hardships, has never felt more triumphant, more sure of his power and of the One True God's protection. For the first time, in a poem he writes on the wall of a roadside temple, instead of the regular character "Wu," which he has always previously used for "I," Hong refers to himself as "Zhen," "I the ruler," a term forbidden to ordinary subjects of the Qing, for its use is traditionally restricted to the emperors of China, and to them alone. By placing this character as the first word of the first line of his poem, Hong further emphasizes his own sense of his newfound glory; he reiterates this mood by using the same imperial personal pronoun twice more in the last four lines.

> I the ruler, in the high heavens, am the Heavenly King;
> You, here on earth, are devil demons.
> Deceiving the hearts of God's sons and daughters,
> You shamelessly dare to let men worship you.
> God has sent me the ruler to descend into the world;
> What will the wiles of devil demons avail you now?
> I the ruler, as commander of the heavenly hosts, will show no mercy:
> You and the other devil demons must quickly flee.[64]

On August 27, 1847, Hong reaches Thistle Mountain and greets the astonished Feng Yunshan and the assembled God-worshipers. His God has brought him home.[65]

JUDGMENTS

For the first month they are together again, during the autumn of 1847, Hong Xiuquan and Feng Yunshan devote themselves to writing. They live in a Thistle Mountain village with the Zengs, a committed God-worshiping family who have supported Feng for over a year already. The two men elaborate the details and the divine significance of Hong's original dream of 1837, and meticulously chart their own travels and the steady growth in numbers of those who have come to share their beliefs in the period since 1843. Hong polishes and adds emendations to the tracts on the Heavenly Way that he has recently been composing in Guanlubu, for now the Bible in its entirety has become available to them, even if much of its message seems to remain opaque. Their writings are distributed for them by the adult son of the Zeng household, whose zeal exceeds even that of his parents. As their writings circulate through the Thistle Mountain area, they win fresh converts for the God-worshiping Society.[1]

Despite Hong Xiuquan's newfound confidence in his majestic powers, expressed in his writings on the temple wall the month before, much of his sense of mission is still focused on the need to banish idols and destroy them. Thus it is that, at least initially for Hong in Thistle Mountain, the most overt use he makes of the Bible study conducted with Issachar Roberts during the summer is of two passages that underline Hong's own feelings, and amplify passages left unexplained in Liang Afa's tracts.

The first of these concerns the way that God chose to transmit His Ten Commandments to Moses on Mount Sinai. Whereas Liang Afa simply wrote that God "sent down" the Ten Commandments to Moses at Sinai, and ordered him to "teach" and to "explain" them to the people of Israel, Hong knows now, after reading Gutzlaff's translation of Exodus, that God wrote these commands for Moses "with His own hand." He knows too that it was "with His own mouth" that God said to Moses, "I am the Lord of All and the Supreme God; you people must on no account set up any images of things in heaven above or on earth below, or kneel down and worship them."[2]

The second passage Hong now uses is drawn from Psalm 115, which puts the Lord's prohibitions against idolatry even more strongly than Liang—with all his lengthy commentaries—chose to do.

> Not unto us, O Lord, not unto us, but unto thy name give glory, for thy mercy, and for thy truth's sake. Wherefore should the heathen say, Where is now their God? But our God is in the heavens: he hath done whatsoever he hath pleased. Their idols are silver and gold, the work of men's hands. They have mouths, but they speak not: eyes have they, but they see not: they have ears, but they hear not: noses have they, but they smell not: they have hands, but they handle not: feet have they, but they walk not: neither speak they through their throat. They that make them are like unto them; so is every one that trusteth in them.[3]

In rewriting or embellishing his version of his dream, Hong also incorporates new elements that overtly attack Confucius. As recently as in his "Moral Exhortations" written in 1846 and 1847 Hong still had praise for Confucians, or at least for those Confucian scholars—and a handful of their rulers—who themselves over the past millennia had had the courage to protest at China's slow slide to superstition and idolatry. His only regret was that they did not go far enough: "One cannot say these people did not have acute awareness; but what they destroyed, burned or criticized was limited to certain lascivious shrines, Buddhist practices, and improper sacrifices, so that everything they did not destroy, burn or criticize remains with us to this day."[4] Now Hong incorporates an element of anti-Confucianism into his dream of 1837, adding a long passage of dialogue that shows the Sage in a foolish or dubious light. In this expanded version of the dream, Hong's Father, the One True God, praises both the Old and the New Testaments as being "pure and without error"; by contrast, all the Confucian books are condemned by God for their "numerous errors and faults" and are accused of bearing "the ultimate guilt for inciting the demons to do wrong." God adds the charge that Confucius, through his books, "muddled and confused" the people of China, so that his reputation exceeded the True God's in that land. And Jesus adds the criticism that Confucius caused harm to Jesus' own younger brother, Hong Xiuquan. At first "arguing stubbornly" against these charges, Confucius at last falls silent. Then comes the fall:

> Confucius, seeing that everyone in the high heaven pronounced him guilty, secretly fled down from heaven, hoping to join up with the leader of the demon devils. The Heavenly Father, the Supreme Lord and Great God, thereupon dispatched Hong Xiuquan and a host of angels to pursue Confucius and to bring him, bound and tied, before the Heavenly Father. The Heavenly Father, in great anger, ordered the angels to flog him. Confucius knelt before the Heavenly Elder Brother, Christ, and repeatedly begged to be spared. Confucius was given many lashes, and his pitiful pleas were unceasing. Then the Heavenly Father, the Supreme Lord and Great God, considering that the meritorious achievements of Confucius compensated for his deficiencies, granted that he be permitted to partake of the good fortune of heaven, but that he never again be permitted to go down to the world.[5]

Now joined through heavenly experience to the ranks of those who condemn Confucius, Hong also draws from the tradition of the Heaven-and-Earth Society, which uses his own name in cipher form to elaborate their own claims. Now it is God Himself, not brothers of the rival society, who invoke Hong's majesty through the mystery of an arcane puzzle. God, in the revised dream, chants twice to Hong, His son. In the first chant God explains how Hong's new name Quan is composed of coded elements drawn from the characters for world and rule and treasure, punningly recombined. The word for "one thousand" also, "less one line, is now attached to Hong's person when one speaks of him." One thousand less one line has three variants, since the Chinese character for "one thousand" has three strokes. Two of these variants do not yield recognizable characters in the Chinese language, but the third yields a symmetrical cross, the same word used to translate the crucifix on which Christ died for all on earth. A third pun links Hong's name to the character for "sun," while a fourth couplet defies interpretation to the uninitiated: "One long, one short, constitutes your given name / There is a knife which has no handle and no sheen."[6]

In a second coded chant, God offers Hong a clue to his understanding of the book that he will read on earth, and that will bring him to true knowledge, but not before he has walked in darkness several more years, and been mocked, humiliated, and slandered by those on earth:

> The cow's hoof is one-oh-five:
> People's eyes can see the flagon in the wine.
> See your face, eighty measures long!
> In other places too one truly is alone.[7]

Such a poem hardly seems the sort of thing to chant when bandits stop one and ask, "Where are you going to and whence do you come?" It seems too complex to remember for the uneducated, and too esoteric to be taken for a line of conversation. But an implication is floating in the code, an implication that Hong now knows new secrets beyond those of his earlier life, and beyond those Liang's tracts and then the Bible gave him.

The son of the Zeng family with whom Feng and Hong are staying is already famous, as a God-worshiper, for the zeal with which he has ridiculed and even defaced the images in local shrines. He joins with Feng and Hong when they pray to the One True God, asking Him to confer on them a strongly defended base area where they can all settle in peace. Whether because they receive an answer to that prayer, or because the Zeng family needs a breathing space from looking after them, in October 1847 Feng and Hong move to a village a mile and a half away, still deep in the mountains, to the home of another faithful God-worshiper, Lu Liu. Here, with the Zengs, they form a plan to smash the most important and immoral idol they have yet encountered.[8]

This spirit, who is described by the locals as being "amazingly effective," is called King Gan, and at least five temples or shrines have been erected in his name near Thistle Mountain. Like so many local presiding deities, his roots are historical, or at least are given the appearance of so being. When Hong questions the locals about this spirit's efficacy and origins, they answer him as follows: In the district of Xiang, some miles to the northwest of Thistle Mountain, there once lived a man named Gan, who put all his trust in a local magician or geomancer. Seeking reassurance about the future of his family line, Gan was told of the perfect burial site for himself and his descendants, but, said the geomancer, the site would bring maximum good fortune only if it was first sanctified by a "bloody burial." To assure the future of his line, Gan thereupon acquired the site and killed his own mother, so that she should be the first buried there, and prove the prophecy correct. Gan's other recorded actions were little better in Hong's eyes. It was said that Gan forced his sister to have intercourse with a local wastrel, and that he loved to listen to the lascivious songs of the mountain men and women, songs that roused them up to commit immoral acts.[9]

Since then, the local villagers tell Hong, King Gan has proved his power in many ways: those speaking ill of him are seized with a mysterious sickness of the bowels, which can be cured only by the lavish sacrifice of pigs and cattle to King Gan. Once, when the local magistrate was passing by King Gan's temple on official business, the force of the spirit pulled the magistrate out of his sedan chair, and prevented his departure until he gave King Gan an embroidered dragon robe. Even worshipers going to his temple to burn incense or light oil lamps in his honor bang gongs loudly as they approach, to prevent any chance of bumping into him by accident.[10]

In the past, Hong Xiuquan cleared his schoolrooms of Confucian tablets, purged his home of the little shrines and spirits he considered improper, and challenged the spirits in other shrines with poems of defiance posted on their walls. But now he decides to take more aggressive action, for this "clearly is the demon devil, and my first task is to save the people in the community," as he tells his friends.[11] Accompanied by Feng Yunshan, the idol-smashing Zeng, and his newfound host Lu Liu, and grasping a stout bamboo pole in his hand, Hong sets out for the most important of the temples erected in King Gan's name, just over a day's march away. After resting nearby, the men are at the shrine next morning. Shouting abuse at the bearded image of King Gan in its dragon robe, and striking at it with his staff, Hong lists ten counts of immorality of which the idol has been guilty. This is the selfsame devil demon that the Heavenly Father and One True God, on Hong's journey to Heaven ten years before, ordered him to slay. "Now do you recognize me the ruler?" shouts Hong. "If you recognize me, then straightaway you had best go back down to hell." And with his willing helpers, Hong topples the image from its resting place, stomping its hat, pulling out its beard, shredding its dragon robe, digging out its eyes, and breaking off its arms. Festooning the desecrated shrine with their triumphant poems, and posting on the wall a manifesto of defiance to the devil demon Gan, Hong signs his name: "Taiping Heavenly King, Ruler of the Great Way, Quan." The next day, the four men are home on Thistle Mountain.[12]

The incident greatly enhances Hong's local reputation, and Feng's too, as leaders of the God-worshipers. It also builds local anger against them. When the desecration is discovered, local gentry offer a reward for the arrest of those who did it. Despite the fact that there have been complaints in the past about the God-worshipers as troublemakers, the local magistrate has no desire to get embroiled with fractious mountain dwellers, and he takes no action. Hong savors his triumph a little longer, but in December 1847 he leaves Thistle Mountain and returns to his friends the Huangs, back in the valley at Sigu village. Exasperated by the magistrate's inaction, a local licentiate called Wang Zuoxin sends a group of village militia up into the hills, and "arrests" Feng Yunshan, holding him captive in a local temple. Feng's host, Lu Liu, assembles a group of God-worshipers and frees Feng. The degree holder reinforces his militia and attacks the Thistle Mountain area once again, this time seizing both Feng and Lu. He takes them down to Guiping township, and hands them over to the magistrate in person, for trial.[13]

The accusations that Wang Zuoxin levels against the God-worshipers cover a wide front. They have pledged themselves into a brotherhood, he charges, which now numbers in the thousands. Through their magical books they trample down the local gods of the land and grain. The Zeng family should be rigorously investigated for the evildoers they have been secretly harboring. For more than two years the God-worshipers have been deluding the country folk, leading them astray through their religious teachings and practices. They wish their believers to follow the teachings in a foreign book, called "An Old Testament," thus abandoning the laws and regulations of the reigning Qing dynasty. They have desecrated temples and overturned and smashed to pieces the incense burners that are used in worship of the local gods along the shores of the rivers that flow through Guiping county. Describing the procedures by which he has acted, the licentiate Wang Zuoxin explains that first he invited the "local elders" to check with him if the charges were true. Convinced that they were, he then assembled a militia to make the arrest, and held Feng Yunshan in the temple till he could be handed over to the mutual security forces. It was at this point that the Zeng clan leaders and Lu Liu assembled their own men and counterattacked, forcibly releasing Feng. This prompted Wang's own second assault on the God-worshipers in which he recaptured Feng and took Lu Liu into custody as well.[14]

Feng Yunshan's defense is both moral and legalistic. Firstly, the God-worshipers are a simple religious group, in no way planning to cause trouble in the area, but merely seeking to worship their God in peace. To prove this, he gives the examining magistrate copies of the God-worshipers' books and a summary of their doctrine. At the same time, he reminds the investigators that since the new treaties with the Western powers ended the old Canton system and the restrictions on foreign religion, proclamations by the governor-general of the two provinces of Guangdong and Guangxi have been hung in front of the churches of Canton and in other public places, quoting the emperor's edict giving freedom to foreign missionaries and Chinese people to worship the One True God.[15]

Wang Zuoxin's "invitations" to the "elders," his "assembling" of the militia force, and his "arrest" of Feng Yunshan are typical of the actions of the various well-off families who live in the fertile farmlands that lie between Thistle Mountain and the township of Guiping as the God-worshiper ranks are growing. These local leaders are adept at trying to protect their home areas from traditional enemies of law and order, and more recently both from the Heaven-and-Earth Society and from the water pirates who are entering their inland rivers from the sea. Now they add the God-worshipers to the list.[16]

The ancestors of many of these influential families had migrated from eastern China at the time of civil war and fragmentation that accompanied the collapse of the Ming dynasty in the 1640s. Settling land, much of it taken by military force with connivance of the local authorities from the Yao inhabitants of the region, or bought at the cheapest prices, they assembled groups of Chinese migrant tenants to work their land and produce surplus crops of rice and grain that could be shipped in bulk down the rivers to Canton. Since many of this merchant elite were Hakkas, their success brought tension both with poorer Hakkas and with local Chinese families aspiring to higher levels of education and economic power. By the end of the eighteenth century such Hakka elite families might possess estates of hundreds of acres, as well as owning stores in several market and county towns, and bulk shipping businesses for rice transport.[17] With their large incomes, such family heads could educate their sons to obtain the licentiate's degree with ease, and in many cases also to win the higher national degrees; if they lacked the intellectual power to pass the examinations, these sons had wealth enough to purchase degrees from a Qing government always short of funds, and even to purchase offices in neighboring provinces.

Because they maintained their personal registration at the sites of their former homes, the men from such families could often serve in office in the Guiping region, even though technically one could not serve as an official in the province in which one lived.[18] Such trans-provincial family linkages gave them extra prestige and influence with incumbent officials even when they themselves were not in office. And further local solidarity and lineage strength came from their building of assembly halls and lodges in the various market towns where family members congregated to run their overlapping businesses, putting some of their income into the central lineage treasury to maintain an impressive level of sacrifices to their ancestors.[19]

Since the various clerks and underlings in the bureaucracy were always after the merchants' money—even going so far as to press loans upon them, connive at bandit raids on merchant shipping, or set up entrapments through prostitutes, to force them into debt and hence dependency—the fates of these wealthy families depended on the local officials' support, as their grateful testimonies hung in the local temples showed. The officials, for their part, were willing to take the merchants' side because the smooth transfer of bulk grain from Guangxi to the Canton delta region was seen as a high economic priority. Official support made "business smooth, life stable, and left nothing to worry about while trading."[20] The merchants' influence could, through intermediaries, reach to the emperor himself, and bring crucial tax relief in troubled times. Merchant money, paid out judiciously, could also bring relief to their communities from bandit gangs and military procurers who, left unpaid, would take the grain and livestock and even kidnap local men or women.[21]

Intricate marriage connections were forged among these wealthy families, whose own dialects, lovingly preserved, acted as further buttresses to their local solidarity. Concurrently, they strengthened their reputation among both Hakka and non-Hakka local inhabitants by their construction of irrigation works, embankments, and bridges, paving the streets of the towns in which they lived, building multistoried cultural and religious halls (one soared five stories high), and establishing local schools and libraries. It was the members of such elites who were "the elders" Wang Zuoxin "invited" to check the charges against the God-worshipers, and by this period they were forming their own "pacification groups."[22]

The most important of these families, in the fertile farming area of Jintian that lay on the road and river route between Guiping and Thistle Mountain, assembled seventy of their members to serve as "elders" in their pacification group. In their ranks were several Hakka migrants who had made their money from lead mines and pawnshops as well as farming.[23] Such families of "elders" protected their long-range interests by imposing rigid limitations on lineage spending and expenses, as shown by the surviving records of one such family in Gucheng village, at the foot of Thistle Mountain. This elite family's rules for self-discipline were not so different from those Hong Xiuquan was slowly forming for his God-worshipers: they forbade all their lineage members to visit prostitutes, tried to curb their gambling or drinking, and threatened with "incarceration for life" any family member who took opium. They controlled their lineage costs through meticulous regulations, estimating their expenses in *jin*, one *jin* being roughly equivalent to a month's wages for a poor artisan or farm laborer, but a comparative trifle to a wealthy landlord or merchant:

> As for all the expenses of the entire household, receiving a bride into the household must not exceed 30 *jin,* and giving a daughter in marriage must not exceed 20 *jin.* Make the cost of attending a school the same as giving a daughter in marriage, and make the cost of taking an examination the same as receiving a bride. The closest friends of the family can be invited in a small group and drink together, but do not accept gifts from them, and do not invite lots of other guests.
>
> As for the cost of a funeral, for an elderly family member, do not exceed 40 *jin.* For others, do not exceed 20 *jin.* Do not use musical instruments for the ceremony, do not prepare expensive food for the funeral banquet, and do not have a Buddhist service for carrying a coffin out of the house. Follow these rules for any auspicious and inauspicious matters of the house. . . . The monthly amount of grain and rice for our house must not exceed 700 *catties* [about 1,000 lbs]. The volume of cooking fuel must not exceed 1,500 *catties.* The oil that is used for lamps and cooking must not exceed 20 *catties,* and salt must not exceed 10 *catties.* Soy sauce, vinegar, and tea leaves must not exceed 200 copper cash, and vegetables must not exceed 100 copper cash per day. . . . If there is anybody in this village or market area who goes ahead on his own and builds a temple or collects money from people and holds a festival for gods, do not list his name, because he is violating the rules. As for the building of bridges and paving of roads, make donations only if the project is confirmed to be beneficial, and is within our ability to pay.[24]

Such careful money management, in turn, gave them added prestige within the community, and extra money to contribute to formal militia organizations and to local county projects. Obviously, their community as a whole would be resistant to God-worshiping recruitment in a way that upland villages of Thistle Mountain would not, whether or not each was dominated by Hakkas who felt in some ways isolated either from the non-Hakka Chinese or from the local Yao tribesmen.[25]

Furthermore, there was a self-defining snobbery built into the leader-ship levels of the pacification groups and those who enforced the local law-and-order contracts in the name of the state: to be a leader in the pacification group was to be a member of the elite, and being in the elite entitled one to lead the pacification group. They were people who claimed to be "loved by the officials as if they were their sons and younger brothers" and in return "they respected the officials as if they were their fathers and elder brothers."[26] The methods they employed to identify, isolate, and eventually punish secret-society brothers in the Heaven-and-Earth Society could be applied unchanged to the God-worshipers: in each case what was required were finer distinctions than those based merely on factors such as socioeconomic status or educational level and examination success:

> The regulations of the *baojia* [village registration groups] blend the rich, the poor, the wise, and the foolish in a given village all together into one group and enforce the same rules upon all of them. Meanwhile, niceties of ranking are all confounded and different levels of knowledge are discounted. To lump everyone together indiscriminately like this is as if one were cooping up chickens and ducks with a flock of fabulous *luan* birds and cranes, or as if organizing tigers and leopards to be in a group of dogs and goats. Their differences in background, and their mutual suspicions, would be obvious to everyone. If one wants to group people together, one should first choose those who belong to the same kind, then make a compact among them, and so give strength to their hearts. That is to say, through the compact, they will be able to gather together all their resources, and make the best possible use of them.[27]

To refine the categories properly, the same village regulations stated, one had to distinguish those who are truly "talented and knowledgeable" from those who are "foolish and cowardly" or "violent." Associated categories separated out those "who know things" from "those who are afraid of things" and those "who like things to happen"—the implication being that this last group were "troublemakers," linked specifically to the "wandering bandits from Guangdong province."[28]

"Guest people" in a village—the phrase might mean Hakkas or could mean simply immigrants or outsiders in some cases—had to be checked out with especial care, and literally expelled from their villages if they proved to have bandit contacts. Every single person in every local village should be registered by name, household, family, occupation, relationship, marital status, and status as "native" or "visitor." Anyone "trusted by the whole village" would be rewarded with the label of "publicly registered" and issued with a certificate to that effect to be hung on their door. Those not worthy of such trust would be given no such certificate, pending further investigation.[29] Found lacking by these standards are certain power-

ful and extremely wealthy people, like the Wei family of Jintian, who
have been excluded by this pattern of discrimination from membership in
the pacification groups, and in return have refused to make more than the
most token contributions to local public projects, and become eager members of the God-worshipers, who do not make the same kinds of distinctions.[30]

There is a tight meshing of the pacification groups and the government,
and even though by no means all those who lead such groups have passed
the examinations at even the licentiate's level, anyone who has passed is
likely to be in a leadership position. And few if any of those who have
passed the examinations join the God-worshipers. Though there are many
God-worshipers who are literate, they come from among the failed candidates, or from those who make their literacy serve in the edges of society:
those employed in junior positions in the magistrate's office or who can
read the law codes enough to help plaintiffs in certain legal cases, some
who practice types of medicine that demand a knowledge of old texts,
merchants and pawnshop owners, clerks in shops or small businesses, and
even—in a strange reversal of roles—those who secretly act as substitutes
and take the examinations for men eager for the titles who have no hopes
of passing.[31]

While Feng is still in Guiping prison, trying to construct a meaningful
defense, Hong Xiuquan has been safely out of harm's way, down in Sigu
village with his distant relatives the Huangs. The charges against Feng
are too serious, and the forces arrayed against him seem too powerful, for
Hong to win his friend's freedom with a simple elegant literary petition
to the magistrate, as he had for the Huangs' own son on his first visit
to Guangxi in 1844. So instead Hong decides to press the curious new
international law aspects of Feng's defense by going to Canton city to
plead the case of Feng in person before the current Manchu governor-
general of Guangdong and Guangxi provinces, Qiying, by coincidence the
very man who negotiated the 1842 treaty with the British on which Feng
bases his claims for pardon. There is urgency in Hong's journey, for magistrates customarily use harsh tortures on their prisoners in cases involving
"heterodox beliefs," and the prisons themselves are often death traps of
disease—Lu Liu has already died, from either illness or maltreatment.[32]

When Hong gets to Canton in the spring of 1848, he finds that Governor-general Qiying is no longer there, having been summoned to Peking
by the emperor for a special audience. Hong visits his own family briefly,
but does not linger. Within a month he heads back to Thistle Mountain,
bearing the bad news of his mission's failure to Feng. Feng, in the mean-

time, has powerfully argued his cause and that of the God-worshipers
with the local officials in Guiping county, and his arguments (backed by
cash gifts to the magistrate from the local God-worshipers) have led to his
release. But as the cost of his freedom the local officials of Guiping decide
to remove Feng from their jurisdiction. They categorize him as "an unemployed vagrant," and order him to return under escort to Guanlubu, his
village of birth and registration. So in the early summer of 1848 Feng and
Hong pass, somewhere on the road or river, perhaps only a few feet apart
as they head in different directions to find each other.[33] Now it is Feng
who is with his wife and sons again after three years away, free to preach
in his home. And Hong once again is far from his wife and daughters,
and his father, who is ill and old.

In Thistle Mountain, the feuds, the fighting, the trial, Feng's release
and Hong's return, all bring new passion to the God-worshipers. Now it
is the local mountain dwellers, used to their local shamans' practices, and
witnesses in the past to spirit possession among their number, who have
the celestial visions.[34] It is in the late spring of 1848, while both Hong and
Feng are absent from Thistle Mountain, that a Hakka charcoal burner
called Yang Xiuqing, drawn to the God-worshipers by his poverty and
their message of salvation, becomes the mouthpiece for God the Father,
who speaks now through Yang's voice as Yang enters a trance-like state,
a voice that Hong accepts as authentically divine on his return to Thistle
Mountain. It is in the autumn, when Hong has been back some months,
that Xiao Chaogui, a Hakka peasant, also among the poorest of the poor
and devoted to the new religion, becomes the vehicle by which Jesus
Christ speaks to his younger brother Hong, and to all his other followers
on earth. Again, Hong accepts this second intermediary with Heaven.
Xiao's trances, in which Jesus speaks through him, can last an hour or
more; but others, both men and women, have shorter dreams of Hong's
impending glory.[35]

Jesus comes back to earth many times in 1848, and through the mouth
of Xiao brings varied messages to Hong Xiuquan and the God-worshipers. He sings them songs newly composed by God; and patiently teaches
God's poems to the congregation, word by word.[36] At other times his
message is doctrinal, as when he repeats the point that Hong has already
mentioned in his own writings, that only their Father has the right to bear
the name of Di, "Ruler of All," while both Jesus and Hong Xiuquan must
claim no title higher than that of *zhu,* or "lord."[37] Jesus tells Hong that
the Buddhist Goddess of Mercy, Guanyin, also lives in Heaven, and that
though God will not allow her to descend to earth again, because her

message can be misunderstood, He knows her heart is good, and permits both Hong and Jesus to call her "sister."[38]

Jesus tells Hong of all the events in Heaven since Hong left eleven years before. They talk of Hong's young son, conceived and born in Heaven, but still unnamed, who lives in Heaven with his grandmother, the wife of God. They talk of the boy's mother, the First Chief Moon, of how she lives in turn with her divine in-laws, or with Jesus and his wife, and of how she yearns for her husband to come back to her. Once the First Chief Moon herself comes back to earth and chides Hong sadly—in Hakka idioms—for his protracted absence. She talks of the kindness shown to her and her son by Jesus' wife, and of Jesus' five children, three boys, two girls. Jesus' boys at eighteen, fifteen, and thirteen are older than Hong's heavenly son, as is Jesus' older girl, now sixteen years old. But Jesus' younger daughter was born since Hong was last in Heaven, and thus Hong's son has at least one younger playmate.[39]

The air of Thistle Mountain is thick with other holy visits, dreams, and portents. A martial host descends from Heaven and fights the bandits who plague the village of Sigu, home of Hong's friends and loyal supporters. Another time it is angels in yellow robes who descend to earth, and save Hong in the nick of time from devils carrying firearms, which they have aimed at him. At Siwang village, east of Thistle Mountain, it is Hong's celestial wife, the First Chief Moon, helped by her angels, who saves him from a mortal danger.[40]

While the God-worshipers are at their prayers, kneeling in their mountain churches open to the winds, from time to time, a contemporary records, "one or the other of those present was seized by a sudden fit, so that he fell down to the ground, and his whole body was covered with perspiration. In such a state of ecstasy, moved by the spirit, he uttered words of exhortation, reproof, prophecy."[41] Those who travel up to Heaven take the Eastern Road, as Hong did in his dream. They see God in His majesty, still with black dragon robe, high-brimmed hat, and golden beard, as Hong too saw Him.[42] They see the chief of the devil demons, square-headed and red-eyed, and learn that he is indeed the same as the demon devil of the Eastern Sea and the devil king on earth they call Yan Luo.[43] As God did to Moses on the Mount at Sinai, writing the tablets of the laws "with His own hand," so now "with His own hand" he identifies the demon king to Heaven's travelers.[44] And not unlike the way Jacob wrestled with the angel through the night near the brook of Jabbok, so does God allow Xiao, the poor peasant who serves as the vehicle for the voice of Jesus, to wrestle with the generals of the Heavenly Army, using the technique that the mountain Hakkas with their powerful fore-arms call "forming the iron-hand bridge."[45] In all their travails, in all their battles, God and his son are with them, watching and advising.

After the New Year's festivals of 1849, Hong travels home to Guan-lubu, and learns that his father has just died, asking to be buried by the God-worshipers' rites. By the traditional Confucian rituals of mourning for the death of a parent, there are two essential paths Hong should now follow: for the three years of grief he should not cut his hair, and during the same period he should abstain from sexual intercourse even with his wife. These rules are meant to show the homage and respect one owes to the dead, who brought one into this world and nurtured one for the expanse of time one now returns to them by abstinence and grief. It is a time to tend the corpse and see to the grave's good ordering, to study and reflect. The rule that a man should not trim his hair or shave during the same period has a similar purpose of self-abnegation and respect, but poli-tics have given the regulation a strange new twist. For since their conquest of China in 1644, the Manchus have ordered every Chinese man to follow the Manchu customary practice of shaving the front of the head, and braiding the rest of the hair behind in a long queue. Those failing to do so are branded as rebels and punished with death. But since 1644, in times of mourning, instead of being punished if they do not shave their fore-heads and braid their hair, Chinese and Manchus are sternly punished if they do shave, and hence appear to put Manchu practice ahead of ancestral virtue.[46]

Hong follows one rule, but not the other. He lies with his wife as soon as he returns to Guanlubu, and does not shave his head. In the heat of early summer, when it is clear that his wife is pregnant, he says farewell to her. And, with his hair now thick above his forehead and flowing around his neck and shoulders, he leaves with Feng Yunshan once more for Thistle Mountain.[47]

9

ASSEMBLING

 By the late summer of 1849, when Hong and Feng are back in Guangxi, there are four distinct centers of the God-worshipers, grouped in a rough semicircle to the north and the west of the district city of Guiping. The four regions—measuring from their outer edges—cover an area some sixty miles from east to west, and eighty miles from north to south. One of the centers remains on Thistle Mountain, but now includes the prosperous village of Jintian on the plain at the foot of the mountains. One encircles the area of Sigu village, where Hong long found support from the God-worshiping Huang family. One, more to the northwest, includes a network of mountain villages under the jurisdiction of Xiang township, where Hong and Feng destroyed the image of King Gan. And one newly expanding area, northeast of Thistle Mountain, sprawls through the Penghua Mountain chain, incorporating the little market towns of Penghua and Huazhou.[1]

Though the God-worshipers themselves are still seen by their neighbors and by the officials of the Qing state as mainly a religious group, not yet an emergency calling for direct military suppression, the area as a whole has been racked by at least a dozen risings of bandit groups connected to the Heaven-and-Earth Society. China itself has more than enough troubles in other regions, but Guangxi has become a focus for the court's concern, and messages of anxiety and resolve are constantly speeding between the southern officials and their rulers in Peking.[2] The decision the same year by the commanding officers of Britain's China fleet—based mainly in Hong Kong—to make a final, all-out assault on the Chinese pirate bases in the South China Sea, brings yet more chaos. As the pirate bases are systematically destroyed, their boats blown up, and their storage bases and safe havens burned, the surviving pirates move upriver to Guangxi from the sea, linking up with those who followed the same route some years before.[3]

The four God-worshiping areas are separated from each other by intermediate zones of rugged territory that are controlled either by hostile, non-Hakka local inhabitants, by bandits, or by wary local officials. Journeying between the four areas is not easy. Hong Xiuquan, like other leaders of the God-worshipers, travels at night, between eleven in the evening and dawn, in a tight-knit group with covered lanterns, "all bunched together so that no one is out in front, and no one lingers in the rear."[4] When one day in early autumn Hong violates these safety procedures, and rides off on horseback before his designated companions have collected together, he is yet again accosted by robbers, and lucky that he survives unharmed. For this impetuosity, he is publicly reprimanded by his elder brother Jesus—speaking through the lips of Xiao Chaogui—who asks how Hong dares to break such a simple order, devised by the Lord for the protection of the true believers. Hong is contrite, and offers up a public apology.[5]

Despite the risks, the leaders of the God-worshipers are always on the move. For their believers are scattered in isolated villages, and the True Religion blurs constantly with local folk practices, beliefs, and shamanic voices, just as the "converts" themselves are often suspect for their motives, devotion, or sincerity. Hong is aware of the dissensions between local groupings, and one of his tasks is to examine the prophetic utterances they have issued in their trances or their ecstasy, to "judge the spirits according to the truth of the doctrine" and to ascertain if possible which were true and which were false, which indeed "came from God and which from the devil."[6] Some believers have undergone apparently miraculous cures, and if these cures come from Yang Xiuqing speaking with the voice of God, or Xiao Chaogui speaking with the voice of Jesus, then surely there is "earnestness and sincerity." But others speak against the word of God and "[lead] many astray," or act "under the influence of a corrupt spirit." In

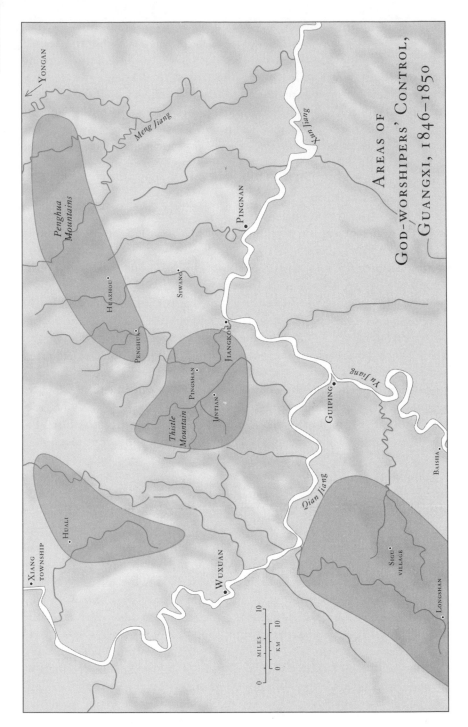

AREAS OF
GOD-WORSHIPERS' CONTROL,
GUANGXI, 1846–1850

such difficult cases, no one, according to Hong's contemporaries, "was so able as he to exercise authority, and carry into effect a rigid discipline among so many sorts of people."[7] In the Taiping's own text that records this era of Hong's work, Jesus declares (through Xiao), "It is because the hearts of the congregations are not totally committed to belief in the Doctrine that I want Hong and you others to go to different areas and dwell there. . . . Those who currently believe the True Doctrine are few indeed—they may revere half of it, but they reject the other half. Are you able to win over all their hearts?" And though the leaders duly respond, "We cannot win them over completely," they accept the charge that Jesus gives them.[8]

Another reason for constantly traveling among the four base areas of the God-worshipers is money, the money for living expenses, for printing tracts, for helping the destitute or the victimized who are beginning to drift to the four areas from the surrounding countryside, for making or buying the simple weapons that are needed for local defense, for establishing emergency grain supplies in the face of the famine conditions endemic to the region, and for buying the freedom of those God-worshipers unfortunate enough to be imprisoned. Local gentry like Wang Zuoxin, angered by the disruptive and destructive effects of the God-worshipers on their communities, and by what they felt were affronts to fundamental Chinese moral values, were able in 1847 and 1848 to have Feng Yunshan imprisoned, and his colleague Lu Liu so mistreated that he died in prison. In the summer of 1849, following another clash and flaring of local angers, Wang Zuoxin is able to have two more God-worshipers confined to jail. One of the captives is the same young man Hong Xiuquan successfully petitioned the magistrate to release five years before, but now angers are deeper and stakes higher, and neither elegant petitions nor the arguments from international treaty law used to free Feng Yunshan are of any use. To raise the money needed for the two men's release, the leaders of the God-worshipers invoke the sufferings of Jesus on the cross, pointing out that though such suffering purified the sufferer, and might have to be endured by all God-worshipers in their quest for salvation, it was still right to evade it for the captured brethren. Xiao Chaogui, speaking again with the voice of Jesus, suggests that all those with stores of rice donate half of them to try and buy the men's release.[9]

At other times the God-worshipers exhort their congregations with moral arguments, blaming them for weakness of will, stinginess, and for cheating Heaven if they withhold their cash.[10] They also urge certain of the wealthiest families among the God-worshipers, like the Shi clan, whose home is near the Huangs' in Sigu village, to give major donations to effect the release of the imprisoned men, telling the potential donors that it is the express will of God that they make these donations. In many of these exhortations the leaders now refer to God by the oddly informal name of the Old One on High; by doing this, the petitioners seem to have been emphasizing that this was all an extended family matter.[11] At yet other times, without great subtlety, the appeals for cash donations from the congregations are made in the same breath as decrees ordering savage punishments for those guilty of immorality. Either enough money cannot be raised or the officials cannot be bribed, for the appeals for funds for these particular men's release stop by the end of the month, when the God-worshipers learn that their two imprisoned friends have been beaten or tortured to death. But within a month, two more prominent God-worshipers are arrested at local gentry urging, and the process has to begin all over again.[12]

This whole grim episode shows that during 1849 the God-worshipers could not yet rely on a strong financial base, and underlines the importance of those wealthy families who had already joined the movement. One of these was the Shi family, Hakkas who provided not only large amounts of money but in the person of one of their young men, Shi Dakai, only nineteen at this time, gave Hong Xiuquan a passionately devoted follower, who was later to become one of his finest generals. The Wei family, from Jintian village, owned large holdings of rice paddy, and also operated a pawnshop or shops; they were apparently drawn to the God-worshipers because despite their wealth they were unable to rise in the local hierarchies, owing to their lowly status as the "runners" or junior lictors in the local government office, and because they were of mixed blood, having at some stage in the past intermarried with local Zhuang tribesmen. There was also the Hu family, who often gave shelter to Hong Xiuquan and had extensive landholdings in both Pingnan and Guiping districts, as well as having held minor military office.[13] Yet the God-worshiping leaders, at least through the month of February 1850, did not want such backers' generosity to be widely known; and in that month, when the Hus offered to sell off their land, and to donate the proceeds along with their other property to the God-worshipers, so as to "further the Heavenly Father and Heavenly Elder Brothers' enterprise," they were warmly thanked for their loyalty and generosity but asked to keep the gift "completely secret" for the time being.[14]

Perhaps the agonizing and ultimately fruitless quest during 1849 for the release of their two imprisoned followers was the decisive factor that drove the God-worshiper leaders into a formal anti-government stance. Ever since his dream of 1837, Hong Xiuquan had been preaching against the "demon devils," even though it was never quite clear who these devils were, whether they were the physical forms of the followers of the devil king Yan Luo himself, or benighted Confucian scholars who closed their eyes to truth, or Taoist and Buddhist priests, or the shamans of local folk cults, or the sinners and idolaters who broke the various versions of Hong's or God's commandments. Sometimes Hong was totally inclusive in his definitions, as in remarks he made at Guanlubu in 1848 or early 1849: "Those who believe not in the true doctrine of God and Jesus, though they be old acquaintances, are still no friends of mine, but they are demons."[15] At other times his definitions edged into broader zones of criticism, closer to the Protestant idea of predestination, as in one of his favorite chants, which he composed during this same period:

> Those who truly believe in God are indeed the sons and daughters of God; whatever locality they come from, they have come from Heaven, and no matter where they are going they will ascend to Heaven.
> Those who worship the demon devils are truly the pawns and slaves of the demon devils; from the moment of birth they are deluded by devils, and at the day of their death the devils will drag them away.[16]

By the end of 1849 or the beginning of 1850 it is the Manchu conquerors of China, and those officials serving them, who are now often identified specifically as the demons to be exterminated, and the Qing courts where God-worshipers are brought to trial on "trumped-up charges" are now described by Hong as presided over by "demon officials."[17] Part of the change lies in Hong Xiuquan's own mood. At this same time he is reported to have said, "Too much patience and humility do not suit our present times, for therewith it would be impossible to manage this perverted generation."[18] Perhaps Hong thinks indeed that the God-worshipers have shown more than enough patience in the face of local hostility, or the local officials' connivance with that same local hostility.

If the time for "patience and humility" was over, and if many people had become "the pawns and slaves of the demon devils," one could see the Chinese people as the enslaved ones and the Manchus as the demon devils. Such thinking was common in secret-society groupings such as the Heaven-and-Earth or Triad Society, with their mystical evocations of the fourteenth-century founder of the Ming dynasty, and their widely announced hopes of a Ming "restoration" that would overthrow the ruling Qing. Hong claimed not to accept all these myths, though his thoughts followed parallel tracks. He told his followers, "Though I never entered the Triad Society, I have often heard it said that their object is to subvert the Qing and restore the Ming dynasty. Such an expression was very proper in the time of Kangxi [ruled 1661–1722], when this society was at first formed, but now after the lapse of two hundred years, we may still speak of subverting the Qing, but we cannot properly speak of restoring the Ming. At all events, when our native mountains and rivers are recovered, a new dynasty must be established."[19]

In an eight-line poem written in the year 1850, Hong Xiuquan invokes images from the great founders of the Han and Ming dynasties to underline his political mood of excitement and belatedness: Both these earlier dynastic founders were men from poor farming families who had risen by courage and tenacity to overthrow tyrannical rulers and found new dynasties that endured for centuries. Both were famous for fighting against alien conquerors or invaders. According to popular stories Liu Bang, while engaged in the bitter military campaigns that led ultimately to his establishment of the Han dynasty in 202 B.C., had been so exhilarated by the winds that sent clouds scudding above his head, likening their rapid motion to his own troops, and seeing an omen that his armies would carry all before them, that he laid out ritual wine on an extemporized altar to salute the wind's passing. While Zhu Yuanzhang, who was forty years old by the time he overcame his numerous rivals and founded the Ming in 1368, liked to compare himself to the autumn-blooming chrysanthemum, which comes into its splendor only when the other apparently more vivid flowers have flourished and faded. As Hong wrote:

> Now at last the murky mists begin to lift,
> And we know that Heaven plans an age of heroes.
> Those who brought low our sacred land shall not do so again;
> All men should worship God, and we shall do so too.
> The Ming founder tapped out the rhythm of his chrysanthemum poem,
> And the Han emperor poured out wine for the singing wind.
> As with all deeds performed by men since ancient times,
> The dark clouds are scattered in reflected light.[20]

In February 1850 a change seems to occur in the shape of the God-worshipers' military organization or at least in the language with which it is discussed. From this month on there is talk of the God-worshipers having an "army" on the march, moving between the four areas where they have their bases, an army that demands careful tactical planning, feeding, and other logistical support. There are set piece attacks on pre-pared "demon" positions. Loyal "troops" who have traveled from distant places have to be replaced, and allowed time to rest up, unless ten or twenty of them choose to volunteer for further combat. Troops from "nearby places" can stay in action for a few days longer. Reports of mili-tary action have to be carefully written up by the commanders and taken to Hong Xiuquan's temporary home in the northeastern Pingshan base area, where Hong is recovering from a leg injury that prevents him from riding on horseback. Hong's base area is now sometimes called "the court," and Hong himself referred to as the "Taiping king." Tempers flare at some of the leaders' strategy meetings, as they argue about whether to press on with a given attack or to retreat. Food supplies run out, with no prior warning being given to commanders in the field, causing desperate hardship.[21]

A record of conflict from Baisha village, a few miles east of Hong's temporary home of Sigu and just outside the southern area of God-wor-shipers' control, shows many of these elements in place at once: the vio-lence slowly growing, from squabble to threat to confrontation, with the concern over arms and supplies constantly cutting into the narrative. The enemy driving the people of Baisha into the God-worshipers ranks are first described as "demons," and might be government-supported non-Hakka local families, or local bandit groups allied to such families. In the main part of the narrative, they are simply called "bandits," or "outsider bandits."

> Heavenly Brother asked Luo Nengan about the real situation in Baisha. He answered, "Li Desheng left his plowing buffalo with Lin Fengxiang to be fed. The outsider bandits from Lingwei village tried to extort money from Li Desheng, but the latter refused. So two of the bandits stole Li's buffalo from Lin Fengxiang's, but Lin got it back from them. He did not hurt the bandits during the fight. Next day, forty or fifty bandits went to Lin's house, yelling and trying to provoke a fight. Eight of us, while preparing our meal, saw the bandits begin to shoot their guns. Five of us grabbed our own weap-ons, and chased them; they escaped, leaving behind two cane shields, a box of gunpowder, and five guns. The second time, two hundred bandits showed up and we defeated them with fifty-eight people. They escaped and left three cane shields, a box of gunpowder, two guns, and one 'cat-tail-shaped' gun. Now we have assembled one hundred eighty brothers in Baisha."
>
> Heavenly Brother asked Luo Nengan how they could supply enough food for the army. Luo: "The relative of Li Deshang, Wu, donated two thousand *dan* of rice."

Heavenly Brother: "Who arranged the horses?"

Luo: "Qin Rigang."

After Heavenly Brother asked Luo many questions, He bid Luo to return and temporarily disband his troops, just retaining a dozen or so. Heavenly Brother: "When you go back, don't worry! Everything will be taken care of by Heavenly Father's and Heavenly Brother's Heavenly Army. You can defeat one thousand people with ten people; if they dare come again, we will send more troops to fight them. . . ."[22]

Given the colossal amount of grain these new Baisha allies could offer—two thousand *dan* would have been over one hundred tons—they would be invaluable allies in case of a major attack or siege by Qing forces. Yet the God-worshiping leaders were still clearly cautious about massing so many people in the central base areas that they would prompt immediate reprisals.

Inevitably the leaders of the God-worshipers worry about the potential loyalty of followers such as these: some call the new recruits "brothers," some call them "demons." Sometimes Jesus, through Xiao Chaogui, is asked for his opinion, and declares the newcomers good people, worthy recruits to the Taiping cause, people who will "support the kingdom." Hong Xiuquan often remains unconvinced, believing that the true goal of these strangers from afar is to "destroy the army."[23]

Regardless of such suspicions, there are mass baptisms of the new arrivals, four hundred at a time one day in late February 1850, after they have been preached to at some length, and taught the secret code names for their leaders. As to the hierarchy of the top leadership, as it is now emerging, the faithful are told that "those who sincerely acknowledge Hong Xiuquan are in the presence of the Old One on High; those who sincerely acknowledge Feng Yunshan, [Yang] Xiuqing, and [Xiao] Chaogui are in the presence of Old Elder Brother." The converts are told to live with patience and sincerity, to convert their wives and children, so that all may live as children of God before their final entry into Paradise.[24] For their part, the leaders undertake to receive all the sincerely faithful into the God-worshiping ranks, whether or not they bring "ritual offerings" with them, for all are equal before the Lord, and each family's lacks or surpluses are the common concern of all.[25] By early April 1850 Hong Xiuquan sometimes wears a yellow robe, a garment only emperors are allowed to assume, though he wears it in secret, inside the home of the believer with whom he is sheltering.[26]

The transcript of the initiation of one God-worshiper into the nascent Taiping forces has been preserved in a Taiping text. This particular ceremony takes place on April 9, 1850, at Hong Xiuquan's base—or retreat—in Pingshan. (The convert, Tan Shuntian, later became one of the Heavenly King's senior officers.) The main questions are posed by Xiao Chaogui, acting as mouthpiece for the Heavenly Elder Brother, Jesus. Hong Xiuquan is present, but acts as observer only, seated—in the absence of any other furniture in this isolated mountain home—upon the bed. The Taiping's own record of this encounter runs as follows:

Heavenly Brother declared to Tan Shuntian: "Tan Shuntian, do you know who is talking to you now?"

Tan Shuntian: "You, Heavenly Brother."

Heavenly Brother: "Who is that person sitting on the bed?"

Tan: "It is Second Brother [Hong Xiuquan]."

Heavenly Brother: "Who sent him here?"

Tan: "Heavenly Father."

Heavenly Brother: "Why did Heavenly Father send him here?"

Tan: "Heavenly Father sent him to become the King of Great Peace [Taiping]."

Heavenly Brother: "What is meant by: 'adding starlight brings the view of Holy Father'?"

Tan: "It means if we have our Second Brother [i.e., Hong Xiuquan], we will be able to see Heavenly Father."

Heavenly Brother: "Who is 'Rice King'?"

Tan: "It is Second Brother."

Heavenly Brother: "You should acknowledge him. In Heaven you should trust Heavenly Father and me; on earth you should follow his instruction; you must not be stubborn and willful, but follow him obediently."

Tan: "With all my heart I will follow Heavenly Father, Heavenly Brother, and Second Brother."

Heavenly Brother: "Who is 'Two Stars with Feet Up'?"

Tan: "It is East King [Yang Xiuqing]."

Heavenly Brother: "Who is 'Henai'?"

Tan: "It is also East King."

Heavenly Brother: "You should recognize East King since it is he who is the mouthpiece of Heavenly Father. All nations on earth should listen to him."

Tan: "Yes, I know."

Heavenly Brother: "Shuntian, at times of hardest testing do you lose your nerve or not?"

Tan: "I do not lose my nerve."

Heavenly Brother: "You should remain faithful until the end. It is just as
    it is with sifting rice, one watches it with one's eyes and then sepa-
    rates out the grains. The Taiping course is set, but caution is still
    essential. The basic plan must not be divulged to anyone."
Tan: "I will obey the Heavenly Command."

The next day, Tan received his formal baptism.[27]

    As the troubled times draw more and more men and women to the
God-worshipers' ranks, the Taiping leaders must not only feed and protect the newcomers but also protect their own reputation for virtue, and
stop both licentiousness and dissension in their own ranks. Hong's original
commandments had been strongly critical of sensuality, and now these are
reinforced by examples from the Bible and Mosaic law. It is early in 1850
that the Taiping leaders begin to make pronouncements hinting that men
and women should be separated, in the interests of decency and the common good. Feng Yunshan, Hong's close friend and founder of the God-
worshipers, who has left his wife and children at home in Guanlubu, is
held up as the model for male behavior. A woman, Hu Jiumei—probably
a daughter of the wealthy Hu family that had donated their possessions
to the God-worshipers—is announced to be the paragon of female behavior. God Himself, through His son Jesus, sends poems down to earth in
their honor, brief classical poems each of four seven-beat lines, that make
mnemonic puns on the chosen models' names, and point out their virtues.
Thus the poem for Hu Jiumei as the paragon for women plays on the
idea that the homophone for Hu's name is another character that means
"lake":

    Women observing Hu, a well of pure water,
    Will long remember that pure repose as they boil up their tea.
    The mountain birds can be large or small, the trees make no distinctions;
    Each red flower has a single bud, dwelling among men.[28]

Speaking through one of the congregation, God's wife also comes to earth,
with her own exhortations to the God-worshipers: "My little ones, above
all heed the instructions of God the Father. Next, heed the instructions of
your Celestial Elder Brother. In general, be faithful and true, and never
let your hearts rebel."[29]
    Such moral exhortations are backed by stern examples of public punish-
ment for wrongdoers. One God-worshiper named Huang Hanjing, who
is discovered to have been having sexual relations with a woman, is con-

demned to a beating of 140 blows with a heavy pole. The woman he slept with—even though Huang had either kidnapped or abducted her in some way—receives 100 blows.[30] Given the shock and loss of blood from such beatings, this number of blows could amount to a death sentence.

The webs of divine and earthly family relationships inevitably intertwine in these heavenly messages and practical instructions. When Xiao Chaogui, for example, spoke as the voice of Jesus, he would naturally address Hong Xiuquan as his "younger brother." But in earthly life, Xiao had recently married a female relative of Hong Xiuquan's, perhaps a cousin, and so the two men were bonded together as "brothers-in-law." If Xiao wished his wife to be more obedient, as he apparently did at times, then he could do so in the voice of Jesus demanding that his "blood relation" obey her husband.[31] Instructions from on high, parallel to those given to Hu Jiumei, could also be given in the name of God or Jesus to other God-worshiping women prominent in the organization, as in the case of those for the "second daughter" of the Chen family, Chen Ermei. Such messages had the force of divine decrees, as in the case of the one of January 30, 1850: "Chen Ermei, women must know how to keep out of the way: men have quarters that should be left to men, and women have quarters that should be left to women. Senior or junior sisters-in-law should also keep a proper balance, for the older ones have things to do that would not be suitable for younger sisters-in-law, just as the younger have things to do not suitable for the older. It is never good for them to compete with each other."[32]

From such pronouncements grows the Taiping policy of separating men and women altogether into separate camps and units, until such time as all will win their Heavenly Kingdom and be reunited. But as the Taiping develop this policy it results not merely in restricting women's lives but also in the formation of women's army units, and in establishing the rights of women to serve as officials in the Taiping bureaucracy. The fullest explanation of this policy's rationale from a Taiping text is the following:

Moreover, as it is advisable to avoid suspicion [of improper conduct] between the inner [female] and the outer [male] and to distinguish between male and female, so men must have male quarters and women must have female quarters; only thus can we be dignified and avoid confusion. There must be no common mixing of the male and female groups, which would cause debauchery and violation of Heaven's commandments. Although to pay respects to parents and to visit wives and children occasionally are in keeping with human nature and not prohibited, yet it is only proper to converse before the door, stand a few steps apart, and speak in a loud voice; one must not enter the sisters' camp or permit the mixing of men and women. Only thus, by complying with rules and commands, can we become sons and daughters of Heaven.[33]

Hong Xiuquan gradually came to apply the idea of the separation of the sexes not only to unmarried men and women joining the Taiping but even to husbands and wives within the Taiping ranks. Such a doctrine, if rigorously enforced, would obviously make procreation impossible until the Taiping created their projected Heavenly Kingdom. This would have advantages for a large army, with many civilians, on the march, but it would be the final blow to any lingering adherence to Confucian views of filial piety toward ancestors with their emphasis on production of a male heir. Hong Xiuquan himself might well have been rendered more receptive to a policy of separation by gender by the news he received in January 1850—rushed to him from Guanlubu—that his wife, Lai, whom he had left at home pregnant when he returned to Thistle Mountain, had given birth to a boy, on November 23, 1849, and that both mother and son were strong and well.[34] Hong names the boy Tiangui, "Heaven's Precious One."

For five months after receiving this news Hong appears absorbed with the world of God-worshipers, and seems to have no special concern over his family. Then, in the middle of June 1850, despite the perils of the journey, he suddenly summons them to join him in Thistle Mountain. Hong does not go in person to Guanlubu, but sends a small delegation of three trusted followers he has known since his earliest visits to Guangxi. One of these men is a physician, who carries always his box of medicines with him as he travels, to quell the suspicions of any government patrols they might encounter.[35] These three men carry a letter to his family, and though we do not have the letter, we know the effects are immediate. Within days, most of Hong's close family members have packed up or disposed of their possessions, and begun the long trip from Guanlubu to the Thistle Mountain base area. Given the advanced age of some members of the group, and the fact that Hong's baby son is still less than eight months old, it is probable that they travel by boat or by litter. (The adults in Feng Yunshan's family choose not to leave their homes, though they do send Feng's two sons to join their father and the God-worshipers.)[36]

What prompts Hong to this decisive action at this particular time is not completely clear. A number of factors may have flowed together in his mind. For one, the kidnapping of God-worshipers' children for ransom was becoming a nightmarish part of life, and Hong may have feared for his family's survival if they stayed in Guangdong.[37] Also there were famine conditions in parts of Guangdong province, including the region around Hong's original home district of Hua. Furthermore, Hong has developed an apocalyptic view of the fate of mankind, claiming that God told Hong that in the thirtieth year of Emperor Daoguang's reign (equivalent to the Western 1850), He would "send down calamities; those of you who remain steadfast in faith, shall be saved, but the unbelievers shall be visited by pestilence. After the eighth month, fields will be left uncultivated, and houses without inhabitants; therefore call thou thy own family and relatives hither."[38]

In addition, in May 1850, Yang Xiuqing, the spokesman through whom God's messages had for more than a year been relayed to the God-worshiping faithful, and who had been claiming to cure the sicknesses of all true believers by absorbing their sicknesses into his own body, himself fell ill with a mysterious yet shocking malady: he "became deaf and dumb, pus pouring out of his ears and water flowing from his eyes; his suffering was extreme."[39] Taiping sources later said this illness had two causes: Yang's "weariness" from redeeming his followers from harm, and God's determination "to test the hearts of us brothers and sisters." But at the same time, those not aware of these twin causes considered that Yang had "become completely debilitated by illness." If Yang had in some ways been constricting Hong Xiuquan's freedom of action, as many both then and later believed, his spell was now temporarily broken, and Yang remained in his "debilitated" state until early September 1850, when he suddenly recovered.[40]

Xiao Chaogui, too, almost ceased to speak in the name of Jesus during the whole spring and summer of 1850. Later that summer Xiao was described as being afflicted by some kind of ulcers or running sores, which cut back his activities, and perhaps this painful scourge had already caught him. Conceivably, also, he was chastened by Yang's illness and God's silence, and preferred not to speak if Yang could or would not.[41] Compared with the flood of celestial edicts earlier and later in the year, there were only two messages from Jesus during this period, both brief: on May 15, when Hong Xiuquan nervously asked him, "What is the demon devil Yan Luo doing at this time?" Jesus replied, "He has been cast down and bound, and is powerless to cause trouble. Let your heart be at ease, let your heart be at ease."[42] And on June 2 Jesus urged Hong, along with key supporters, to stay out of sight "while the demons killed each other. Once they are completely exhausted, then of course the Heavenly Father and Heavenly Elder Brother [Jesus] will give you clear orders on what to do next."[43] This elliptical statement may well refer to the massive campaigns of bandit suppression that Qing government forces were finally initiating around the Guiping area, campaigns that would bring both opportunities and fresh dangers to the God-worshipers.

It is July 28, 1850, in the afternoon, when Hong Xiuquan and his family are reunited, at a little village in Guiping district. There is Hong's wife, Lai, their two daughters, and their baby son, whom Hong now sees for the first time. There is Hong's recently widowed stepmother. Hong's elder brother Hong Renda and Renda's wife and family have obeyed the summons, as has Hong's wife's uncle. Hong's eldest brother and wife, and other cousins and children, are on the way. The family is further increased by various male members of the Lai family who live near Guiping. Since Hong's wife is a Lai, they now claim relationships as Hong's "brothers-in-law," claims that Hong accepts.[44] Accompanying the group of relatives are three more of Hong's most trusted friends, two men and one woman: Qin Rigang, a Guiping native and sometime soldier and miner; Chen Chengyong, a wealthy landlord from a nearby town who has brought his whole family into the God-worshipers' camp; and one of the daughters from the same Huang family who had helped Hong so often.[45] It is this woman—perhaps initially assigned by Hong to watch over his women family members as they traveled—who has offered up the Huang family residences to the large and disparate group. Asked if she and her family can afford to support so many people—despite the numerous brothers and sisters of the God-worshipers they have aided in the past—she answers, Yes, with the Lord's help, and that of his son Jesus, they can.[46]

Xiao Chaogui, silent for months, now resumes his mediator's role, and with the voice of Jesus summons the new arrivals individually to their duties as God-worshipers and protectors of their relative the Heavenly King. Hong's elder brother, Hong Renda, is told to be cautious over whom he trusts, and not to let people scare him. He and his brother will fight for the rivers and mountains of China together; as one enters his Heavenly Kingdom, so will the other; as one gets food or clothing or the tribute offerings of the myriad nations on the earth, so will the other, as each partakes of their glory under God on High.[47] Hong's stepmother, Li, is told to instruct and watch over her daughter-in-law and the children, and to maintain their integrity, till she comes at last "to dwell in her golden palace built of golden bricks."[48] Hong's eldest daughter, now a little over twelve years old, is told to trust in the teachings of her grandmother, mother, earthly uncles, and her uncle Jesus. The other in-laws receive their suitable instructions. And to Hong Xiuquan's own wife, Lai, come special words, in light of the special tasks confronting her: "Lai, with all your heart obey the Heavenly Commandments, and strive to bring honor to your husband, and preserve his reputation. Your husband is not as other men, so rejoice at your good fortune, cleave to this your husband; you are not as other women, you must discipline yourself with extra vigor, be filial to your parents, and obedient to your husband. Leave the education of your children to your older sister-in-law. It is no light task to be the wife of the Taiping Lord of all the countries on this earth."[49]

For a month the Hong family live together near Guiping township, sheltered by the Huangs, but it is a dangerous and fugitive existence, with the possibilities of arrest or betrayal at every turn. As anxiety mounts for the group's safety, Wei Changhui, whose own wealthy clan have made the market town of Jintian a safe haven for the God-worshipers, negotiates and plans with other leaders to bring the group northwards. This is no mere matter of assembling a small group at night and proceeding on mountain tracks with covered lanterns. There are numerous sedan chairs to be hired, boats to be found, supplied, and placed at the right spot on the riverbank, away from prying eyes. There are elaborate stories to be made up, and rehearsed, so that if they meet Qing patrols all in the party can state with conviction where they have come from and whither they are going. Stupid mistakes are made, which nearly wreck the venture, and the Heavenly King loses his temper and has to apologize. But by August 28, 1850, they have crossed the broad river near Guiping and reached the Jintian base area, ready as a family to build the Heavenly Kingdom.[50]

10

EARTH WAR

 There is no precise moment at which we can say the Taiping move from tension with the Qing state to open confrontation, but clearly in 1850 their provocations mount steadily until war becomes inevitable. It is in February 1850 that Hong and his closest associates begin to use martial language when talking of their followers. In April of that year Hong dons a robe of imperial yellow. In late July, Jesus tells Hong to "fight for Heaven," "to take responsibility for all the rivers and mountains," to "show the world the true laws of God the Father and the Heavenly Elder Brother," and to realize God has given him "full authority" to rule his kingdom. "In such a venture," says Jesus, "you must take the long view, not just focus on what is in front of you."[1] By August and September, the various Taiping leaders are beginning to assemble and arm groups of troops, and move them to the Jintian area.[2] In mid-October, arrangements are made to keep beacons and signal lights burning through the night around Hong Xiuquan's base area, so that the alarm can be instantly given in case of enemy attack.[3] On October 29 Hong sends out a more general mobilization order, telling all his followers to prepare for action, though still he urges secrecy upon them. While it would be premature "to proclaim Hong Xiuquan openly as leader, or to unfurl the banners," the God-worshiping brothers are told to begin to draw up plans, with those in the base area strengthening their defenses, while those in the outer areas not only make military preparations but "buy up gunpowder in bulk. When the general call goes out, then will be the time for all forces to unite."[4]

The "bulk buying" of gunpowder would surely be a provocation, for such purchases might well be noticed and reported to the authorities, given the God-worshipers' enemies among non-Hakkas and the local gentry. But this is seen as a calculated risk, a decision to end the period of surreptitious arms manufacture that has been going on for some months, especially in the Jintian village area, in which families like the Weis have set up front operations where simple arms are made by night, wrapped, and hidden in one of the myriad ponds that speckle the area.[5] And though there is no separate Taiping banner to unfurl as yet, the rudiments of a system of signal flags for different military units have already been designed by Feng Yunshan and one of his friends.

Feng's fundamental strategy is to build up units from the lowest levels systematically, and to identify each by clear markings and banners. Thus 4 men are to be under a corporal; 5 corporals and their men, a total of 25, are to be under a sergeant, who has his own square identifying flag, two and a half feet high. Four sergeants with their troops, 104 in all, are commanded by a lieutenant, with his own somewhat larger banner, and so by gradations up through captains and colonels to generals, who at full strength would have divisions of 13,155 troops under their command.[6] Individual units are also to be identified by different-colored triangular flags, labeled with their base area in bold characters. In addition, the corporals have insignia, five inches square, on the back and front of their shirts or coats, identifying them by platoon and battalion, while privates have four-inch-square insignia, which give their squad and platoon of affiliation and their personal identifying codes. In every squad, to help standardize battle orders, the same four code names are given to the four soldiers, one being given the name "Attacking," one "Conquering," one "Victorious," and one "Triumphant." Signals for emergency use when flags cannot be seen at night are made by sound, using gongs and rattles, in an ingenious series of combinations, to differentiate each large unit from every other.[7]

Some of this organization, particularly the arrangement of the men in small-sized units with a clearly identified chain of command, is taken by Feng from the *Zhouli,* or "Rites of Zhou," a text with a complex history of composition and transmission, allegedly detailing the administrative and military structures of the duke of Zhou, the efficient and moral minister of one of China's earliest dynasties, who was deeply admired by Confucius. Feng even uses exactly the same terms for his units and their commanders as those in the *Zhouli,* and almost the same number of soldiers in each unit—the only discrepancy probably reflecting an ambiguity in the original text.[8]

Other commanders of local God-worshiping forces find these classical echoes either unnecessary, or pedantic, and an irritation with textual punctiliousness is clearly expressed by both Xiao and Yang, ascribing their views, as customary, to Jesus and to God. The two men's sparring for prestige is obvious at times, expressed in their complaints that each is being forced by the other to "lose face" in public, since as Xiao says of Yang "men need to keep face just as trees need their bark."[9] Some Taiping leaders speak up for the need for scholarship and knowledge, branding Xiao and Yang as "hardly literate"; but Xiao and his friends in turn mock the misplaced "scholarship" of those who seem to prefer "antiquated texts on astronomy and geography" or classical poetry to the practical experience and useful knowledge of men who have "an unusually good understanding of things."[10]

In preparation for potential conflict, units of God-worshiping troops are now assembling under their various commanders on a regular basis, and reciting aloud the entire Ten Commandments as they are listed in the Bible, with glosses and expansive commentaries provided by Hong Xiuquan himself. Even if the God-worshipers recite the commandments correctly, they can be publicly beaten for violating their basic premises, or for showing sarcasm or ignorance of God's wider purpose.[11] The Ten Commandments themselves become the basis both for daily life and for future hope, as Hong Xiuquan explains in a poem to his followers, and its accompanying commentary:

In your daily life, never harbor covetous desires;
To get caught in the sea of lust leads to the deepest grief.
In front of Mount Sinai the injunctions were handed down,
And those Heavenly Commandments, earnest and sincere, are full of power today.
Repent and believe in our Heavenly Father, the Great God, and you will in the end obtain happiness; rebel and resist our Heavenly Father, the Great God, and you will surely weep for it. Those who obey the Heavenly Commandments and worship the True God, when their span is ended, will have an easy ascent to Heaven.

Those who are mired in the world's customs and believe in the demons, when
they come to their end, will find it hard to escape from hell. Those sunk in
their beliefs in false spirits will thereby become the soldier-slaves of false spirits;
in life they involve themselves in the devil's meshes and in death they will be
taken in the devil's clutches.

Those who ascend to Heaven and worship God, they are God's sons and daughters; when they first came to earth, they descended there from Heaven.[12]

The public recitations of the commandments are a part of the constant
probing by the God-worshiping leaders, a probing made urgent by the
swiftly rising number of new recruits to their ranks. In late 1850, this
influx becomes almost unmanageable, as two human movements number-
ing thousands of people converge on the Jintian base area. One of these is
made up of Hakkas from four different neighboring areas, driven—like
their brethren of Baisha—to seek shelter in the main base area because of
the ever-rising local levels of violence directed against them by local non-
Hakkas, by local gentry and officials, and by bandits of various kinds.
Ironically, the last of these categories forms the second human wave—
bandit groups themselves, no fewer than eight according to accounts at
the time, who converge on the Jintian region because of the massive campaign now being coordinated against them by the Qing government.[13] At
least two of these bandit groups are led by women, and one by Big-head
Yang, the Macao mixed-blood pirate who was central in causing the disruptions in Guangxi that gave such impetus to the growth of the God-
worshipers in the middle 1840s.[14]

In early December 1850, regular units of the Qing forces, working with
local gentry-led militia, and coordinated by their commanding officer in
Guiping township, begin aggressive campaigning in the northeastern-
most of the four God-worshiping base areas, the safe haven provided for
Hong and his family by the Hus in Huazhou village. The Qing have not
yet identified Hong Xiuquan as the God-worshipers' leader, and they are
acting on vague information that troublemakers are there. Nevertheless,
they come dangerously close to capturing him. Crossing the broad river
that flows past Guiping, the government troops bypass Jintian and converge on Huazhou from the south, via the village of Siwang. The terrain
is treacherous, and the approach difficult—one narrow mountain track,
with steep ravines to one side, sheer mountain walls to the other, a perfect
place for ambushes. So while making a show of strength, the Qing troops
content themselves with closing off the village by driving hundreds of
sharpened bamboo stakes at an angle into the track and the adjacent

slopes, making egress impossible. Alerted to the danger, Hong sends loyal messengers out by mountain tracks to the northwest, who then circle back to Jintian and warn the other Taiping leaders. Moving with dispatch, the God-worshipers attack the Qing forces from the rear, routing them, removing the stakes, and bringing Hong and his family safely back to Jintian. In the conflict there is heavy hand-to-hand fighting, and as many as fifty government troops and militia are killed, among them a deputy police magistrate, Zhang Yong. In the name of their God, the Taiping have now killed a "demon" who officially represents the ruling regime.[15]

Jintian village is crowded and in chaos from the masses of Hakka refugees, bandit recruits, local God-worshipers, and fresh recruits recently arrived. There are so many new arrivals that—despite the stock-piled grain resources of groups like the God-worshipers from Baisha—by early December conditions in Jintian have reached near famine levels, and the God-worshipers and their allies are reduced to a daily ration of thin rice gruel. Some of the bandit troops defect in the face of this hardship, while the Taiping leaders try to keep morale high among their own troops by pointing out that this deprivation is a simple trial, devised by God and His son Jesus, "to test the determination" of their followers on earth.[16]

It is no surprise, after the killing of one of their officers in the line of duty, that the Qing attempt a second strike, this time more thorough and more massive. On December 31, 1850, a much larger Qing force, commanded by a dozen veteran officers and supplemented by some local militia, which has marched northeast from Guiping in three columns, crosses a tributary of the Xun River and establishes a base area command post only five miles from the village of Jintian. The Taiping forces, now with their recent recruits and bandit allies at least ten thousand strong, march a mile east of Jintian and take up three coordinated defensive positions in a wide arc between the Qing forces and Jintian, with Yang Xiuqing commanding the troops on the left flank, extending to the point where Caicun Bridge spans the Thistle River; Xiao Chaogui on the right flank, centered on Pangu Hill; and Hong Xiuquan and Feng Yunshan commanding the center.[17]

The complicated defensive formation adopted by the Taiping troops shows they are confident in their battle readiness and in the communications system they have devised. Each major Taiping encampment has its own signal flag, depending on its strategic location: red for the south, black for the north, blue for the east, and white for the west. The center has a yellow banner, as well as a duplicate of the other four banners. With these large flags as the main signals, backed by smaller triangular flags to

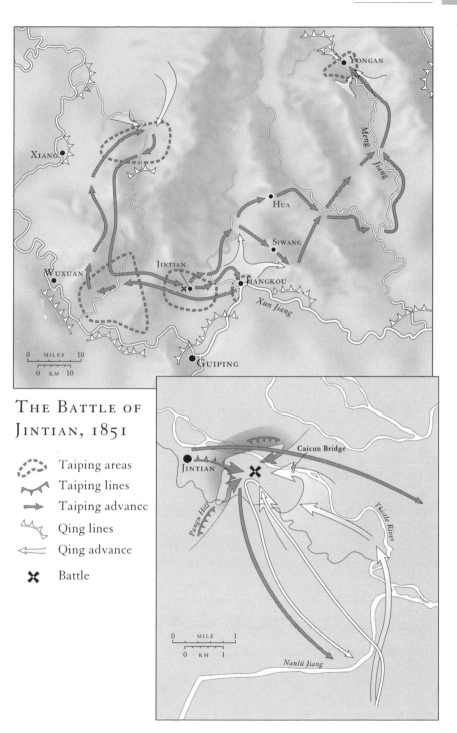

XIANG

YONGAN

Meng Jiang

HUA

SIWANG

JINTIAN

WUXUAN

JIANGKOU

Xun Jiang

GUIPING

0   MILES   10

0   KM   10

THE BATTLE OF JINTIAN, 1851

Taiping areas
Taiping lines
Taiping advance
Qing lines
Qing advance
✖   Battle

JINTIAN

Caicun Bridge

Pangu Hill

Thistle River

Nanlü Jiang

0   MILE   1

0   KM   1

request troop reinforcements, complex instructions can be conveyed even in the heat of battle, and at considerable distance. As a Taiping manual explains the system:

> If the demons on the east side prove very active and the eastern station wishes to draw soldiers from the west, they shall add a small triangular white flag to the great blue banner. This signal shall be transmitted to the center which will in turn transmit the signal to the western station. Thereupon the officers in command of the western station shall quickly lead their soldiers to the east to help destroy the demons. Or if they wish to draw soldiers from the south they shall add a small red flag to the great blue banner. When this signal is transmitted to the south, the officers in command of the southern station shall quickly lead their soldiers to the east to help destroy the demons.[18]

With only minor adjustments, this same system can be used if the demons attack on two fronts at once. For instance, if the east and south come under attack at once, the center will hoist both the blue and the red banners, alerting the west and north commanders to prepare to relieve their embattled brothers.[19]

Fighting begins the next day, January 1, 1851. As the Manchu colonel Ikedanbu tries to force his seven battalions through the center of the Taiping line, Xiao and Yang curve in from the flanks in a coordinated assault, severing Ikedanbu from his rear guard, and trapping him against a small hill. The Qing forces soon begin to break, and the break becomes a rout, with a dozen officers and three hundred or more dead on the Qing side. The horse of Colonel Ikedanbu skids on the bridge as its rider flees the scene of his defeat. Ikedanbu is pounced on by Taiping foot soldiers and cut to death. Next day, reinforcements sent by the commanding officer in Guiping are also defeated, and the remaining Qing troops pull back across the river.[20]

January 11, 1851, is Hong Xiuquan's birthday, but there is little time to celebrate, for despite their astonishing victory the Taiping forces are again in disarray. There are massive arguments and quarrels with the various Heaven-and-Earth Society recruits, who rebel against the excessive levels of discipline in the Taiping forces, and also perhaps at the absence of promise of further loot or income. To clarify his own position, just after the victory the Heavenly King, Hong Xiuquan, summarizes all his various preceding pronouncements into five simple orders:

1. Obey the [Ten] Commandments.
2. Keep the men's ranks separate from the women's ranks.

3. Do not disobey even the smallest regulation.
4. Act in the interests of all and in harmony; all of you obey the restraints imposed by your leaders.
5. Unite your wills and combine your strengths and never flee the field of combat.[21]

With resources dwindling, and with the disturbing news that Big-head Yang, the woman leader Qiu Erh, and several other secret-society leaders have not only abandoned the Taiping camp but offered their services to the Qing forces in exchange for official positions and pardons, Hong and his fellow leaders decide to abandon Jintian, and move to a base with better defensive possibilities. Their choice falls on the prosperous market town of Jiangkou, fifteen miles to the east, on a fork of land where two rivers converge, making it a good base both for controlling commerce and for supplying reinforcements. Since Jiangkou is also the chosen base for Big-head Yang's renegade forces, as well as the hometown of Wang Zuoxin, the gentry and militia leader who so often crossed and harried the God-worshipers in the past, the town offers a nice focus for revenge. By mid-January the Taiping have left Jintian, ahead of any counterattacking Qing forces, and by the end of the month they have taken over Jiangkou and refurbished their forces. They are crucially aided in this endeavor by the one major Heaven-and-Earth leader who has not defected, the sincere God-worshiper Luo Dagang; from this time onward Luo becomes one of Hong's key advisers, bringing the Taiping crucial skills in the command and execution of water-borne campaigning, navigation, and supply.[22]

But Jiangkou is too well chosen for the Qing to allow the Taiping to keep it as their base. This time, learning from past defeats, the newly appointed coordinating general for all Guangxi forces, Xiang Rong, with two other generals commanding troops from Yunnan and Guizhou, leads three massive columns of troops by land to Jiangkou, supported by two water-borne columns—some ten thousand troops in all. By mid-February they have reached the Jiangkou area. For three weeks the Taiping hold the town, but the forces against them prove too strong, and in early March the Taiping leaders slip out of the city at night and head back to their original base areas near Guiping, settling in the area of Wuxuan township, west of Guiping. During their retreat, the city of Jiangkou is burned to the ground, each side blaming the other for the disaster.[23] For the rest of the spring of 1851 the fighting is bitter in the region, if sporadic.

It is in the midst of this chaotic period, perhaps in March 1851, that Hong Xiuquan declares the formal existence of the Taiping Heavenly

Kingdom, a concept long promised yet long delayed. Oddly, however, there is no single ceremony, not even any single day, to point to, and the Taiping themselves never celebrate any particular anniversary for their founding. An unexplained illness of Hong Xiuquan in the spring—described in one Taiping source as the "pestilence"—may have further delayed the dates of key decisions on organization. But from this spring-time on, the year known in the West as 1851, and to the Qing dynasty as the first year of the Emperor Xianfeng, is called by the Taiping themselves the First Year of the Taiping Heavenly Kingdom.[24]

Starting from March 30, 1851, a new kind of public ritual is inaugurated, one that combines celestial advice on the kingdom, rewards for the virtuous, and stern punishments for the backsliders. On this day, Jesus (through Xiao) talks of the growing strength and complexity of the Heavenly Kingdom now on earth, and his special desire "to discipline those who disobey the Heavenly Commandments." After this introduction, Jesus gives voice to a fuller exposition of confidence in the Taiping kingdom's future:

> All of you should be at ease and try your hardest. When undertaking this Heavenly enterprise, you cannot take all the weight on your own head. This enterprise is directed by Heaven, not by men; it is too difficult to be handled by men alone. Trust completely in your Heavenly Father and Heavenly Brother; they will take charge of everything, so you need not worry or be nervous. In the past I tried to save as many mortals as possible from among those who were threatened with destruction by demons. Now we have so many followers of God, what should you fear? Those who betray God won't be able to escape Heavenly Father's and Heavenly Brother's punishment. If we wish to have you live, you will live; if we want you to perish, you will die, for no one's punishment will be postponed more than three days. Every one of you should sincerely follow the path of Truth, and train yourselves in goodness, which will lead to happiness.[25]

Following this statement Jesus gives his blessings to a long list of Taiping leaders and staff officers—some twenty-three in all—who are taken to Heaven and initiated into its mysteries. Jesus then gives specific instructions to the five military leaders, identified by their army corps: front, left, rear, right, and wing—in other words, to Hong's five associates Yang, Feng, Xiao, Wei, and Shi. They are told that disobeying a military order is the same as disobeying the word of God, of Jesus, or of the Heavenly King, Hong Xiuquan. To underline this sense of discipline, an opium smoker in the Taiping ranks is publicly tried—"Can you fill your stomach by smoking opium?"—savagely beaten (with "one thousand blows" according to the text), and then given a last meal of glutinous rice before being publicly executed. Another battalion commander is given one hundred blows for not being watchful for traitors within his own unit, and Jesus then gives each commander authority to "kill any such rebels before reporting them to higher authorities, since killing these rebels won't lessen the strength of our armies, whereas having rebels in our army ranks harms the entire kingdom." No units, Jesus emphasizes, are free from such traitors, so eternal vigilance is needed.[26]

A brief reminder to all the faithful of Hong Xiuquan's kingship, and of the awe due to him as the ruler of the world sent down by God, is given by God Himself, speaking through Yang Xiuqing, on April 15, 1851.[27] Then, on April 19, while the Taiping troops are still fighting for survival in the same area of Wuxuan, another solemn meeting is held, containing the same general elements as that of March 30 though in different order: a public trial of a wrongdoer followed by mass expressions of devotions and religious commitment and a general pronouncement on policy. This time, the wrongdoer is a man who has abused his trust as the bodyguard to the family of the Triad leader and pirate-turned-Taiping general, Luo Dagang, by stealing a golden ring and a set of silver toothpicks from Luo's wife while she was in a religious trance.[28] Like his opium-smoking predecessor the previous month, the thief is to be given one thousand blows, prior to receiving his final meal of glutinous rice and being consigned to the executioner's sword and "a life in hell." The solemn ceremony this time is for all the unit commanders, at the army, divisional, and battalion levels. Jesus' words on this occasion are not only remembered; they are made a written part of one of the Taiping movement's most sacred texts:

> All of you, my younger brothers, must keep the Heavenly Commandments and obey military orders; you must be harmonious with your brothers. If the leader has more to do than he can manage, let his subordinates assume some of the duties; if the subordinates cannot carry out their duties, then let their superiors take on some of them. You must absolutely not consider people as enemies and hate them because of some chance sentence they uttered that you then committed to memory. You should cultivate goodness and discipline yourselves. When you are in a village you must not ransack people and their possessions. In combat you must never flee from the field when going into battle. If you have money, you must recognize that it is not an end in itself, and not consider it as belonging to "you" or "me." Moreover, you must, with united heart and united strength, together conquer the hills

and rivers. You must clearly discern the road to Heaven and walk upon it. At present there is some hardship and distress; yet later you will naturally be given high titles. If, after receiving these instructions, there are any of you who still violate the Heavenly Commandments, still disobey military orders, still willfully contradict your superiors, and still, when advancing into battle, flee from the field, you should not blame me, the Heavenly Elder Brother, if I give orders for your execution.[29]

From this time on, also, as a heightened proof of the religious discipline now to be expected, those who fail to attend meetings when summoned, or even those who are late, or stumble in their responses to the religious ritual questions, can be beaten with one hundred blows, dismissed from their military posts, or both.[30]

The frustrating, circular fighting over all-too-familiar ground continues through the spring and summer heat of 1851. The most important of the battles is one the Taiping fail to win. Seventy miles to their south, on April 19—the same day as the major Taiping trial and rally—God-worshipers from a fifth base area have crossed the border from Guangdong province and managed to seize the town of Yulin. The leader of these God-worshipers, Ling Shiba, a Guangdong native, is known to the Heavenly King. Ling had been converted to the God-worshipers' religion while laboring as a migrant indigo gatherer in the Pingshan Mountain area, between 1848 and 1849, and became a passionate believer. Moving between his Guangdong native place in Yixin township and the Thistle Mountain base area, Ling converted hundreds to the cause, and prospered in business. Early in 1850 he sold all his accumulated land—paddy field, unirrigated land, and mountain land—and put all the proceeds, more than 340 ounces of silver, into the common Taiping treasury.

Even earlier than other leaders in Thistle Mountain, Ling began secretly to make and stockpile arms, store gunpowder, and prepare red cloth and sashes for his fledgling army. But when he approached Hong Xiuquan in the summer of 1850, asking to join him in Jintian, he was told to wait for a more propitious time. While waiting, he built up his military base by holding off the local militia, and roused popular support by seizing granaries and opening them to the poor, and by posting placards in villages attacking the greed and selfishness of local landlords and officials. Now, in mid-1851, with three thousand or more of Ling's troops holding Yulin and ready to move north to join up with Hong, the times are propitious indeed. But realizing the fateful nature of this planned union of Taiping forces, the Qing generals concentrate all their resources to stop

Ling from moving north, and to stop Hong's troops from moving south. Despite repeated attacks on the Qing lines, neither army of the God-worshipers can break through.[31]

The key figure in preventing the linkup between Hong Xiuquan's troops and Ling's is the same former pirate leader Big-head Yang, whose riverine forces prevent all Hong's attempts to cross the Qian River. And by June 1851 the incessant counterattacks of the Qing and local militia troops force Ling to abandon Yulin, and to retreat back eastward into Guangdong. To strengthen their morale after this setback, Hong's Taiping troops are told in mid-June to shed their doubts and fears, and not only to protect their "kingdom" as it is now constituted, or to look to eternal rewards in Paradise at God's right hand, but to fix their sights on the coming "Earthly Paradise," or "Heaven on earth" (*xiao tian tang*), where all God-worshipers "would receive rewards beyond their expectations." Though the exact location of this yearned-for place is not disclosed, this is the first indication Hong Xiuquan has given that the Taiping forces may soon have a permanent base in which they and their families can live in joy and peace.[32]

The Qing forces keep up their pressures throughout the Taiping base area, and despite these promises of an Earthly Paradise Taiping morale begins to sag. Taiping leaders single out for praise the women's units, which with some divine help repulse formidable militia attacks.[33] But instructions issued to unit commanders at the newly instituted roll calls for soldiers suggest that attrition is taking its toll: a name board is now to be prepared for each unit, with the names of soldiers assigned to the unit written on it. Those who have "ascended to Heaven" since the fighting began—that is, have died in combat—have their names marked with a red dot; those who are ill are marked with a red circle; those wounded are marked with a red triangle; and those who have recently deserted are marked with a red cross. "Thus," says the Taiping instruction, "the person who calls the roll, upon reading the name board, will know immediately the number of available soldiers."[34] In his constant hunts for traitors in the Taiping ranks Hong—aided at times by timely warnings from Jesus relayed to earth by Xiao Chaogui—orders public executions for those caught, and placards hung around their necks, reminding all that "Jesus our Elder Brother showed us the treacherous heart of this demon follower."[35]

By mid-August 1851 Hong and the other Taiping leaders have come to a difficult decision. Despite the hallowed role of Thistle Mountain in their movement's founding and growth, they must make a breakout. To do this successfully calls for extraordinary secrecy and meticulous planning. Special orders are given forbidding any record of the discussions about the decision; even so, there is obviously bitter disagreement, and many God-worshipers are castigated for their selfishness and pettiness as the time for departure approaches.[36] It is Hong Xiuquan who has to explain this collective decision to his followers, and he does so in both celestial and strategic terms:

> In the various armies and the various battalions, let all soldiers and officers pluck up their courage, be joyful and exultant, and together uphold the principles of the Heavenly Father and the Heavenly Elder Brother. You need never be fearful, for all things are determined by our Heavenly Father and Heavenly Elder Brother, and all hardships are intended by our Heavenly Father and Heavenly Elder Brother to be trials for our minds. Let every one be true, firm, and patient at heart; and let all cleave to our Heavenly Father and our Heavenly Elder Brother. The Heavenly Father previously made a statement, saying, "The colder the weather, the more clothing one can remove; for if one is firm and patient, one never notices such things." Thus, let all officers and soldiers awake. Now, according to a memorial, there is at present no salt; it is then correct to move the camp. Further, according to the memorial, there are many sick and wounded. Increase your efforts to protect and care for them. Should you fail to preserve a single one among our brothers and sisters, you will disgrace our Heavenly Father and Heavenly Elder Brother. . . .
>
> Whenever the units advance or pitch their tents, every army and battalion should be equally spaced and in communication, so that the head and tail will correspond. Use all your strength in protecting and caring for the old and the young, male and female, the sick and the wounded; everyone must be protected, so that we may all together gaze on the majestic view of the Earthly Paradise.[37]

Once again, there is no sign of where the Earthly Paradise lies. But there are indications of its general direction, since the breakout is made to the northeast. In military terms, the maneuver is stunningly successful: fast, disciplined, coordinated, and leaving the Qing troops off-balance. But it is ruthless too, for the masses of the God-worshipers are told to burn their houses as they prepare to leave, as proof of their total commitment to the Taiping cause. And as each village is abandoned, it and the surrounding hills are combed for hidden supplies of food that will be needed on the march.[38] The vanguard land forces of the Taiping are led by Xiao Chaogui and Shi Dakai, and the river forces by Luo Dagang; they move swiftly up the Meng River valley toward the walled city of Yongan, some sixty miles north-northeast of Thistle Mountain. Unable to work out what route the Taiping are taking, two pursuing columns of Qing troops move either too far to the west or too far to the east to stop them. Hong Xiuquan, guarded by Yang Xiuqing's central army, moves behind the vanguard by river, with his family. Feng Yunshan and Wei Changhui are given the dangerous task of guarding the rear of the massive column.

The city of Yongan, though stoutly walled, is unprepared for such an onslaught, and not strongly defended. The Taiping vanguard forces reach the edges of Yongan on September 24, 1851, and in a strategy later lauded in Taiping accounts, they bewilder and shatter the nerves of the city's defenders by riding their few horses around the city walls with baskets of rattling stones to amplify their sound and exaggerate their numbers, and by lighting and hurling into the city, throughout the night, a large store of fireworks that they have found in the suburbs. The next day, with the city's residents dazed and sleepless from the explosions, fumes, and colored lights, the Taiping forces train what cannon they have on the city's east gate, and send scaling parties over the walls—some protected from the defenders' fire by coffins held on long poles over their heads, others laying ladders horizontally onto the walls from the roofs of nearby houses that the defenders have failed to demolish. By evening, eight hundred Qing troops are dead, and their senior officers have been killed or have committed suicide. It is September 25, 1851, and fourteen years after Hong's first celestial battle the Taiping have acquired a solid earthly city.[39]

THE
FIRST CITY

 Yongan is a good-sized walled city, home to a large population; before the Taiping arrived, it was also home to the magistrate and his extended staff, but now they are dead or fled. Hong Xiuquan, entering the city on October 1, 1851, a week after its capture, at once takes up residence, with his family, in the former magistrate's residence. With its spacious courtyards, reception rooms, library, and the ornamental streams and ponds around the private family quarters, it must seem like a paradise indeed after the years of hiding and fighting.[1] But Hong realizes that all the exhausting maneuvering and marching and the presence in the Taiping ranks of new and untried troops, as well as former secret-society members, have created serious risks of looting and other abuses by his followers. So his first official act in the city is to issue a warning and an exhortation, combining the need for order with the promise of the new community.

> An order to officers and soldiers of all ranks in each army corps and battalion:
> All of you must think of the public good, not of your private interests;

and with single-minded determination cleave to your Heavenly Father, Heavenly Elder Brother, and myself. From this day on all soldiers and officers are ordered that, every time you kill demons or capture their cities, you must not hoard away for yourself the gold and valuables you find, the silks, and other precious objects, but must hand over everything to the sacred treasury of our Heavenly Court. All violators will be punished.[2]

Such an order surely helps in preventing abuses by the Taiping troops, but it is also essential to gain the active loyalty of the people of Yongan and those in the surrounding villages, many of whom are Hakka, but still frightened and suspicious. The Taiping leaders spread the word that they have no desire to harm the people, only to kill the demons and follow the commandments of the Lord in Heaven. The people of Yongan are reassured that they do not have to join the Taiping armies, or adopt the God-worshipers' religion. It is enough if they follow certain rules of behavior toward the occupying troops, one of which is to hang a simple circlet of bamboo strips above their house doors as a sign that they welcome their occupiers. Special rewards are given to those in Yongan or nearby villages who bring members of their communities to promise obedience to the Taiping, who report on the movements and morale of the "demon troops," who make contributions of cash and grain, or help the Taiping transport military supplies. To temper this generosity with rigor, swift execution is promised to any in Yongan who provide supplies to the demon troops, enroll in local anti-Taiping militia units, and take advantage of the exigencies of war to rape women or plunder and murder local residents.[3]

To further bolster local support, the Taiping try to get the city and village markets functioning as they were before the Heavenly Army arrived, and to ensure that all goods obtained from the locals are properly paid for at current prices. In cases of wealthier landlords fleeing from the area to avoid expressing loyalty to the Taiping, the Taiping send out sizable groups of troops to raid the fugitives' homes and seize their grain stores, livestock, salt and cooking oil, and even their clothing. In one of these raids, some two thousand Taiping troops—both men and women—move against the Li and the Luo families, and need five days and nights to list and carry away the families' accumulated stores. On other occasions troops are sent to cut the grain from landlords' fields. Some of these purloined goods are shared out among the local villagers, and the remainder deposited in the Taiping's common treasury in Yongan city.[4]

The idea of all things being pooled in common in this "sacred treasury" draws both on past Chinese historical traditions and on the voice of Jesus from the Sermon on the Mount: if the Heavenly Father is omnipotent and creates all things, then of course His delegates on earth can furnish all supplies to all their followers.[5] But those showing such a communal sense—whether out of love for their fellow beings, or fear of reprisals if they disobey—also need reassurance that their courage will be rewarded on this earth. Accordingly Hong's second imperial pronouncement in Yongan, issued on November 17, orders all the sergeants in the Taiping army to make a meticulous recording of the performance of the twenty-five corporals and private soldiers under their personal command. Courage in battle and obedience to orders will be marked with a circle against each man's and woman's name; cowardice and disobedience, with a cross. As each record book is filled, it is to be passed up the chain of command to the senior generals themselves, when all the circles and crosses will be tallied. Those of the highest merit will be rewarded with the highest offices when the Taiping army at last makes its home in "the Earthly Paradise." As with the promises made earlier in June and in August, no indication is given yet of where or when this Earthly Paradise will be found.[6]

To prepare for that projected event, Hong Xiuquan uses the breathing space provided by Yongan to declare the advent of Taiping time, by promulgating a new calendar first devised by Feng Yunshan some three years earlier. This Taiping calendar rejects the dates prepared by the astronomers in the Qing court, which set the rhythms for the festivals and seasons of the country as a whole. Nor does it follow the exact contours of the Western countries' calendar, which Hong Xiuquan (and probably other Taiping leaders) would have been familiar with in Canton, despite that calendar's Christian structuring. Instead, it reaches back to China's early classical texts, and combines them with some aspects of the West, to create a year of 366 days, divided into twelve months and seven-day weeks, with the odd-numbered months having thirty-one days, and the even ones thirty days. Though the familiar Chinese twenty-four solar terms are kept, and the lunar mansions, the new calendar with its Sabbath day for prayer and rest is believed to be purified of its old superstitious elements, which are now seen to have been no more than "the demons' cunning scheme to deceive and delude mankind." By contrast, the new calendar, with "its years, months, days, and hours all determined by our Heavenly Father," will ensure that every moment of future Taiping time is both "happy and peaceful."[7]

On December 4, 1851, in a third decree, Hong Xiuquan makes his promises broader and grander. Honorary hereditary titles are granted to all those officers who have already given their lives in the Taiping cause. And for the living, who have been fighting for the Taiping, there are—

depending on their rank—awards of the caps and coats worn by officers, or of the ceremonial cowls worn by the sergeants. Hong promises too that all loyal followers shall be treated with equal dignity, henceforth, until the day they reach that Earthly Paradise of which Hong has spoken thrice before. At that joyful time, more honorary titles will be handed out, and all "in dragon robes and horn-encrusted girdles" will be welcomed in Hong's Heavenly Court.[8]

To supplement these promises of future bliss, the Heavenly King drafts lists of ritual titles and ranks for the Taiping leaders, along with the correct terms of address to be used for each of them, their wives, and their children. Hong Xiuquan's own son, Tiangui, now two years old, is to be called "the Young Monarch, of ten thousand years." Hong's future sons, as many as there may be, shall be called "Heir to the Heavenly King, for one thousand years." Hong's daughters shall be known as "Princesses." The senior generals shall be called "Excellencies," the medium officers and sergeants addressed as "Your Worship." Their male children shall be called "Sons of the Just," and "Sons of the Commander," and their daughters be known as "Jade" or "Snow." Women commanders shall be termed "Chaste Ones," and the wives of officers as "Noble" with terms appropriate to their husband's rank: "Noble Lady," "Noble Beauty," "Noble Nurse," and "Noble Bride."[9]

The same decree provides the forms of the honorific titles for each of the five senior God-worshiper leaders, those celestial voices and military commanders who have brought the Heavenly Army from its fragmentary life in Thistle Mountain to the heart of Yongan city: Hong Xiuquan, as Heavenly King, is hailed as the Lord of Ten Thousand Years. Yang, as the East King, is Lord of Nine Thousand Years, and Xiao, West King, Lord of Eight Thousand Years; Feng, South King and Lord of Seven Thousand Years, while Wei, the North King, will be Lord of Six Thousand Years, and Shi Dakai, still in his early twenties but proven again and again in combat, shall be Wing King and Lord of Five Thousand Years. The honorific terms by which they were known in the previous months— "Kingly Fathers," or "Wang-ye"—will be dropped, for *ye* is part of the Lord's name Jehovah (Ye-huo-hua), and to suggest that such earthly men share in this fatherhood partakes of the "twisted usage of our mortal world" and has proved "somewhat offensive" to the Lord God Himself.[10]

Following similar logic, Hong Xiuquan declares that he himself must never be addressed as "Godly" *(di)*, "Supreme" *(shang)* or "Holy" *(sheng)* but only as "Sovereign" *(zhu)*, while the word *wang* itself—"prince" or "king"—will be used for no other mortals but these Taiping chosen ones. To underline the special status of these leaders, in Taiping texts henceforth all references to those figures in China's past who used to be called *wang* or king will be written with a character that has the addition of the "dog" component on its left-hand side; in regular usage this character is pronounced "kuang" and bears the basic meaning of "wild" or "cruel."[11]

While Hong drafts the decrees that are meant to reassure his followers that their hardships and self-denial will be rewarded, it is Yang and Xiao—speaking this time as the two "chiefs of staff" of the "Taiping Heavenly Kingdom," rather than as the voices of God and Jesus—who give the rationale for the battles that the Taiping now are fighting. What the Taiping faithful are now experiencing, they tell their followers, is the fourth manifestation of God's divine rage and power. The first manifestation was when God—"spiritual father, father of the soul, omniscient, omnipotent, and omnipresent"—having created all the heavens, earth, and living things in six days, sent down a great flood for forty days and forty nights. The second manifestation was when He rescued the Israelites from the land of Egypt. As the third manifestation, He sent His own son, "the Savior, Lord Jesus," to be born on earth, suffer, and redeem the sins of men. And as the fourth, he sent an angel to bring Hong Xiuquan up to Heaven, where Hong received his orders to kill the demons, rule the world, and save the people. To help Hong in this task, both God and His son Jesus descended regularly to the world, "manifesting their innumerable powers" and "exterminating great numbers of the demons in pitched battles." The leaders of these demons are the new emperor of China, the "Manchu devil Xianfeng, descendant of barbarians," and his ally the old serpent devil. These two and all their slavish minions have misled many true Chinese, and even the members of the Hong brotherhoods of Triads and the Heaven-and-Earth Society, although at their secret-society initiations these men had "formed blood pacts to exterminate the Qing, with united hearts and strengths."[12]

In appealing to the secret-society followers of the Taiping, the leaders admit that some of the purity of the earliest God-worshiping congregations has been lost. They also imply that they know there are traitors in the ranks, and indeed much of the prestige of both Yang and Xiao springs from their using their heavenly voices to identify and condemn Taiping turncoats secretly working for the Qing, or planning to desert to them. Some of these schemes go back six months or more, and involve hundreds of men, elaborate deceptions, and dual allegiances, as when Qing supporters pretend to be Taiping loyalists hiding out in Qing encampments until they can enter Yongan to "serve" the Heavenly King. On several past occasions such suspected traitors were executed or savagely beaten—even during the most difficult months of campaigning that preceded the capture of Yongan—and new cases are constantly coming to light, even within Yongan's walls.[13]

There is of course no certainty that Yongan, despite its greater size, will prove a firmer base than those earlier ones around Guiping. For though the approximately twenty thousand Taiping troops have defended Yongan with greater care than any base before—they have ringed the walled city itself at a distance of about one mile with peripheral defensive earthworks, set up a second line of patrolled defenses that reaches far beyond these earthworks into the countryside, put their boats to patrol the nearby river Meng, and erected high wooden towers to act as watching posts and bases from which to launch projectiles—the Qing armies are not leaving them in peace.[14] More and more Qing troops have gathered, forming a massive armed base camp to the southwest of the city, and a smaller encampment to the northwest. They are backed by local provincial officials, militia groups, and defected bandits, so that the total government forces exceed forty-six thousand by the end of 1851. Even though these troops are not that reliable—many of them are often willing to trade clandestinely with the Taiping, bartering meat, fish, and pickles with the enemy under cover of dusk or the smoke of their campfires—nevertheless at regular intervals they have been launching probes or full-scale counterattacks, either to cut the Taiping lines of communication to north and south or to move against the now fortified villages that serve as the Taiping's defensive outposts.[15]

It is on December 10, 1851, that the Qing forces under General Ulantai launch their fiercest counterattack yet on Yongan. Wary, after more than a year of failed or inconclusive campaigning against the Taiping, they concentrate on one limited objective, the village of Shuidou, a Taiping supply depot and fortified outpost on the river, at the very southern tip of the Taiping's outer defensive perimeter, where Taiping land armies can keep contact with Luo Dagang's river fleet. At least five Qing columns take part in the assault, which is successful: the fort is overrun, and the supplies burned. The Taiping attempt to save the depot by rushing two relief columns from Yongan and the inner line of defenses, but the Qing troops beat them off. At this point, prudently content with their minor victory, the Qing forces pull back to their base camp.[16]

Xiao Chaogui, who for three years has served as the voice of Jesus, is wounded in this battle; the evidence for this is the voice of Jesus, as recorded in one of the Taiping's own confidential records:

In the first year of the Taiping, 10th month, 18th day [December 10, 1851, in the Western calendar] the Heavenly Elder Brother [Jesus] showed his compassion and came down to earth in Yongan. Because the West King [Xiao Chaogui] while killing the demons had received several minor wounds—none of them too serious—the Heavenly Elder Brother wished to reassure the Heavenly King and his followers, and therefore issued them this sacred instruction: "My little ones, console your Second Elder Brother [Hong Xiuquan], reassure him and give him solace, for [Xiao Chao] Gui, his brother-in-law, has received this pain. It is not serious."

When Yang Xiuqing, Feng Yunshan, and Shi Dakai hear of this, they cluster around the wounded Xiao Chaogui, who gives them the same reassurance. Their response shows the extent of their disquiet:

We obey Your instructions. We Your humble disciples have all been blessed by the fact that our Heavenly Elder Brother long ago manifested His great goodness by atoning for our sins. Now [Xiao] Chaogui, our brother-in-law, [Lord for] eight thousand years, has also on behalf of humankind endured this suffering. We Your humble disciples beseech God the Father and our Heavenly Elder Brother to cherish him with Your most especial care, so that he may recover soon, and show us all the extent of Your heavenly goodness.[17]

The response, given in the voice of Jesus, is that the army as a whole should be reassured that this is "nothing serious," and that all the Taiping troops should "advance with spritely steps and all their courage, uniting their minds and uniting their strength, to exterminate those demon devils."[18]

Two days later, on December 12, far from being reassuring, the news about Xiao seems worse: the "scars from his wounds have not yet healed." Jesus descends again, to talk to another leading Taiping general, Wei Changhui, who was not present on December 10. As the other senior commanders have done, Wei begs Jesus to make special allowances for Xiao, and to relieve Xiao of his "serious pain," and to grant him a swift recovery. Wei also calls Xiao by his new honorific name "eight thousand years." Jesus responds with an ambiguous speech: "Fulfillment as a man does not come from a life of ease; a life of ease does not lead to fulfillment as a man. The deeper your suffering, the more awe-inspiring your reputation. Let your mind be at rest. Whether those demon devils fly or change their form, they will never escape the hands of the Heavenly Father and Heavenly Elder Brother."[19] Thereafter, in the Taiping record, with the exception of a few murmured words of encouragement to the troops five months later—"Keep your courage up, be of good cheer"—Jesus comes no more to earth, and his voice falls silent.[20]

There is a mystery here. According to surviving Taiping sources, Xiao dies a full nine months after this, in September 1852, during the Taiping attack on Changsha city. In the intervening period, he is given military assignments, noble titles, and listed as directing campaigns. The Heavenly King, Hong Xiuquan, in one of his most sacred texts, "The Book of Heavenly Decrees and Proclamations," issued to his subjects in 1852, quotes Jesus' comment that "the deeper your suffering, the more awe-inspiring your reputation," but he does not link it specifically to Xiao's wounds or death.[21] Is Xiao in Yongan perhaps incapacitated in some way, so weakened that he is kept in seclusion, so as not to destroy his followers' morale or allow people to think that God and His son have abandoned the Taiping? Is that why Jesus issues no more reassuring or didactic statements, and passes no more judgments on Taiping policies, as he has so often in the past? Has Yang Xiuqing, Xiao's Thistle Mountain neighbor—and like Xiao among the very poorest and least educated of the senior Taiping leaders—who has been speaking so confidently with the voice of God since his own long illness, and exposing hidden traitors in the Taiping midst, won some kind of power play? Has Xiao been silenced by a Taiping coup rather than by Qing spear thrusts or bullets?

If there has been some kind of power struggle, it is Yang Xiuqing who is the winner. For on December 17, a week after Xiao is wounded, Hong Xiuquan, with no comment on Xiao's state of health, issues his full enfeoffment of the five kings, including Xiao as "West King." At the end of the proclamation, Hong grants to Yang, the East King, "supervisory power" over the other four kings, clearly promoting him above the rest in the earthly Taiping hierarchy.[22]

Military training and moral instruction continue side by side as the Taiping, their final destination still not announced by the Heavenly King, seek to strengthen their ranks. In a new summary of military conduct, rules for the behavior of troops, both male and female, in Yongan or the base camps as well as on the march, are spelled out in simple form. As the Taiping now have access to printing facilities, these are copied in large bold type, easy to read and easy to remember. Among the rules are the following:

> Make yourselves thoroughly acquainted with the Heavenly Commandments and with the regulations on praise, on morning and evening worship, and on thanksgiving, as well as with all the issued edicts.

Observe the separation of the men's camps from the women's, and let there be no exchanges of personal affection.

Do not speak falsely of the laws of the state or regulations of the Sovereign, nor pass on rumors concerning military secrets or army orders.

Let every officer and soldier, regular or volunteer, from fifteen years old and upwards, carry with him the necessary military accoutrements, provisions, cooking utensils, oil and salt; let no spear be lacking its shaft.

Let no able-bodied officer or soldier, regular or volunteer, usurp position or title and ride in a sedan chair or on horseback; neither let anyone improperly impress the people into his service.

Let all officers and soldiers, regulars or volunteers, retreat to the side of the road and cry out, "Long live the Heavenly King and his son, the East King and his son, or the other princes" as the case may be; and let none stray out among the royal conveyances or the horses and sedan chairs of the royal ladies.

Let no officer or soldier, male or female, enter into the villages to cook rice or seize food; let no one destroy the dwellings of the people or loot their property; also let no one ransack the apothecaries' or other shops, or the offices of the various prefectural and district magistrates.

Let no one improperly coerce the people outside our ranks who sell tea or cooked rice to carry burdens for them; let no one fraudulently appropriate the baggage of any of his fellow soldiers throughout the army.

Let no one set fire to the dwellings of the people, or urinate in the middle of the road or in private houses.

Let no one unjustly put to death the old and the weak who don't have the strength to carry burdens.[23]

The Taiping leaders use the carved wood-block printing facilities of Yongan to publish this and several other moral and military texts.[24] To simplify their religious message, and make the unfamiliar history from another world accessible, the Taiping leaders create their own version of the basic and venerable Confucian educational primer, the *Three Character Classic*. Both style and content suggest the author is Hong Xiuquan himself. In its Confucian version, the simple rhythms of the verses, with only three characters per line, and the carefully selected roster of basic Chinese characters, encourages literacy and religious knowledge at the same time. In its Taiping form, in the same format, the primer fills the same functions, but with a new religious focus. Rather than the story of God's anger as shown in the examples of Noah and the flood, or the destruction of Sodom, this basic Taiping text dwells on the survival of Israel and the flight out of Egypt, as presented in Exodus. The parallels of this saga to the Taiping flight and survival must have struck all the true believers:

It is said that long ago
There was a foreign country
Which worshiped the True God—
Israel.

Their twelve tribes
Traveled to Egypt.
God protected them,
And their descendants flourished.

After the Egyptians turn against the Israelites, God rains plagues on Egypt, and helps Moses lead His people to safety:

By day in a cloud,
By night in a pillar of fire,
The True God
In person saved them.

He caused the Red Sea
Water to part in two;
To stand like walls,
That they might pass between.

The people of Israel
Walked straight ahead,
As though on dry ground,
And thus saved their lives.

When their pursuers tried to pass,
The wheels fell from their axles;
The waters joined up again,
And they were all drowned.

Thus the Great God
Displayed his great powers,
And the people of Israel
Were all preserved.

When they came to the wilderness
And their food was all gone,
The Great God
Bade them not be afraid.

He sent down manna,
In abundance for each of them;
It was sweet as honey,
And all ate their fill.[25]

The primer then echoes the version of religious history Hong first wrote on Thistle Mountain during 1845, telling how the Chinese themselves, once believers in the True God, fell away from God's law and His word, until first Jesus and then Hong were sent down to earth, to destroy the demon devils and save the world from evil.

To reinforce both the handbooks on military discipline and the moral injunctions, Hong issues his own extended version of the Ten Commandments as God presented them to Moses at Mount Sinai. In line with the need for order in the city of Yongan, Hong emphasizes the problem of sexual impropriety and other antisocial acts, and presents his own paraphrase of the seventh commandment:

> The Seventh Heavenly Commandment: Thou shalt not commit adultery or be licentious.
> In the world there are many men, all brothers; in the world there are many women, all sisters. For the sons and daughters of Heaven, the men have men's areas and the women have women's areas; they are not allowed to intermix. Men or women who commit adultery or who are licentious are considered monsters; this is the greatest possible transgression of the Heavenly Commandments. The casting of amorous glances, the harboring of lustful thoughts about others, the smoking of opium, and the singing of libidinous songs are all offenses against the Heavenly Commandment.
> A poem reads:
> Lust and lewdness most certainly constitute the worst of sins;
> Those who become monsters or demons, are truly pitiable.
> If you wish to enjoy true happiness in Heaven,
> You must curb your desires and painfully reform.[26]

By the end of February 1852, Hong Xiuquan has ordered enforcement of this commandment to "all soldiers and officers throughout the army, high-ranked or low, male or female," and instructed the five kings and other senior commanders to carry out constant checks into their own units, to find any offenders against the seventh commandment. All those caught "as soon as discovered shall be immediately arrested, beheaded, and the head displayed to the public. There shall assuredly be no pardons."[27]

In making this firm declaration about morality for the Taiping followers, Hong Xiuquan has no compunctions about excluding himself, for clearly he enjoys the company of women. In the edict giving the correct titles for the five subordinate kings and the other Taiping officials, he orders that his wife Lai, the mother of his oldest two daughters and of his eldest son, Tiangui, be always addressed as "niangniang" or "empress."

But in the following sentence of the same edict he adds that his other "senior imperial consorts" shall be addressed as "wang-niang," "princess-consort."[28] The names of these new consorts are never clearly listed in any Taiping sources, but the Heavenly King must have chosen the first of them by February 1851, during the difficult campaign that followed the retreat from Jiangkou. For in that month, all the various "sisters-in-law" of the Taiping leaders were ordered to show no trace of jealousy to the Heavenly King, or to complain about his behavior—all those doing so would be put to death. Such "sisters-in-law," given the structure of family relationships established among the other Taiping leaders and Jesus, would have included Hong's own first wife, Lai.[29]

This problem of jealousy is alluded to in another moral tract that Hong issues in Yongan, the "Ode to Youth," a lengthy poem in lines of five characters that outlines the basic patterns of deference and obligation owing to God, His son Jesus, and to all the members of human families according to their positions—parent, child, in-laws, or married couples. Though most of these are bland, or at least conventionally predictable, the stanzas on husband and wife are more personal in tone:

> The way of the husband is founded on firmness.
> In loving his wife he must have his own methods.
> If his wife is a jealous shrew
> He must never give way to fear or panic.
>
> The way of the wife lies in her obediences.
> She should not go against her husband's control.
> If she's the one who rules the roost
> It will bring misery down on the whole family.[30]

Hong Xiuquan himself, in the regulations issued in Yongan on correct nomenclature for various ranks in the Taiping hierarchy, refers to the correct titles to be given to his various "royal fathers-in-law" and "royal mothers-in-law," showing that his relationships with several women were common and accepted knowledge. Given Hong Xiuquan's "imperial" rank, perhaps this is not seen as being at variance with the morality and chastity that he imposes on his subordinates.[31] But Hong has no intention of allowing gossip and speculation about his private life to spread among his followers. As he puts it in an edict issued the following year, all those who discuss the "family name, personal names, or comparative ranking" of the imperial consorts, or filter information into or out from the women's palace quarters, shall be instantly beheaded.[32]

The military fervor in Yongan, the constant exhortations and preaching, the titles and the promises, cannot hide the Taiping's deadly predicament. Despite the morale problems of the assembled Qing forces, the numbers of the government troops around Yongan grow steadily, and their repeated attacks whittle away at the Taiping outposts on the defensive perimeter. Regular Taiping sorties against the Qing base camps, though fought with great courage, are not successful, and slowly the Qing construct their own encircling wall around the city, severing the last Taiping supply routes and sources of food. The Taiping troops are forced to get their salt by boiling and filtering the soil from the floors of the former official salt depot of Yongan city, and to experiment with various methods for obtaining the sulfur and saltpeter needed for the manufacture of gunpowder. Among these are the crushing and filtering of old building bricks in an attempt to obtain the saltpeter accumulated there, and the manufacturing of a chemical compound with the properties of sulfur by repeated boiling in alcohol and evaporation of either dogs' blood or horse dung.[33]

Surely this cannot be the Earthly Paradise, although it has served its purpose, and given the Taiping time to harden their discipline and formulate their doctrines. By the early spring of 1852, Hong and the Taiping leaders are preparing plans for their breakout. Either they keep these plans so secret that even the hidden Qing informers do not know about them, or the informers have all been identified and killed in the relentless hunts for traitors conducted by Yang Xiuqing. On April 3, Hong Xiuquan issues a new proclamation in poetic form to all the men and women officers in his ranks, a proclamation that those used by now to his diction might correctly interpret as the call for a strategic withdrawal:

Let the devil demons hatch their myriad schemes;
How can they escape the sure hand of our Heavenly Father,
Who in six days created all the rivers and mountains?
Each of you who believes in the Spiritual Father will be a bold warrior.

High Heaven has appointed you to slay the demon devils;
The Heavenly Father and Heavenly Elder Brother constantly watch over you.
Men and women officers, all grasp your swords,
And give no heed to changing whatever clothes you happen to be wearing now.

Unite your hearts, rouse your courage, and together slay the demons.
Forget about your valuables and your bundles of possessions.
Divest yourselves of worldly affections and uphold high Heaven,
Shimmering in the light from the golden bricks and golden mansions.

In high Heaven, in majestic splendor you will enjoy happiness.
The least and the lowliest shall all don silks and satins,
The men wear dragon robes and the women be garlanded with flowers.
Let each be a faithful officer, glorying in the battle.[34]

On April 5, 1852, in a carefully planned mass exodus, beginning at ten in the evening and ending before dawn, the main body of the Taiping army and their dependents leave the east gate of Yongan, where Qing defenses are weakest, cross the narrow stream that flows by the gate, and climb up into the mountain passes, heading toward the north. Before leaving the city, they have studded the ground with homemade mines made of gunpowder and charcoal, packed into wooden tubes and wrapped in inflammable hay or cotton wadding. As the rear guard leaves the city, it ignites long fuses made of plaited grasses or corn silk, and the erratically spaced explosions, smoke and din that follow help confuse the Qing pursuers, just as the noise and glare of the fireworks had eased the Taiping capture of the city some six months before. The Taiping have also tied lumps of old metal and broken pots to dogs and pigs, and the terrified animals running through the smoking streets compound the din and confusion.[35]

Despite these attempted diversionary tactics, close to two thousand people in the Taiping rear guard, trying to hold off the main Qing force, are trapped and slaughtered in the retreat. To avenge the deaths of so many of their companions, the units of the Taiping army that have marched ahead into the mountains turn back and, in the driving rain that has begun to fall, bury more mines in the soft soil of the pass, and bundle great piles of rocks into rough-and-ready cages of woven bamboo, which they secure to trees on the steep mountain slopes. As the Qing troops, closely bunched together, struggle up the rain-slick pass, the Taiping explode the mines and slash the ropes holding the cages, maiming or crushing hundreds of the enemy. They then open fire and charge, routing the Qing forces completely and leaving almost five thousand enemy dead. The surviving Taiping forces seize the reprieve offered by this providential victory, and tramp up deeper into the mountains, sliding through the rain and mud toward their still unidentified promised land.[36]

12

THE HUNT

There are no shortcuts to the Earthly Paradise, especially when one has no idea where it is. The towns, hills, streams, and valleys of China spread out before one, in all directions. The demons, always at one's heels, can dictate the rhythms of one's march, but not its purpose.

As they leave Yongan and climb into the hills, the Taiping number around forty thousand. From the dead and dying demons they have seized Qing uniforms, banners, insignia, pouches, and other items. They have also found and carried off a cache of gunpowder, at least ten large loads, a crucial addition to their nearly exhausted stores. However ingenious, the extraction of saltpeter from old bricks and the attempts to make sulfur from blood or dung are inadequate for their needs on the march, which include the gunpowder for muskets, for mines, for cannon mounted on their boats, and the extra supplies for blasting down the walls of demon towns. Siege warfare should be easier for them since over one thousand experienced miners, employed once in Guangxi but now jobless, have joined them in Yongan.[1]

As they leave Yongan, do they advance or retreat? The question is maybe not the right one. The point is that, with God's help, they have survived again. And also with the help of Big-head Yang, who as a bandit deserted them at Jintian, and as a Qing officer during the summer of 1851 stopped their troops from uniting with those of Ling Shiba; by 1852 Yang has realized that the Taiping presence helps his own prestige, and though he controls the Meng River south of Yongan he lets the Taiping move upstream to the north, and makes no attempt to use his stronger fleet to race up the river and cut the Taiping route to Guilin.[2]

It is a mixture of chance and strategy that leads the Taiping forces toward Guilin, the capital of Guangxi, sheltered in its rice-rich valleys among the vivid forested peaks of karst and limestone. Guilin is a major city with strong defenses, and the walls will not fall as easily as those of Yongan. But the routes back into southern Guangxi are blocked by Qing forces, and with well-equipped Qing garrison armies holding cities to both the west and the east, it is the best Taiping strategy to drive straight through the center, moving from village to village rather than attacking other towns.[3]

Luo Dagang, proven by now to be one of their subtlest and most inventive commanders, suggests the Taiping proceed with guile. He orders several hundred of his troops to don Qing uniforms—seized from the prisoners or stripped from the fallen troops outside Yongan—and with Qing banners flying to approach Guilin in marching order, and bluff their way past the unsuspecting guards. By the chance of war, though no one in Guilin has yet heard that the Taiping have left Yongan, a commanding general is hurrying to Guilin with that news when he sees the marching troops dressed like his own army. Realizing that no Qing troops can or should be there, he gallops ahead of the Taiping columns and beats them to Guilin, alerting the defenders and ordering the great gates closed.[4]

For thirty-three days the Taiping besiege Guilin, concentrating their attacks on the southern edge, but they can neither break through nor undermine the walls, nor can they starve out the city for they do not have enough troops to surround Guilin completely. But camped on the banks of the fast-flowing Li River, they are able to rest their forces and seize large numbers of boats, to make up for those that had to be abandoned on the Meng River when they left Yongan. It is during the Guilin siege that the Taiping develop the strategic and logistical skills to make themselves a power on the water as well as on the land. A few weeks into the siege, they have already amassed a fleet of forty or more large river vessels. It is on these ships that they store their munitions and their grain reserves, the cash and treasure from looted houses, along with the noncombatant women, and the children. This tactic frees up the stronger Hakka women and other male troops from tedious guard duty and lets them join in active combat, while dependents and supplies can be swiftly moved if danger threatens.[5] Land batteries of cannon are there to hold back the ships of Big-head Yang if needed, but he does not press the attack with vigor. The other Qing river forces stay mainly to the south, fearing the Taiping might try to double back and join up with Ling Shiba or other supporters in western Guangdong.[6] By mid-May, the siege still unsuccessful, the Taiping pay a massive bribe to Big-head Yang to leave them unpursued; with their now well-honed skills, they execute a swift withdrawal along two routes, one by land and one by water, and continue their journey to the north.[7]

The choice of direction has now become a fateful one, for north of Guilin the Taiping forces cross one of China's great strategic and geographical divides, the band of hills and mountains where the river systems that flow from north to south have their source; on the far side of the range, a different group of rivers flows from south to north. So having traveled some sixty miles north of Guilin, to the northern end of the navigable section of the Li River, the Taiping troops come to the ancient but still serviceable canal at Xingan city, which links the Li River to the northward-flowing river Xiang. From here, the Xiang River flows straight through the heart of Hunan province, and thence, via the wide waters of the Dongting Lake, directly to the Yangzi River itself.

Astonishingly, Qing forces have left Xingan virtually unguarded, and the Taiping enter it on May 23 without a fight. But they do not have the time to linger there, for the journey north draws them with greater urgency, and the Qing are in pursuit. Thus they push on immediately to the river junction city of Quanzhou, which the Taiping vanguard reaches the next day, on May 24. Unlike Xingan, Quanzhou is strongly guarded, but since it is not the Taiping goal, their troops march and sail past the walls. In their midst, comfortable in his ornamental sedan chair, sits Feng Yunshan, the South King, the closest friend of Hong Xiuquan and founder of the God-worshipers in Thistle Mountain. Idly, a Qing gunner on the Quanzhou walls takes aim at the gaudy target and fires at the unseen passenger within. The casual shot has a deadly accuracy. The ball smashes through the chair's ornamental coverings, seriously wounding Feng.[8]

When Xiao Chaogui, the West King and voice of Jesus, was struck by the demons at Yongan, there was confusion among the leaders and the sound of contradictory voices. But at Quanzhou, the news of Feng's mortal wound spreads unstoppably through the ranks, and the Taiping forces

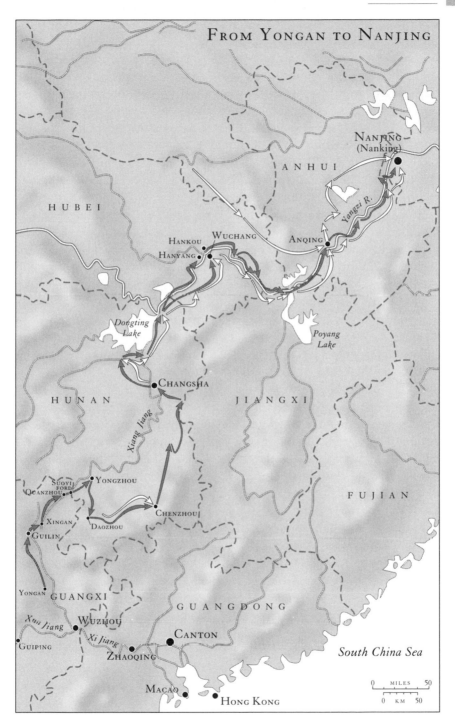

FROM YONGAN TO NANJING

NANJING
(Nanking)

ANHUI

HUBEI

Hankou
Hanyang
Wuchang
Anqing
Yangzi R.

Dongting
Lake

Poyang
Lake

Changsha

HUNAN

JIANGXI

Xiang Jiang

Suoyi
Ford
Quanzhou
Yongzhou

FUJIAN

Xingan
Guilin
Daozhou
Chenzhou

Yongan
GUANGXI

GUANGDONG

Wuzhou
Canton

Xun Jiang
Xi Jiang

Guiping
Zhaoqing

South China Sea

Macao
Hong Kong

0   MILES   50
0   KM   50

seem to act as one. Breaking their march, massing around the city walls, for over a week the Taipings launch assault after assault, while the neighboring Qing commanders, scared of the Taiping ferocity, linger in their camps and refuse to give the city aid, despite the anguished pleas of the city magistrate, written with his own blood. Finally breaching the gate and walls on June 3, the Taiping force their way into the city and attack everyone inside without quarter. They have never acted thus before. Within two days almost all of Quanzhou's residents, except for those who fled in time, are dead.[9]

Leaving the gutted city on June 5, the double Taiping columns continue north, apparently intending to proceed down the Xiang River to the provincial capital of Changsha. As before, they follow the dual tactic of one line of river vessels and a parallel marching column, for the time being on the western bank. Now more of the foot soldiers can travel by water, for their fleet of boats has expanded once again. They have seized at least two hundred craft of different sizes anchored off Quanzhou at the time of the siege.[10] Tired and careless after the siege and slaughter in Quanzhou, the Taiping move swiftly on their way without the careful procedures of advance reconnaissance that they usually follow on the march through unknown terrain. So it is that only five miles north of the city they blunder straight into the trap set for them by a local militia leader, Jiang Zhongyuan.

Jiang Zhongyuan is the earliest exemplar of a new kind of antagonist the Taiping must now confront, a man backed by more resources and with infinitely more important family and bureaucratic contacts than local landlords like Wang Zuoxin and the God-worshipers' other enemies in the Thistle Mountain region. Jiang is a scholar from southern Hunan, just two years older than Hong Xiuquan. His first experience with organizing local militia troops came in the late 1840s, before the Taiping had yet appeared, as he sought to protect his home and lands from Yao tribesmen and other disaffected groups. These rootless men drew strength and inspiration from millenarian sects like the "Black Lotus" or from local secret societies like the "Cudgels," which combined elements of martial arts with Buddhist beliefs and vegetarian dietary practices.[11] Such groups had been expanding their forces in Jiang's native Hunan for years, gaining recruits as drought conditions worsened and corrupt local magistrates connived with local grain merchants to manipulate distributions from the local granaries so as to drive the already exorbitant rice prices still higher.

One of Jiang's purposes in raising a local militia was preemptive, to keep his own kinsmen out of these potentially rebellious organizations.

The members of such defensive militia groups were, as in Guangxi, a complicated mix: representatives of powerful lineages, local farmers, the unemployed, and semiprofessional soldiers who had no strong local ties but sought a military sponsor to guarantee them a steady income. Jiang's militia numbered around two thousand men by the late 1840s, and though his successes brought him career preferment and a posting in a distant province, the militia were kept partly intact by Jiang's brothers and family friends from the educated Hunanese elite.[12] When in 1850 Jiang returned to his Hunan hometown following his father's death—as Qing ritual practice demanded—his previous skills were brought to the attention of the Qing commanders, who summoned Jiang and his militia to aid in the siege of Yongan and the relief of Guilin, even though it meant traveling far from his home base. Jiang did take part, briefly, in both those campaigns, though he was mortified by the hesitancy of the various Qing government forces to take decisive or concerted action.[13]

The ambush that Jiang lays is just beyond the Suoyi ford on the Xiang River, five miles north of Quanzhou. At this point, where the river makes an abrupt eastward turn, it is about one hundred yards wide and fairly shallow, but the current is swift and the riverbed is crisscrossed by an intricate tracery of sandbars that make navigation difficult. The west bank is hilly and thickly wooded, with trees and shrubs growing down to the water's edge. It is here that Jiang oversees the blocking of the stream with cut trees and logs, through which huge iron spikes have been driven to hold them in place, making the river impassable to vessels. Meantime he positions his troops on the west bank, among the dense trees.[14]

Swept along the river by the swift stream, the first Taiping vessels in the column sail through the sandbanks and round the bend in the river straight into the great barrier of tethered tree trunks. As hails of shot are poured on them, and their stranded vessels set afire, the boats behind, unable to halt, pile into those in front. Each arriving vessel compounds the confusion, while the fire spreads from boat to boat and the trapped troops and sailors—joined by their comrades who have been marching along the west bank—flounder across the river to the eastern shore. Had Jiang had more troops at his command, and had one of his fellow military commanders not reneged on his promise to set up a similar ambush on the eastern edge of Suoyi ford, the Taiping force might have been wiped out. As it is, the Taiping casualties are colossal: three hundred boats are burned, sunk, or captured, and around ten thousand of their troops are killed or drowned, many of them the original God-worshipers from Guangxi who gave the movement so much passion and energy. Among the dead is the South King, Feng Yunshan, who succumbs to his wounds.[15]

Abandoning the remaining vessels, Hong Xiuquan and the Taiping troops cut across the wooded hills beyond the east bank of the Xiang River and trek into Hunan province, hoping to seize the prosperous river city of Yongzhou by surprise. But the Qing have cut the bridges and pulled all boats over to the farther shore. With no clear destination open to it, the whole army veers south again and finding the city of Daozhou unprepared for its sudden change of direction, and weakly defended, occupies it on June 12.[16]

Here the Taiping stay, either in the city itself, or campaigning, raiding, and destroying temples in the vicinity, for a month and a half. The leaders must not only restore morale but also attract new recruits to make up for their stunning losses. The greatest potential sources for such recruits are also the most problematical: the members of the various groups who—for ethnic, economic, political, or religious reasons—have turned against the state and its officials, and seek an often rough-and-ready version of a better life. In wooing such people directly, the Taiping leaders are taking a calculated risk, for whether or not such men will make true God-worshipers, or care about the Taiping's Heavenly Kingdom, has to remain unknown.

The proclamations posted in southern Hunan are issued in the names of Yang Xiuqing and Xiao Chaogui, the East and West Kings, who have already begun to prepare such materials in Yongan. The rhetoric they employ to denigrate the Manchu rulers and their minions is both forceful and personal. The ruling emperor himself, Xianfeng, is referred to as "the Manchu demon" and "the Tartar dog," of "barbarian origin," and the "mortal enemy of us Chinese." By serving him, the followers of the Heaven-and-Earth Society are reminded, they not only obey the "old serpent devil" and shun the "glory of the Great God"; they violate their own blood oaths, which pledged them "with united hearts and united efforts to exterminate the Qing."[17] But avoiding all references to the cause of restoring the Ming dynasty, which some secret-society brothers still espouse, Xiao and Yang urge on them the duty of supporting Hong Xiuquan, the "True Sovereign," in his goal of "founding the state."[18]

In their earliest recruiting efforts, in the Guiping region of Guangxi, the Taiping leaders had begun to talk of a common "sacred treasury" and the need to donate to it. The secret societies, too, in the same areas as the God-worshipers, constructed their own appeals, often as songs or jingles, with a powerful social message:

The people at the top owe us their money;
The people in the middle are content to snooze.
The people at the bottom should go with us—
For that's far better than renting an ox to plow some worn-out land.

Playing on the same theme, the Taiping had their own version in Thistle Mountain jingle:

Those with millions owe us their money,
Those who are half poor–half rich can till their fields.
Those with ambitions but no cash should go with us:
Broke or hungry, Heaven will keep you well.[19]

Now Yang and Xiao expand these ideas and relate them specifically to Manchu abuses and callousness:

Whenever floods and droughts occur, [the Manchus] do not show the slightest compassion; they sit and watch the starving people wander by until the bleached bones grow like wild weeds, for they desire to reduce the numbers of us Chinese. Moreover, throughout China the Manchus have unleashed grasping officials and their corrupt subordinates to strip the people of their flesh until men and women weep by the roadsides, for they desire to impoverish us Chinese. Official posts are obtained by bribes, and punishments bought off with money; the rich hold the power and heroes despair.[20]

This oppression is one of the main reasons that the Taiping armies are on the march: "On behalf of God above we shall avenge those who have deceived Heaven, and for China below we shall free the common people from their miseries. We must wipe away the foul air of the Qing dynasty so that we can together enjoy the happiness of Taiping."[21]

The Taiping proclamations tie mockery of the Manchus to mockery of their racial ancestry and their pretensions:

We have carefully investigated the Manchu Tartars' origins and have found that their first ancestors were a white fox and a red dog, who copulated together and from their seed produced this race of demons. As their numbers grew they mated together since they had no proper human relationships nor civilization. Availing themselves of China's lack of real men, they seized the country, established their own demon throne and placed the wild fox upon it; in their court the monkeys bathed and dressed. We Chinese could not plow up their caves or dig up their dens; instead we fell in with their treacherous plots, bore their insults, and obeyed their commands. Moreover, our civil and military officials, coveting their awards, bowed and knelt in the midst of this pack of foxes and dogs. Now, a little child only three feet tall may be extremely ignorant, but point to a pig or a dog and tell him to bow down to it and he will redden with anger.[22]

In other passages, Yang and Xiao link social humiliation to sexual subservience:

Chinese people should look like Chinese; but now the Manchus have ordered us to shave the hair around the head, leaving a long tail behind, thus making the Chinese appear to be brute animals. The Chinese have their own Chinese robes and hats; but now the Manchus have instituted buttons of rank on the hat, barbarian clothes, and monkey caps, discarding the robes and headdresses of former dynasties, in order to make the Chinese forget their basic origins. The Chinese have Chinese family relationships; but the former false demon, Kangxi, secretly ordered the Ta [Tartars] each to control ten families and to defile the Chinese women, hoping thereby that the Chinese would all become barbarians. The Chinese have Chinese consorts; but now the Manchu demon devils have taken all of China's beautiful girls to be their slaves and concubines. Thus three thousand beautiful women have been ravished by the barbarian dogs, one million lovely girls have had to sleep with the malodorous foxes; to speak of it distresses the heart, to talk of it pollutes the tongue.[23]

The manifestos also invoke the kind of numerological wordplays that the secret societies use so often, and that Hong Xiuquan and the Taiping kings also use to emphasize their prestige. In telling their followers that "the demons' fortune of three by seven has ended," the Taiping leaders refer to an astrologer eighteen hundred years before, who predicted that in "three by seven decades," or 210 years, the dynasty in which he lived would come to its end. Applying the same time frame to the Qing, who founded their dynasty in 1644, this would make 1853 the year of the Manchu fall. In that year "the true sovereign of nine by five" would rule triumphant—in other words, Hong Xiuquan. For the reference here is to the first hexagram of the *Book of Changes,* which declares, "Nine in the fifth place means: Flying Dragon in the Heavens. It forces one to see the Great Man." The Confucian commentary on this line elaborated that "things that accord in tone vibrate together. Things that have affinity in their inmost natures seek one another. Water flows to what is wet, fire turns to what is dry. . . . Thus the sage arises, and all creatures follow him with their eyes."[24]

It is in this same spirit of dignity and emancipation, of shared fellowship in the knowledge that all Chinese are God's children, even if they have unwittingly or even willingly served the Manchu demon, that the Taiping armies are fighting. Those who reject the Taiping message after it is offered to them will be "caught in the demons' net of delusion and in death become slaves and underlings of the demons, to bear their debaucheries and evil poisons, to become bloated with leprosy, to become ugly and evil ghosts eternally consigned to the eighteenth layer of hell." For those who repent and join the Taiping, and for their descendants, there will be "unlimited happiness, eternal dignity, and eternal honor."[25]

The numbers drawn to the Taiping in Hunan, at least in part because of these messages, are large: according to one man serving in their ranks, in the three cities briefly held after the disaster at Suoyi ford, the Taiping gained respectively twenty thousand, "twenty or thirty thousand," and "several thousand" new recruits, bringing a total of at least fifty thousand new troops to their army.[26] These secret-society recruits, toughened by years of hardship in this area of Hunan, and speaking the local dialect, can infiltrate towns ahead of the Taiping forces, posing as local militia members or as traveling merchants, and thus gauge the defenders' strength. Holding some of these cities for a day or two, dodging others altogether, and acquiring the mules and pack horses wherever they find them to speed their land advance, the Heavenly King, his Taiping veterans, and the new recruits drift between various prosperous towns in southeast Hunan.[27]

It is Xiao Chaogui, once the voice of Jesus, still the West King, and apparently recovered from his wounds, who breaks this circle of indecision. In late August 1852 he leaves the city of Chenzhou, the current base for Hong Xiuquan and the Taiping forces, and with a small force of two thousand troops or less, cuts across Hunan by land, reaching the city of Changsha on September 12. For six days he leads his men in pounding at the walls and gates on the southern face of the city with cannon and explosive, and showering the city with fire-tipped arrows. Changsha's defenders are not much more numerous than Xiao's small force, for most of the Qing troops have been ordered deployed elsewhere, and Xiao's impetuous attack has been unexpected, the other Taiping armies having shown no signs of marching on the city. But the walls and gates are strong, the defenses skillfully coordinated. The West King, with his robes of office, and his fluttering banners, is a tempting target. On September 17, as he leads another in his series of attacks, a marksman from the walls fells him with a shot.[28]

Jolted by the news of Xiao's death, which reaches him a week later, the Heavenly King leads his entire army north, to press the siege at Changsha. He reaches the city walls in early October, after a ten-day march, and sees for the first time the powerful city which—but for the shattering ambush at Suoyi ford—might have been his four months before.[29] His delay has been a crucial one to the city's defense; whereas only five to eight thousand troops were there when Xiao Chaogui made his surprise attack, Xiao's near success galvanized the state to send massive reinforcements, so that by the time Hong and his troops arrive the defenders' ranks have swollen to thirty thousand or more, and within another month reach fifty thousand. These new Qing arrivals are backed by the necessary resources: twenty thousand pounds of gunpowder, as many pounds of shot for their guns, and several heavy cannon to be mounted on the city walls.[30]

The defenders of Changsha are coordinated in their resistance by the governor of Hunan, Luo Bingzhang, whose official residence is in the city. Luo is from Hong Xiuquan's home county of Hua, and his life has been everything that Hong's has failed to be. Twenty years older than Hong, Luo excelled at his classical studies and converted his scholarship into examination success, rising by turns through every stage of the hierarchical challenges, from the county level to the provincial, and thence to the national level, where he attained the topmost degree of *jinshi* in 1832, ranking twenty-seventh in the second class, the highest-ranking student from the whole of Guangdong province. For this achievement he was selected for service with the elite of scholars in the Hanlin Imperial Academy in Peking. Scholarly, honest, meticulous, Luo rose steadily in the ranks of the Qing bureaucracy, as Hong dreamed, preached, traveled, and began to gather the brethren in Thistle Mountain. At almost exactly the time that Hong donned his yellow robe and won his first great battle at Jintian, Luo was chosen by the emperor as Hunan governor and posted to Changsha.[31] As governor of Hunan, Luo was blamed by Emperor Xianfeng for the Taiping victories in the southern part of his province, but he was not recalled. Instead, following a common Qing practice, he was "dismissed from office but retained at his post," and despite the formal appointment of a new governor in his place, he received a special commission as "Coordinator of the Changsha Defenses."[32] Now Luo watches from the walls as Taiping troops try, for two full months, to bring the city to its knees and kill the demons who are based within it.

The siege of Changsha is thus partly the story of two wills clashing, one steeped in the successful practice of Confucian virtue, one confidently in touch with God the Father. It is also a battle of techniques, as the

Taiping perfect their skills at building floating pontoon bridges to hold their forces together. They span the wide, swift waters of the Xiang that flow past the westward wall of Changsha with just such a bridge. While Shi Dakai, the Wing King, opens a second front to keep other Qing forces at bay to the west of the city, the two long stretches of this bridge give the besieging Taiping troops easy communication with each other, as well as access to a narrow island west of the city walls where they can camp and beat back any boats that seek to approach the city from the south with reinforcements.[33]

In their attempt to take Changsha, the Taiping use the skills of the Guangxi miners who have joined their ranks over the previous two years, as well as thousands of miners from Hunan who have recently come over to them. Gunpowder is no longer a problem, for they have accumulated massive supplies in southern Hunan. As the Taiping miners dig and sap the walls, the defenders sink great wooden vats into the ground to serve as their listening posts, often using blind men, whose ears have grown unusually acute, to listen for the far-off sounds of burrowing and pinpoint the miners' progress to the garrison troops. Though the Taiping seek to confuse these secret listeners by the constant banging of drums outside the walls, the distractions are not enough, and each time a tunnel is near completion, it is smashed open from above by the Qing defenders with huge iron balls, crushing those within, or else flooded with water or with excrement to flush out the exhausted sappers.[34] Of ten major tunnels attempted by the Taiping at Changsha only three are completed, and though explosions within these successfully bring down stretches of the city wall, the Taiping still cannot fight their way past the defenders, whose ranks have swelled to fifty thousand by November, for as at Guilin the Taiping forces are too small to surround the city completely and prevent relief columns from arriving.[35]

By late November 1852, with no victory in sight, but with thousands of boats acquired from the city wharves and the maze of connecting streams and rivers around Changsha now in Taiping hands, Hong Xiuquan orders the siege abandoned. As the Taiping fleet and army move north, they use these newly captured ships to capture other ships, and the awesome sight of marching men to lure new recruits into the Taiping ranks. They also develop a new idea, that of coordinating mobile floating fortresses with land forces and cannon that can be swiftly moved from land to boat and back again.[36]

Like the land troops before a battle, the naval forces develop a system by which each unit of a given fleet has its flags—the forward sections fly triangular red flags from their mastheads, the center sections triangular yellow flags, the rear sections triangular black flags. For recognition at night, sound signals are used: two drumbeats at regular intervals mark the lead ship; one gong stroke the command ship with heavy cannon aboard; three drumbeats for the ships of the rear guard.[37] Three gong beats from the commander's ship, regularly repeated, mean the signal to untie cables and prepare to sail; four gong beats mark the signal to anchor. Ships must always anchor in lines, not in the form of a cross; they must keep their guns cleared and pointed up or downstream. Small Taiping patrol boats move through the fleet at night, carrying lanterns and searching for spies or signs of fire. Shore patrols perform similar tasks, with each soldier carrying a gong to sound the alarm—the horns, which some soldiers used to carry, have been abandoned since soldiers "frightened at the approach of demons" might lose the ability, through fear, to blow a clear warning call. On shipboard, however, blasts blown on the horn are always used to signal the presence of demon vessels.[38]

Probing unknown waterways is difficult as well as dangerous, and lack of care can swiftly lead to disaster, as the catastrophe at Suoyi ford showed all too well. Though all contingencies cannot be anticipated, many are spelled out in the Taiping's battle manuals:

When troops move by the water route, they must act with extreme care, for rivers are wide, and there are numerous branch channels and creeks and small inlets. Disaster may result if they take a wrong turn. Before the forces move out on an operation, all military equipment must have already been installed aboard the ships. Then a fixed date for departure shall be set and the soldiers notified of it.

A plan for moving the ships must first be drawn up. The assistant general shall select several soldiers of the water force who are familiar with the river route and keep them at his side. They shall first list carefully all the branch channels and small creeks along the river. If on a given night they are to anchor the ships at a certain place and there are ten branch channels at that spot, the assistant general must assign beforehand a certain number of small boats, each carrying five or six of the brothers [Taiping soldiers], equipped with guns and military supplies, to proceed in advance of the main troops. When they come upon a branch channel, two of the small boats shall be moored at the diverging point. When the other ships arrive at this place, they shall sound one signal on the rattle and two signals on the gong, instructing the ships to proceed straight ahead and not to enter the divergent channel. For fear that the people aboard the ships will not be able to distinguish the small boats at night, they shall hang three small red lanterns on each boat, besides giving the signal of one sound of the rattle and two of the gong.[39]

The leaders of the Taiping river forces are from the south, but the owners and crewmen of the captured boats are often from Hunan, and can be trusted to know the rivers well. In the land forces, both leaders and the central groups of fighting men and women are also from the south, but as one of them observes, when over fifty miles from home one loses one's bearings, and has little choice but to move on blindly, following one's orders.[40] The newly joined troops have unproven loyalties, and tricks and traps are frequent. As with the river forces, full precautionary measures are taken:

> When the troops are starting on a march, it is of first importance to calculate the distance of the march. For example, if it is intended to proceed to a certain place or to attack a certain city, the approximate distance between the objective and the present location must be investigated thoroughly. Then from among the troops a number of men who are thoroughly acquainted with the route must be selected, from whom can be learned the distance from the present location to the town and the distance from that town to the next village. These facts shall be clearly recorded on paper so that the facts are as intelligible as one's own palm. Make several copies. . . .
>
> If there are none of their own soldiers who are familiar with the route, when they arrive at a particular location, they shall first seize one of the locals to be a guide. However, they must investigate carefully whether the man actually knows the route before his service is employed. Obviously one cannot just seize a man at random and tell him to lead the way, for care must be exercised against possible treachery. When the army arrives at a junction of two or three routes, the correct one is easy to distinguish in the daytime, but it is very difficult to distinguish at night. Therefore, the officer in charge must investigate carefully in which direction a given road leads and which road is the correct one. Then the officer in charge must send a personal aide to take a station at the junction, holding a signal flag in his hands. When the heavenly troops arrive he shall shout in a loud voice that one is the right road and the other a branch route, thus clearly indicating to the heavenly troops the correct route to follow, so that they will not go the wrong way. Moreover, lest the heavenly troops suspect the soldier with the signal flag of being a spy and not believe him, the commanding officer must first issue him credentials bearing the assistant general's seal.[41]

Discipline of the troops on the march is equally important. The general policy guidelines issued at Yongan are supplemented by precise rules that every soldier, veteran or raw recruit, can follow. Rice and other foods for the coming day are cooked in the predawn hours, before breaking camp. The troops march out at dawn, carrying with them their cooked food for the noon meal. No fires may be lighted along the way to reheat food, nor may the troops shelter or cook in villagers' houses. The march generally ends between five and seven in the evening, and then troops can prepare an evening meal.[42]

In a campaign of spectacular coordination and skill, after leaving Changsha the Taiping armies crisscross northward down the Xiang River toward the Hubei capital of Wuchang, taking to the land when least expected, abandoning fleets of hundreds of boats at one spot only to seize new fleets a thousand strong when they descend upon some unsuspecting river town, cutting bridges as they pass them to delay pursuit, recruiting the boatmen along with the boats to check the Qing, throwing up pontoon bridges where no other bridges had existed, then removing them and floating them downstream to use again. In twenty-five days of constant moving and fighting, despite the dependents and the families, the equipment, weapons, gunpowder, munitions, treasure, grain, salt, oil, and religious texts, they cover three hundred miles.[43]

Bursting out across Dongting Lake to the banks of the Yangzi River, and moving swiftly east downstream, instead of at once attacking the strongly walled and massively guarded city of Wuchang, the Taiping leaders in a surprise maneuver send their troops to the north shore and seize the two wealthy but poorly defended commercial towns of Hanyang and Hankou. With these two bases in their hands, the Taiping construct two huge floating bridges across the Yangzi, so they can attack Wuchang on its weaker northern face, which fronts the river. The Hubei governor orders his garrison to burn all the homes outside the Wuchang city walls, to give them clearer fields of fire, and tries to rally the inhabitants of Wuchang by promising them lavish cash rewards for every Taiping soldier they capture: twenty ounces of silver for every male Taiping head with hair so long one can tell it belongs to a veteran soldier, and ten ounces for each Taiping head with the shorter hair of recent recruits to the rebel ranks. Like the Changsha defenders, too, they block all the city gates with earth and rocks, and create sunken listening posts to pinpoint the undermining of their walls. But the people are sullen and resentful of the destruction of their homes, and seem sympathetic to the Taiping message; the defense crumbles, and the city falls to the Taiping on January 12, 1853, the greatest prize that they have ever won.[44]

The huge city becomes a proving ground for all the social policies the Taipings have been developing since they retreated from Yongan in the spring of 1852. They seize for their common treasury the immense stores of wealth found in the homes of the Qing officials. They commandeer the military supplies from the armories, and take from the various Qing treasuries in Wuchang sums so huge they bedazzle the mind—well over one million ounces of silver in all. The property of the wealthy citizens and merchants who have fled is also taken for their treasury, and those residents who choose to stay in the city are told to offer a tithe of all their assets—whether jewelry, gold and silver bullion, copper cash, rice, ducks, clothes, or tea—to the public treasury. The jails are opened and the prisoners freed, common soldiers of the Qing disarmed, and new Taiping militias of the able-bodied citizens formed to guard the city walls.

All inhabitants of Wuchang are urged to follow the God-worshipers' religion, divided up according to their sex, and organized under sergeants in groups of twenty-five, men in one squad, women in another. Execution is the penalty for those who stray from one camp to the other. Even those preexisting families from which the men have been recruited to guard the walls are told to leave their homes, the women and children placed in women's hostels, and the old and infirm sent to special houses of their own. For all, whether active combatants, cloistered women, or sequestered elderly, daily rations are allocated, three-tenths of a pint of rice, and a small container each of salt and oil. The Taiping allow no trade of any kind within the city walls, but to supplement their meager public diets, soldiers and their families are allowed to shop outside the city gates, where local farmers congregate to sell fresh river fish and shellfish, chicken and pork, flat cakes and dumplings.[45]

The emperor, in despair and rage, has barely begun to issue the edicts that threaten punishments to all his baffled and defeated officials—a litany that in scope and intensity has been unwavering since Yongan fell over a year before—when unexpectedly on February 10, 1853, the Taiping leave the city, taking with them the huge stores of gold and treasure, and tens of thousands of new followers, both men and women.[46] They have acquired at least two thousand more boats in the lakes and rivers near Wuchang, and absorbed their crews into their ranks. While the campaign continues at this breakneck pace, they excuse all sailors working for them from the sexual segregation they impose on their own troops, and let all who have their families on board keep them there, just as long as they will serve. The sailors need not even let their hair flow free, like Taiping braves, but may keep them in the Manchu queue if that is what they prefer.[47] For speed, speed is everything. The forces all arrayed. The current swift. The leaders still have not publicly said where the Earthly Paradise lies, but to them as to their followers the next stage on the journey there has now become the city of Nanjing, six hundred miles down the Yangzi to the east, the soul of China's richest province, the center of its scholarship, the capital of the founding emperor of the Ming dynasty almost five hundred years before.[48] Along the six hundred miles of river are garrisons, forts, ships, loyal ministers and generals, and Qing armed forces moving in pursuit. The Taiping seem not to care. They race down the river in their great armada, columns of soldiers on the shore, pausing briefly for supplies and to empty the treasuries in the cities that surrender, bypassing those that offer stout resistance, crossing the river altogether to avoid the few major cities where organized resistance might check their rushing flood.[49]

Ahead of the main forces, the Taiping leaders send spies and agents to infiltrate the towns and villages on the route, and spread their message of solace and salvation. Some of these messages promise swift execution for looters and others who use the battle world for crimes. Gentry members are told to remove any honorary tablets or insignia they have received from serving the Manchus, but are reassured that once the Taiping armies seize Nanjing new examinations will be held to select the worthy. All are assured that if they simply write the character for *shun*—"obedient"—and post it beside their doors, no harm will come to them. Buddhist and Taoist monks are threatened with beheading if found in their temples; all their property, like that of the gambling-shop owners and brothel keepers, will be confiscated and given to the poor.[50] For everybody on the route of march, passive acceptance is the recommended stance:

> The Heavenly King is the younger brother of the Lord, Jesus Christ, descended into the earthly world. Because the people of the world are deluded by the devils, the Heavenly King was by design born into the world to save the people of the world. Therefore, he is called the Saviour. Those who are trapped and become devils are like men who are contaminated by sickness. Further, the East King was born to advise the people to revert to righteousness, and to cure their sickness. Therefore the East King is called the Teacher of Advice and Consolation and the Redeemer from Sickness. The Taiping troops practice the Way of Heaven, save people, and do not harm people. After the unification of the rivers and mountains there will be a universal three-year exemption from [land] taxes in cash and grain. The rich should contribute money, the poor should offer up their strength. After the great enterprise is finished all will be rewarded with distinctive and hereditary official positions. Wherever we pass we will concentrate on killing all civil and military officials, and soldiers and militiamen. People will not be harmed and they can certainly pursue their livelihood as usual, and

THE
EARTHLY
PARADISE

 The Earthly Paradise is not just one place. It is the whole of China, wherever the Taiping Heavenly Army can reach the people and destroy the demons, so that all may live together in perpetual joy, until at last they are raised to Heaven to greet their Father.

Hong Xiuquan, the Heavenly King, and Yang, the East King, and other leaders have developed the military ideas of Feng Yunshan and combined them with their experiences at Thistle Mountain, Yongan, and Wuchang, to create their own ideal system. Just as in the Taiping armies there are four private soldiers under every corporal, and five of these little units under every sergeant, so now in the Earthly Paradise at large there shall be four families linked to every corporal's family, and twenty-five such family units under the guidance of every sergeant. Each one of these communities shall build a public granary, and also a chapel for public worship, in which the sergeant shall make his dwelling. Every Sabbath day, the corporal shall take his own family and the four others under his command to the chapel, to worship there, and men and women shall sit in separate rows as they listen to the sermons from the sergeants fairly buy and fairly sell. At the time when a city is taken if all families close their doors we can guarantee an absence of incidents. If you assist the devils in the defense of a city and engage in fighting, you will definitely be completely annihilated.[51]

Within thirty days of leaving Wuchang, the Taiping vanguard covers the six hundred miles of river route and reaches the edges of Nanjing. The walls are vast, rising forty feet or more above the flat riverbanks and twisting through the hills that girdle the city to the east. They also extend for almost twenty-five miles in circumference, too huge to be defended in depth, as the British noted in their surveys made several years before, at the time of the Opium War. The northwest corner near the river seemed to them the most vulnerable part, while raiding parties sent up into the surrounding hills with cannon or artillery could hold the inner city at their mercy.[52]

The Taiping are no lesser strategists, and see the same possibilities for attack. They sap. They surround. They threaten. They infiltrate. They spur the hatred for the Manchu conquerors and urge the city's population not to do the demons' work. On March 19, 1853, they breach the walls on the northwestern corner with a series of huge explosions and their first patrols enfilade the streets, though one tragically mistimed explosion kills hundreds of Taiping warriors as they charge through the open gap. Other forces scale the southern gate and walls and move through the prosperous residential quarters there, routing the remaining Chinese defenders. On March 20 the Manchu garrison troops hold fast in their inner citadel as the Taiping troops converge. The Taiping press around the inner citadel and launch a fresh assault. There are perhaps fifty thousand Manchus there, but few of them are trained or battle-ready veterans. As their walls are breached they turn on themselves and their families, setting fire to their homes and committing suicide even as the Taiping burst into their garrison quarters. The smoke rises, the carnage continues for days as the Taiping hunt and slay all surviving demons.

On March 29, all preparations completed, there is the sound of music. The people of the city prostrate themselves at the roadside as Hong Xiu-quan in yellow robe and yellow shoes is carried into the city by sixteen bearers in his elaborately ornamented golden palanquin. Above the palanquin nod the effigies of five white cranes. In front march the long columns of his victorious troops. Behind him, astride on their horses, are thirty-two women, with yellow parasols.[53]

and sing praises to the Heavenly Lord. Every seventh Sabbath day, all senior officers, from the generals to the captains, shall visit one of the churches of the sergeants under their command, both to preach to them and to check that all in their congregations work hard and obey the Ten Commandments. Every single day the children will go to the chapel to hear their sergeants expound the Bible and the sacred Taiping texts.[1]

By day the people will work their land, but all must serve, when time allows, as potters, ironsmiths, carpenters, and masons, according to their skills. As to the land of China, all shall divide it up amongst themselves, with one full share for every man and woman aged sixteen and above, and half a share for every child below sixteen. All the land will be graded according to its productivity, and the shares handed out accordingly, with each person receiving land of varying richness, from best to worst. When the land is insufficient for the people's needs, the people will be moved to where the land is plentiful. Let every family in each unit rear five chickens and two sows, and see to their breeding. Let mulberry trees be planted in the shelter of every house, so all can work at raising silkworms and spinning silk. Of the products of this labor—food or cloth, livestock or money—let each corporal see to it that every family under him has food for its needs, but that all the rest be deposited in the public treasuries. And let the sergeants check the books and tally the accounts, presenting the records to their superiors, the colonels and captains. For "all people on this earth are as the family of the Lord their God on High, and when people of this earth keep nothing for their private use but give all things to God for all to use in common, then in the whole land every place shall have equal shares, and every one be clothed and fed. This was why the Lord God expressly sent the Taiping Heavenly Lord to come down and save the world."[2]

From the public treasuries, gifts shall be made to every family at times of birth, marriage and death, according to their need, but never in excess of one thousand copper cash, or one hundred *catties* of grain. No marriage should be treated differently because of the family's wealth, and these rules shall apply to all of China, so that each community has a surplus in case of war or famine. And at every ceremony, the sergeant shall lead his families in the worship of the One True God, making sure that no superstitious rites from days of old are followed.[3] From every family unit with a living male head, one person shall be chosen to serve as a soldier in the army; but the widowers and widows, the orphans and the childless, the weak and the sick, need not serve, but will receive food for their needs from the public treasury.[4] As births and new marriages or the Taiping's advances lead to new families joining the ranks, from every five such families a new corporal shall be created, and from every twenty-five a new sergeant, and so on up the ranks. Reports of merit even of the humblest soldier shall also be passed up the ranks from sergeant to lieutenant and so to the Heavenly King himself, so that promotions can be made and rewards given. All officers and officials, even the highest, shall be reviewed every three years, and promoted or demoted according to performance.[5]

Though all of this ideal system cannot be implemented at once, at least the listings and the rosters can be prepared and reviewed so that when the times allow, the Taiping leaders will be ready to act. From the earliest days of the Taiping's entry into their Heavenly Capital of Nanjing, censuses have been taken of the people, and the lists kept up to date and duly passed up through the ranks.[6] From the details entered on a specific family record, such as that of the Liangs, one can see whence they have come, the extent of their loyalty, and who is left still to serve. Liang himself, now thirty-four, born and raised in Guiping, joined the Taiping forces at Jintian in August 1850; in September he was named a sergeant, in October raised to captain. After the capture of Yongan he was raised to colonel and then to general, in which rank he still serves. His father is deceased in Guiping, his mother is a general of the women's Fourth Rear Army. His wife holds a position in the office of court embroideries; his sister is an official messenger in the North King's court. His children still are under age. Of his three brothers, one has died in combat, two are currently not serving in the Taiping army.[7]

The military rosters, by contrast, do not list every family member, but give the age and provenance of each soldier, so their commanders can check their careers and capabilities at a glance. Thus Sergeant Ji, in the Thirteenth Army's forward battalion, now twenty-six, is also a Guiping man, who joined the Taiping at Jintian in September 1850, and rose to sergeant after the capture of Wuchang. His assistant sergeant Wang, only eighteen years old, was born in Wuchang and joined the Taiping when they took the city in January 1853, and named to assistant sergeant after the capture of Nanjing. Sergeant Ji's five corporals are aged nineteen, thirty-five, twenty-six, thirty, and twenty-three, and are all from the provinces of central China, not from Guangxi. The private soldiers in their squads range in age from seventeen to fifty-one. Six other men are listed as soldiers in the platoon, but classified as "off-the-registers" because of youth or age. One of these men is fifty-nine, the other five are youngsters, whose ages range from eleven years old to fifteen.[8]

Not everyone flocks eagerly to the Taiping ranks. Households are often

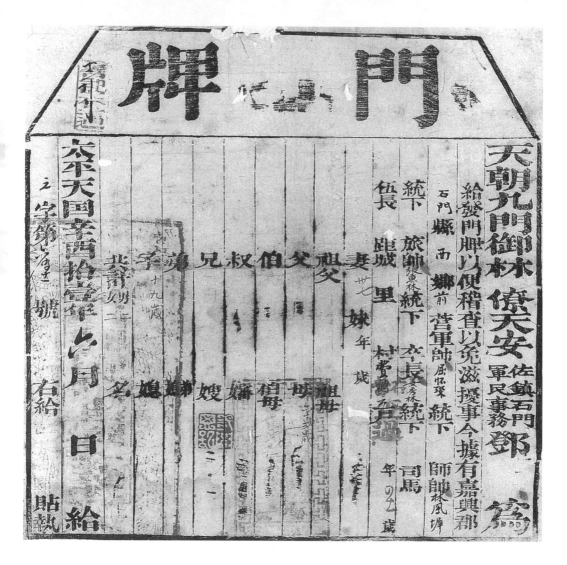

Taiping household register. Registration forms of this kind were issued by the Taiping authorities to all households in the areas that came under their control. The information on such forms enabled the local Taiping military commanders (whose names are entered on the right-hand side of the form) to calculate taxes due, and the availability of family members for military service. In this example, the household head is listed as being a certain Fei Heyun, aged forty-one, resident of a village in the western sector of Shimen county (some fifty miles northeast of Hangzhou in northern Zhejiang). With Fei live his wife, aged thirty-seven, his mother of sixty-two, and a son aged nineteen. To prevent any chance of the form being tampered with, a column on the left records that this household contains two male and two female residents. The document is dated the sixth month of the Taiping Kingdom's eleventh year, equivalent to July 1861 in the Western calendar, when the Taiping were at the peak of their expansion into the coastal region of China.

reluctant to register their members, and prevaricate for weeks, sometimes until threatened with death for their delays. Some Nanjing residents hide out in their own or close friends' homes, on some occasions walling off back areas of their courtyards and trying to conceal their family members there. Some hide themselves in closets if the Taiping come, while others simply live in the wooded hills of deserted areas of the city, the huge extent of which makes such a fugitive existence possible even in the midst of the Taiping's own Heavenly Capital.[9] One ingenious merchant establishes special institutes to manufacture luxury embroideries and face powder for the women's quarters of the Taiping leaders, which assures the workers he employs of special perquisites and freedom to roam in search of rare materials, for the Taiping women dress boldly and garishly, and are heavily made-up, despite the puritanical pronouncements of their leaders. The same merchant, emboldened by his success, gets permission to assemble squads to gather firewood in the outer suburbs, and transport it to the capital in boats; many use this brief taste of freedom to vanish altogether into the countryside.[10]

In areas recently occupied by the Taiping, where the locals are not known at all to the occupiers, the local villagers and townspeople are left free to choose their own corporals, sergeants, and lieutenants, by whatever criteria they choose. They are even handed the blank forms in bulk, so they can circulate them in their neighborhoods, and omit none of the information on family members that the Taiping require of them. Once the rosters have been checked by Taiping officers, each household is issued an official doorplate with the relevant information written on it, to be publicly displayed as proof they have complied with the regulations of the Heavenly Kingdom.[11]

The problems of dealing with the followers of non-Taiping religions are handled by the leaders in different ways. Taoists and Buddhists get short shrift: the numerous Taoist and Buddhist temples within Nanjing's walls, many of them treasures of architecture centuries old, are burned to the ground. The statues and images are smashed, the priests are stripped or killed. Those who survive must conform to the new Taiping religion, and Taiping soldiers preach the new religion with drawn swords in their hands, to underline the message.[12] But the Chinese Muslims in Nanjing are not attacked so savagely, and the mosques already established in the city are allowed to stand.[13]

One group of religious Chinese in Nanjing are in a position of particular ambiguity, because of their apparent closeness to the Taiping troops' beliefs—these are the Catholic converts, who number about two hundred.

In the brief days of siege before the Taiping storm the city, these families store all their valuables for safekeeping in the mansion of the Ju family, for they are the wealthiest Catholics in the city. But one day after the Manchu citadel has fallen, the Ju family home is commandeered as the residence for a senior Taiping official, and all the property is confiscated for the common treasury. At least thirty of the Catholics are burned in their homes or cut down in the streets, during the first harsh days of chaos, before order is restored.[14]

The survivors gather in the Catholic church, where Taiping soldiers find them; when the Catholics refuse to recite the prayers according to the Taiping liturgy, they are given a three-day grace period, but warned that thereafter death will be the penalty for those who still resist. Good Friday is on the twenty-fifth of March in 1853, and as they begin their service of the adoration of the cross Taiping soldiers burst into the church, breaking the cross and overturning their altar. The seventy to eighty Catholic men, arms tied behind their backs, are given a rapid trial before a Taiping judge, and condemned to death unless they say the Taiping prayers. They refuse, expecting martyrdom. But for no clear reason a reprieve is given, and while their womenfolk and children gather in the church, the men, still bound, are locked in a nearby storehouse, where they spend their Easter Sunday. By the day after Easter, twenty-two of the Chinese Catholic men have recited the Taiping prayers, finding nothing in them that specifically contradicts their faith. The others, still obdurate, are sent off to serve at the front as soldiers—where ten desert—or as laborers.[15]

In order to make all the necessary registration forms, and also to print enough Bibles and copies of the Taiping sacred texts for all the sergeants who need them for their reading and preaching, it is necessary to marshal the forces of the printing industry of Nanjing. The ranks of the local printers are swelled—after the Taiping capture of Yangzhou in April 1853—by numbers of Yangzhou craftsmen relocated to Nanjing, some of them masters at using metal movable type, fonts of which had been brought north by officials once stationed in Canton. The headquarters for these Taiping printing operations, suitably enough, are in the former Temple of the God of Literature, revered by Confucian scholars.[16]

The forms are easy to make, and require little skill, but the word of God is a different matter. It seems to be chance—or the fact that this is the particular edition that the Heavenly King has with him for several years for his own use and study—that leads the Taiping to rely on the version of the Bible translated by Karl Gutzlaff in Hong Kong, rather than any of the various other versions available, including later corrected versions by Gutzlaff himself.[17] The first book of the Bible that the Taiping publish is the *Book of Genesis,* chapters 1 through 28, from the creation of the world through Jacob's dream of the ladder, on which the angels ascended and descended to and from Heaven. Though Genesis has fifty chapters altogether, the Taiping leaders close this opening volume with the words of the True God to Jacob at the end of chapter 28, for these will have especial force to anyone among the Taiping faithful who can read or hear:

> And he dreamed, and behold a ladder set up on the earth, and the top of it reached to heaven: and behold the angels of God ascending and descending on it. And, behold, the Lord stood above it, and said, I am the Lord God of Abraham, thy father, and the God of Isaac: the land whereon thou liest, to thee will I give it, and to thy seed; and thy seed shall be as the dust of the earth, and thou shalt spread abroad to the west, and to the east, and to the north, and to the south: and in thee and in thy seed shall all the families of the earth be blessed. And, behold, I am with thee, and will keep thee in all places to which thou goest, and will bring thee again into this land; for I will not leave thee, until I have done that which I have spoken to thee of.
>
> And Jacob awaked out of his sleep, and he said, Surely the Lord is in this place; and I knew it not. (Genesis 28:12–16)

Even though the Chinese translation is not that fluid or perfect—and at times not even clear—the Taiping block carvers are instructed to print all twenty-eight chapters directly from Gutzlaff's text, just as they find them, not excluding the numbers of each verse that are inserted among the columns. There is only one exception, something the Taiping leaders find so shameful that they cannot put it in their people's hands. That is the last eight verses of Genesis 19, where Lot, after the destruction of Sodom and Gomorrah, and the death of his wife, retreats with his two surviving daughters to a cave above Zoar. Hong himself knows full well, from his Confucian texts, and his experiences at Thistle Mountain and Guanlubu, the paradoxes that can attend the filial child who seeks to perpetuate the family line. But this story is different from any in the Chinese tradition, as Lot's eldest daughter speaks to her sister:

> And the first-born said unto the younger, Our father is old, and there is not a man in the earth to come in unto us after the manner of all the earth. Come, let us make our father drink wine, and we will lie with him, that we may preserve seed of our father. And they made their father drink wine that night: and the first-born went in, and lay with her father; and he perceived

not when she lay down, nor when she arose. And it came to pass on the next day, that the first-born said unto the younger, Behold I lay last night with my father: let us make him drink wine this night also; and go thou in, and lie with him, that we may preserve seed of our father. And they made their father drink wine that night also: and the younger arose, and lay with him; and he perceived not when she lay down, nor when she arose. Thus were both the daughters of Lot with child by their father. (Genesis 19:31–38)

Faced with the moral implications of such a passage that they have no means to explain away—especially given their own insistence on the force of the seventh commandment—the Taiping leaders cut the verses altogether, continuing the Bible story with Genesis 20. In practical terms, the cut is easy, for the offending verses fall at the end of a chapter, and there is no problem of continuity between Lot's flight from Zoar and the story of Abraham and Abimelech, which follows.[18]

With at least four hundred men in Nanjing employed in the job of transcribing the characters and carving the blocks, the Taiping work moves swiftly forward. The rest of Genesis is published, and Exodus too, by the summer of 1853. By winter, with the numbers working on the printing project grown to six hundred craftsmen, the Taiping complete Leviticus and Numbers from Gutzlaff's version, faithfully transcribing the long lists of odd-sounding names and the minutest dietary and sacrificial details, and making no further cuts, for there is less that they find shocking here. Amidst the maze of technical details, one can find important reinforcement for the Taiping's own precise regulations for the listing and organizing of the faithful, even though in the Bible the troops are older, and women are not included:

> And the Lord spoke unto Moses in the wilderness of Sinai, in the tabernacle of the congregation, on the first day of the second month, in the second year after they were come out of the land of Egypt, saying, Take ye the sum of all the congregation of the children of Israel, after their families, by the house of their fathers, with the number of their names, every male by their polls; from twenty years old and upward, all who are able to go forth to war in Israel: thou and Aaron shall number them by their armies. And with you there shall be a man of every tribe, every one head of the house of his fathers. (Numbers 1:1–4)

Also that winter the Taiping publish the first of the Gospels, that of Matthew, in its entirety.[19]

Nanjing is, for now, the Heavenly Capital, and to protect it the great

Taiping armies are divided into three: one to defend the city itself, one to sail and march back up the Yangzi River to recapture and consolidate control over the cities bypassed—or captured and abandoned—in the headlong rush downriver in the spring of 1853, and one to march overland to the north, cutting through the heartland of China and threatening Peking itself.[20] In either December 1853 or January 1854 those with enough education to write a polished essay who have stayed on in Nanjing are invited by the Taiping leaders to submit essays on the three major strategic decisions that Hong Xiuquan has taken: the selection of Nanjing as the capital, the Taiping printing and publishing program, and the altering of place-names in China.

In praising the choice of Nanjing as the Heavenly Capital, the various scholars assemble a range of reasons: the direct intervention and support of God and the Elder Brother Jesus are of course central factors. But also emphasized by many are more mundane topics: the city's high, thick walls, its full granaries, its favorable topography—"like a crouching tiger and a coiling dragon"—the "elegant, simple, and generous" customs of its inhabitants, and the prosperity of its markets and its agricultural hinterlands. Others write of Nanjing's admirable river communications, the city's reputation as a "realm of happiness," its "concentration of material wealth" and location as a prime grain-producing area, the wideness of its streets, its historical resonance as a prosperous and fortunate city, and its natural role as the end of a geographical and temporal sequence that brought the Taiping armies from Thistle Mountain through Yongan to Wuchang.

Riskily but boldly, one of the scholars, a native from the Guiping area of Guangxi who once passed the licentiate's examination that Hong Xiuquan failed, brings up the problem of the right to rule. Across all time, he writes, since God first created Heaven and earth, there have been those who have turned against their rulers; thus "regicide and usurpation were frequent, and chaos and change continued until the present." But this process, far from being repeated by Hong, was by his goodness brought to a close. For "our Heavenly King personally received God's mandate and will eternally rule over the mountains and rivers. The righteous uprising in Jintian signaled the formation of a valiant and invincible army, and the establishment of the capital in Nanjing lays an everlastingly firm foundation. The capital is called the Heavenly Capital in accordance with Heaven's mandate, and our country is called the Heavenly Kingdom in consonance with God's will."[21]

In praising the printing in Nanjing of an official list of Taiping publica-

tions, each marked with the royal seal of approbation on the title page, the scholars serving the Taiping again speak much of divine will and of Hong's majesty. "When Heaven produces an extraordinary man, it must have an extraordinary task for him to do. When Heaven has an extraordinary task, it must have an extraordinary treasure to facilitate its completion." But some talk with more precision of the need to purify the Chinese language after its corruption by the "demonic language and barbarian words of the Tartar dogs."[22] Other scholars praise the use of such seals on the books as a proof of authenticity at this early period of the Heavenly Kingdom when "authenticity and falsehood of books are hard to distinguish." Particularly when such books are circulated among the armies in the field, "suspicion may be mixed with belief and the demons use all sorts of tricks." Furthermore, since the restructuring of literature and of culture is one of the prime proofs that a true leader has once more emerged on earth, spreading such clearly authenticated books will show all people, great and small, near and far, that such a new leader is now come.[23] Yet other scholars link the word of God on earth as exemplified in three books especially, the Old Testament, the New, and Hong's own proclamations. With these three circulating in authenticated editions, "the road to Heaven is now in sight," and the day of their "secrecy" will be over; all other works such as those by Confucius and his follower Mencius, along with the "various philosophers and hundred schools," can be safely "burned and eliminated, and no one be permitted to buy, sell, possess, or read them."[24]

The third public task given to the scholars assembled in Nanjing is to comment on Hong Xiuquan's proclamation that henceforth the city of Peking be named the "Demon's Den," and the province of Zhili, in which Peking is situated, be called the "Criminal's Province." At once arcane and direct, Hong's purpose here is to brand the very language given to the region where the Manchus dwell as tainted and improper. Peking, the administrative capital of the Manchu empire, is set in the northern province of Zhili, a name that can be interpreted as "correct" or "attached." Since "the demons have defiled that region," writes Hong, "and the ground they tread is involved in their crimes," the name must be changed to "Zuili," "criminally attached province." Similarly Peking, "the northern capital," must also be abandoned as a name, since there can be no capital other than Nanjing, the Southern and Heavenly Capital. In all military reports and future orders, the former Peking shall be called Yaoxue, the "Demon's Den." When all the demons have been exterminated, the original name of Peking will be restored. And when all in the Criminal's Province "have repented of their sins and begun to worship God our

Heavenly Father," then the Criminal's Province too will have its name changed. But in honor of this transformation it will be given, not its old name, but a new one, "Province Restored to Goodness."[25]

The scholars all praise the celestial wisdom of this proclamation, and their arguments complement each other and overlap. In condemning the more than two hundred years in which the northern region has been occupied by the Manchus, they point to the region's perversions, its dishonesty, its love of idolatry and rejection of the One True God, its gambling and opium smoking, and the slavish nature of the Chinese living there. They also imply that the Manchus are now driven into a corner, and that this is the last area left to them. "With such a small territory," they ask, "how can the demons resist the heavenly troops?" In "their ludicrous self-importance" the Manchus have named their "caves and dens" as an upright province. But having behaved so unpardonably, they have been condemned for all time by the Heavenly Father and Heavenly Elder Brother, Jesus. "Their crimes are too flagrant to be tolerated, and their viciousness is so excessive as to make their extermination certain." Thus the area that the Manchus think they can call their own is in fact "a prison erected by Heaven."[26]

Behind Hong's proclamation, however, lies a deeper truth, a truth about language. Almost all the writers acknowledge in a general way the importance of changing the names to "Demon's Den" and "Criminal's Province," and praise Hong for his wisdom in doing so. But only one, Qiao Yancai, later to be rewarded with the highest honors in the Taiping's newly instituted examination system, gives a slightly fuller explanation of *why* this should be so: "The world has long been deluded by these demonic Tartars, and it is imperative that they be soon destroyed. But before we destroy these people, we must first destroy their bases. And before we can destroy the power of their bases, we must first destroy the bases' names."[27]

It is not only place-names that have this kind of force and resonance. When the presence of the devil demons runs through other names, then they too are changed. Thus Xianfeng, the reigning emperor and by definition leader of the earthly demons, whose name in its correctly written form means "united in glory," has his name rewritten with a dog component added to the original characters, so all can see his dog-like nature. And the word *Ta,* used unflatteringly already as a way to refer to barbarian nomads or "Tartars," is also given a dog component so that all Manchus are mocked alike. The temples where both the Manchu demons and the Chinese idolators worship their false gods are also given their own mocking character, a new coinage that shows that the truth is absent within them.[28]

Other words are freshly created because certain components are too tainted to be used. The words for "soul" and "spirit" fall into this category, whether their basic meaning concerns our animal, sentient, or inferior souls that bind us here on earth, or the spiritual, upward-tending divinely oriented souls that are ours throughout eternity. When the component in such words is *gui,* used commonly for the dead, the spirits and the demons, it is removed, and the simple component for "human being" is used instead. Thus it is our human nature, not our demonic one, that urges us toward our God.[29]

Some characters that represent the forces of the highest good must of course be retained, if no impurity adheres to the composition of the character, but they must then be forever tabooed for any other use. *Ye, huo,* and *hua* are three of these, for they are the ones used to represent the word Jehovah; the characters used to transliterate "Jesus" and "Christ" are also banned from all other use, and accepted substitutes are clearly stipulated, as are those for "Heaven," "holy," "spirit," "God" and "Lord," and "elder brother." The words for "sun" and "moon" must also be written in an altered form, for the original characters in all their purity are reserved for Hong Xiuquan himself, the Sun, and his true wife in Heaven, "the First Chief Moon." The personal names of all five Taiping kings are tabooed from other use, whether like Feng Yunshan and Xiao Chaogui they have left this mortal life, or like Yang and Wei and Shi Dakai they still lead the Taiping troops in earthly combat. The family name of Hong Xiuquan himself, the Heavenly King, also is forbidden to others, replaced by different characters with the same pronunciation.[30]

Yet Hong's name can be incorporated in newly coined characters when their majesty is great enough. The character for the "rainbow" of God's covenant with Noah, pronounced "Hong," like the Heavenly King's own name, is banned from general use. But the new character created in its place, of a rain cloud above and a flood (or Hong) beneath, reminds all who read of the disasters striking earth before the covenant was made. Other characters that can be ambiguous or even sound obscene if pronounced with the Cantonese, Guangxi, or Hakka accents of many of the God-worshipers are changed accordingly. Three of the terms for cyclical days in the calendar are changed for these reasons, and euphemisms are designed for certain basic human functions. For the government of the Heavenly Kingdom, too, certain new words are created: a word for "true unity," another for "pure justice," one for "glory," and one for "distribution by boat of needed food supplies."[31]

The inclusion of a word for "food supplies" in such a list highlights a material problem for the Heavenly Kingdom. Since Yongan, or even earlier, the Taiping have been drawing largely on contributions—some given from religious fervor, others coerced—and from the loot of captured cities put into the common treasury. The huge city of Nanjing, lying in the midst of fertile farmlands, densely cultivated, offers ample food for a time, but there are too many Qing armies in the area to enable the Taiping faithful to establish the units of five families led by their corporals and guided in morality by their sergeants in any permanent form. And questions still remain about the permanence of the Heavenly Capital. If the northern armies overthrow the Qing, will not the Demon's Den, as Hong has promised, be freed from its opprobrium, and the Criminal's Province blossom anew as Province of Restored Goodness?

To highlight the differences between the Heavenly Capital and the Demon's Den, Yang Xiuqing, the East King, has told the Taiping faithful that it is not yet time to end their period of sexual separation.[32] Men who force themselves on women, even if they are veteran soldiers from Guangxi with accumulated merit, must be executed, and even married couples arranging for clandestine reunions, when caught, are sternly punished. Some will seek to avoid these prohibitions by resorting to prostitutes, but that too is strictly forbidden, and enforcement backed by group involvement; those who work as prostitutes, or those who use them, will not only themselves be executed but so will their families. Anyone in the community reporting such improper acts to Taiping authorities, however, will receive special rewards.[33] Male homosexuality is punished with similar severity; if the partners are both aged thirteen or older, both shall be beheaded. If one is less than thirteen, he shall be spared and his partner beheaded, unless the child was an active partner, in which case he too is killed.[34] Even the sending out of clothes by the men to be washed or mended by women in the town is carefully scrutinized and may be harshly punished, for "with this type of intimate contact, love affairs between them cannot be prevented." To avoid the chance of sin, all men should wash and mend for themselves.[35]

Like Wuchang, the city of Nanjing is divided into blocks of men's quarters, and those for women and their children. Within these blocks, as far as practicable, people are arranged, by sex and occupation, into their groups of twenty-five, called *guan*. The world of city life is naturally different from the countryside, and within Nanjing itself the dream of labor shared in common yields to specialization, to keep the people and their leaders sheltered, clothed, and fed. Thus among the *guan* are those for bricklayers, carpenters, and decorators; for tailors and shoemakers; for millers, bakers, soy sauce and beancurd makers; and, in a sense overarching all others, those for medical care, fire fighting, and the burial of the dead. All these workers are meant to labor for the public good, and draw their food from the common treasury.[36] The women are marshaled under their own female leaders—older Guangxi veterans—and clustered in buildings near the Xihua Gate in squads of around twenty-five also called *guan*. The numbers of women under Taiping control grow dramatically, as the cities around Nanjing are seized and occupied by Taiping troops.[37]

To make these newly captured cities true bastions of defense, all commerce and traveling merchants are forbidden inside their gates, and the women and children are shipped off to the Heavenly Capital, leaving the teenage boys and fighting men to guard the walls of the garrison towns. The common treasury sees to the maintenance of these uprooted people in Nanjing. In the stripped-down cities, as also in Nanjing, to preserve security all regular trade and markets are forbidden within the city walls. Whatever supplies can be found must be bought at the stalls clustered around the city gates, where the local farmers soon set up stands for meat and fish, and even teahouses; though the Taiping officers, always watchful, often order that even these little shops be separated by sex, some for male and some for female customers. These stocks can be supplemented by foraging or purchase in the countryside, and by privately arranged barter or trade.[38]

The people of the Heavenly Capital react to these new impositions in many ways—some stay in hiding, some plan to flee, some plot to poison or overthrow the occupiers, others join the Taiping ranks with varying degrees of passion, yearning for the restitution of some family life.[39] There are extra employment opportunities for many people, since though the lieutenants, sergeants, and corporals supervise the lives of their dependent families at the local level, the Taiping kingdom now has a growing bureaucracy of men and women, all with their own staffs and assistants. As the East King explains the situation in a message to Hong Xiuquan: "As a consequence of the great mercy of the Heavenly Father and the Heavenly Elder Brother in sending our ruler, the Second Elder Brother, down into the world to be the true ruler of the ten thousand countries under Heaven, and to establish the Heavenly Capital, heavenly affairs have daily increased in complexity and in number, and people are needed to assist in the administration."[40]

The six central government ministries, with their elegant archaic names drawn from the *Rites of Zhou*—the Ministries of Heaven, of Earth, of Spring, Summer, Autumn, Winter—are largely honorific, the real work being done in the more than fifty departments and agencies ranked under them. These oversee the treasuries and granaries that supply the Heavenly Kingdom. They provide the personnel to supervise the storehouses of gunpowder and shot that supply the armies on campaign, to manufacture war vessels, to provide the robes and embroideries for the kings and their palace women, and to preserve the heavenly decrees and other sacred texts. There are also staff positions for the procurement of cooking oil, salt, and firewood, for the goldsmiths, and for the supplying of fresh water.[41]

Sometimes the various skills must flow together, as with the symbols and calligraphy of the new hats that the Taiping rulers design for themselves. The ceremonial hat for Hong will have a fan-shaped front and be decorated with twin dragons and twin phoenixes. The other kings may each have twin dragons as well, but only a single phoenix. On the upper part of his hat the Heavenly King—and he alone—shall have the embroidered words "the mountains and rivers are unified" and on the lower part the words "the heavens are filled with stars." The three other surviving kings shall each have one line of embroidered calligraphy: for East King Yang, the characters "Lone Phoenix Perching in the Clouds"; for North King Wei, "Lone Phoenix Perching on the Mountain Peak"; for Shi Dakai, the Wing King, "Lone Phoenix Perching on the Peony," accompanied—as a gesture to his youth?—with a single embroidered butterfly.[42]

One group of skilled practitioners constantly in demand are doctors, for most of the scholars specializing in these arts left Nanjing for the shelter of Shanghai or other cities as the Taiping troops approached. In a great city such as Nanjing, there is always the danger of disease, but to the city's normal needs are added now the exigencies of war, with the attendant wounds, the presence of many additional women and their children, some separated from their families at short notice in nearby towns, and the East King, Yang Xiuqing, whose problems with his eyes and ears had kept him from the front lines of leadership for a time in Thistle Mountain. Thus the Taiping proclamations, issued by the North King, invite all those living in Taiping areas who have skills at curing diseases of the eyes, handling children with convulsions and other illnesses, and special knowledge of obstetrics to make their names known to any Taiping commanders in their area. Those doing so will be given special escorts to the Heavenly Capital and—if their skills are real—high-ranking office and a huge cash payment of ten thousand taels (each tael roughly one ounce) of silver. Their term of service completed—the length of time is nowhere specified—they will "be sent back to their native place in peace."[43]

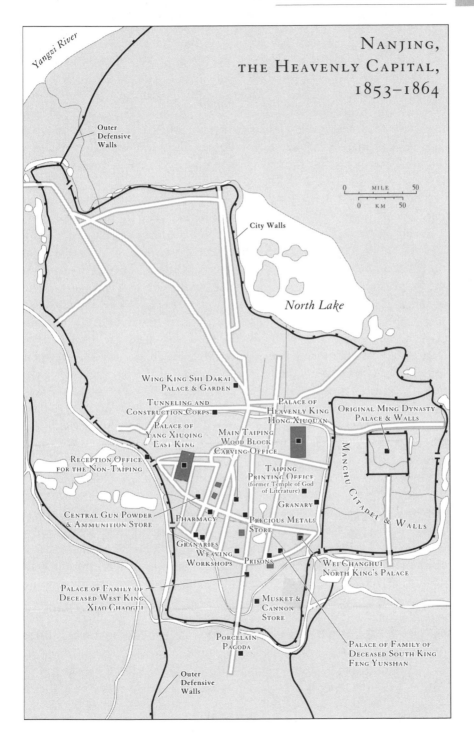

Yangzi River

NANJING,
THE HEAVENLY CAPITAL,
1853–1864

Outer
Defensive
Walls

City Walls

0   MILE   50

0   KM   50

North Lake

WING KING SHI DAKAI
PALACE & GARDEN

PALACE OF
HEAVENLY KING
HONG XIUQUAN

TUNNELING AND
CONSTRUCTION CORPS

PALACE OF
YANG XIUQING
EAST KING

MAIN TAIPING
WOOD BLOCK
CARVING OFFICE

ORIGINAL MING DYNASTY
PALACE & WALLS

RECEPTION OFFICE
FOR THE NON-TAIPING

TAIPING
PRINTING OFFICE
(former Temple of God
of Literature)

MANCHU CITADEL & WALLS

GRANARY

CENTRAL GUN POWDER
& AMMUNITION STORE

PHARMACY

PRECIOUS METALS
STORE

GRANARIES
WEAVING
WORKSHOPS

PRISONS

WEI CHANGHUI
NORTH KING'S PALACE

PALACE OF FAMILY OF
DECEASED WEST KING
XIAO CHAOGUI

MUSKET &
CANNON
STORE

PORCELAIN
PAGODA

PALACE OF FAMILY OF
DECEASED SOUTH KING
FENG YUNSHAN

Outer
Defensive
Walls

The North King expresses regret that doctors have not responded in the past to Taiping pleas, but hopes now that the higher rank and cash payments will be sufficient inducements. "None should hide their talents," for they were given to them by God "for benefit of all mankind."[44] Enough doctors are attracted by these or other means at least to staff the hospitals for the seriously ill—known, so as not to discourage the patients, as "institutes for the able-bodied"—and to provide some basic medical care in each of the sixty zones into which the Heavenly City has been divided. Others are assigned to the neighboring garrison towns, to help those wounded in combat.[45]

The Heavenly Capital needs fitting palaces for the kingdom's rulers. Part of the Taiping plan is implemented here, in that all those with skills at carpentry, masonry, and decoration are called to pool their skills and labor to create the palaces. Ten thousand people work for six months on the splendid palace built for their Heavenly King, ten times grander than the former magistrate's residence in Yongan. This palace rises on the site of the former governor-general's mansion, at the center of the northern side of the main residential city.[46] After the first few days of the occupation, the leaders move into the main city, using what is still salvageable from the old buildings in the ravaged Manchu citadel to decorate their grand new palaces. When Hong's almost completed palace complex accidentally burns down, in late 1853, as many more hands—some from Nanjing and some from neighboring provinces—are recruited to rebuild among the ruins, and to decorate the walls and pillars with the colorful paintings of birds, animals, and mountain scenery that the leaders seem to value most.[47]

Much of the energy and cost for building goes not into palaces but into defense of the Heavenly Capital, or the newly conquered or reconquered towns that lie beyond. Within Nanjing, the great city gates are at first cleared of the obstructions and the sacks of earth put there by Qing troops in their fruitless defense. But within a few days, under the constant threat of counterattacks by government forces, the gateways are reinforced with stone, and the passageways through them narrowed so that only one file of people at a time can pass through; the gates themselves are repaired, and additional gates built in front of or behind the existing ones, so that one leaf at a time can be opened without rendering the whole defensive system vulnerable. Emplacements for cannon—two per gate—are constructed, and special encampments reinforced with palisades for the gunners and the other troops on gate duty. At intervals across the city, and beyond the walls in the forward defensive encampments, wooden watch-towers are raised, to a height of thirty or even forty feet. Here veteran soldiers stand the watches, supplied with colored flags to make the signals that can warn from which direction any demon attacks are launched.[48]

The smaller towns nearby—though lacking Nanjing's mighty walls and gates—are defended with a care designed to give even the largest demon army pause; the houses near the city walls are burned or torn down to remove the possibility of cover, and the open spaces crisscrossed with ditches, palisades, and felled trees with obtruding branches. Whole areas are honeycombed with small round holes, a foot across and two feet deep, lightly camouflaged with grass or straw, so that any rapid movement or transportation of heavy loads is impossible. Between these barriers lie fields of sharpened bamboo stakes, their spikes four inches or so above the ground, so sharp they rip bare feet and go through any shoe, so close together that only by moving slowly one step at a time can one pass through them. Tens of thousands of such stakes are made and sharpened by the civilian populations of the occupied towns, working as ordered through the nights. Where stone for walls is lacking, the doors and floors of all the city houses have been commandeered and fastened in serried rows to two high lines of posts, five feet or so apart, and the space between them filled with pounded earth.[49]

Beyond the walls of the heavenly havens, in the land the Taipings pray will soon become the Earthly Paradise, the war is one of guile and cruelty. Just as the demons find it hard to pierce walls so defended, so the heavenly troops are cautious when they venture forth to cities abandoned by the enemy. The Taiping troops are warned by their commanders, "The demons sometimes bury gunpowder and shot under the ground and camouflage it with straw, fresh earth, or bamboo leaves. Sometimes they conceal a bow and arrow so that anyone coming in contact with it releases the arrow. Sometimes they conceal spikes or iron nails under wooden bars, or sometimes they dig pits." Umbrellas, apparently abandoned on the ground, conceal shot and gunpowder in their handles, which are triggered when the umbrella is opened. Precious objects lying on the ground are linked to fuses and explode when one picks them up. Even innocent-looking documents may contain concealed arrows or explosives that fire or erupt when the document is opened. Such demon tricks "cannot be detected by the eye," the troops are told. Anticipation and wariness are the only methods of defense.[50]

Secure for now behind the stakes and walls and ditches, with the watchers in their towers around him, and his women at his side, Hong Xiuquan surveys his kingdom. He knows that the naming of all under Heaven is now within his personal purview. It is his royal writing brush that contains all things, all mysteries. As once the vocabulary of China's children was learned from the *Thousand Character Essay,* which gave the essence of the language to those who had mastered their "Three Character Classic," so now the subjects of the Heavenly King will learn from Hong's own "Imperially Written Tale of a Thousand Words" not only the history of their origins but the very words with which to phrase them:

> Our Great Lord God
> Is One. There is no other.
> In the beginning He showed his skills,
> Creating Heaven and earth.
> When the myriad things were all
> complete
> He gave life to men on earth,
> Dividing lightness and darkness
> So day and night came in succession.
> Sun and moon each shone their light,
> Stars and constellations formed an order.
> The winds reached to the four directions,
> Fierce and harsh they blew.
> Far off, the clouds gathered
> And rain fell from the void.
> After the flood waters ebbed away
> God in compassion made a Covenant:
> Never again to send such a deluge—
> The rainbow would stand as His sign.
> He slew the devils, wiped out the demons,
> Thunder crashed and lightning struck.[51]

Now that Hong's name is in the rainbow, he partakes both of God's wrath and of His mercy. The proof of this, for the Heavenly King, is in the present:

> The capital is established near Zhong Mountain;
> The palaces and thresholds are brilliant and shining;
> The forests and gardens are fragrant and flourishing;
> Epidendrums and cassia complement each other in beauty.
> The forbidden palace is magnificent;
> Buildings and pavilions a hundred stories high.
> Halls and gates are beautiful and lustrous;
> Bells and chimes sound musically.

The towers reach up to the sky;
Upon altars sacrificial animals are burned.
Cleansed and purified,
We fast and bathe.
We are respectful and devout in worship,
Dignified and serene in prayer.
Supplicating with fervor,
Each seeks happiness and joy.
The uncivilized and border peoples offer tribute,
And all the barbarians are submissive.
No matter how vast the territory,
All will eventually be under our rule.[52]

14

THREE
SHIPS

There are three large foreign ships moored off the Shanghai waterfront as the Heavenly King enters his Earthly Paradise: the *Hermes,* the *Cassini,* and the *Susquehanna.* The first is British, the second French, the third American. Over the weeks preceding and immediately following Nanjing's fall, the local Qing officials have been asking the foreigners to intervene, to help maintain law and order in the Yangzi valley, or failing that at least to guard the Shanghai gates with reliable troops and suppress piracy on the river. Far from their home government's reassuring presence, each of the ships' commanders has to decide whether to intervene or not, and if so to what extent.[1] As the French captain of the *Cassini* puts it in a journal entry, in such a situation "one can either perform a real service or commit stupid mistakes."[2]

Over their shared dinners on one another's vessels, the captains and the consuls of the three nations discuss far into the night their national strategies and feasible options, and whether or not to summon their missionaries from other towns to find shelter under their guns in Shanghai.[3] Rumors of every kind about the atrocities committed in Nanjing swirl through the countryside, and Shanghai is filled with terrified inhabitants—the mere appearance of four long-haired rebels in one neighboring market town sets off a stampede of fear in which twenty-seven Chinese are trampled to death.[4] The British and Americans pledge themselves to form a defensive militia and to dig trenches and gun emplacements at strategic points around their own settlement areas, though they differ on how to approach the crisis: the British land seventy sailors in early April, and put them in a fortified house on the edge of Soochow Creek, while the Americans decide not to send men ashore until disaster actually happens, though they do make exceptions for the members of their ship's band, who charm all assembled at the theater with their spirited renderings of "The Young Reefer" and "Harlequin Golden Lily." As for the French captain, he decides to land his men only if the life of the French consul is threatened.[5]

When in late April 1853 the British plenipotentiary, Sir George Bonham, gives orders to sail the *Hermes* to Nanjing, it is to the chagrin of the captain of the American vessel, which has just run aground attempting the same feat.[6] Bonham is egged on by the most influential British merchants in Shanghai, worried over the total disruption of all commerce, but also by simple human curiosity.[7] The few items of information that the Westerners have gathered on the Taiping over the previous two years, drawn mainly from the period of the Taiping's occupation of Yongan, have been vague and contradictory, blurring the lines between the secret societies and the God-worshipers, muddling the names of the Taiping leaders, and attempting to ascertain if they are really Christians or not.[8] In Canton, Issachar Roberts, prompted to recollection by Hong Xiuquan's victories, now underplays his refusal to give Hong baptism, and writes in a local newspaper that Hong Xiuquan, during their period of study together, had "maintained a blameless deportment." Roberts recalls Hong clearly enough to give the first physical description of the Heavenly King recorded by a Westerner: "He is a man of ordinary appearance, about five feet four or five inches high; well built, round faced, regular featured, rather handsome, about middle age, and gentlemanly in his manners." Hong may have made his name as a "destroyer of idolatry," writes Roberts, but seems now to act "something in the capacity of a prophet" and appears to be "struggling for religious liberty."[9]

The question, to the British especially, whose trading interests and investments in Shanghai's buildings, docks, and trade are estimated already at around twenty-five million pounds sterling, is whether the Taiping offer greater chances for current stability and future expansion of trade than the reigning Qing.[10] For the time being, as Bonham writes to the Foreign Office from Shanghai on the eve of Hong's entrance into Nanjing, he has decided "not to interfere in any shape in favour of the Chinese Government, as I feel confident that any such interference on my part could only prolong the struggle."[11] The need to imprint this stance of British neutrality firmly on the Taiping mind by a personal visit is uppermost in Bonham's mind, since at least one wealthy American merchant has already leased one of his vessels to the Qing forces, as have several Portuguese traders in Macao, while the Qing intendant in Shanghai has also been buying up on his own initiative any foreign vessels that he can find.[12]

The British consul's own interpreter, T. T. Meadows, who tries to keep abreast of all the latest news or rumors on the Taiping, concurs that foreign interference on behalf of the Qing would "only have the effect of prolonging hostilities and anarchy for an indefinite period"; while if the British stayed on the sidelines, it was "highly probable" that the whole of China's southern provinces and the Yangzi valley would be solidified by the Taiping "under the rule of a purely Chinese dynasty as one internally strong State."[13] At the same time the interpreter Meadows, making a reconnaissance trip on his own across country to the banks of the Yangzi, and coordinating his observations with the reports of his own personally dispatched "Chinese messengers" and his Chinese-language teacher, concludes that the Taiping forces consist of thirty to forty thousand original "long hair" insurgents and their eighty thousand to one hundred thousand later additional recruits and "pressed men." They are, as a rule, "puritanical and even fanatic," punishing rape, adultery, and opium smoking with death, placing their women in separate buildings, and with "the whole army pray[ing] regularly before meals."[14]

As a result of these various baffling reports, Bonham feels "unwilling to rest" until he has personally ascertained "the intentions of the insurgents towards foreigners." The task will be difficult, perhaps dangerous, because the Qing officials have taken their own initiative by spreading proclamations that "the ships of the barbarian volunteers" are all now on the Qing side, and that the British are all "filled with a strong feeling of common hatred to the rebels" and themselves ready to pay all the necessary expenses needed to "exterminate" the Taiping.[15]

The departure of the British armed steamship *Hermes* for Nanjing on April 22, 1853, is thus a scouting expedition that might or might not become the basis of policy formation. But rapidly it also becomes something else, a battle for dignity. Sir George Bonham has many responsibilities and many titles: he is superintendent of foreign trade, governor of

Hong Kong, and the minister plenipotentiary to China of the British crown. But Hong Xiuquan is the Heavenly King presiding over the Celestial Capital. In the delicate balance of prestige and power, while it is certainly all right for the interpreter Meadows and even perhaps the *Hermes*'s captain, E. G. Fishbourne, to meet with lower-ranking Taiping officials, for Bonham only a meeting with Hong Xiuquan himself or one of the other "kings" will permit a conversation between equals to take place. The Taiping response on April 28 to Sir George Bonham's request for such a high-level meeting is not encouraging:

> Commands are hereby issued to the brethren from afar that they may all understand the rules of ceremony.
> Whereas God the Heavenly Father has sent our Sovereign down on earth, as the true Sovereign of all nations in the world, all people in the world who wish to appear at his Court must yield obedience to the rules of ceremony. They must prepare representations, stating who and what they are and from whence they come, after previous presentation of which only can audience be accorded them. Obey these commands.[16]

Bonham's response, delivered orally to the Taiping, is preordained: the "improper mode" of the document and the "very objectionable manner" in which it was written could not be accepted; "it was further stated to them in plain terms that productions of this nature could not for an instant be tolerated by the British authorities."[17]

As the interpreter Meadows elaborates in a conversation with the Heavenly King's brother-in-law Lai,

> ... while the English had, for 900 years, adored the Great Being whom he called the Heavenly Father, they on earth acknowledged allegiance to but one Lord, the Sovereign of the British Empire; and that, under no circumstances whatsoever, would they for an instant admit fealty to any other, though they were quite prepared to recognize as the Sovereign of the Chinese whomsoever the Chinese themselves might choose or submit to as such.[18]

Bonham, using the "boisterous" weather on the Yangzi as his excuse, but in fact fearing that some "difficulties in the way of ceremonial" might precipitate a quarrel with the Taiping leaders, stays on the *Hermes*, expressing his willingness to meet there personally with any of the subordinate Taiping kings. When they send Hong Xiuquan's brother-in-law Lai, Bonham stays on his ship and communicates in writing only, reasserting both Britain's neutrality in the current conflict, and reminding the

Taiping leaders of the provisions of the Nanjing treaty of 1842—to which the British intend to adhere—and their firm determination to defend their property in Shanghai should any Taiping troops decide to attack that city. In the event, Bonham never goes ashore in Nanjing.

The interpreter Meadows, however, and Captain Fishbourne, do go ashore, and are well received and permitted to travel some distance within the walls. They are also granted lengthy interviews by the North King and the Wing King in a residence in the northern part of the city, not far from where the *Hermes* rides at anchor. After initial attempts to intimidate the two men—they are marched between double rows of Taiping retainers, ordered to kneel, remove their swords, stand while the officials remain seated, and to watch as the guides who had led them this far are publicly beaten for their daring—the interpreter Meadows responds to the North King's question whether he worshiped "God the Heavenly Father" by repeating his response that "the English had done so for eight or nine hundred years," and the atmosphere at once changes.[19] As Meadows then records his conversation with the leader who first sheltered Hong Xiuquan six years before in the hills to the east of Thistle Mountain:

> He stated that as children and worshippers of one God we were all brethren; and after receiving my assurance that such had long been our view also, inquired if I knew the "Heavenly Rules" (Teen teaon). I replied that I was most likely acquainted with them, though unable to recognize them under that name, and, after a moment's thought, asked if they were ten in number. He answered eagerly in the affirmative. I then began repeating the substance of the first of the Ten Commandments, but had not proceeded far before he laid his hand on my shoulder in a friendly way, and exclaimed, "The same as ourselves! the same as ourselves!" while the simply observant expression on the face of his companion disappeared before one of satisfaction as the two exchanged glances. He then stated, with reference to my previous inquiry as to their feelings and intentions towards the British, that not merely might peace exist between us, but that we might be intimate friends.[20]

To Captain Fishbourne, the Taiping he meets seem "clever, decided, and determined" but also "civil and good-humored." They accept the Bibles (both English- and Chinese-language versions) that he offers them with a grave and moving gratitude, and look thoughtfully through copies of the *Illustrated London News* that he gives them, and are delighted when he says they can take copies home with them. Taiping visitors gaze in admiration through the spyglass that he demonstrates for them, and clamber up the ship's rigging or examine the ship's steam boilers and engines when Fishbourne at times allows them on board the *Hermes*. The Taiping are pleased to see the Westerners wear their hair long, like themselves, and one brave youth even takes off Sir George Bonham's top hat to see if the plenipotentiary himself has the same hairstyle as the rest. Informal trade flourishes, the Taiping trading jade and silver for the crewmen's two-edged swords, and offering to trade silver for musical boxes.[21]

Despite the formalism of the initial Taiping document on Britain's sub-servient status, the apparent sincerity and openness of the Taiping troops and officers they encounter seems to lull the British into a sense that all is moving calmly in the direction of mutual understanding. They spend their time working on their diplomatic statements and collecting copies of all the Taiping publications they can find—amassing twelve in all.[22] Accordingly the reply to their diplomatic initiatives that they receive on board the *Hermes* on May 2—hand-delivered by the Heavenly King's brother-in-law Lai—leaves them dumbfounded. The missive is signed with the names of Yang Xiuqing, East King, using his fully panoply of titles, and of the West King, Xiao Chaogui (no Westerners are yet aware that Xiao died in combat at Changsha eight months before). As translated rapidly for Bonham by the interpreter Meadows, Yang's message reads:

A decree to the distant English, who have long recognized the duty of worshipping Heaven (God), and who have recently come into the views of our royal master, especially enjoining upon them to set their minds at rest and harbour no unworthy suspicions.

The Heavenly Father, the Supreme Lord, the Great God, in the begin-ning created heaven and earth, land and sea, men and things, in six days; from that time to this the whole world has been one family, and all within the four seas brethren: how can there exist, then, any difference between man and man; or how any distinction between principal and secondary birth? But from the time that the human race has been influenced by the demoniacal agency which has entered into the heart of man, they have ceased to acknowledge the great benevolence of God the Heavenly Father in giving and sustaining life, and ceased to appreciate the infinite merit of the expiatory sacrifice made by Jesus, our Celestial Elder Brother, and have, with lumps of clay, wood, and stone, practised perversity in the world. Hence it is that the Tartar hordes and Elfin Huns so fraudulently robbed us of our Celestial territory (China). But, happily, Our Heavenly Father and Celestial Elder Brother have from an early date displayed their miraculous power amongst you English, and you have long acknowledged the duty of worshipping God the Heavenly Father and Jesus Our Celestial Brother, so that the truth has been preserved entire, and the Gospel maintained. . . .

Now that you distant English "have not deemed myriads of miles too far to come" and acknowledge our sovereignty; not only are the soldiers and officers of our Celestial dynasty delighted and gratified thereby, but even in high heaven itself Our Celestial Father and Elder Brother will also admire this manifestation of your fidelity and truth. We therefore issue this special decree, permitting you, the English Chief, to lead your brethren out or in, backwards or forwards, in full accordance with your own will or wish, whether to aid us in exterminating our impish foes, or to carry on your commercial operations as usual; and it is our earnest hope that you will, with us, earn the merit of diligently serving our royal master, and, with us, recompense the goodness of the Father of Spirits.

Wherefore we promulgate this new decree of (our Sovereign) Taiping for the information of you English, so that all the human race may learn to worship Our Heavenly Father and Celestial Elder Brother, and that all may know that, wherever our royal master is, there men unite in congratulating him on having obtained the decree to rule.[23]

In a curt reply to "the Insurgent Chiefs," Bonham rejects the document, "part of which," as he puts it, he is "unable to understand, and especially that portion which implies that the English are subordinate to your Sovereign." Should either the Taiping or anyone else, he adds, "presume to injure, in any manner, the persons or property of British subjects, immediate steps will be taken to resent the injury in the same manner as similar injuries were resented ten years ago, resulting in the capture of Chinkiang, Nanking, and the neighbouring cities." (The British had, in fact, not captured Nanjing in 1842, merely threatened it with their artillery, but this is not the time for historical niceties.)[24] Ordering the anchors of the *Hermes* raised, Bonham has Fishbourne set full steam for Shanghai, which they reach in thirty-three hours. On the way to Nanjing the week before, when nervous Taiping garrisons, misled by the Qing propaganda, fired on the *Hermes,* Bonham practiced complete restraint and refused to run out his guns. On the homeward journey, when the same thing happens, he orders the *Hermes* to return the fire.[25]

Bonham's mind is now made up. While the cultured missionary-interpreter W. H. Medhurst reports to him, after perusing the twelve Taiping tracts acquired in Nanjing, that the Taiping appear to be "in some respects better" than the Europeans, Bonham brushes the suggestion aside. As he tells his superiors in Whitehall, the Taiping religion appears to him a "spurious revelation," with a true Old Testament base perhaps, but "superadded thereto a tissue of superstition and nonsense."[26]

The reports and tracts brought back to Shanghai by the *Hermes* fascinate the foreign community and cause new waves of speculation, defensive preparations, and bewilderment. One wealthy British wit—acting as if Hong Xiuquan has deposed the ruling dynasty—renames his racing pony *"Rebel Chief* late *Emperor,"* entering it for the May races, which it wins. [27] The Qing officials are also perturbed by reports that Bonham has traveled to Nanjing to "dine with the Taipings," but are reassured by Bonham in a personal note that such was not the case.[28] The French, who have their own sizable foreign area in Shanghai, are anxious to repeat the initiative of the British but find it hard to make the journey to Nanjing, since there is only one French steam-driven man-of-war in the region, the *Cassini.* The captain of this vessel, François de Plas, is not only an experienced career officer but a recent convert to the Catholic faith, who successfully petitioned the French government to assign him a ship in which he might visit "every point of the globe in which pious missionaries have tried to spread God's word."[29] In France in 1851 de Plas slowly assembled a group of officers and midshipmen who shared his sentiments and goals, and traveled in person to Rome, where the Pope blessed his project. For de Plas, the *Cassini,* with its two paddle wheels driven by 200-horsepower engines, six cannon, specially constructed chapel, and crew of 120, is a true vessel of God.[30]

De Plas is torn constantly by his own desire for action, the need to defend the Catholic community farther down the coast in Ningbo as well as those in Shanghai, visits for patrol purposes or refitting the ship to Macao and Hong Kong, and the contradictory instructions and requests of the French consul in Shanghai.[31] The confusion of the period is compounded when, in September 1853, Chinese secret-society members—not acting in any coordinated way with the Taiping armies—seize much of the Chinese city of Shanghai, causing the Qing officials either to flee or to take refuge with the foreigners in their special concession areas. Though the foreign community has prepared for such a contingency some time before with the training of militia and the construction of ditches and communicating roads, the disruption of trade leaves them in continuous anxiety.[32] For the French residents, there are several complicating factors. Firstly, the French concession area is the actual neighbor of the Chinese city, where the secret societies now hold sway, and hence it is almost impossible to avoid daily tensions and clashes, or problems over sharing out the jurisdictions of roadblocks and bridge defense with the British. Secondly, the French have taken it upon themselves, ever since the treaty settlement of 1842, to be the guardians of the Catholic missionaries in China. Hence the grim news of the maltreatment and the killings of Cath-

olic Chinese converts by the Taiping in Nanjing and other cities, gives de
Plas an added urgency to go to Nanjing, and see if he can get some formal
diplomatic agreements and promises of religious toleration more effective
than those acquired by Bonham.[33]

Captain de Plas also has trouble on his hands as he tries to moor the
Cassini in such a position off the Shanghai waterfront that its guns can
cover both the newly built Catholic cathedral at one end of the stretch and
the French consulate at the other, while attempting at the same time to
avoid the erratic fire kept up in the waterway between the boats of the
secret societies and the Qing waterborne forces.[34] The immense ransoms
demanded by secret-society members from the Chinese Catholic converts
in Shanghai—as much as ten thousand taels from certain wealthy families
of the faithful—further compound his problems of when or how to intervene to protect his charges. And, as a strictly private agenda of his own,
de Plas lives in hopes that the recently widowed British consul, Rutherford
Alcock, a man of "elevated soul and an upright heart," will soon be converted to Catholicism for he seems to de Plas to be "not far from abjuring
his protestant faith."[35]

It is only in November 1853, six months after the British return, that
Captain de Plas receives permission to attempt the voyage to Nanjing, to
make a reconnaissance and help the French diplomats meet with the Taiping leaders. To his alarm, instead of the consul or a junior diplomat
coming with him, the French minister M. de Bourboulon decides to make
the journey in person, and to bring his wife with him. His wife, an
Englishwoman and a Protestant, takes pleasure in denying the divinity of
Jesus and insisting that he is nothing more than a great philosopher. Thus
what might have been a simple if risky venture becomes one fraught with
diplomatic and personal niceties. The minister placates de Plas by telling
him the goal of the journey is nothing less than "the extension of French
protection over the Catholics" of Nanjing.[36]

Leaving Shanghai on November 30, the *Cassini* is after a few hours
shrouded in fog at the mouth of the Yangzi, and forced to anchor. Even
after the weather clears, it is a delicate journey because of the deep draft
of the vessel, the officers' and crew's lack of familiarity with the shifting
sandbars and unpredictable currents, and the great flotillas of small
junks—one of two hundred sails, another of close to three hundred—
which despite the presence of numerous Qing patrol boats still crowd the
river as they carry supplies to the Taiping capital or the outlying cities the
God-worshipers control on the Grand Canal and the river shores. Not
until December 6 do the French reach Nanjing, and anchor in the river
outside the walls.[37] Soon the *Cassini* is filled with Taiping emissaries,

dressed in red and yellow robes, their hair hanging long around their faces below their scarlet hoods or turbans, or sometimes stuffed into a cloth bag or pouch around their neck. To the French Jesuit priest Stanislas Clavelin, who is on the *Cassini* to serve as an additional interpreter, the Taiping seem "honest and polite." Told of the French desire to have an interview with Taiping leaders, they take a day to decide, but the affirmative response comes by nightfall.[38]

Next morning Taiping guides with horses are at the waterfront to meet them. De Bourboulon's legation secretary and Clavelin, with his Chinese catechist to help in translation, and two ship's officers, make up the party, which rides for close to an hour and a half to the sound of gongs and under fluttering Taiping banners, past the city's huge outer walls, till they enter through the main western gate, and ride several miles more through the wide main avenue. Among many burnt-out houses, the shops are closed and silent. Groups of women pass, some richly clad, on their way to their units of twenty-five in the women's camps, loaded with the rice they have collected from the public treasury near the river bank. To Clavelin they seem to show "a calm resignation, a little sad no doubt, but nevertheless much less so than [one] would have expected, considering the sacrifices of all kinds that they have had to make."[39] A group of thirty young Chinese teenagers, finely dressed and mounted on well-formed ponies, caper around the Frenchmen, who are told these are the children of the Taiping leaders. Once a man presses close to Father Clavelin and opens his hand for a second, showing the priest a rosary clasped within, and making a rapid sign of the cross. It is the first evidence of the survival of Chinese Catholics in the city, among the God-worshipers.[40]

Other things about the Taiping order impress the French observers: the severed heads of opium smokers hanging in cages on the walls; the constant printing of the Pentateuch and Matthew's Gospel, and the holding of new examinations based on these and other religious texts; women petitioning for warmer clothing in the winter cold and being granted it from the common store, and the lanterns burning in the women's quarters through the nights. The impossibility of buying a set of Taiping clothes from anyone in Nanjing, since no one will trade such goods for cash, shows the Taiping control over economic life. The ten shots fired from cannon twice a day when the Heavenly King is at his prayers, and the apparent sincerity of other Taiping followers in their prayers and services, give an air of sanctity to the city.[41] When finally summoned to the audience hall to meet with Taiping officials, the French are startled by the contrast with the mixed desolation and bustle of the rundown streets:

> With the aid of torches which lit up the room, we saw on each side a large
> number of onlookers; and at the end, in front of us, the two ministers who
> would receive us. Their splendid robes of blue satin, richly enhanced, on the
> chest mainly, by magnificent embroideries, their red boots, diadems wholly
> of carved gold on their heads, their grave and dignified bearing, and a large
> retinue forming a second rank behind them; all, in a word, contributed to
> giving to this interview a character of dignity and grandeur. . . .[42]

The mood of the meeting is encouraging. The Taiping officials talk of
their religious doctrines, their Heavenly King and his mission to stamp
out idolatry, and call the Frenchmen "friends" and "brothers." Not only
can de Bourboulon meet with their highest ministers, they promise, but if
he has "serious interests to discuss" he can meet with the Heavenly King
himself.[43]

When de Bourboulon enters Nanjing on December 10, he is presented
with a diplomatic predicament equivalent to that faced by Bonham: for
the Taiping representative Qin Rigang, one of the leading Taiping generals and a close friend and confidant of Hong Xiuquan, is seated in a single
chair upon a raised dais, from which eminence he gestures the French
legate to one of a row of chairs below him. The slight is too obvious to be
accepted. De Bourboulon demands a chair upon the dais of the same kind
as Qin's. Qin demurs. But just as the audience is about to be called off, a
compromise is reached—the two men and their staffs will talk "infor-
mally" in an adjacent room. There de Bourboulon enquires closely into
the Taiping's religious beliefs, seeks guarantees for the well-being of Chinese Catholics under Taiping control, and reminds Qin both of France's
neutrality in the current conflict and of her prior treaty agreements with
the Qing that are still in force with Emperor Xianfeng. He makes no clear
offers of forming a new treaty of formal agreement with the Taiping
state.[44]

This reticence, along with the invocation of Emperor Xianfeng's name
and title—*huangdi,* or "emperor," being reserved by the Taiping for God
alone—leads swiftly to exasperation. Though de Bourboulon in person is
spared, the wrath falls on his interpreter Clavelin, who is summoned to a
special meeting with Taiping officials and treated to a sarcastic and angry
diatribe. The Taiping logic is forceful; if the French revere the Qing ruler
Xianfeng so much, they must be his friends; if they are Xianfeng's friends,
they must see the Taiping as rebels; if they see the Taiping as rebels, then
they are the Taiping's enemies; and so, in conclusion, "the better to help
your friend you have come to spy on us, and to acquaint yourselves with
the strengths and weaknesses of our position."[45]

As if to reinforce this new and harder line, after several days of silence a message is brought to the *Cassini* on December 13. It is from the North King himself, "ordering" the French to visit his palace and receive his "verbal instructions." De Bourboulon, rejecting both the language and the tone of this Taiping summons, accepts the failure of his mission, and steams back to Shanghai on December 14.[46]

But in his final report to the Foreign Ministry in France de Bourboulon remains more buoyant than Bonham after his earlier rebuffs. Admitting that he has not really achieved either the religious or the diplomatic results he hoped for, de Bourboulon still considers that the new intelligence he has gained more than makes up for those frustrations:

> What stands out most for me from all that I have seen is the strength of this revolutionary movement, which promises nothing less than to accomplish a complete transformation, at once religious, social and political in this immense Empire, by tradition a land of custom and immobility. Whatever doubts may exist about its ultimate success, whatever obstacles the indifference of the masses and the resources of the Tartar dynasty may yet oppose to the rebellion's triumph, it is clear to me that this revolt is one of formidable character and proportions; that it is led by men who, be they fanatical or ambitious, have faith in the success of their venture, and who, besides their audacity, have in their favour ideas, a strength of organisation, tactics, in short a moral force which gives them great superiority over their adversaries. . . .[47]

As to de Plas, on his return to Shanghai he learns that the *Cassini* is to be replaced by another warship and that he has been posted back to France: he feels his mission of bolstering the faith has been achieved, and he looks forward to greeting his mother once more, the mother to whom he has written almost weekly throughout the voyage, and whose letters in return have tracked him, to his joy, around the world:

> Aboard the *Cassini,* Shanghai, December 27 [1853]
> My dear mama,
>   The departure of the *Cassini* has been a bit delayed by unexpected events, but it seems that our mission in this country is now completed. . . .
>   I went just once into Nanjing, to accompany M. de Bourboulon, who himself had just one interview with ministers there. That town, once so flourishing, inspired in me a feeling of sadness similar to that which one feels in visiting the ruins of Pompeii. The area enclosed within the fortifications is immense, but I doubt if even one-third is inhabited. The ramparts, still in good condition, encircle hills covered with trees where one sees not a single

dwelling; they are at least forty or fifty feet high, but if they seem formidable to the Chinese they would not be so to Europeans. . . .

One cannot deny it: there is, in the relations of these Guangxi people with each other a family air which seems to justify the name of "brother" that they give each other. Thus all their homes are shared in common, and their food and clothing are held in public storehouses. Gold, silver, and precious goods are all placed in the treasury. One can sell nothing, buy nothing. It is up to the leaders to see to all the different needs of their subordinates. Is it not admirable that a population of over one million can be thus clothed and fed in the midst of a civil war, and in the face of an armed enemy who besieges their city!

But now, what should one make of such a state of affairs? Will China change her masters and her religion? The insurrection of these Guangxi people is, one cannot deny it, an event of the gravest import. Let one call these people "rebels" or "brigands" as much as one wants, they have nonetheless gnawed the empire to its heart. . . . Only God can say what the future has in store for China, and for Catholicism in this land.[48]

One touch of grace at his departure is the formal abjuration of her Protestantism by Mme. de Bourboulon, and her solemn reception into the Catholic church. Alcock, however, has not succumbed.[49]

On first reaching Shanghai in March 1853, Captain de Plas had met both Sir George Bonham and the American minister Humphrey Marshall. He found the latter to be a man who liked to "follow a frank and tough line of conduct" in his dealings with the Chinese, and was touched when Marshall asked him if the *Cassini* would accompany the U.S. vessel *Susquehanna* on her projected voyage of reconnaissance to Nanjing. At the time, de Plas felt he could not take the responsibility for such a decision, given the weak state of the defenses of Shanghai.[50] As it happened, the *Susquehanna* had already run aground near Shanghai, despite the presence of two Chinese pilots on board, and been forced to abandon the attempt. De Plas noted that Marshall, angry at the British coup in getting to Nanjing first, vowed to make a second attempt to reach Nanjing as soon as he could get a vessel with a shallower draft than the *Susquehanna* put at his disposal.[51] The subsequent demands by Commodore Perry for the assistance of all available ships in Far Eastern waters for his celebrated journey to Japan, and Perry's temporary selection of the *Susquehanna* as his flagship, frustrated Marshall's desire. De Plas dined with Perry, in August 1853 after his return, and gave full details of this initial American foray to Japan, and in December de Plas noted Perry's departure on the second voyage with three warships, the *Susquehanna, Mississippi,* and *Powhatan.*[52]

Marshall, despite his "frank and tough" approach, was also a stickler for the letter if not the spirit of the "neutrality" commitment made by the United States under the treaties signed in the 1840s, contenting himself in the spring of 1853 with collecting Taiping printed materials and sending them back to the Department of State for reference.[53] When Hong Xiuquan's teacher, the American Baptist Issachar Roberts, received an invitation in Canton from Hong to visit Nanjing, he at once asked Marshall in Shanghai for his permission; Roberts claimed the opportunity was parallel to that made to Paul in Acts 11:9—"And a vision appeared to Paul in the night; there stood a man of Macedonia, and prayed to him, saying, 'Come over into Macedonia, and help us.'" But Marshall expressed his disapproval on the ground that such a trip violated the terms of the United States agreement with the Qing. Undeterred, Roberts collected the passage money from a sympathetic merchant in Canton, and traveled to Shanghai with a son and cousin of Feng Yunshan, the deceased South King, who had been in hiding in the south.[54]

Once in Shanghai, Roberts repeated his request to Commissioner Marshall, who this time rebuffed him in even stronger terms, threatening (according to Roberts) to hang him if he tried. But in a private conversation with an American friend, Marshall said, "Why could not the infernal ass go without saying anything to me about it? Of course I had to tell him 'no.' My position compelled me to take that stand under the treaties, but I should have been delighted to have him go and bring back some reports of the rebels, which I could rely upon."[55] With the encouragement of Captain Fishbourne, and some local merchants, Roberts nevertheless decided to risk it and hired a small boat with a medical missionary acquaintance, Charles Taylor. They got as far as the lower reaches of the Yangzi River before they were stopped by a Qing patrol boat and ordered back to Shanghai.[56]

No American group has yet reached Nanjing by the spring of 1854, when Robert McLane replaces Marshall as U.S. commissioner, and announces that he will attempt the journey to the headquarters of "the Revolutionary Army" in Nanjing, using the *Susquehanna*. Roberts at once asks if McLane will take him, but the new commissioner rejects Roberts' request, though he does take two other Protestant missionaries with him. After carefully studying everything he can find on the previous delegations by Bonham and de Bourboulon, McLane leaves Shanghai on May 22, 1854, reaching Nanjing on the twenty-seventh.[57]

Most of the formal American correspondence with the Taiping forces is sent in the name of the *Susquehanna*'s captain, Frank Buchanan. As has been the case with both the *Hermes* and the *Cassini*, Taiping garrisons, unfamiliar with the markings or flags of foreign vessels, and constantly jumpy that Qing forces might be traveling in their wake or under their protection, fire warning shots as the *Susquehanna* approaches. But despite the study McLane says he has made of the French and British experiences, and despite the Taiping explanation that they have never seen the Stars and Stripes before, Buchanan is in no mood to trifle with the Taiping:

> Sir, . . .
>
> I will tomorrow morning send a boat on shore at 11 a.m. for the answer to my communication delivered to you today by an officer from this ship, and I have to insist that this answer shall contain a full and satisfactory apology for the heedless and insulting demonstration, of your battery, on shore this morning. If the fullest and most satisfactory apology is not made by you in response to my demand, I shall not hesitate on my return from Nanking, to resist the insult offered to the Flag of the U.S.
>
> At one o'clock tomorrow I shall weigh anchor and proceed to Nanking, and then represent to your Ruler Taiping-Wan the insolence of those at Chin-Kiang-Fu, who have been so insensible to the proprieties and obligations of friendly national intercourse, and the respect which the Flag of the U.S. must always command, more especially from those whom we have fully informed of the friendly and neutral character of that Flag, as you were by me, in my communication of this morning.
>
> I send you here enclosed a drawing of the Flag of the U.S., that you may never mistake it hereafter.
>
> Very respectfully
> Your obdt. Servt.
> Frank L. Buchanan[58]

The relationship grows no more cordial over the next few days. Unclear over the reasons for the U.S. vessel's visit—Buchanan and McLane refuse to answer other requests for clarification—the Taiping, through formalistic responses by medium-level officials, stall over all Buchanan's requests tendered on McLane's behalf. The American desire to visit the famous porcelain pagoda south of the city (which, Clavelin had noted, was "located close to the retrenchments built at the foot of the walls to protect the city against imperialist [i.e., Qing] attacks" and hence was considered restricted territory), is deferred pending the East King's permission.[59] An American visit to explore the city of Nanjing is held off until the Americans can show they have someone "who understands the language and reads the characters" so that they would "know the rules and customs of our Heavenly Kingdom."[60] Tempers are not improved when a young midshipman, impatient with confinement, climbs over the city wall on his own exploring trip.[61] The desire of McLane "to communicate with His Excellency Yang" and to make known "the friendly intentions" of the United States is not even passed up the chain of command, on the grounds that Buchanan "presumed to employ terms used in correspondence between equals" instead of those befitting a country "on the ocean's borders" that "ought to come kneeling" and show "the principles of true submission."[62]

The heart of the response received from two senior Taiping officials, as translated by the American Protestant missionary E. C. Bridgman who is acting as one of McLane's interpreters for the trip, clearly states the Taiping view of their cause:

> Our Sovereign, the T'ien Wang [Heavenly King], is the true Sovereign of Taiping of the ten thousand nations in the world. Therefore all nations under heaven ought to revere Heaven and follow the Sovereign, knowing on whom they depend. We are especially afraid that you do not understand the nature of Heaven, and believe that there are distinctions between this and that nation, not knowing the indivisibility of the true doctrine.
>
> Therefore we send this special mandatory dispatch.
>
> If you can revere Heaven and recognize the Sovereign, then our Heavenly Court, regarding all under heaven as one family and uniting all nations as one body, will certainly remember your faithful purpose and permit you, year after year, to bring tribute and come to court annually so that you may become ministers and people of the Heavenly Kingdom, forever basking in the grace and favor of the Heavenly Dynasty, peacefully residing in your own lands, and quietly enjoying great glory. This is what we, the great ministers, sincerely wish. You must tremblingly obey; do not circumvent these instructions.[63]

Captain Buchanan responds at once that he finds this message "couched in language so peculiar and unintelligible as to cause [him] much astonishment," and that he accordingly encloses "a historical memoir of the U.S. of America, together with a drawing of their National Flag, which his excellency, the Commissioner, desires may be submitted to your Chief authorities, to prevent any misapprehension on their part."[64]

That same day of May 30, at noon, a party of eight Americans leaves the *Susquehanna* without Chinese permission and travels on foot along the west wall of Nanjing. Denied entry to the city by the guards at the various gates, they push on farther than either the British or the French had presumed to do, curving around below the southern wall to the marshes and an abandoned fort that stands there, and passing through an almost ruined and deserted suburb before coming out at the famous porcelain pagoda.[65]

The pagoda tower itself is still intact, with its shining porcelain tiles, but the circular stairway that once led to the summit of the nine-story structure—and would have given a clear field of fire or observation over the city—has been ripped out, and lies in a heap of rubble at the foot of the building. The myriad Buddhist images that once graced the building—idols that they are to the Taiping—have all been defaced and mutilated, and the decorations stripped from them. An attempt by one of the bolder Americans to clamber up and remove the golden sphere from the pagoda's summit is foiled almost before it begins, although the bravado of the attempt long lingers in Taiping minds.[66] The result of this unauthorized excursion is that all eight Americans are arrested by Taiping officials and face a series of tense interrogations, both in the suburbs and subsequently in the city, for the remainder of the day and into the evening. The Chinese interpreter used by the Taiping grows so terrified of the menace in the exchanges that by the end he is too frightened and tired to be coherent, so the final questions are put in writing. It takes the issuing of three sets of permits and papers by three separate Taiping officers before the small groups of Americans are taken out through the western gate, and returned to the *Susquehanna*.[67] While they are being interrogated, a note is delivered to their ship stating that the Taiping authorities will not guarantee that those making similar unauthorized trips in the future might not be killed by Taiping troops.[68] The next day the *Susquehanna* raises anchor and leaves the city.

Summarizing these events to the secretary of state, McLane dwells on the unreasonableness of the Taiping beliefs and practices, their "monstrous misapprehension of scriptural truth," and their incapacity to see any foreign intercourse in "terms of equality."[69] But when he comes to balance off the Qing against the Taiping, it is hard for him to see either side as the worthy one:

> Thus is presented the melancholy spectacle of an enfeebled and tottering imperial government, ignorant, conceited, and impracticable; assailed at all points by a handful of insurgents, whose origin was a band of robbers in the interior, whose present power is quite sufficient to drive before them the imperial authorities . . . but who are, nevertheless, unworthy [of] the respect of the civilized world, and perhaps incapable of consolidating civil govern-

ment beyond the walls of the cities captured and pillaged by a multitude excited to the highest pitch of resentment against all who possess property or betray a partiality for the imperial authorities.[70]

The only solution to McLane seems to be to "enlarge the powers and duties" that the United States exercises in China, so as to enforce the current treaty stipulations and prevent the abuse of the flag. By "such enlargement of the *protectorate* character of the existing treaty, the interior should be opened to us, where we would extend the moral power of our civilization and the material power necessary to protect the lives and property of our people."[71] Such an activist policy would enable the United States "to give a truly Christian direction to that movement, which though now shrouded in heathen darkness, is yet founded on the text of the Bible," and also to "offer to the American manufacturers a market more valuable than all the other markets of the world to which they have yet had access."[72]

The Taiping leaders, for their part, have now had a chance to meet with the representatives of the three most important Western commercial and missionary powers in China. Despite the apparent closeness of their shared religion, the gulf has grown, not narrowed. The Taiping's own view of their favored status under God clearly weighs at least as heavily in their minds as the brotherhood of all mankind.

15

THE SPLIT

 What magic intersection of timing, fate, and providence can found our Earthly Paradise upon the rock? The homage demanded from the foreign visitors, and the excoriation of Emperor Xianfeng and all his followers as demon dogs and foxes, cannot hide the realities of boundaries that shift in response to the exigencies of war, and of a Heavenly Capital that turns in upon itself.

The Taiping leadership has followed an ambitious strategy, which has worked only in part. To capture the Demon's Den of Peking city, they have dispatched in May 1853 a dedicated Taiping army of some seventy thousand veteran Guangxi men and new recruits on a northern march, but God has not blessed the enterprise. The Qing forces have kept them guessing with false intelligence reports designed to suggest the advance of huge Qing armies to the south, while their real troops and local militia forces mount spirited defenses of small towns, slowing the marchers unexpectedly. The terrain of northern China is unfamiliar, and progress further hampered by the Qing government's appointment of a special officer whose only task is to keep all boats on the northern shore of the Yellow River as the Taiping troops approach, making it impossible for them to repeat the triumphs of their earlier 1852 campaigns on the Yangzi.[1] Even when the Taiping troops do capture medium-sized cities, Qing commanders have now been instructed to burn all their stocks of food and gunpowder if the Taiping storm their walls—and though some are reluctant or too tardy to comply, those who do so reduce the chances of the Taiping resting and restocking their supplies. Forced much farther to the northwest than they have planned, the Taipings at last cross the Yellow River, but are caught unprepared by savage winter weather, which freezes many in their tracks or leaves them maimed from frostbite—"crawling on the snowy, icy ground with their legs benumbed"—for they are southerners, and not equipped with proper winter clothes. Reinforcements, sent to their aid, are also checked or turned back by local Qing forces, for the Taiping have not kept a main supply route from north to south open and defended at any point on the vast battlefield.[2]

Astonishingly, by late October 1853 one of the thrusting Taiping columns pushes to within three miles of the outskirts of Tianjin, from which they might have opened up a path to nearby Peking, but they can get no farther. New Qing and local forces, including Mongol cavalry, are sent against them. Despite the initial enthusiasm of many local people for the Taiping message, and the military help of secret societies and the members of new rebel organizations like the Nian—who are also locked in struggle against their landlords and the government—the Taiping blunt their popularity. Their search for food and clothing grows desperate, and the massacre of all one town's civilian population sends a wave of fear ahead of them.[3]

Swiftly though the Taiping can build defensive redoubts, for they are veterans at this kind of warfare—throwing up earthworks, digging ditches, and crisscrossing open ground with foxholes in a single day of frenzied work—the Qing are learning to encircle these encirclements, recruiting thousands of local laborers from the farming population to build a solid ring around the Taiping forces. By May 1854, with the remnants of the Taiping vanguard forces thus encircled, the Qing commander orders a long ditch built to divert the waters of the Grand Canal to a dried-out riverbed that flows near the Taiping fortified position. The work takes a month, but slowly as the water enters its new channel the Taiping camp turns to mud, and then to a lake; the soldiers can neither sleep nor cook, their gunpowder is waterlogged and useless, and as they climb onto roofs, cling to ladders, or float on homemade rafts, the Qing troops pick them off in groups and execute them. So, ingloriously, die the warriors after fighting and marching over a one-year period for close to two thousand miles.[4]

Had the northern campaign had full call on all Taiping resources, per-

The Taiping northern campaign of 1853–1855. In the summer of 1853, after Nanjing was consolidated as the Heavenly capital, Hong Xiuquan sent an army north to seize the Qing dynasty's capital of Peking. By October, the Taiping army of around thirty thousand men reached the suburbs of Tianjin, less than seventy miles from their goal, but here they were checked by the Qing forces and slowly driven back. After vainly fighting to hold a succession of towns, the Taiping northern army made a last stand in the Grand Canal city of Lianzhen, where they held out during an eight-month siege until they were annihilated in March 1855.

These four illustrations are from a series of ten, probably commissioned from a local artist by the grateful merchants of Tianjin as a gift to the victorious Qing commander, General Senggelinqin. The pictures show the Taiping being burned and driven out of two towns, until Senggelinqin surrounds their last bastion of Lianzhen with a ring of earthern walls and gun emplacements. In the last illustration, the defeated Taiping general Lin Fengxiang is shown kneeling before Senggelinqin, whose supply trains, camels, cavalry horses, and gun positions are all clearly delineated. Lin was subsequently executed. *Credit: Harvard-Yenching Library, Harvard University*.

haps it might have succeeded, and the criminals' province been renamed. But it is matched by a parallel campaign to the west, planned and executed on a similar scale; swiftly, also, this western campaign splits into two, as part of the army fights for a strategic base in Anhui province, on the northern shore of the Yangzi River, while the other part moves upriver to recapture Wuchang city, and extend the Taiping river and supply lines to China's southern hinterland. This Wuchang campaign then subdivides, as one group of Taiping armies regains, loses, and recaptures yet again the city of Wuchang, while others push southward into Hunan, seeking once more to seize Changsha. This Hunan campaign splits in its turn, as General Shi Dakai swings south to attack Jiangxi province, southwest of the Heavenly Capital.

Some of these campaigns succeed and some do not: Changsha cannot be taken, nor can Hunan be held, for the gentry of Hunan have learned in full measure how to recruit, train, and pay militia armies, while Zeng Guofan, a Confucian scholar-bureaucrat at home to mourn his parents, joins forces with the reinstated governor Luo Bingzhang, and by integrating their land and naval forces slowly build a formidable fighting force.[5] Wuchang, however, is recaptured by the Taiping general Chen Yucheng, aged eighteen at the time, nephew to a senior Taiping veteran but already a brilliant military strategist. The city becomes their inland base, easy of access up the Yangzi River from the Heavenly Capital.[6]

In Anhui province, the battles swirl for years around the strategic city of Luzhou, held for a time by another gentry leader, Jiang Zhongyuan, hero of Suoyi ford, promoted for his valor to be Anhui governor. The Taiping seize the city at last, having developed a new strategy of digging double tunnels one above the other, and lining them with explosives attached to time-spaced fuses. After the first explodes, the Qing defenders rush to mend the gaping holes, and are just completing their repairs as the second explosives fire, killing the wall menders and reopening a gaping hole through which the Taiping charge. Jiang commits suicide. But though the Taiping hold Luzhou stubbornly for twenty-two months, until November 1855, they are at last starved out, betrayed, and stormed.[7] In Jiangxi province, Shi Dakai links up his forces with tens of thousands of Triad Society troops who have been fighting for possession of Canton city and, though failing in that endeavor, have escaped northward up the river Gan. Uniting these various armies, and receiving clear support from the local people, Shi makes most of the province a center of Taiping government and a rich source of food supplies, save for a small circle of land around the city of Nanchang on Poyang Lake, where Zeng Guofan, sent

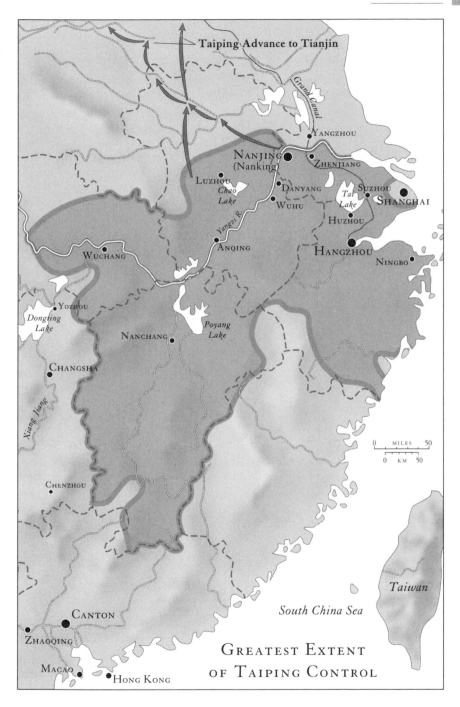

Taiping Advance to Tianjin

Grand Canal

YANGZHOU

NANJING
(Nanking)

ZHENJIANG

LUZHOU
Chao
Lake

DANYANG

SUZHOU

Tai
Lake

SHANGHAI

WUHU

HUZHOU

Yangzi R.

ANQING

HANGZHOU

NINGBO

WUCHANG

YOZHOU

Dongting
Lake

Poyang
Lake

NANCHANG

CHANGSHA

Xiang Jiang

0   MILES   50

0   KM   50

CHENZHOU

Taiwan

South China Sea

CANTON

ZHAOQING

GREATEST EXTENT
OF TAIPING CONTROL

MACAO

HONG KONG

there from Hunan, just manages to hold the city's defenses intact.[8]

With all these massive campaigns in progress, the constant shift of victories and defeats, the endless search for new recruits and supplies, the Taiping can do little toward the east of their Heavenly Capital, even though the resources there are rich. Indeed even as they threaten and hold cities hundreds of miles away, the Qing press hard upon their central base. It is all the Taiping's locally based forces can do to hold Zhenjiang, less than forty miles downriver, the key to the approaches to the Grand Canal and the Heavenly Capital; while Qing garrison armies are encamped in force in the hilly countryside just a few miles outside the walls of the Heavenly Capital, in a series of interlocking bases from which the Taiping have never had the time or resources to dislodge them. These Qing troops are so near that they are able to keep secret communications open with anti-Taiping loyalists within the city, and to enforce the rules on their own dress and customs, so that local farmers bringing their produce to the informal markets outside the city gates often still have the shaved forehead and long plait of hair mandated by their Manchu masters.[9]

Of the surviving Taiping kings, only Shi Dakai, the Wing King, is constantly occupied in the field, directing and personally leading the different phases of the western campaigns. The Heavenly King, Hong Xiuquan, as spiritual leader, bestower of rewards and punishments, and ultimate supervisor, stays in his palace. Wei Changhui, the North King, acts as coordinator for the defense of the region around the Heavenly Capital, and sees to its food supplies. General administrative supervision is in the hands of the East King, Yang Xiuqing, who also acts as coordinator of all the military campaigns. Other Guangxi veterans, mainly from Thistle Mountain and Guiping, have mansions in the city and have been enfeoffed with noble ranks—they serve either in the field or as senior officials in the Heavenly Capital.[10] But despite the formidable system of post stations and communications both by land and by water that the Taiping rapidly establish—with post stations ten miles apart, special bureaus to chart the weather, and couriers carrying their special seal of a flying horse surrounded by clouds, and disguising themselves as merchants or peasants when demon patrols are blocking the routes—the fronts change so often along with the areas controlled by the Taiping that most generals on specific campaigns have to be left a wide area of initiative. The river town of Wuhu, for example, some fifty miles upriver from Nanjing on the south shore of the Yangzi, and an important center for commerce and communication, changes hands eight times between 1853 and 1855 alone.[11]

It is at the end of December 1853 that Yang Xiuqing changes the rules as they have begun to coalesce, and begins to speak once again publicly as the voice of God. This is the first clear move in a sequence that will take Yang himself and thousands of other Taiping followers to their death. The timing and the precise motivation for the change are ambiguous. The news from the northern expedition is bad but not yet disastrous, and Yang has ordered massive reinforcements to move north from Yangzhou; the western expedition has temporarily stalled, but has already achieved remarkable successes; and the French have visited Nanjing on the *Cassini* and left again without making any offers of support despite Taiping encouragement.

The visitation is announced abruptly, in the middle of a working day, after the North King and other senior officials have conferred with Yang about their administrative duties. Four of Yang's palace women officials, with their assistants, are the only ones with him, and it is to these women that God first speaks through Yang's mouth. God's message to these women is that Hong Xiuquan, the Heavenly King, has grown both harsh and indulgent with his power: harsh to the women who serve in attendance on him, and indulgent to his son the Young Monarch, now four years old. In particular, four of the palace women who work for the Heavenly King—the message names them individually—should be released from their palace duties with Hong and sent to live instead in the palace complex of Yang, the East King. Their duties could be taken over by any of Hong's other palace women. By the time the North King and the other Taiping officials arrive, God has returned to Heaven, so kneeling they receive the message from the women of the court. In a second swift visit through Yang, this time at the court of Hong Xiuquan, God orders the Heavenly King to receive forty blows of the rod for his derelictions. Only when Hong prostrates himself to receive the blows does God forgive him and return to Heaven.[12]

The charges of harshness and indulgence are then discussed by Yang Xiuqing: the Young Monarch, Hong's four-year-old son, is self-indulgent and willful—he plays in the rain, despite the possible harm, and that must be stopped. He smashes presents that he is given, and that too must cease, lest as a ruler in the future he abuse the people.[13] The harshness to the women has also taken various forms: when palace women dig an ornamental pool for Hong, he treats it as a general might a military operation, ordering them to work through rain or snow. The concubines have been allowed to sneer at and scold the women officials, preventing them from doing their duty in the palace, and when the women officials are attending to such details as repairing palace rooms or sweeping the protected inner gardens, the Heavenly King is always criticizing and interfering, terrorizing those who work for him. In his anger, too, Hong has kicked or otherwise punished his royal concubines, even when they are pregnant. However serious their crimes, none should be disciplined by violent means until her time is up and the child is born.[14]

These are the East King's elaborations of God's words, but on this and another occasion two days later he gives his own related thoughts, couched in the form of a "loyal memorial" from a concerned minister rather than as the direct commands of God. Yet it is clear that Hong is expected to respond to Yang as if Yang's own words were God's. In the running of the Taiping kingdom, the most important change is that Yang now arrogates to himself the power to decide all cases that might call for the death penalty. Yang also would refer back to Hong Xiuquan those cases in which clemency might be granted. Thus Hong's "naturally severe disposition" and tendency to order "wrongful executions" would be mitigated by Yang's sensitivity to "unredressed grievances" that would linger in the Heavenly Capital if people were "hastily put to death." The result of this new arrangement would be that "the Heavenly Father's intent in fostering human life will be eternally displayed, and the spirit of gentleness and tranquility will be handed down through all eternity."[15]

On two other matters in the same December meetings Yang overturns previous decisions of Hong Xiuquan, both seeming inconsequential, but each cutting, in some way, at the heart of Taiping practice or belief. One is an appeal to Hong to lessen the severity of prohibitions of "family visits" among those loyal Taiping women followers who "forgot their homes for their country, and forgot themselves for the public good." The "single-minded devotion" of such loyalists should be rewarded by allowing them "home visits" once every twenty or thirty days, or maybe every Sabbath, so they can see to their children, attend to their elderly in-laws, and "serve their husbands."[16] As to the world of ritual and pomp, here also changes should be made. Dragons, for example, with their ritual implications of imperial glory and grandeur, should be separated out from "demons" with whom they have been indiscriminately lumped by Hong Xiuquan as Heavenly King, in his passion for extirpating demons. Yang states that dragon palaces, dragon robes, and dragon vessels are all honorable, and should not be confused with the devil serpent of the Eastern Sea and his demon minions, who betray the souls of men.[17]

This discussion—or conflict—over ritual goes back to the roots of the formation of the God-worshipers in Thistle Mountain, or perhaps earlier to Hong's visions of 1837. For in that vision, and as constantly retold in Taiping texts, and even revisited in the minds of Hong's disciples, the figure of God the Father was wearing a black dragon robe in Heaven.[18] In 1849, Hong's loyalest followers were promised that if they persevered and were victorious one day they would wear dragon robes and horn belts, whereas if they did evil they would be killed.[19] During the early campaigns of 1850, Hong's own rural retreat was euphemistically known as the Golden Dragon Palace, and was visited by all the leading Taiping commanders, including Yang Xiuqing.[20] Hong Xiuquan defends himself by saying to Yang that their Elder Brother, Jesus, long before in the Thistle Mountain area came down to earth and announced that "dragons are demons" although "the dragon of the Golden Dragon Hall was not a demon but a truly precious creature," and Hong chose to focus on the first part of these remarks and not the second.[21]

One of the inner Taiping texts, not yet distributed to all the Taiping followers but known to Hong—and surely to Yang as well—quoted Jesus' remarks in the Pingnan Mountains, autumn of 1848, as follows:

> "Hong Xiuquan, my own younger brother, can it be you do not know the astral prophecy of the dragon demon? The dragon of the sea is this same leader of the demon devils, and he that the people of the world call the devil Yan Luo is that same dragon of the Eastern Sea. He is the one who can change his form, and deceives the souls of those who live on earth. When you some time ago came up to Heaven, and together with the great army of the Heavenly Host fought against that square-headed red-eyed demon devil leader, that too was him. Have you now forgotten that?" And the Heavenly King replied, "I would have forgotten had my Heavenly Elder Brother not reminded me."[22]

In glossing this sacred text in the direction desired by Yang—as Hong forthwith meekly does, with the words "From now on, whenever dragons are engraved by our Heavenly Kingdom or Heavenly Court, all shall be considered as precious golden dragons, and there is no need to regard them with glaring eyes"—Hong has in fact yielded up a point in a longstanding argument over imagery and iconography, and their relationship to idolatry.

It is essential to Hong Xiuquan, if he is to keep his paramount position within the Taiping movement, that the central truth of his journey to Heaven not be disputed. Yang may speak with the voice of God, but Hong has seen and talked with God, recorded the color of His beard and clothes, and has seen and talked with Jesus. Thus when he is presented with a lengthy text in Chinese that argues the Christian doctrine with great force and yet denies that God can have material nature, Hong alters it with care before releasing it as a Taiping sacred text. Hong makes both deletions and additions. He deletes the statement "God is immaterial and invisible," adding instead the sentence "He can be seen only by those who ascend to Heaven." Hong also cuts a longer passage that runs as follows: "God is without form, sound, scent or taste; we can neither observe His form, nor hear His voice, nor feel nor perceive Him by any bodily organs." And Hong substitutes for this and other lengthy passages of similar import remarks designed to humanize the God whom he has seen, such as the homely metaphor "When the house leaks God can observe it." Thus purged and amplified, the text is published as a Taiping sacred work in 1854.[23]

Simpler on the surface, but perhaps deeper in theological implications, is the formal declaration by Hong that henceforth Yang Xiuqing shall bear a new title in addition to those he already possesses. Because of the solace the East King has brought him by his frankness and fearless honesty, says Hong, Yang shall be called the "Comforter" and the "Wind of the Holy Spirit," the phrase that the Taiping use to translate the "Holy Ghost," or third person of the Trinity. By conferring this title, says Hong, he consciously echoes the words used by Jesus, who "addressed his disciples, saying 'At some future day the Comforter will come into the world.'" Hong is here referring to the fourteenth chapter of John's Gospel, which—though not yet published by the Taiping—has been in his possession for several years in Gutzlaff's Chinese translation. According to John, at the end of the Last Supper, Jesus tells his anxious disciples, "I will pray to the Father, and he shall give you another Comforter, that he may abide with you for ever." Jesus also says, "The Comforter, which is the Holy Ghost, whom the Father will send in my name, he shall teach you all things, and bring all things to your remembrance, whatsoever I have said unto you" (John 14:16 and 26).

The phrase "Holy Ghost," so central in the Christian idea of the Trinity, is muted in this early Chinese translation. But there is no denying that when Hong says to Yang that "the Comforter and the Wind of the Holy Spirit spoken of by our Heavenly Elder Brother is none other than yourself," he has ventured into new and difficult terrain, especially since Hong knows well the passage in John's first epistle, where it is written, "For there are three that bear record in heaven, the Father, the Word, and the Holy Ghost: and these three are one."[24]

That Yang, through deliberate manipulation of Hong, is here moving to a higher stage in the Taiping hierarchy can be suggested by the chilling reference to the Comforter that follows those quoted by Hong. For in John's Gospel, chapter 16, verse 7, Jesus also says, "I tell you the truth; it is expedient for you that I go away: for if I go not away, the Comforter will not come unto you; but if I depart, I will send him unto you."

Yang is aiming high, and when you aim high, others must fall. Two of Hong Xiuquan's closest and most trusted associates are also publicly humiliated by Yang in God's December visitations. One of these is the North King, Wei Changhui; the other is the marquis Qin Rigang. Both have been with Hong Xiuquan from his earliest days at Thistle Mountain. Wei, a man with some education, gave all his family possessions to the God-worshipers after they helped him in his local village; Qin, while working as a miner, also studied military arts and became a formidable strategist. For years both men have handled key military assignments for Hong, and Qin is regarded as the senior-ranking Taiping officer after the surviving kings.

Yang uses his claim to speak for God to humiliate North King Wei in many ways. Whenever God appears, Yang's women attendants summon the North King at once with drum calls; if Wei is late, it is the women who relay God's messages to him. When Yang is speaking with God's voice, Wei must kowtow in full prostration before him. When Yang is in a trance in his sedan chair, Wei must walk, not ride, beside him. Even Yang's stewards keep Wei jumping, by refusing to disturb their master to clarify the messages or to see if his trance has ended. Qin has to endure similar humiliations and even has to help carry the East King's sedan up the palace steps.[25]

The December clash between the East and North Kings includes one other confrontation that illustrates how each maneuvers for position with Hong Xiuquan, East King Yang to prove his own morality, North King Wei to show his support of Hong's imperial perquisites. The incident starts when Yang suggests that Hong has more than enough embroideries and robes in his palace, and should economize for a time instead of acquiring more. The North King, ignoring Yang, replies to Hong:

> You, our second elder brother, are the true Sovereign of all nations of the world, and you are rich in the possession of all within the four seas; although robes and garments are sufficient, it will still be necessary to be constantly engaged in making up more.

To this clear challenge to his own authority, the East King responds as follows:

I beseech you, our second elder brother, to pardon this younger brother's crime and permit this younger brother to memorialize straightforwardly. If apparel were insufficient, then it would be necessary to make up more; but if it is said it is sufficient, it will be better to delay the making up of more, and then we can see the second elder brother's virtues of economy and love of man. Why should our younger brother Zheng [the North King] memorialize on the necessity of constantly making up more clothing?

Faced by these conflicting claims, the Heavenly King praises Yang, saying:

Brother [Yang Xiu]Qing! You are certainly what the ancients called a bold and outspoken minister. And you, brother Zheng, although you may have a sincere regard for your elder brother, are not so straightforward and open in your statements as our brother Qing; for which he is to be much more commended. Later, in the reign of the Young Monarch, all who are ministers should imitate the example of our brother Qing in speaking straightforwardly as he has done this day; thus will they fulfill their duty as ministers.[26]

The humiliation of Marquis Qin is more indirect, but after he and the East and North Kings have been treated to a banquet by the Heavenly King, in honor of their presence at God's visit, he is firmly reminded by Hong that he is not in the inner circle of Hong Xiuquan's "brothers" and that such special grace, rare already, will not be repeated once Hong Xiuquan has departed this world, for Qin is, and will remain, only a "minister" and not a king.[27]

This distancing of Qin does not however mean that Yang accords North King Wei the same kingly dignities he claims for himself, any more than he does Shi Dakai, the Wing King, who in any case is away most of the time directing the western campaign and poses no current threat to Yang. What Yang has done, with Hong's apparent agreement, is structure an inner "family" of four brothers, with Jesus the eldest, Hong Xiuquan the second, and Yang himself the fourth. (The third place in this sequence was either allotted to the South King, Feng Yunshan, now safely dead, or to Hong's eldest son, Tiangui, still only four years old.)[28] In an abbreviated history of the Taiping movement and its beliefs, written by two of Yang Xiuqing's close advisers and issued on his personal orders in 1854, Yang is described as being "personally ordered by the Heavenly Father to descend into the world, to become the Senior Assistant and the Chief of Staff of the Heavenly Kingdom, to save the hungry and redeem the sick, and to rule the younger brothers and sisters of all nations throughout the world."[29] In the same text Yang's "Holiness" is distinguished from the "eminence" of the other kings, just as the "kindness and liberality" of Yang the Comforter is separated from the mere "tolerance" of the other kings.[30]

On March 2, 1854, God pays another visit to earth through the mouth of Yang. This time, His message is in two parts. One part is again directed against the veterans from Guangxi, especially those of the highest ranks, just below the kings; three of these men are manacled and lectured on duty and morality before they are released. Two other men, senior Guangxi veterans, are brought forward and accused in front of all their colleagues of sleeping with their wives on four or five occasions, instead of following the Taiping prohibitions of sexual love until such time as final victory over the demons has been won. One of these men—now a minister at court, and in earlier days the collaborator with Hong Xiuquan on the expanded Taiping version of the Ten Commandments—is given a pardon after he makes a full confession. The other is condemned to death, along with his wife, by being beheaded in public, on the grounds that they tried to suborn their female staff from revealing the news of what they had done.[31] In making his accusations, God through Yang reminds the Taiping officials of the penetrating power of his vision, which has led him to unmask traitors in the Taiping ranks on crucial occasions in the past, both in the Guiping region and in occupied Yongan. By pinning this scrutiny to the intimate activities of the bedchamber, Yang even more strongly makes the point that no one can escape God's all-seeing eyes and Yang's network of informers.[32]

In the second part of his March message God speaks through Yang of the fundamental virtues that are embedded in China's classical texts. God first states his position elliptically, through a riddle-like couplet:

The heroes of old are never lost to us,
For their achievements have been preserved for us in the pages of books.

Once the Taiping officials, on God's urgings, have done their best to explain this utterance, God through Yang gives his own elaboration:

"You should ask Fourth Brother [Yang] to notify your Heavenly King that among the ancient books which were condemned as demonic are Four Books and Thirteen Classics which advocate Heavenly feeling and truth. These books exhort people to be filial and loyal to their country. For this reason, East King requested me to order the preservation of those books. You should keep the books in compliance with truth, filial piety, and loyalty, but destroy those which celebrate sensual desire and absurdity. Historical writings throughout the ages, in venerating good and condemning evil, have inspired filial piety and loyalty among people, motivating them to kill rebellious officials and prodigal sons. The absolute moral standard which they advocate is crucial to social mentality and ethics. Moreover, since I created Heaven and Earth, most of the faithful men and heroes I have sent down have been responsible persons. These heroes are not necessarily demons, so their names are recorded in various writings and last forever. How could you destroy those books and erase the names of these figures? I have sent down the Heavenly King to rule the world. This is the right time for our heroes to help establish the Heavenly Law and exterminate evil. Those who remain loyal to Heaven are also motivated by immortal fame which will inspire later generations to be loyal. Also, there is no need to avoid the word *shen* (god); the same goes for many words which before were regarded as taboo. From now on, the dragons drawn from Heavenly Court should be guarded by five paws, since four paws signify a demonic serpent. The chief minister can adopt the phoenix as his symbol."

All the woman officials kneeled down and listened to the Heavenly Decree. Each of them promised to follow the Heavenly Father's instruction. The Heavenly Father returned to Heaven.[33]

In thus reasserting that certain core values of the Chinese past are preserved for all time in the Confucian classics, and can be ignored only at the Taiping's peril, Yang is striking at the heart of the doctrine that Hong Xiuquan has put together across so many years. Originally, it was Hong himself who was the scholar, filling his early pronouncements with echoes from his reading and Confucian moral judgments. But slowly the versions of his vision of 1837 came to contain more details of God's anger with Confucius, and even of Confucius' public humiliations; in the Thistle Mountain years, Jesus, through the mouth of Xiao, also joined in the chorus of condemnation. This was made clear in an account of a visit by Jesus to the Taiping mountain retreat in the winter of 1848:

Heavenly King asked Heavenly Brother: "How is Confucius doing in Heaven?"

Heavenly Brother: "When you ascended to Heaven, there were a few occasions on which Confucius was bound and whipped by Heavenly Father. He once descended unto the world and instructed people with his writings. Although he had some good points, he often made great mistakes. All his books should be burnt during the Age of Great Peace [Taiping]. However, since Confucius can be generally regarded as a good person, he is allowed to enjoy happiness in Heaven, so long as he does not descend again."[34]

A similar message, linked to anti-Manchu patriotic slogans designed to win over secret-society membership, was reiterated during the campaigns of 1852 and 1853, in the names of both Hong Xiuquan and Yang Xiuqing. But now, with the city of Nanjing, with its large population and many scholarly inhabitants, as the temporary—perhaps permanent—Heavenly Capital, Yang seeks to establish his own reputation as the preserver of eternal values. His declarations to Hong, which have been recorded and distributed to the people of Nanjing, not only show his special powers as God's mouthpiece but are also larded with references to the role of the virtuous ministers and moral exemplars drawn from the Confucian classics, especially to the central text, the Confucian *Analects*.[35]

In so appealing to mainstream Confucian values Yang Xiuqing also shows an awareness of the deep unhappiness of many people—both the educated elite and the uneducated—with the Taiping occupation. Gentry militia leaders like Zeng Guofan, who are now building up their own regionally based army forces in a sustained effort to hold back the Taipings, have shown themselves fully alive to the importance of this war over moral values, and able to fight back with pronouncements of their own. As Zeng phrases it in a proclamation widely distributed in central China at this time:

> Since the days of T'ang, Yu, and the Three Dynasties, the sages of all ages have been sustaining the traditional culture and emphasizing the order of human relationships. Hence, ruler and officials, father and children, high and low, honored and humble, were as orderly in their respective positions as hat and shoes which can never be placed upside down. Now, the Yueh [Taiping] bandits steal some dregs of foreign barbarians and adhere to the religion of God; from their fake king and fake ministers down to the soldiers and menial servants, they address one another as brothers, alleging that only Heaven can be called father. Aside from this, all the fathers of the people are brothers and all the mothers are sisters. The farmers cannot cultivate their own fields to pay taxes, because it is said that all the land belongs to the Heavenly King. The merchants cannot do their own business to make profits, because it is said that all the commodities belong to the Heavenly King. The scholars cannot read the classics of Confucius, but they have others called the doctrines of Jesus and the book of the New Testament.
>
> In short, the moral system, ethical relationships, cultural inheritance, and social institutions and statutes of the past several thousand years in China are at once all swept away. This is not only a calamity in our great Qing Dynasty but is, in fact, the most extraordinary calamity since the creation of the universe, and that is what Confucius and Mencius are crying bitterly

about in the nether world. How can all those who study books and know the characters sit comfortably with hands in sleeves without thinking of doing something about it?[36]

Yang's reassertion of certain traditional Chinese values overlaps with the Taiping discovery of a plot to open the gates of Nanjing secretly to the Qing forces encamped outside. The leader of this conspiracy, Zhang Bingyuan, is a holder of the licentiate's degree that Hong had failed to pass, an alert and inventive man, who by the time his plot is discovered in March 1854, has recruited in person and through intermediaries, an estimated six thousand disaffected soldiers and Nanjing residents. His plan secretly to open one of the eastern city gates at dawn so the Qing troops can storm inside is foiled only by the dilatoriness and suspicions of ambush by the Qing commander. There is also a disastrous muddle in which one party plans its armed link according to the Taiping calendar while the other calculates according to the traditional Qing calendar; since the two calendars use the same terms for dates that are in fact six days apart, the mistake is discovered only when it is too late.

Yang's subsequent uses of the power he has wrung from Hong Xiuquan in December 1853—to be the ultimate arbiter of death sentences in legal cases—is given ironic substance by Zhang Bingyuan's fatal subtlety. For when Zhang is first arrested, and charged with attempted treason by a Taiping informer, he convincingly insists the informer is an opium addict, who acted as he did because he was afraid that Zhang would turn him over to the authorities. For this crime the informer is executed on Yang's orders before all his charges against Zhang have been substantiated. When the main plot is unraveled and Zhang is interrogated by Yang's agents, he blithely lies again, naming thirty-four of the most talented Taiping military officers as his co-conspirators. Only when all thirty-four have been summarily executed do the Taiping leaders find they have been duped into doing themselves much of what Zhang himself had hoped to achieve. The final execution of Zhang can not atone for all these Taiping dead.[37]

The contradictions in Taiping text and policy are now so pronounced that they can hardly be concealed. But it is not only on Confucian ground that the battle is being joined. In the biblical world as well tensions and ambiguities are pressing to the fore. Hong Xiuquan, as God's second son and Jesus' closest younger brother, obviously has a kind of primacy over Yang as "fourth brother." Yet with Xiao Chaogui now long dead and the voice of Jesus stilled, Yang's double claims as voice of God and "Comforter and Wind of the Holy Spirit" give him two places in the structure of the Christian Trinity, while Hong has consistently and consciously denied the nearness of any force to God Himself. Just as Jesus himself is lesser than his father, so is the Comforter and Wind of the Holy Spirit only an emanation rather than an equal force. Moreover, though other Taiping leaders have traveled up to Heaven, and met at intervals with the Father, Son, and others in the holy families, it is Hong Xiuquan's revelation of 1837 that is the decisive one, with his vision of the golden bearded God in black dragon robe, and his special nearness to Jesus' wife and children, his elder sister-in-law, and his son Tiangui's first cousins. But how can such claims be balanced or evaluated in all their complexity, since no one in the Taiping leadership has training in theology, and Issachar Roberts has been banned from visiting the Heavenly Capital by the American commissioner, punctilious about the neutrality of the United States in the current war?

Providence, which works in many ways, gives Yang an opportunity to test the waters. It is the British who occasion the opportunity. Frustrated by their experiences with the *Hermes* in 1853, they have sent no more formal diplomatic visits. But in late June 1854 they can no longer contain their curiosity. Claiming the need for the British in Shanghai "to ascertain whether a supply of coals can be provided for the public service" from the Taiping, since coal is rumored to be stored in Wuhu, which has been intermittently under Taiping control, the British minister sends a small mission under Captain Mellersh of the *Rattler* to investigate the options. The two junior British diplomats assigned to the mission are further instructed to find out everything they can about the current state of Taiping life and belief—"their political views, their forms of government, their religious books, creeds and observances, their domestic and social habits, and all facts respecting them which seem entitled to notice."[38]

Reaching Nanjing on June 20, 1854, the British are denied permission to enter the city or its suburbs, and no Taiping come to their ship. Frustrated, they submit to Yang, the East King, thirty questions on a wide variety of topics—trade prospects, troop numbers, laws, tariffs, initiation rites, examinations, the common treasury, separation of males from females, opium prohibitions, ranks of nobility—and two intrusive ones on a matter of different import: what does it mean when Hong Xiuquan says he is Jesus' younger brother; and why, among his many titles, does the East King include those of "Comforter" and "Holy Ghost"? Yang's answer comes promptly, in a large yellow envelope, one foot wide and eighteen inches long. Though often evasive or elliptical, on the questions relating to Hong's identity and his own titles he is more direct, and the British interpreter at once translates Yang's answers:

> To your enquiry (as to whether and why I received the appellation of "the Comforter," "the Holy Ghost" and as to the meaning of the titles "Honae Teacher" and "Redeemer from Disease") I reply, that the Heavenly Father appeared upon earth and declared it as his sacred will that the Eastern Prince should redeem the people of all nations upon earth from their diseases, and that the Holy Ghost should enlighten all their blindness. The Heavenly Father has now pointed out the Eastern Prince as the Holy Ghost, and therefore given him the title of "Comforter, Holy Ghost, Honae Teacher and the Lord who redeems from disease," so that all the nations of the earth may know the confidence placed in me by the Heavenly Father in his mercy. . . .
>
> To your enquiry (whether you are to infer by the designation given to Jesus of Celestial Elder Brother and that given to the Celestial King of Second Elder Brother, that the latter is actually the child of God, or that he is so only by allegory) I reply, that the Celestial King is the second son of God, truly declared to be by the Divine Will of God. The Celestial King likewise ascended up to Heaven in his own person and there again and again received the distinct commands of God to the effect that he was the Heavenly Father's second son and the true sovereign of the myriad nations of the globe. Of this we possess indubitable proof.[39]

In return, Yang poses fifty questions of his own to Captain Mellersh; in their range and nature, the first thirty of them show with great clarity the questions that are troubling the Taiping Celestial Court about their heavenly claims. The East King writes:

> The questions I have to ask are these—
> You nations having worshipped God for so long a time, does any one among you know,
>
>   1. How tall God is, or how broad?
>   2. What his appearance or colour is?
>   3. How large his abdomen is?
>   4. What kind of beard he grows?
>   5. What colour his beard is?
>   6. How long his beard is?
>   7. What cap he wears?
>   8. What kind of clothes he wears?
>   9. Whether his first wife was the Celestial Mother, the same that brought forth the Celestial Elder Brother Jesus?

10. Whether he has had any other son born to him since the birth of Jesus his first born?
11. Whether he has had but one son, or whether, like us mortals, a great many sons?
12. Whether he is able to compose verse?
13. How rapidly can he compose verse?
14. How fierce his disposition is?
15. How great his liberality is?

You nations having worshipped God and Jesus for so long a time, does any one among you know,

16. How tall Jesus is, or how broad?
17. What his appearance or colour is?
18. What kind of beard he grows?
19. Of what colour his beard is?
20. What kind of cap and clothes he wears?
21. Whether his first wife was our elder sister?
22. How many children he has had?
23. Of what age is his eldest son?
24. How many daughters has he had?
25. Of what age is his eldest daughter?
26. How many grandsons has God at this moment?
27. How many granddaughters has God at this moment?
28. How many heavens are there?
29. Whether all the Heavens are of equal height?
30. What the highest Heaven is like?[40]

The remaining twenty of Yang's questions refer to specific problems of interpretation of New Testament passages, to the role of the "Comforter," to the nature of the Taiping mandate from God to destroy the Manchus, and the significance of Britain's alleged stance of neutrality. With a sharper touch, in the fiftieth question Yang notes, "You have the audacity to presume to impose upon us in spite of ourselves, and without any sense of propriety to represent that your object in coming to the Celestial Kingdom is the desire to get coals."[41]

The small group of foreigners on the *Rattler*—none of whom has theological training either—form what they sardonically call "a synod" with Captain Mellersh for the purpose of answering Yang as well as they can, locating apposite passages to answer specific points, and moving thoroughly through all fifty of his questions. For questions one to eight, the answer is that God has neither height nor breadth. On nine to eleven, God as spirit does not "marry," and has no son but Jesus. For twelve to fifteen, God is always merciful, and nothing to Him is impossible. On sixteen to twenty, the New Testament gives no information. On twenty-one to twenty-seven, references to the "marriage of the Lamb" as found in Revelation can only be understood figuratively, as the "union of believers with Christ." Twenty-eight to thirty are unknowable.[42] But though these answers to the specific questions are courteous and thorough, the British "synod" 's summary of their conclusions and reflections reads harshly indeed to Yang:

> In reference to your closing declarations, such as that God has specially commissioned you and your people to exterminate the imps—that your sovereign is God's own son, and the uterine brother of the Celestial Elder Brother—that he is the true sovereign of all nations—that you, the Eastern King, are appointed by God to the office of the Holy Ghost, the Comforter—I think it right to state to you distinctly that we place no faith in any one of your dogmas to this effect, and can subscribe to none of them. We believe only what is revealed to us in the Old and New Testaments, namely, that God the Father is the creator and Lord of all things—that Jesus is his only begotten son—that he came down into the world and became flesh—that he died on the cross to redeem us from our sins—that after three days he rose again from the dead, and ascended into heaven, where he is ever one with God—that he will appear once again hereafter to judge the world—that those who believe in him will be saved—and that those who do not believe in him will be lost—that the Holy Ghost is also one with God—that he has already been manifested among men, namely, shortly after the ascension of our Lord—that now those who pray for his influence will receive him in their hearts and be renewed thereby—and that these three, the Father, the Son and the Holy Ghost, are the one and true God.[43]

And the Englishmen reiterate, in conclusion, that in all problems of doubtful interpretation Yang should follow Christ's simple injunction: "Search the Scriptures, for in them ye think ye have eternal life, and they are they that testify of me."[44]

This letter is sent to the East King on June 29, 1854; next day the *Rattler* leaves Nanjing for Shanghai, where the vessel docks on July 7. The Taipings have not allowed them to ship a single lump of coal, but safely stowed on board are copies of the latest books to have left the Taiping presses, Leviticus, Deuteronomy, and Joshua, which carry the story of the wandering tribes of Israel from the death of their leader Moses to their final entry into the Promised Land, which he was fated never to see. Also on the ship is Hong's revision of the text on the nature of God, with its painstaking attempt to argue for the propositions that the "synod" has just refuted.[45] That same day of July 7, in Nanjing, God speaks again through the mouth of Yang. The message is brief and unprecedented in the history of the Taiping movement:

> "Your God has come down to you today for one reason and one reason only: namely to inform you that both the Old Testament and the New Testament, which have been preserved in foreign lands, contain numerous falsehoods. You are to inform the North King and the Wing King, who in turn will tell the East King who can inform the Heavenly King, that it is no longer useful to propagate these books."[46]

When God, through Yang, asks the assembled Taiping officials to comment, there is little for them to say. One veteran Taiping general protests that he, being illiterate, can hardly consider the merits of such a decree; another, who has a scholar's training in the old society, and senses what answer Yang really seeks, replies that "there can be no mistakes in the sacred instructions of Our Father or Our Eldest Brother," clearly implying that the messages relayed to earth by Xiao and Yang are the pure revelation, while the written text itself can be seen as suspect. God replies through Yang: "Those books are neither polished in literary terms nor are they fully complete. You must all consult together, and correct them so that they become both polished and complete."[47]

The challenge to Hong Xiuquan, and to his followers, is unmistakable: the biblical word of God, which has carried them all so far, is now to be altered by the hands and minds of men. But the words of God as revealed through Yang are correct in every detail, and none shall presume to alter them.

16

THE
KILLING

 The Bible printing stops, while Taiping leaders start to probe for errors and produce a version that can reconcile their visions with the text. The northern expedition falters, dies. The western expedition, driven from Hunan, consolidates its forces nearer home. Qing forces oust the Triad rebels from Shanghai, and reclaim the Chinese portion of the city as their own. A large Qing army remains assembled near the eastern walls of Nanjing. The Taiping program continues to be preached in town and countryside, but it is hard to collect the tithes or unify the families in their squads as the fighting swirls around them. Harder still to maintain the separation of the sexes; in early 1855 the formal ban is dropped, and married couples begin to meet without restraint, though couples meeting clandestinely out of wedlock still face execution.[1] Even some convicted opium smokers are spared the death penalty by God and Yang if they can show it was the demon devils who led them astray, though the Heavenly King still warns against the folly of addiction in a rhyming edict:

One smoke endlessly follows another; there is never satisfaction.
Why follow this stupid practice, transforming yourselves into living demons?

To sicken or die as you give up smoking is preferable to being executed—
To stop being a ghost and become human again must be the better way.[2]

Yang Xiuqing, East King and Comforter, is often ill in 1855. That does not stop his steady accretion of new powers. When he is too ill to move, he issues injunctions from his "golden bed." Sometimes, when God speaks to him, it is not in open revelation but safely in his dreams, and Yang reveals the contents of the dream the next day, treating it directly as the word of God, and expecting all to do the same.[3] When God does come down to speak through Yang directly, the pomp of the occasion grows: now imperial relatives walk on each side of Yang's palanquin in their full court robes of state, for he has formalized the roles of family members, and brought new order to their ranks within his palaces. As well as "golden" gongs and drums, "sacred guns" salute him with their cannonades as he travels on his way. All kneel to greet him, and although in the harshest winter cold, in bitter wind or snow, all need not wait for hours outside the palace for his arrival, none may slight the basic rules of protocol. Terrible is God's anger, expressed through Yang, if on one of His nocturnal visits to earth the Heavenly King's women attendants dawdle in throwing open the mighty palace gates—these being so numerous and so heavy that they sometimes simply cannot open fast enough to please.[4] Sometimes, now, it is Hong Xiuquan who must go to the entrance of his palace and greet the East King there, kneeling at his own threshold to receive the heavenly messages, while Yang stays seated in repose. On occasion Hong even goes himself to Yang's own palace when Yang is indisposed.[5]

Yang's interference in Hong Xiuquan's daily life is unremitting. Hong is blamed for lack of filial piety toward his mother by not allowing his palace women to serve her as they should.[6] Yang takes the moral position that the older mothers and wives of loyal Taiping veterans are being neglected, and forced to do the hard work in their lodgings by themselves; he orders women from the royal palaces to be assigned to help them, whether by gathering fuel or tilling in their gardens.[7] Even the role of Hong Xiuquan's beloved son Tiangui, already named as his heir apparent, is undercut by Yang. For Yang's own young son is allowed to intervene when Yang talks to God the Father, showing conspicuous filial piety by crawling forward on hands and knees to plead his father's cause before his "Heavenly Grandpapa."[8]

As has been true for several years, Yang makes political decisions in arbitrary ways. When Hong Xiuquan tries to fill the depleted ranks of his attendant kings, by naming two of the most trusted veteran commanders from Guiping days, Qin Rigang and Hu Yihuang, to be kings in place of the dead Feng and Xiao, at first Yang acquiesces, but when the two are temporarily checked in battle in the west, Yang deprives them of their newly awarded titles.[9] North King Wei is constantly summoned, at any hour of day or night, to hear the relaying of God's instructions, and threatened with public beatings for his laziness if he dares delay. Qin Rigang, one of the new kings so soon deposed, is accused by God of "failure in fulfilling his duties" and threatened with both prison and enslavement.[10] Those decreed by Yang to be guilty of "grossly violating the law of Heaven" meet death as "lighted Heavenly lanterns," being soaked in oil and set afire.[11]

Senior military officers are flogged if they fail to pay proper homage to the officials from Yang's household they encounter on the Nanjing streets; and if they refuse to express regret for their behavior, but with "hearts filled with hatred reply in abusive words," they are executed.[12] Members of Yang's palace staff, accused by him of neglecting their duties while he is ill, or of allowing improper conversations in the palace, are also publicly executed.[13] God feels the need to return to earth through Yang, and give a brief explanation for these killings: "These rebels betrayed Heaven and deceived the East King. Didn't they realize that the East King, their older brother, fell ill to atone for their sins? They dared to act with disdain and play deaf in the palace. Now their treacherous hearts have been treated thus!"[14]

In military affairs the East King's role—even when he is ill—is also paramount. As senior chief of staff, perhaps in sporadic consultations with Hong Xiuquan, it is Yang who coordinates the far-flung campaigns. He sends massive reinforcements—futilely it turns out—to try and save the beleaguered northern expedition. He approves the campaigns to recover Wuchang, and advance to Hunan, and in 1855 coordinates the armies sent to Anhui province and Jiangxi. He realizes too the crucial importance of the city of Zhenjiang, on the south bank of the Yangzi River, fifty miles downstream from Nanjing, to guard the approaches to the Heavenly Capital as well as access to the Grand Canal. Thus when the Qing forces launch an all-out campaign to retake Zhenjiang, Yang responds by sending massive reinforcements and all the ammunition that can be spared, as well as generals of outstanding experience and ability. The result, after savage fighting, is a great Taiping victory and the relief and reinforcement of the city.

It is Yang also, when the troops are still exhausted and nursing their heavy casualties from that protracted battle, who decides with great strategic insight that this is the time to launch an all-out assault on the vast Qing base camp that spreads around the eastern flank of the Heavenly Capital itself. Though protesting vehemently, and close to open disobedience, the tired generals rally their soldiers and in three days of savage fighting in the month of June 1856 use the element of surprise and all their battlefield experience to hit the base camps in succession with such impact and success that more than ten thousand Qing imperial troops are killed or routed, their encampments all destroyed, and their discredited leaders sent fleeing scores of miles to safety. The Qing commandant, Xiang Rong, who has been dogging the Taiping's heels since the campaigns in Yongan and Guilin five years before, broken by this last humiliation, falls ill and dies.[15]

The East King views these victories as proof of his powers, and his ambitions grow accordingly. It pains him to see his titles less than those of the Heavenly King, whose glory as "Lord of Ten Thousand Years" outshines Yang's "Nine Thousand Years" by what seems to Yang too large a margin. Planning with care, Yang sends the generals most loyal to the Heavenly King on important new assignments, even though they and their troops are still not fully rested up: Shi Dakai to Hubei province in the west, Qin Rigang to Danyang in Jiangsu, and Wei Changhui, North King, to Nanchang in Jiangxi. Once they have left Nanjing city with their troops, Yang tells his Heavenly King that he too would like the title of "Ten Thousand Years." Without his loyal commanders near him, the Heavenly King is trapped, but pretends to accede. He suggests Yang's coming birthday, still two months away, as the time for this auspicious event. And then, somehow evading Yang's omnipresent spies, Hong sends trusted messengers to Shi and Qin and Wei, ordering their instant return to the Heavenly Capital to thwart this design at treason.[16]

By the strangest of coincidences, the best description of what happens next comes from a restless Irishman, who can barely read or write, and whose name is no longer even known to us. After the months he spends in Zhenjiang and Nanjing during 1856, the Irishman dictates his story that same year to a ship's officer named Reynolds. Reynolds is a man who knows China well and believes in the truth of the Irishman's strange tale. So do experienced missionaries living in Shanghai.[17]

The presence of an Irishman in the Taiping base areas in 1856 can be explained by the desperate nature of the times. The strict neutrality laws that the diplomats try and follow cannot prevent a certain number of rootless men from drifting into the Taiping camp to offer their services to the Heavenly King. From the earliest days of 1853, Westerners have been selling guns and ammunition to the Taiping, along with their services.[18] Amongst such mercenaries one finds "3 black men," perhaps from India, for all are described as British subjects, who have made their way to Zhenjiang to join the Taiping.[19] Some Englishmen continue in the lucrative if risky business of trading forbidden war goods with the various rebels by using false bills of lading, gunpowder being itemized as "Chinese snuff" and Enfield rifles as "umbrellas."[20] Even the simpleminded can play such games, like the Englishman discovered by the mate of the *Hermes,* but not taken seriously, for he seemed "too stupid-looking ever to have been in a ship of war."[21] An American named Drinker begins to recruit a small army of foreign mercenaries—many of whom are British—in the Canton region, till prevented by the joint action of the British and Americans.[22] To the British governor in Hong Kong, these exemplars are only a sampling of "a host of filibustering cutthroats and deserters (subjects of the Queen) who, under the pretence of joining the patriots, are committing every species of robbery and outrage."[23]

Such adventurers are not just drawn from British ranks: the French captain de Plas has placed in irons on the *Cassini* a French deserter, who tries to pretend he is an Italian, and observes large numbers of deserters crewing on an American ship, the *Challenge,* where they far outnumber the Chinese seamen.[24] An Italian, known by the name of Antonie, or Antonio, has joined the Taiping as early as 1853. He is a powerful man, whose pride is a sword weighing almost twenty pounds—his specialty lies in pretending to fall down dead on the battlefield till Qing troops approach his body, at which point he leaps to his feet, decapitating several of the astonished enemy. His foreign status gives him special dispensations, for the Taiping allow him "money for his Opium pipe and Grog of which he seemed very fond."[25] There are at least five "Manilamen," long haired and dressed in Chinese style, and worshiping God the Taiping way, also stationed in Zhenjiang. They serve as executioners for their Taiping masters, one of them being assigned to kill women found guilty of breaking the Taiping laws.[26]

The Irishman knows his weapons well, and is flexible in his allegiances, having been fighting for a time with the Triad rebels in Shanghai, and for a period with the Qing. Choosing, for obvious reasons, not to stay on in Shanghai when the Qing recapture the Chinese city, he makes his way overland to Zhenjiang, where, knowing no Chinese, and interpreters being rare, he shows his loyalty to the Taiping leaders by kneeling on the ground before them, and by participating in their religious services, both before each meal and on the Sabbath day.[27] The advent of the Sabbath is

announced in a way that even illiterate Westerners and Chinese still puzzled by the new Christian weekly calendar cannot miss, with large flags
hung across the main streets of the town.[28]

Arriving in April 1856, just after the triumphal raising of the Zhenjiang
siege, with an American companion, Charles Thompson from Boston, the
Irishman is first assigned to help supervise the collection of rice supplies
from Yangzhou on the Grand Canal. For a full month, dressed now in
Chinese clothes, he works at this task, estimating that thirty thousand
Chinese, men and women, old and young, have been conscripted for the
labor. When that area is exhausted, he ranges farther afield with the Taiping troops and a body of one hundred cavalry, throwing up temporary
earthworks to defend themselves from Qing patrols as they scour the more
distant countryside for stores of grain. He estimates that the colossal foraging party gives the Taiping forces in Zhenjiang two years' food supply.
Nanjing itself reputedly has enough grain stored to withstand a six-year
siege.[29]

In May, two more Europeans join them. The four Westerners are
assigned to the main Taiping army commanded by Qin Rigang as it fights
successively against the remaining Qing encampments near Zhenjiang,
where the Taiping obtain massive supplies of ammunition and many cannon, prior to returning to Nanjing for the triumphant strike ordered by
the East King against the Qing encampments there. In the hard-fought
battles these Western observers note the finer points of Taiping battle
technique: their speed at throwing up defensive works, their use of mobile
pontoon bridges, their courage under fire, and their strategy of collecting
all flammable material from houses around a given Qing emplacement
and ringing it with fire, then cutting down the Qing troops one by one as
they flee the blazing circle. The Irishman also notes the Taiping practice
of destroying every "large building" that they find—these being presumably temples, the homes of the wealthier landlords, or the headquarters of
local officials—while leaving intact all those "belonging to the poor," even
though the villagers "would all flee on our approach" in any case. In
one of these engagements his Boston friend, Charles Thompson, is fatally
wounded in the chest, dying after ten days, although no fewer than three
doctors in the Taiping service attend his wounds. As he "frets" before his
death, Charles Thompson tells the Irishman he would rather spend three
years in a United States prison than three months longer with the Taiping
troops.[30]

Having proven his loyalty and effectiveness, the Irishman and one of
his new companions are summoned to meet General Qin Rigang himself.

Qin offers them horses for their use, and a transfer to Nanjing. Accepting the offer gladly as indicating a rise in status, they travel to the Heavenly Capital and—after careful scrutiny from the guards and several hours' delay—are allowed inside the gates. Here they meet again with General Qin and his associate General Hu Yihuang, the two "kings" added to the roster by Hong Xiuquan but soon to be demoted by Yang Xiuqing. After being carefully searched for concealed arms, the two Westerners are taken to audience with the East King, Yang Xiuqing. Unable to speak Chinese themselves, they can do no more than observe that not only do all those present kneel before the East King and utter a short prayer, but that everyone is also made to kneel whenever either of Yang's two young sons, aged three and seven, are present in the room with their father—as long as ten minutes at a stretch on some occasions.[31]

By the summer of 1856 the Irishman has found an English-speaking interpreter living in Nanjing, a Chinese man "formerly a carpenter at Canton," so when he is next summoned with his friends for an audience with Yang Xiuqing, whom the Irishman refers to simply as "Number 2," the dialogue is somewhat more protracted:

> The next morning about six we were brought up before No. 2, who enquired how we fought thinking we only used our fists—We shewed him, we could use both a sword and firearms, upon which he gave us a stick and we shewed him the cuts and guards as well as we knew. We told him we only used our fists when we were drunk, showing our meaning by lifting a cup and motioning to be drunk. They made us go through a little pugilism, which amused the second King very much, he laughing heartily. They brought us an English pistol asking me to fire it off—placing a piece of paper against a wall some fifty yards distant. I put the ball into the centre—No. 2 standing behind me while taking aim appeared nervous while I was using the weapon.
>
> Looking round and taking notice of his Palace which was very extensive, he asked us whether our Emperor had one similar to his, to which we, of course, answered—No![32]

The Irishman finds Yang himself to be a not unattractive figure: "He was up early and retired late—and appeared to get through a mass of business. In person he was a fine noble looking man, with a pleasant countenance and mild affable manner."[33]

Given comfortable lodgings by the East King in the house of one of his brothers-in-law, not more than fifty yards from the East King's own palace, the Westerners—though they pine for action—pass the next three months in enforced idleness. Sometimes they sing whatever songs they know, to pass the time, and their host, amused, provides them with wine, which he keeps in his mansion despite the prohibitions and likes to drink himself. In the main, as the Irish narrator puts it, there is little to do "but wander through the city, amusing ourselves as well as circumstances would allow us." To their surprise, the women seem to roam around quite freely, at least when they are at work, carrying bricks and stones, wood, and rice. Not all entertainments are banned, and they see, on two occasions, "very long processions formed of dragons, and representations of all sorts of animals made of paper."[34]

Though trade is formally banned within the city, the Westerners note there seems to be a fascination with Western objects—musical boxes, gloves, umbrellas, and watches and clocks, which are sold on "almost every street." Pistols are on sale too, and the Westerners are able to buy not only a sword but a "Deane and Adam's revolver."[35] Two examples of these latest Western manufactures are given the pride of place outside Hong Xiuquan's palace, a spot one might expect to be reserved for the decorative spirit tablets that protect the palaces and mansions of the wealthiest Chinese: "two handsome brass 12 pdr. [pounder] shell guns, marked Massachusetts 1855, with American oak carriages," in perfect condition, down to their "gutta percha buffers," and the wads "attached to the tomkin." Bought by the Qing for use against the Triad rebels in Shanghai, and transferred to the garrison force outside Nanjing, the guns have now been dragged into the Heavenly Capital and this honorable resting place.[36]

The two foreigners also acquire, from somewhere, a Chinese "boy" who speaks Portuguese and English and gives them greater mobility and familiarity with the city through his skill with languages.[37] During this period the generals who first hired him have all been sent away on campaigns by Yang, so the Irishman is ignorant of the plots and counterplots that are swirling all about him. It is not from these Westerners but from a Taiping text that we know the East King's last utterances in God's name—two brief and anguished cries on August 15, 1856, unlike anything he has said before. The first, at dawn: "Qin Rigang is helping the demons, Chen Chengyong is helping the demons, ensuring that the city of your God is set aflame. There is no way to save it." And at noon: "The officials in the Court can acquire no strength, for they do not with true reverence worship the Lord their God."[38]

We cannot tell, from our current vantage point, whether this cry of frustration refers to defeats in the field just suffered by Generals Qin and

Chen; or to some knowledge Yang has acquired through his omnipresent informants that these and other generals are heading back toward the Heavenly Capital at the urgent summons of their Heavenly King; or simply to his intuitions of impending catastrophe to himself and his plans. But the same Irish mercenary does leave a gentler but still haunting picture: "The last time we saw him [Yang] he was lecturing in a public place to about three thousand Canton men . . . who were all on their knees. We heard they had hesitated to go out to fight."[39]

On September 1, 1856, around midnight, the North King, Wei Changhui, having handed over command of the Jiangxi campaign to subordinates, reaches Nanjing, with about three thousand of his veteran troops. General Qin Rigang, having had less distance to go, is already in the city, with selected troops from his army, the victors of the summer battles both at Zhenjiang and outside Nanjing itself. After swift consultations with Hong Xiuquan's brother-in-law, and Hu Yihuang—the other recently deposed king—and a brief talk with Hong Xiuquan himself, the two generals decide not to wait for Shi Dakai but to move at once, before Yang can rally the more than six thousand troops in the city who are believed totally loyal to him. Led by the North King, so long humiliated by Yang Xiuqing, the troops storm Yang's palace, and cut Yang down before he manages to flee—into a "hollow wall" that he has prepared for such emergencies, according to one account. Then, despite a prior agreement with Hong that Yang should be the only one to die, in a few murderous hours, Qin's and Wei's troops slaughter every one of Yang's family and followers who can be found in his palace, male or female, of whatever rank or age or occupation. Yang's own head is severed and hung from a pole in the street.[40]

Wakened by the sound of cannon fire at four in the morning, the Irishman and his friend, sleeping near Yang's palace, hurry at once to the street door of their residence, but the streets are lined with troops from Qin's and Wei's armies, who will not let them leave their lodging. By daybreak, when they are able to make their way to Yang's palace, they find the streets full of corpses—"the bodyguard, officers, musicians, clerks and household servants of No. 2"—and the palace being looted. Within a few hours the huge complex is "completely gutted."[41]

There remains, for Hong Xiuquan as for Wei and Qin, the problem of the six thousand or so loyal followers of the dead East King, many of them veterans from Thistle Mountain, who are still at large, scattered across the entire city of Nanjing. Though many of these soldiers have been loyal God-worshipers for five years or more, it is not clear whether their deepest allegiance is to Yang or to Hong. One can risk being wrong about their future conduct, or one can preempt the question. Hong Xiuquan, in consultation with the North King and the other generals, decides not to take the risk. The plan they arrive at is devious and effective. In an angry edict the Heavenly King denounces the senseless slaying of all Yang's family and palace staff, and the bloodbath and looting that have followed. North King Wei and General Qin Rigang are arrested and made to kneel with chains around their necks in front of Hong's palace gate. Hong's palace women issue forth with a huge proclamation written in vermilion ink on a length of yellow silk, seven or eight feet long. The edict sentences the two men to a savage punishment of five hundred blows, the same punishment once meted out to traitors in the Taiping ranks during the Thistle Mountain days. The Heavenly King's decision is read out in clear, commanding tones, by Hong's palace women at the gate, and some of the East King's surviving followers press close to read the message while others listen with attention. All of Yang's followers are invited to witness the beatings, which are to be administered inside the walls of Hong's huge palace. As the blows begin to fall on the erring generals, who are kneeling on the ground in the outer courtyard of Hong's own palace, Yang's surviving followers crowd in to watch. They leave their arms at the gate, as is customary for security, and are seated in comfort in two long halls on either side of the central courtyard. When it is estimated that almost all are there, the doors and gates are closed, hemming them in. The beatings stop. Yang's followers are trapped.

Among the guards at the front of the Heavenly King's palace are the Western mercenaries. As the unnamed Irishman then tells the story:

> Next morning at daylight the doors and windows of these prisons were opened, and several powder bags thrown in on the prisoners, while the entrance was strongly guarded. In one house the soldiers entered with little resistance and massacred the whole, but in the other the prisoners fought with the bricks from the walls and partitions, most desperately for upwards of six hours before they were got under. In addition to musketry, a two pounder discharged grape at them.—These poor devils then stripped themselves, and many were seen to fall from sheer exhaustion. At last Nos. 5 and 7 [Wei and Qin] called upon their men to draw their right arms from their sleeves, so as to distinguish them from No. 2's men; they then rushed in and massacred the remainder—We shortly after entered, and, good heavens! such a scene, the dead bodies were in some places five and six deep; some had hung themselves and others were severely scorched from the explosions of the powder bags thrown in.—These bodies were removed from this to a

field and remained uncovered.—After this every master of a house in the city had to give an account of how many men, women and children were residing under his roof, to every one of whom was given a small chop [seal imprint] which they wore on their breast, and if they found any of No. 2's men they were to secure them—For several weeks these people were brought to the execution ground in parcels of fives, tens, hundreds, and thousands, who were all beheaded. All the women and children also, any one who had eaten of No. 2's rice suffered.[42]

Even after this horrendous slaughter, neither Wei nor Qin is satisfied, and the killing continues for three months, until thousands more have lost their lives, including all five hundred of Yang's former palace women and female retainers.[43]

Shi Dakai, the Wing King, has had to travel much farther than Wei or Qin to reach Nanjing, from far up the Yangzi River, near Wuchang. He reaches the Heavenly Capital in early October, having been informed on the way of the incredible slaughter. Revolted and angry, Shi meets with North King Wei, and blames him for the excesses of the killing, warning that such action will only lead to Qing victory. Wei, furious in his turn, suggests that Shi may be in Yang's camp, or a traitor for the Qing. Warned by friends that he too may be assassinated, and finding the gates closed against him, Shi slips out of the city in secret, the same day on which he entered it. Late that night, Wei and Qin surround Shi's mansion, as they had the East King's, and force their way past the guards. Finding Shi gone, they kill his wife and children, and all his retinue.[44]

Moving back upriver, west of Nanjing, Shi Dakai rallies the troops loyal to him, along with the troops of other disaffected generals and the forces of various Triad organizations. Shi is the most popular of all the Taiping commanders, despite his youth, and is able to consolidate a force of close to one hundred thousand men in all. With this huge force at his back, and the river to give him mobility, he turns his tracks once more to Nanjing, telling his Heavenly King that only the heads of Wei and Qin can satisfy him now. Alerted to this newest danger, North King Wei dispatches General Qin to block Shi's march, blows up the hallowed porcelain tower to deny Shi's artillery a commanding height from which to shell the city, and lays plans to imprison Hong Xiuquan. But before Wei can complete his plans, Hong assembles his own loyal elite bodyguard of troops, and has Wei killed, sending Wei's head to Shi. Qin is killed soon after, lured back to the city by a ruse.[45] Placated by these events, though they hardly compensate for the loss of his family and his closest friends,

Shi enters Nanjing again in pomp and majesty, to a hero's welcome, in December 1856.

Almost as Shi arrives, the Irishman and one of his companions decide the time has come to depart. They have seen enough. "Finding matters at sixes and sevens," as he tells his interlocutor Reynolds, "and beheading the order of the day, we thought it best to leave these rebels to themselves."[46] The two mercenaries dress themselves in Chinese clothes and reach Shanghai ten days later after a risky journey by wheelbarrow, on foot, and in a rented boat, helped and sometimes fleeced by local peasant guides. Entering Shanghai, they find to their complete bewilderment that it is only December 20, 1856. The impact of their experiences has distorted all their sense of time: "So completely had we lost all dates, that we imagined the year of 1857 had advanced to about February."[47]

FAMILY

CIRCLES

 Never for a moment, now that Yang is safely slaughtered, does Hong fail publicly to revere him. In proclamations for the remaining years of the Taiping kingdom, Yang's role as Voice of God and Comforter is remembered, his princely title of East King always used. One of Yang's brothers, who somehow survives the killing, is honored and enfeoffed in the nobility.[1] And though Yang's sons have all met their fate, Hong gives his own second son, Tianyou, to be the East King's posthumous adopted son, to keep Yang's family line alive. So that Jesus, too, can have his line maintained on earth as well as through his heavenly children, Hong also names his eldest son, Tiangui, the Taiping heir apparent, to be Jesus' adopted son.[2]

These grandchildren of God are joined by the two surviving sons of the dead West King, Xiao Chaogui. The two boys merit inclusion in this select group since Xiao, married to one of the Heavenly King's female cousins, had been awarded the title of Heavenly Brother-in-law, and hence Xiao's two sons can be seen as nephews to Jesus and to Hong Xiuquan, and grandchildren to God. Given special recognition in view of their father's heroic death, these two sons of Xiao are regularly invoked first among all the family in the state documents issued by Hong Xiuquan.[3]

Besides creating from among the children and the dead this inner core of relatives linked directly by marriage or descent to the Divinity, in the crisis of trust and confidence that follows the murderous months of 1856 Hong turns back to the adults of his own immediate family for solace and support. The two men he feels he most can trust are his own two elder brothers, Hong Renfa and Hong Renda. In 1850 they and their families made the hazardous journey from Guanlubu to join him in Thistle Mountain, and since those days they have campaigned at his side and served him loyally in his court. With only Shi Dakai left alive of the original five subordinate kings, Hong seeks to swell the numbers again by promoting his brothers to make up the lack, and he names Renfa as "Peace King" and Renda as "Blessings King." Lest this seem a slight to Shi Dakai, he raises Shi's title at the same time from "Wing King"—which always bore a slightly peripheral air when contrasted to the basic compass points of the earlier kings—to "Righteous King." When Shi unexpectedly declines the new honor, Hong is in a quandary, and takes what seems to be a diplomatic course: Shi is left with his "Wing King" title, to which Hong adds the title of "Lightning of the Holy Spirit" to match that once held by Yang, while the two brothers are transferred to a new order of nobility just below the kingly level.[4]

The compromise pleases no one. Shi resents the power still given to Hong's brothers, whom he believes to be incompetent. The brothers resent Shi's status as the lone survivor of the earlier order, and do everything they can to undercut his power. Thus although for almost half a year, in 1857, Shi more or less runs the region of Nanjing, it is a solitary and lonely kind of rule, with all his family gone: he is reported to live "in seclusion" and not to receive oral messages but only petitions in writing. These he answers during the night, having his staff affix his responses next morning on the wall outside his residence.[5] In the later recollections of a Taiping general familiar with this period in Nanjing, "When the Wing King returned to the Capital, the whole court recommended that he take over the government and the people welcomed this; but the Sovereign was not pleased and would only employ [his brothers] the Peace Prince and the Blessings Prince. . . . The people at court were very displeased at the Sovereign for using these two men. They had neither talent nor planning ability; but they were versed in the Heavenly Doctrines and in no way disagreed with the Heavenly King's ideas." According to this same general, Li Xiucheng, it was the brothers' "suspicions and obstruction" that "forced" Shi to leave Nanjing, a defection that left "no one in charge at court."[6]

Shi Dakai departs peacefully from Nanjing in the summer of 1857, taking his most loyal troops with him. Whatever his personal animosity toward Hong's brothers may be, he does not put it into clear words, and his loyalty to his Heavenly King does not seem to have been affected by their behavior. The manifesto that Shi posts in the cities through which he passes gives as his reason for leaving his desire to continue with the campaign in the west and expand Taiping power there, "in order to repay the Sovereign's grace and kindness." The real reason is phrased by Shi in an elliptical form that would doubtless be clear to those who knew the full story, but would have left all others in the dark:

Shi, of the Heaven-ordained Taiping Heavenly Kingdom, Lightning of the Holy
    Spirit, Commanding General of the Entire Army, and Wing King:
I regret my lack of talent or wisdom,
And thus being unworthy of the favor shown me by the Heavenly Kingdom.
But, having vowed to express my loyalty and integrity,
My humble heart has but one purpose:
Above, that I may face August Heaven;
Below, that I may bear witness to the men of old.

Last year, amidst the disaster and turbulence,
I hurried in anguish back to the Capital.
Confident that my unwavering loyalty
Would be clearly understood by my Holy Ruler.
However, things were not quite so,
And imperial edicts were issued one after another.
Dark suspicions abounded on all sides,
How can my own brush record them all?

Because of this, I am determined to exert my utmost,
To lead a military campaign and reemphasize my sincerity.
I shall endeavor to reward those who walk with God,
In order to repay the Sovereign's grace and goodness.[7]

With Shi Dakai's departure—he was never to return—Hong is in a predicament. "Morale declined and there was no unified policy," in General Li's words. "Each went his own way. The Sovereign did not place complete confidence in anyone. He had been frightened by the East, North and Wing Kings, and dared not trust other ministers, but placed all his trust in members of his own clan."[8]

Yet the Qing forces are unable to take advantage of these inherent weaknesses in the Taiping ranks. With their main besieging camps around Nanjing smashed in the 1856 campaigns, and with their own morale and finances at a low ebb, the Qing also face two new distractions: one is the growth of a second major rebellion, this time in northern China, that of the Nian, which severs communication lines to the south and makes any coordinated assault on the Taiping almost impossible. The other is the slow drift of the Qing and British once again into a state of open warfare over the problems of residence of foreign merchants in Canton, the levels of tariffs to be imposed on foreign goods, and the stationing of a permanent diplomatic representative in Peking. Just as the Nian bring an end to the regular use of the Grand Canal as a supply route to the north, British sea power severs the last main lines of contact on the sea, effectively leaving the local regional commanders in the south and center of China to formulate their own strategies to deal with the Taiping.[9]

The financial records from the treasuries of Emperor Xianfeng's own imperial household show the incredible straits to which the Qing court is reduced: suspending orders for the silks and porcelain that are such a conspicuous proof of imperial glory, canceling both wedding and funeral stipends for the Manchu Banner troops and their families, melting down "golden" bells—assays proved these to be only three-tenths gold, five-tenths silver, and two-tenths copper by volume—to make into small gold ingots of five to fifteen ounces with which to buy food and essential supplies, and melting bronze ritual vessels and Buddhist statues to make coins. The court also forces contributions by rank and seniority from all officials, reduces staff in selected government departments to economize on salaries, and cancels all repairs to palace buildings.[10] By 1857 some Imperial Banner families have reached starvation levels of a few pounds of relief grain a month, and the emperor allows his Banner soldiers to found their own banks and rice stores in an attempt to shield military personnel from the effects of the dramatically increasing prices.[11] Even so the Qing armies might have been able to crush the Taiping altogether, at this time of disarray, had it not been for the Qing leaders' reiterated insistence that all the veteran Taiping troops from the Guangxi days would be executed if captured, with no exceptions. This meant that even those wavering in their loyalty to the Heavenly King had every incentive not to give up the fight.[12]

"The clan" in which general Li feels that Hong places "all his trust" includes not only Hong's brothers, Renfa and Renda, his sister, and the family of his senior earthly wife, Lai. There are also the eight sons of his eldest brother, and the two sons of his second elder brother. Hong himself has two other young sons besides the two who have been named the adopted sons of Jesus and of Yang Xiuqing, and as many as eight daughters by various consorts, many of whom are married—though following Chinese practice several of these marriages are arranged ones among children, who have not yet reached puberty and begun to live together.[13] There are also dozens of cousins from the Hong family in Guanlubu and other areas of Guangdong and Guangxi, many of whom trekked to Thistle Mountain to join Hong Xiuquan in the beginning of his movement, or fled their homes later when Qing troops moved in on Hong's ancestral home to destroy the family gravesites and arrest or blackmail any living relatives they could find. Commencing in 1856 and 1857, these men are named by Hong to honorific titles in the newly established category of the Taiping "Imperial Clan."[14]

In regulating the numbers of wives for his most senior associates, Hong Xiuquan has shown himself broad-minded: the East and West Kings were each allowed eleven (though whether in fact or as a posthumous honor is not made clear); the junior kings and Hong's own brothers could have six; senior officials three, middle-rank officials two, and junior officials and the common people one each. As Hong explains to those who might feel frustration at this system: "Don't be jealous. The Heavenly Father made Adam, and linked him with Eve. This at first was right, there was one man and one wife." But later, when God and Jesus descended to earth, "by their grace it was given to me to increase the number of wives." There would be no retroactive punishments for those who, carried away by the ending of the marital intercourse prohibitions in 1855, had in their enthusiasm exceeded the quotas due to them by rank: "Those who before this Edict have exceeded their allowance (or who have more than one) I shall overlook it."[15]

Freed by the murder of the East King from obtrusive scrutiny of his palace affairs, the Heavenly King can now run the extended family of his palace women in any way he chooses. Hong's palace complex in the heart of Nanjing is a universe in its own right. In the imperial palaces of China's rulers, the administrative duties and much of the service for the emperor and his women were performed by eunuchs, while non-castrated males were restricted to the outer edges of the court, beyond the inner gates, where they staffed the regular bureaus and defended the palace walls. The Taiping employ no eunuchs, so Hong's inner palaces are run entirely by the women themselves, under his general supervision. The approximately two thousand women working there are divided into three main categories—the female ministers and bureaucrats; the female maids and attendants; and the women of Hong's immediate family, from his mother,

mother-in-law, and senior consort Lai, to the many other consorts he has drawn into his chambers on the long road from Thistle Mountain to his Celestial Kingdom. According to his son Tiangui, Hong Xiuquan had eighty-eight such consorts in Nanjing.[16]

Hong's son Tiangui, nine years old by Chinese reckoning in 1857, is considered too old by his father to stay any longer within the inner palace. He is given four wives of his own, and sent to live with them in the outer palace, forbidden even to see his own mother or sisters. But yearning for their company Tiangui sometimes, when his father is preoccupied with court business, manages to slip back into the palace, and visit with them.[17] Tiangui, like his brothers and sisters, is bound by the stern rules their father has drawn up for their behavior, and made them learn by heart: at four, the boys are no longer allowed close contact with their older sisters; at seven, they can no longer sleep in their mothers' or other consorts' beds; they must also stay ten feet or more away from their sisters, and learn to bathe themselves; by nine they should not even see their grandmothers. Their sisters' separation from their brothers is similar: after five, they must never be touched by their brothers, and after nine they stay entirely with the women and are not meant to see even their younger brothers any more.[18]

In the Eden from which he has just banished his son, Hong Xiuquan creates the rules of order for his women of all ranks and classes. The rules are at once meticulous and intimate, spread ruminatively across five hundred stanzas of Hong's discursive verse.[19] There shall be no weeping in this garden, no long faces, and no raised and angry voices like dogs barking. No one will be jealous.[20] A perfect order will prevail, as each woman sees to the task assigned her in the duty rosters;[21] there will be no leaving the precincts without permission, roll calls will be taken when the gong sounds once, the palace will be locked at night, and night inspectors make their rounds.[22] Hong does not like the noisy use of gongs and drums, for all loud and sudden noises are upsetting to him, although they have their role in sounding the hours and rhythms of the day. But he likes to hear the fuller, deeper sounds of an organ, which has been found in the city and taken to his palace, where it is kept under lock and key when not in use.[23] And most of all he enjoys the gentle, plaintive music of the plucked string *Qin;* to him, this is the truest sound of the Kingdom of Heavenly Peace, and he orders that *Qin* music sound through the palace every evening from twilight until after midnight, and that all the palace women practice their music when they are not attending to their other duties.[24]

In Hong's palaces, everything must be clean, to avoid the dangers of fire or disease. Leprosy is a terror that has struck the palaces before, leaving "faces swollen, black and filthy, bodies putrid." No piles of rubbish may be left around, all spittoons must be emptied carefully and neatly at every change of shift, and all flying insects must be kept away from Hong's own person, especially in the evening. One attendant fans them away from Hong's head, and one from his feet. The fan must not be nearer than five inches to his body, and never may it touch him.[25] The bathhouse must be another world of cleanliness and order: no women may go there when not on duty, and those who use it must be recorded on a roster of attendance and afforded perfect privacy.[26]

When Hong himself is at his ablutions, the women always prepare four sets of clean and scented towels, some of yellow and some of white silk, and when the weather calls for it the towels are heated. His handkerchiefs, sweat towels, and cloths for face and beard are always clean and regularly changed.[27] One group of attendants is assigned to the care of his upper body, one for his lower. His beard is trimmed, his hair is combed and neatly coiled, his nose is wiped, his feet and lower parts kept clean, and the area "near his navel" cleansed with special care.[28] The two attendants assigned each morning to his dressing, may stand directly in front of him, and face him, but like every other woman in the court they may not raise their eyes higher than his shoulders, and never meet his gaze directly.[29] Making sure not to touch his bared neck, they robe him in his gown, they see to the even hanging of his sleeves to right and left, and smooth the decorative collar round his shoulders. His hat is placed upon his head always by being held at the back, and completely straight.[30]

All the women in the palace, on rising, rinse their mouths so that their breath is fresh, and carefully clean the area round their eyes.[31] Their hands too are always clean. Never may they pluck their brows or hair, never wear outlandish clothes and never bind their feet, but always keep their hair smoothly combed, their topknots neatly coiffed, their dresses bright and clean and trimmed with flowers.[32] As Hong tells them, being pretty is not the point, for when did Jesus or the Heavenly Father mind an ugly woman? It is being well groomed that is essential to one's looks.[33]

When Hong walks forth in his palace gardens, by day or night, his women check that his clothes are warm enough, and may even hold his arm to steady him. If he wishes to ride through the gardens, to see the flowers or hear the birds, they pull the traces of his ornamental carriage with their own hands, watching at all times for bumps, walking slowly, keeping their distance, and remembering that if they swing the front of the carriage to the left then the rear of the carriage will veer out to the right.[34]

Hong maintains a complete ban on all Confucian books, both for his palace women and for his own children. Unmoved by God's message relayed to him by Yang Xiuqing before his death, Hong sees such "ancient" books as "all demonic."[35] But every day, amidst or after their other duties, the women must read the Bible and Hong's poems in conjunction and in sequence: one day a chapter from the Old Testament, followed by some poems, next day a chapter from the New Testament. When reading the Bible, they must pay particular attention to the personal names, which are marked in their editions with a vertical line, and the geographical names, which are marked with two lines, reading them aloud to each other to make sure their pronunciation is correct. Every Sabbath, in addition, they read the Ten Commandments. Those failing to do their reading will be reported to Hong, and severely punished.[36] In addition, at every morning assembly, the women will chant some of Hong's poems aloud, and commit them to memory. They need never hide their admiration for Hong's poetry, so long as they are sincere.[37]

The nights in Nanjing can be long and cold, and the Heavenly King's health and happiness is everyone's concern. Carefully they see to the rugs and quilts and braziers that will keep him warm, prepare his heated ginseng and shaved deer horn to give him strength, massage his head and feet, ankles, arms, and knees to ease the tiredness of his body.[38] On the most private matters of all, Hong gives no precise instructions to his women, but he who calls himself both "fire" and "sun" throughout the cycle of the poems, in echo of the fiery name that once he shared with God, and in honor of his designation as the sun in apposition to his women moons, gives special praise and promise to those who "ease" the flame:

> She who can truly ease the flame repels the demon's snares,
> She who can truly ease the flame is my true wife.
> She who can truly ease the flame shows the greatest mercy,
> She who can truly ease the flame understands the Way.[39]

Such easers of the flame are the "most treasured" of the palace women, the true *niangniang,* or "queens," and the ones who can expect the "highest rewards."[40]

Everywhere in this palace universe Hong's rule holds sway, for he can "never be wrong" as far as his attendants are concerned, any more than God can be wrong to His daughters-in-law, or Jesus to his sister-in-law.

In the awesome presence of these three, the demon devil Yan Luo and his minions "bow their heads like turtles and burrow into the earth."[41] Hong claims that there is now "no secret beating in dark corners" in his palaces, but that does not mean that there is neither fear nor violence among the members of his sprawling entourage, and the women are expressly told not to blame Hong if he shows a violent temper.[42] His anger can be provoked by anything from a misplaced swing of a fan to the late arrival of his hot towels.[43] Anyone making a mistake twice is considered a "habitual offender," and though beating is the commonest punishment—those enduring the blows are expected to look cheerful and even to praise their Heavenly King as the blows fall—those who refuse to acknowledge their guilt may find that the punishment for their stubbornness is death, the woman being first ritually bathed and then carried to the back garden of the palace compound for execution with the "great sword."[44] "If you do not care for your Sovereign," as Hong says bluntly, "there are others who will."[45]

Hong not only has to see to the relationships between the dead, the living, and God the Father, between his earthly relatives and each other, and between his palace women and himself—he also has to heed the relationship between himself as God's younger son and the Bible text that has dominated so much of his life. Even as his women chant their chapter of the Bible each day, Hong has to work with all his heart and mind to reconcile the previously accepted word with the echo of the dead East King's charge—based itself on Captain Mellersh's rejections of the Taiping claims to their personal relationships with God and Jesus—that both the Old and the New Testaments were full of errors and need revising.

Where to start? Hong decides to start at the beginning, in Genesis, and to focus on two basic categories of "errors" that he can both identify and try to set aright. One category concerns God's journeys down to earth; the other involves the interconnections of family members with each other in ways that are not suitable for the Taiping faithful, and surely must be due to the devil's work.[46] As he has been telling his palace women, so brash are the devil demons that they even dare, at times, masquerade as God the Father or as Elder Brother, Jesus, and can thus deceive Hong himself, let alone his more gullible subjects.[47]

To alter the Bible's accounts of God's visits down to earth, and thus to reinforce the claims of Taiping revelation—whether Hong's or Yang's or Xiao's, for all are intertwined and none can stand without the others—is in part a matter of grammar and of emphasis. Thus in Genesis 1:26, where the old Bible says, "And God said, let *us* make man," Hong's altered version reads, "And God said *I* will make man."[48] In Genesis 12, verse 13, whereas in the old Bible Abraham asks Sara, his wife, to protect him from Pharaoh, in Hong's revision Abraham asks "the God of my ancestors" to do the protecting. In Genesis 19, verse 1, when the old Bible reads, "And there came two angels to Sodom at even," Hong's change is even more direct. He writes, "The Lord True God came down to Sodom," and God as visitor and actor in his own earthly presence replaces the angels throughout the story, in verses 13, 15, and 16.[49] At other times the words for "older brothers" or for "younger brother" are inserted into the text, even though not in the old Bible, to heighten the sense of family intimacy.[50] Or, even more boldly, Jesus, identified as "God's *eldest* son" (to leave room for Hong as the younger son), is introduced suddenly into the Old Testament story, as a forceful man of action. One example of such an insertion by Hong occurs in the mysterious verses 24 and 25 of Exodus chapter 4, when Moses is returning to Egypt and his wife, Zipporah, bloodily circumcises their son Gershom. In Hong's version Jesus is in attendance at this event.[51]

Certain aspects of the story of Noah and his three sons are also disturbing to Hong Xiuquan. For here it is the father's drunkenness that is most at issue in Hong's mind, and makes him seek revision. In the early version of the flood, which Hong read in 1843 in the religious tracts of Liang Afa, the story ended with the ark still floating upon the waves, and the reader was never told if its passengers ever came safely back to land. The version of Genesis that now confronts Hong's urgently exegetical eye tells of their landing and of God's covenant, and continues the story this way:

> (v. 20) And Noah began to be a farmer; and he planted a vineyard.
>
> (v. 21) And he drank of the wine, and became drunk; and he was uncovered within his tent.
>
> (v. 22) And Ham, the father of Canaan, saw the nakedness of his father, and told his two brethren outside.
>
> (v. 23) And Shem and Japheth took a garment, and laid it upon both their shoulders, and went backward, and covered the nakedness of their father; and their faces were backward, and they saw not their father's nakedness.
>
> (v. 24) And Noah awoke from his wine, and knew what his younger son had done unto him.
>
> (v. 25) And he said, Cursed be Canaan; a servant of servants shall he be unto his brethren. (Genesis 9:20–25)

Hong's solution is to leave uncut the fact that Noah became a husbandman and planted a vineyard, for the Chinese version sounds innocent enough about these bucolic labors. But the two references to drunkenness and to nakedness in verse 21 have to go. "Exhausted," Hong writes in substitution, "Noah while in a deep sleep tumbled from his bed onto the ground." Only in verse 22 is it explained that by this unfortunate fall he exposed his naked body.* For the Taiping, banned from alcohol as from opium, the fact that a man beloved of God would drink himself to oblivion, and in this state show his private parts to his three sons, is safely smoothed away. A quick erasure of "Noah awoke from his wine" in verse 24 and substitution of "Noah awoke from his sleep" and the revision is complete.[52]

In purging the story of Noah, as he has already done for that of Lot, Hong Xiuquan is removing the taint of immorality and impropriety from the earliest denizens of the Bible. But with Lot's uncle Abraham, as with Abraham's son Isaac, Isaac's son Jacob, and Jacob's son Judah, Hong is entering specific family territory. For as it is written in the very first verses of Matthew's Gospel, Jesus himself is in the direct line of descent from these four, a line of descent that passes down from them through Jesse, David, and Solomon, to Joseph, the husband of Mary, mother of Jesus. As Jesus' younger brother, and the father of the Young Monarch Tiangui, Hong has clear need to make his Old Testament ancestors moral exemplars. Abraham and Isaac do not present major problems to Hong Xiuquan, but in each case he is worried by the way that they lie to Abimelech, king of Gerar, by claiming that their beautiful wives—Sarah and Rebekah—are in fact their sisters. Both Abraham and Isaac fear that Abimelech will kill them if he wants to make their wives his own. But by lying, they not only place their wives in sexual jeopardy; they bring the wrath of God on Abimelech's head. By rather elaborate sleight of hand, Hong recasts these stories so the patriarchs appear blameless and the burden of deceit falls either on the wives themselves or on other intermediaries.[53]

More difficult, for Hong, is knowing what to do about Jacob, whom God the Father himself rewarded with the name of Israel. The old Bible clearly delineates how Jacob first obtains his brother Esau's birthright by use of ruthlessness, and then with his mother's help deceives his dying father, Isaac, and receives the blessing that his father wished to give to Esau. In this case Hong gives up the text as too immoral to be fixed by minor changes, and rewrites all of Genesis 25:31–34, and most of chapter 27.

---

*The effect of this small excision is strong: the brothers' action in covering their father is still convincingly explained, but what the Taiping readers and Noah's sons see in Chinese, in verse 22, is the stark word "nakedness," *luoti;* whereas the Chinese phrase *lushen,* skillfully used to translate the true significance of "he was uncovered" by Gutzlaff in verse 21, which has the same force as the English phrase "exposed himself," is gone forever.

In Hong's version the family values are preserved, and no central deceit is practiced. Jacob does not make Esau "sell" his birthright in exchange for the food to stay alive. Instead, speaking as a respectful younger brother, Jacob gives Esau a brief lecture on the need to respect his birthright, and then agrees to "divide" it with him in exchange for the pottage that Esau craves.[54]

As to Jacob's betrayal of the wishes of his dying father, all is transformed by Hong into an exemplary story of filial piety. Drama is lost, but honor is saved. If there is deceit, it is the fault of Rebekah, Jacob's mother: for it is she who urges Jacob to kill two fine kids from his herds, to make their dying father the meat dish that he loves. Jacob gently reproves her: "My elder brother Esau is the one beloved by my father, and besides that it is correct for the elder brother to be the one who should receive the father's blessing." To which Rebekah replies that what Jacob says is right, but that he in his turn must listen to her words. She makes Jacob wear one of his finest garments, which she scents with myrrh and the fragrance of fresh milk, and gives him the savory dish of goat kid to take to his father.

In the original text of Genesis, the dying Isaac asks, "Who art thou, my son?" and Jacob lies, "I am Esau thy firstborn," completing the deception he has begun by donning Esau's clothes, and placing the skins of the slain kids upon his arms and the soft skin of his neck, since Esau was "a hairy man" and Jacob a "smooth man." In Hong's version, the false hair is gone as well, and Jacob truthfully answers his father's question with the words: "I am your second son Jacob, come to pay reverence to my father. Please sit up, and eat this savory food, and I beg my father to give me his blessing." Touched by the fact that Jacob brought the savory meat of his own volition, whereas Esau had to be told to go out and hunt for it, moved by the sweet smell of his clothes, and equally moved by Jacob's kneeling before him and asking his blessing, Isaac bestows the benediction on his younger son. For Hong, the blessing cannot be sealed with wine, so it is sealed with the broth of the savory meat. Similarly Isaac, in the blessing, no longer offers Jacob a lifetime of "corn and wine." Instead he promises him "corn and wheat" forever.[55]

With Jacob's worst duplicity expunged, Hong can tackle the challenges posed by Jacob's fourth son with Leah—Judah, the fourth in the descent line of patriarchs listed at the start of Matthew's Gospel. Lot's drunken incest could be bluntly excised by Hong because it did not seem to affect the main Bible story. Judah's incest with his daughter-in-law Tamar, even if unwitting, cannot be left standing by Hong, but neither can it be simply excised, since the story of Judah is central to the Bible and the fate of the twelve tribes of Israel. Furthermore, the fruit of Judah's loins, Perez, the twin brother of Zerah, is sanctified by Matthew as the ancestor of Joseph, husband of Jesus' mother, Mary, and Judah himself has been favored beyond all his eleven brothers in his father's eyes, with a magnificent final blessing:

> Judah, thou art he whom thy brethren shall praise: thy hand shall be in the neck of thine enemies; thy father's children shall bow down before thee. Judah is a lion's whelp: from the prey, my son, thou art gone up: he stooped down, he crouched as a lion, and as an old lion. Who shall rouse him up? The scepter shall not depart from Judah, nor a lawgiver from between his feet, until Shiloh come; and unto him shall the gathering of the people be. (Genesis 49:8–10)

The story of Judah and his daughter-in-law Tamar is a harsh and lengthy one, which takes up all of the thirty-eighth chapter of Genesis. It is also the second of Hong's revisions to deal with three brothers—the first was the story of Noah's sons and their naked father. Like Noah, Judah has three sons, Er, Onan, and Shelah. Er marries Tamar, but angers God in some unstated way, and is slain. Eager to perpetuate the line of his eldest son, Judah marries Tamar to Er's brother Onan. Onan, unwilling to have the offspring of his seed return to his older brother's line, "spills his seed upon the ground" and is also slain by God. Judah then betroths the twice-widowed Tamar to his third son, Shelah, who is still a boy. But while Tamar waits dutifully in Judah's home till Shelah comes to manhood, Judah forgets his promise, and when his own wife dies he goes up to the mountains of Timnah to supervise the shearers with his sheep. Tamar is left bereft and still unmarried in the valley.

Even thus far, the story causes Hong moral misgivings. He feels the same distaste as he does for the passage in Matthew 22:24–26, where the Sadducees try to trick Jesus by invoking a similar law to suggest that seven brothers in a row marry the same woman after each one dies childless.[56] Hong tidies that story by simply substituting the phrase "another man" each time the Bible mentions "brothers." Similarly, with Tamar, Hong drops the words for brother and for sister-in-law, implying that Genesis thus fits with Chinese law, by which the firstborn of the younger son's marriage will be posthumously adopted as the heir to Er, securing for him and Tamar the perpetuation of their line. Hong, after all, has done the same with his own sons, having one adopted out as Jesus' son, and one as

Yang Xiuqing's. But what is Hong to do with this continuation of the story, as found in Genesis 38:13–26?

> And it was told Tamar, saying, Behold thy father-in-law goeth up to Timnah to shear his sheep. And she put her widow's garments off from her, and covered her with a veil, and wrapped herself, and sat in an open place, which is by the way to Timnah; for she saw that Shelah was grown, and she was not given unto him as his wife. When Judah saw her, he thought her to be an harlot; because she had covered her face. And he turned unto her by the way, and said, Come, I pray thee, let me come in unto thee (for he knew not that she was his daughter-in-law). And she said, What wilt thou give me, that thou mayest come in unto me?
>
> And he said, I will send thee a kid from the flock. And she said, Wilt thou give me a pledge, till thou send it? And he said, What pledge shall I give thee? And she said, Thy signet, and thy bracelets, and thy staff that is in thine hand. And he gave them to her, and came in unto her, and she conceived by him. And she arose, and went away, and laid by her veil from her, and put on the garments of her widowhood. And Judah sent the kid by the hand of his friend, the Adullamite, to receive his pledge from the woman's hand: but he found her not. Then he asked the men of that place, saying, Where is the harlot that was openly by the wayside? And they said, There was no harlot in this place. And he returned to Judah, and said, I cannot find her; and also the men of the place said that there was no harlot in this place. And Judah said, Let her take it to her, lest we be shamed: behold, I sent this kid, and thou hast not found her.
>
> And it came to pass about three months after, that it was told Judah, saying, Tamar, thy daughter-in-law, hath played the harlot; and also, behold, she is with child by harlotry. And Judah said, Bring her forth, and let her be burned. When she was brought forth, she sent to her father-in-law, saying, By the man, whose these are, am I with child: and she said, Discern, I pray thee, whose are these, the signet, and bracelets, and staff. And Judah acknowledged them, and said, She hath been more righteous than I; because that I gave her not to Shelah, my son. And he knew her again no more. (Genesis 38:13–26)

Hong can see no solution except to scrap the whole story. As with all his other retellings, Hong writes his new version to the same length as the excised passages, so most of the blocks can be reused, unchanged, with the same pagination. In Hong's version, Judah sees a veiled "young woman" (not a harlot) sitting at the roadside. As he enquires after her, she identifies herself as his daughter-in-law Tamar. Startled, he asks what she is doing there, when she should be at his home, in mourning. Plaintively, she tells

Judah that she came all this way to remind him of his promise to marry off Shelah, so Shelah's firstborn could continue Er's line. She was beginning to doubt if Judah would ever carry out his word. Judah apologizes—having lost two sons so young, he naturally, out of father's fondness, had delayed the moment when he should make his third son marry too. But he promises redress at once. Tamar and Judah return home, he arranges Shelah's marriage to a local woman, and soon the new bride announces she is pregnant. Joyfully, Tamar thanks the Lord her God. Hong can now return to the original text of Genesis 38, and continue the story with this new young daughter-in-law of Judah's bearing—as it turns out—twins to Shelah:

> And it came to pass in the time of her travail, that, behold, twins were in her womb. And it came to pass, when she travailed, that the one put out his hand: and the midwife took and bound upon his hand a scarlet thread, saying, This came out first. And it came to pass, as he drew back his hand, that, behold, his brother came out: and she said, How hast thou broken forth? This breach be upon thee: therefore his name was called Perez. And afterward came out his brother, that had the scarlet thread upon his hand: and his name was called Zerah. (Genesis 38:27–30)

Hong just has space at the end to add a sentence of his own to the last verse: "And so Judah chose Perez to continue the elder brother's line, and Zerah to be the son of Shelah."[57]

When Hong gets to work on Exodus, he tries to tidy the present and the future by altering the law of Moses as it relates to these family matters. Hong finds that God's words to Moses concerning physical passion are too broad-minded to act as moral guidelines for the Taiping. According to the original version of Exodus, what Moses recorded ran as follows:

> (v. 16) And if a man entice a maid that is not betrothed, and lie with her, he shall surely endow her to be his wife.
> (v. 17) If her father utterly refuse to give her unto him, he shall pay money according to the dowry of virgins. (Exodus 22:16–17)

Hong rewrites artfully, starting with the same words in verse sixteen, but then switching the passage in a new direction, so that God's words will fit Hong's own definition of the seventh commandment, that against adultery, which he has promulgated as deserving of death for all his Taiping followers:

(v. 16) And if a man entice a maid that is not betrothed, and lie with her, he is breaking the seventh commandment.

(v. 17) If her father knows of the matter, then he must hand over both the woman and her seducer to the officials, to be executed; on no account may he, knowing what has happened, attempt to conceal it.[58]

It is exhausting labor. The Bible is so long, and there are many other changes to be made. But the main story is now more cleanly told and, as much as it can be, the family honor is saved. Hong's own children, his entourage of palace women, and all the future generations of Taiping followers will never know there once was disagreement between Hong and the Bible on these matters of sex and alcohol, nor now can there ever be. On these matters it has been made clear for all to see that Moses, God, and Hong Xiuquan think fruitfully as one.

THE
WRONG
MAN

 On July 2, 1857, just after Shi Dakai has left the Heavenly Capital forever, and while Hong Xiuquan is hard at work with his revisions of the Bible, James Bruce, eighth earl of Elgin and twelfth earl of Kincardine, steams into Hong Kong harbor on the *Shannon,* steam frigate of Her Majesty's navy. The *Shannon* is a magnificent ship, not only one of the swiftest sailing vessels afloat when the wind is fair, but also equipped with a powerful steam-driven propeller that will enable her to travel five days under full steam against the wind on a single hold of coal. She is also the most massively armed ship in Far Eastern waters, carrying no fewer than sixty 68-pounder guns, as well as a complement of 24-pounders, and a large company of well-trained and armed Royal Marines. To Lord Elgin, viewing her among the massed sails of smaller Asian ships is like looking at "a triton among the minnows."[1]

Lord Elgin has been sent from England with a comprehensive assignment as special plenipotentiary of Her Majesty the Queen. He carries instructions from his government either to negotiate with the Qing government or to fight against it if no negotiation seems feasible. Either way, he is to make five "demands": for "reparations of injuries" suffered by British subjects in China and for compensation of financial losses during the recent destruction of the foreign factories outside Canton; for Chinese compliance with the treaties of 1842; for permission to allow the British ambassador to reside in Peking, and communicate directly with Chinese ministers there in writing; and for an increase in trade with China and in Chinese trade with Hong Kong. He is also empowered to explore the Qing government's interest in legalizing the trade in opium in return for the payment by foreign traders of a fixed tariff, and to see if the Qing will agree to allow unrestricted emigration of Chinese women as well as men from her shores, so that Chinese laborers settling overseas could lead a normal family life. Should the Qing be unwilling to discuss these points, then a "measure of coercion" should be adopted, by blockading China's northern ports, blocking the Grand Canal at its Yellow River or its Yangzi River junction, and occupying either Canton itself or other suitable ports and islands.[2]

Lord Elgin—whose father, the seventh earl, had been both praised and execrated for removing the friezes from the Parthenon and selling them to the British Museum—is a proud and talented man. A brilliant classical scholar at Oxford in his youth and later a successful public servant, he has already served as governor of Jamaica and governor-general of Canada by the time he receives his posting to China.[3] Distracted from his assignment during 1857 by the crises of the Indian mutiny, and by diplomatic maneuvering with Japan, in the summer of 1858 he returns to southern China to resume his mission. When the Qing fail to respond to his demands to open up the city of Canton, he shells it thoroughly, attacks and occupies Canton, capturing the governor and shipping him off to imprisonment in Calcutta. Like a wrathful presence he then steams northward with the British fleet, blasting his way past the Dagu forts that protect the approaches to Peking, and forcing the Qing to negotiate terms of abject surrender. Flushed with his string of victories, in October 1858 he returns to Shanghai with his fleet, determined to be the first representative of the British crown to sail the whole way up the Yangzi River to Wuchang, to assert his country's newly won treaty rights, wrested by force from the Qing emperor Xianfeng, and to open trade with China's interior ports.[4]

Ten years before this time, in the Thistle Mountain region, when Jesus descended for the second time to speak to his younger brother Hong Xiuquan through the mouth of the West King, Xiao Chaogui, Hong asked him a simple question: "Heavenly Elder Brother, when the time of the Taiping comes, who will be the commanding generals of our armies?"

The Elder Brother replied, "Feng Yunshan, Yang Xiuqing, Xiao Chaogui all shall be commanding generals. . . . And one of your commanding generals will come from a foreign country." Hong Xiuquan asks, "What is his name?" And Jesus replies, "His name is Cai." Hong asks, "Has he come to China yet or not?" And Jesus answers, "At the present time he is still in his foreign land."[5]

Almost two months later there is a related dialogue: Hong has had a dream that demons with guns attacked him, and he is rescued by angels and heavenly generals. Recounting the dream to Jesus, he asks if it is accurate or not. Indeed it is, says Jesus. Those were troops and generals sent by Heaven who rescued him. And what is the name of that general? Hong asks. "We will let you know later," Jesus replies.[6]

None of the foreign visitors to Nanjing on the *Hermes, Cassini,* or *Susquehanna* seems a fitting candidate for the designation of the foreign general to be sent by God. And certainly neither the Irishman known as Canny, the Boston mercenaries, nor even the tough Italian Antonio is quite of general's stature. But based on his record of destruction of the Qing, Lord Elgin just might be the one.

Steaming with his armed fleet of five warships past Nanjing on November 20, 1858, "on a lovely evening" as "the sun was sinking rapidly," having sent a smaller gunboat ahead to alert the Taiping to his peaceful intent, Elgin has his vessels mistakenly fired on by Taiping gunners, leaving one British sailor dead, and two badly wounded, one losing an arm and another a leg.[7] Elgin's view on this matter is, as he later tells the foreign secretary in Whitehall, "that no human power, and no physical obstacle which could be surmounted, should arrest my progress. It was obviously essential to the prestige of England, that a measure of this description, if undertaken at all, should be carried out; I could not, therefore, recognize in the rebels a right to stop me, nor could I take any step which they might construe into such an admission." Instead therefore of echoing the comparative restraint of the *Hermes* in 1853, Elgin orders the fire returned.[8]

As Elgin explains his state of mind in a journal entry that night, "We have passed the town, but I quite agree with the naval authorities, that we cannot leave the matter as it now stands. If we were to do so, the Chinese would certainly say they had had the best of it, and on our return we might be still more seriously attacked. It is determined, therefore, that to-morrow we shall set to work and demolish some of the forts that have insulted us. I hope the Rebels will make some communication, and enable us to explain that we mean them no harm; but it is impossible to anticipate what these stupid Chinamen will do."[9] Elgin's secretary, in his own journal, records his own thoughts somewhat differently: "It is accordingly arranged that at daylight tomorrow we drop down abreast of the batteries, and hammer them into ruins and their garrisons into submission."[10]

At dawn on November 21, the weather "shrill and biting," the British ships slip silently downriver through the mist to their allotted battle stations. Moving, in some cases, to within fifty yards of the Taiping gun emplacements on both the left and the right banks of the river, the British vessels "pour such a storm of shot, shell, grape, and rockets into the batteries, that our fire of the previous evening seemed mere child's play." From his vantage point up in the "topgallant crosstrees," Elgin's secretary can look right down into the Taiping forts, and "see the men in bright dresses clustering round the guns" and watch the effects of the newly invented "Moorsum shells" as they burst amidst the Taiping troops, scattering their deadly fragments. After an hour and a half, the last Taiping batteries fall silent.[11] Late that same evening, impressed by this startling show of force, a Taiping commander of the Heavenly King's "gun vessels" writes to "Your Excellencies the Foreigners" asking them to help him with their fleet, so that he can destroy the Qing naval forces; in exchange for these services, he would petition the Heavenly King to grant them Taiping noble rank.[12]

In his own message to Lord Elgin, written on yellow silk in the vermilion ink reserved for the Heavenly King's proclamations, Hong greets Lord Elgin in his own way. His message, addressed to "Our foreign younger brother of the Western Seas," consists of 172 lines of seven-character verse, arranged into stanzas, but with the names for God and Jesus raised, as in Taiping practice, two spaces above the text, and Hong's own name raised one. It is true that Elgin's Chinese name is Lai, not Cai, but Hong lives his life by coded rhymes. To set the scene, Hong first offers to Lord Elgin a summary of the Taiping revelation, and a description of Hong's role as Jesus' younger brother and his founding of the Heavenly Capital in Nanjing. The suffering and death of Yang Xiuqing—who always dealt with foreigners in the past—is then spelled out in graphic detail:

> The Father and the Elder Brother led me to rule the Taiping [dynasty]. The Father has deputed the East King to redeem sickness. Thus he was blind, deaf, and dumb, and suffered infinite misery, and while fighting the demons, he was wounded in the neck and fell. The Father had declared beforehand in his sacred decree that when our warriors went forth, [Yang Xiu-] qing would be afflicted, and that when they arrived at the court [Nanjing], he would be assassinated. [The words] of the Father's sacred decree were all accomplished. The Elder Brother gave his life to ransom sinners, so that he

became a substitute for myriads and myriads of people of the world. The East King, in ransoming the sick, suffered equally with the Elder Brother, and when he fell with the pestilence he returned to his spirit-nature to thank the Father for his goodness.[13]

Almost casually, Hong mentions, "The sacred decrees are numberless. I select one or two of them for declaration," for it is always "impossible to know exactly what is in the hearts of the Father and the Elder Brother." For forty-four lines, without identifying them, so familiar are they to him, Hong recalls for Elgin God's prophecies and decrees from the far-off days of Thistle Mountain and Yongan. All these decrees have proved truthful, writes Hong. "Come soon to Heaven, and you will be aware of this." In the realm of prophecy, "the First Elder Brother, Jesus, is the same as the Father," and therefore "not a sentence of his sacred decrees shall be changed."[14]

Still in a verse form of seven-character lines, at line 119 the Heavenly King comes to the heart of his message:

Foreign younger brother from the Western Sea, heed my royal proclamation:
Let us together serve God and our Elder Brother, and destroy the hateful insects.
All that happens on earth is controlled by God, or Elder Brother, and myself.
My brother, join us joyfully, and earn incalculable rewards.

In former days, when I traveled in Guangdong,
I gave a proclamation to Luo Xiaoquan [Roberts] in his chapel.
On that occasion I proclaimed my ascent to Heaven
Where my Heavenly Father and Elder Brother conferred great powers on me.
At this time, has [Luo] Xiaoquan accompanied you or not?
If he has come, let him visit my court and confer with me. . . .

The Kingdom of Heaven is near at hand, yea it is come!
Foreign younger brother from the Western Sea, be of good heart.
When I traveled up to Heaven, I saw my Father's plan:
That the myriad nations would help me mount the altar of Heaven.

What the Father foretold has now come to pass.
On Heaven's behalf put forward all your strength, for it is destined to be so.
For our Father and our Elder Brother, slay the demon devils,
And thus requiting your Father who gave life to you, return victorious from your
    battles.[15]

How could Hong be clearer on the need to work together to extermi-nate the Qing demons, as Elgin has so spectacularly done already? As to the British also firing on the Taiping positions, that was under provocation, and the Taiping gunners responsible have all been executed. Besides, the Taiping casualties have not been as great as it seemed to the observers on the British ships—only three officers and some twenty men have died.[16] Hong's message is sent upriver, to reach Lord Elgin as soon as possible; but since Elgin's flotilla is under full steam, the message fails to reach him before he has passed beyond the areas of the Yangzi River controlled by Taiping forces, and has entered territory recaptured by the Qing. Here the Taiping emissaries with their yellow scroll cannot hope to follow him.[17]

It is only in late December 1858, as Elgin returns from his upriver explorations and his state visits to Qing officials in Wuchang, and reenters Taiping waters, that the Heavenly King's message is presented to him, in an envelope now marked "To our Elder Brother Lai, Special Commissioner from the Great Nation." In a covering note, the senior Taiping official delivering the message says it was entrusted to him by the Heavenly King himself, for delivery to Lord Elgin.[18] Elgin, who has passed bleak days of sleet and snow jammed with all his staff in one of the small gunboats after his flagship ran aground, finds it a "strange document," written "on a roll of yellow silk, about three fathoms long," "a sort of rhapsody, in verse, with a vast infusion of their extraordinary theology."[19] It would, he feels, "be awkward for me to have any intercourse with the rebel chiefs, so I do not, as at present advised, intend to land." Though a missionary has indeed accompanied him, the man is Alexander Wylie, and not Issachar Roberts, so there is no need to respond to Hong's query over that.

Elgin notes privately that those of his party who do go ashore in Nanjing find the city a scene of desolation, through which one can ride as through a "great park." Most of the guards at the gates seem to be unarmed, women roam freely within the streets, and though no shops are open supplies seem plentiful. The senior Taiping officer they meet, a Guangxi man named Li, promises the British that if they will stay the night ashore they "can then visit the court of the Heavenly Kingdom." But no one in the British party follows up on the invitation, and the moment passes. Lord Elgin himself does not go ashore, and gives no answer to the Heavenly King.[20]

19

NEW
WORLDS

 It is in April 1859, during the time of drift and indecision in Taiping government and war following Elgin's visit and departure, that Hong Rengan reaches Nanjing, and greets his cousin the Heavenly King, whom he has not seen since 1849. The Heavenly King is amazed and overjoyed, for Rengan too is family, in both a literal and an emotional sense. He grew up next to Hong's ancestral village and knows his relatives. He was among his cousin's earliest converts, and one of Feng Yunshan's closest friends. He knows Hong Kong. He knows the foreigners and their ways. He knows the Bible intimately, but believes in the revelations of the Heavenly King, and in his cousin's kinship with God and Jesus. And so within days of Hong Rengan's arrival, Hong Xiuquan names his cousin to high rank in the Taiping nobility, makes him a commanding general of the Taiping armies with the honorary title of "Supreme Marshal," appoints him "Leader of the Ministers," "Chief Examiner," "Minister of Appointments," and "Head of Foreign Affairs." And in mid-May 1859, the Heavenly King makes the final leap of faith: he enfeoffs Hong Rengan as king, the "Shield King," to take the place of the other founding leaders who have died.[1]

Hong Rengan has had a strange and often dangerous life since last the cousins met. While Hong Xiuquan built up his following in Thistle Mountain, Rengan continued to take the lower state examinations—five times in all—but always failed. When in 1850 Qing troops raided Hua county to arrest the followers or relatives of Hong Xiuquan, Rengan set off to Guangxi, but he could not get through the Qing lines, and the war was so mobile that he never was able to join his cousin. Leaving Guangxi, but unable to return home, Rengan drifted to Hong Kong, where he began to work for foreign missionaries.[2]

Hearing of the Taiping capture of Nanjing, and their establishment there of the the Heavenly Capital, Rengan traveled—like Roberts—north to Shanghai, but also like Roberts was unable to get through the Qing forces to reach the Taiping base, and the Triad Society occupiers of Shanghai would not help him. So after a brief period during which he "studied astronomy and astronomical calculations in a foreign school"—perhaps with Alexander Wylie, a talented mathematician and astronomer who had been in China since 1847—in the winter of 1854 he decided to return again to Hong Kong and seek longer-term employment with the missionary society there. The trip back, on a steamer that made the entire journey in four days, was a revelation to Hong Rengan, and plunged him into verse:

The ship flies like an arrow through the raging billows;
Swept along in the wind's force, my determination grows all the stronger.
The sea becomes the field of battle, the waves are the military formations;
Their crests toss against the stars and the moon, like billowing banners and flags.[3]

In Hong Kong, Rengan continued for four years to study astronomy and work with the missionaries, and he slowly began to mingle on terms of trust and friendship with many of the talented group of Westerners who crowded the little colony at this time: among those from Britain whom Rengan came to know were James Legge, the first translator of the Confucian classics; William Milne, son of Liang Afa's first teacher and reviser of Morrison and Gutzlaff's Bible translation projects; William Burns, who had just completed his translation of John Bunyan's *Pilgrim's Progress;* and Benjamin Hobson, preacher and physician, author of books in Chinese on surgery, midwifery, and children's diseases. He also re-met Issachar Roberts and several other American Protestant missionaries, among them E. C. Bridgman, who translated for minister McLane on the *Susquehanna*'s Nanjing voyage. Among new acquaintances were a number of German and Scandinavian missionaries from the Basel Missionary Society, including the Swedish-born Theodore Hamberg, a fine orator and preacher, expert in Hakka dialect, and early co-founder of the Chinese Union with Gutzlaff, with whom Rengan shared a brief written record of the Taiping movement's founding, and to whom Rengan dictated a much longer account of the movement's growth and glory. He also talked often with Yung Wing, the first Chinese to have traveled to the United States and received an American college degree, who was trying to work out how to combine his knowledge of the West and China in either the world of administration or business.[4]

Of all Hong Rengan's friends in Hong Kong during this period, the most important was undoubtedly the Scotsman James Legge. Legge, the youngest of the seven children of an Aberdeen tradesman, initially taught mathematics, until he was ordained as a Congregationalist minister and traveled to Hong Kong in 1843, where he headed the Protestant Theological Seminary, which had been founded to "train a native ministry for China." By the time Rengan returned to Hong Kong in 1854, Legge was already well on the way to amassing what has been called one of the most "extensive and important collections of sinological literature in all of the western nations in the nineteenth century."[5] Rengan worked with Legge both as a Christian catechist—to help in the conversion of other Chinese— and as a scholarly assistant. Hong Rengan was lucky in this friendship, for Legge was a man who trusted the Chinese and saw much good in them, and was constantly using his ministry to learn as much as possible: in Legge's words, "Several hours of every day were spent in visiting them from house to house, and shop to shop, conversing with them on all subjects, and trying to get them to converse with me on one subject."[6]

Years later, after Hong Rengan's death, Legge remembered him as "the most genial and versatile Chinese I have ever known, and of whom I can never think but with esteem and regret." And Legge wrote further that Hong Rengan "was the only Chinaman with whom I ever walked with my arm round his neck and his arm round mine." Sometimes they preached together at the same church service, and when Rengan spoke of trying to join his cousin in the Taiping capital, Legge urged him to "remain quietly in Hong Kong as a preacher."[7]

Perhaps it was with Hong Rengan that Legge was strolling in the summer of 1857, as Lord Elgin arrived, and Hong Rengan with whom he shared his thoughts on the future:

> On the 2nd July of that year I was walking out on Caine's Road in the afternoon with a friend, when we saw a steamer coming through Sulphur

Channel. At first we thought it must be the mail, but it proved to be the *Shannon,* with Lord Elgin on board. As she steamed into the harbour, and she and the Admiral saluted each other, and the thunder of their guns reverberated along the sides of the mountain, which were then all fringed with mist, I said to my companion, "There is the knell of the past of China. It can do nothing against these leviathans."[8]

James Legge, because of his formidable knowledge of Chinese language and his theological erudition, had been entrusted by the Protestant missionaries, along with the celebrated translator Walter Medhurst, "to deliberate on the rendering of the names of the Deity into Chinese." This led to a further bond with Hong Rengan, for throughout his long and productive life Legge always championed the use of "Shangdi"—High Lord of All—for the translation of the name of God, a choice that fitted perfectly with the belief of the Taiping, who had consistently used the same term, from the time they named their first assemblies the "Bai Shangdi Hui," God-worshiping Society.[9] As part of his methodology in proving his theological positions, Legge drew heavily on the way that Paul in the Epistle to the Hebrews had elaborated on the story of the priest-king Melchizedek. Such an early Christian methodology seemed to Legge a perfect example of the way later commentators on the Bible message could "confirm the good and supplement the deficient." By this logic, Confucianism was not seen as fully antithetical to Christianity, since the term *shangdi* can be found in various early Chinese texts. Thus in Legge's mind, "progressive revelation in the Biblical text affirms the possibility that God could leave a witness elsewhere in the world, even if this witness was quickly distorted by other corrupting influences."[10]

Along with a small number of other missionaries such as Karl Gutzlaff, Legge also had a special interpretation of the prophetic passage in Isaiah, chapter 49, verses 11 and 12:

And I will make all my mountains a way, and my highways shall be exalted. Behold, these shall come from far: and lo, these from the north and from the west; and these from the land of Sinim.

To these missionaries, "Sinim" referred to China, and implied that for over two millennia God had anticipated including the Chinese people in His kingdom. Legge preached on this very theme in the later 1850s.[11]

The Hong Kong in which Hong Rengan resided during the 1850s—especially the waterfront area of Victoria—was becoming a boom town, despite the pessimism over its prospects that had accompanied its founding in 1841, and the terrible death toll taken of the earliest Western settlers and troops from fever. Legge attributed much of this new prosperity to the dislocations caused by the Taiping and the secret societies around Canton, placing "the turning point in the progress of Hong Kong" to 1852 and 1853. In those years, wealthy Chinese families fled to Hong Kong to escape the fighting and disorder on the mainland; houses were in demand and rents rose; the streets that had been comparatively deserted assumed a crowded appearance; new commercial Chinese firms were founded; the native trade received an impetus. The British Royal Engineers installed well-planned roads, drains, and harbor facilities, and the colonists planted groves of shrubs and bamboo to improve the air; these changes, along with the streetlamps and their staff of lamplighters, the handsome post office where the mail was brought by clipper from Bombay, the new churches and substantial houses, gave some imposing aspects to the new settlement, though visitors grumbled that both rents and the prices in the only good hotel were excessively high.[12]

The little colony itself exhibited the worst and the best of the West and China, and a certain blending of the two cultures. For Chinese as for Westerners there was gambling, work in the illegal opium trade, the coolie trade with its racketeering and kidnapping, savage fights between rival gangs, daring robberies by those who used the colony's new drains as secret channels past the guards above the ground, and a social "order" in which for a time there were more brothels than respectable households. The prevalence of crime and violence meant that "the gallows found constant employment" for Western and Chinese alike, since British criminals guilty of capital crimes were hanged in public along with their Chinese counterparts.[13] But there were also the first successful entrepreneurial Chinese businessmen rising to prominence in trade, property, and in shipping, Chinese studying British law, and young Chinese girls being trained to a high level of English-language competence in special schools. Even if some of these girls, when grown to womanhood, formed irregular liaisons with the Western traders there, for others there was the model of Daniel Caldwell—once the fearsome head of the Hong Kong detectives in charge of suppressing piracy, now promoted to registrar general of the colony—who had publicly taken as his wife a Chinese Christian convert. As a bemused James Legge expressed it, "I sometimes fancy Britannia standing on the Peak, and looking down with an emotion of pride on the great Babylon which her sons have built."[14]

In January 1857 Hong Rengan had a chance to witness one of the more complex cases in the young colony's history—the attempted mass poisoning of the Western residents, which was traced swiftly to the bakery of a Chinese resident of Hong Kong named A-lum. James Legge himself ate the poisoned bread twice—"early in the morning and again at breakfast time"—but survived because the second meal of poisoned bread made him vomit violently. Yet even in the midst of the terror, hysteria, and cries for vengeance, Hong Rengan would have seen that A-lum was not lynched, as many at first had believed he would or should be. Instead A-lum was brought to trial before a British court and acquitted, since he was able to prove that the poison had in fact been placed in the dough by two of his bakery employees, perhaps at the instigation of Chinese in Canton who hated the British for their attempt to enforce their rights of residence in the city. During the trial, and for a short time afterward when he was held in protective custody, A-lum kept order in the jail and supervised the management of the Sunday Christian services there, preparing the prayer books in advance and maintaining "perfect order among all who attended."[15]

Hong Rengan, with money given to him by members of the missionary community, left Hong Kong in the summer of 1858 to travel to Nanjing. The timing of his journey was probably determined by the death of his mother that same summer, which released him from the pressing obligations of filial piety. But since he was, in the deepest sense, moving into the unknown, he left his wife and young son, and one of his brothers, in the care of the Legge family until he should send for them.[16]

Having left his family in safety, Hong risked taking the traditional route that centuries of Chinese had followed, moving north from Canton city up the East River to the Jiangxi border, and then down the Gan River into central China. Here in the autumn of 1858 he linked up with a subordinate general of the Qing commander Zeng Guofan, campaigning in the region. But when the Taiping troops routed the Qing, Hong was unable to move across the lines to join them, and instead lost all his baggage and was forced to flee northwest, to the Huangmei area of Hubei. Ever resourceful, he gained temporary respite and needed funds by serving as medical adviser—perhaps using skills taught to him by Benjamin Hobson—to a Qing magistrate whose son was ill. When he heard the news of Elgin's fleet moving down the Yangzi River after its visit to Wuchang, Hong was able to place aboard a British ship a message to his Hong Kong friends, telling them how he was faring. In early 1859, using his recent wages to buy a stock of goods, he passed back through Qing lines posing as a merchant, and reached the Heavenly Capital in late April 1859.[17]

After living for so long in Hong Kong, Hong Rengan has much to share with his Heavenly King. He presents his thoughts to his ruler in a long memorandum of May 1859. The Heavenly Kingdom needs a post office, so the mail will arrive on time. Tied up in bundles, paid for by the weight, the letters should move in vehicles driven by fire and steam that stop for no one till they reach their destination.[18] New houses should be sturdy, tall, and built in rows, though old houses can all be left the way they are. Banks can be formed to issue notes at 3 percent, speeding transactions and protecting travelers from bandits, for no one seeing merchants pass without their piles of silver will dream they carry money. Roads will be wide and straight and transport swift, the rivers dredged. Five- to ten-year patents can be issued for ingenious manufactures, with the longer time spans for most useful items, but inventors of "useless items" will be strictly punished. The system of life and property insurance, now practiced in foreign countries, can also be used in the Heavenly Kingdom. Houses, ships, merchandise, one's own existence, can each be guaranteed against loss from water or from fire, by payment of a simple premium.[19]

The Heavenly King's notations in the upper margins of his Shield King's memorandum show that he approves of all these things, even if the precise details of how or when they can be implemented are not yet firm. Hong Xiuquan also approves other plans of Rengan's, such as examinations for physicians, the abolition of slavery, the forbidding of infanticide, the banning of all plays and dramas, and an end to laziness.[20]

Only two of Hong Rengan's suggestions are rejected by the Heavenly King, on the grounds that they are not practical at present. One is for the establishment of a network of newspapers in different regions, and of special assistants to the Heavenly King, whose only role will be to make sure that all news from different places in China and beyond reaches him promptly and is free from tampering. In his marginal comment, Hong Xiuquan notes that such a procedure "can not be carried out now, lest the demon devils continue to set us against each other." After the devils are all killed, one can proceed with such a scheme.[21] The other is the suggestion of the Shield King that capital punishment should be left to God's divine judgment, rather than to men, so that all can follow the sixth commandment, which stipulates, "Thou shalt not kill." The Heavenly King responds in a marginal note: "Our Holy Father's sacred edict instructs us to behead the evildoers and sustain those who are upright. Thus killing demons and those who have committed crimes is something that cannot be avoided."[22] But despite the Heavenly King's apparent support for the other new reforms, nothing is undertaken at the time. There are armies on the march, most of the leading generals are away and, as Hong Rengan tells a visitor to Nanjing, nothing could be done till all were reassembled in the capital, "as it required the consent of the majority to any measure before it could be carried out."[23]

Caught between his pragmatic views and his deep and abiding admiration for Hong Xiuquan, Hong Rengan cannot but appear ambivalent to foreign missionaries who meet him. As he rises from his sofa to greet them, says "How do you do" in English, and shakes their hands, he is the affable host. Yet he is dressed in a long yellow damask robe, embroidered with dragons, wears a gilt crown set with precious stones upon his head, has crowds of boys to fan him, and rows of his subordinates before him, dressed in green or yellow robes with their flowing hair bound up in silken kerchiefs.[24] Hong Rengan does not agree with every one of the Heavenly King's articles of faith, he tells the Western missionaries. The two central revelations of Hong Xiuquan, received in 1837 and 1848, most certainly are "real," says Hong Rengan, though it is not completely clear "how they should be understood."[25] He does not, however, believe in the visions of the dead East King, Yang Xiuqing, though Hong Xiuquan "will not allow them to be questioned." As to the meaning of Hong's being the younger brother of Jesus, that is because Hong "regards Christ as the greatest of God's messengers, and himself as second only to him"; and it is in this light that he believes himself to be the brother of Christ and God's son.[26]

If offerings—whether of rice, or tea, or meat—are made to God when the Taiping offer up their prayers, they should be seen as "merely thank-offerings, not propriatory," Hong Rengan explains. Similarly, the burning of written prayers after they have been chanted aloud is the action of those still new to the faith, and will eventually be abandoned. The Lord's Supper is not observed in Taiping territory, and wine is never drunk during religious services; baptism—which may be administered by any of the faithful—consists of a sprinkling of water followed by a washing of the chest. When one speaks of the Heavenly King's birth in terms of his "descending to earth," that should be understood as meaning "nothing more than natural birth, with a divine commission." The Heavenly King does not accept that God is immaterial; to Hong Xiuquan, God *is* material and he "does not brook contradiction on this point." Nor will Hong Xiuquan change any of the terms for God that he has been using in his works. When Hong Rengan protests that the term "True God" should not be used, since God cannot be called either true or false, the Heavenly King rebuffs him. The Heavenly King reserves the final word on all matters of state, "but on most affairs not connected with religion he looks with contempt, remarking that they are 'things of this world' and not 'heavenly things.' "[27]

Hong Rengan's own study in Nanjing, which he allows a visiting Englishman to enter, perfectly reflects the overlays of cultures between his former life in Hong Kong and his current life in the Heavenly Capital. Though the Englishman is sarcastic about the condition of the Shield King's possessions, he still manages to capture the mood and the variety:

> Turning through a small door to the left you come into the Shield King's own Sanctum, which is quite a museum in its way. It is a large cheerful room facing a garden of flowers. The principal article of furniture is a large bed of Soochow manufacture, covered with jade and other ornaments, and hung with yellow curtains. The King takes a siesta in this now and again. Tables line the sides of the chamber, and support a most extraordinary conglomeration of different articles. There is a telescope on a moving pedestal (broken), a gun box (gun gone), three Colt's revolvers (all useless from rust), a box of gun caps, ditto of Vestas, two solar lamps that can't be made to light, and a cake of brown Windsor soap; the Woolwich Manual of Fortification, a book on military tactics, and the Holy Bible; any amount of Chinese books, comprising all those valuable works published by foreign missionaries, quires of yellow paper, five or six clocks, an alarum, broken barometer, heaps of proclamations, ink stones, gold pencils, and dirty rags. On the other side, piles of books suffering from moth, a hat box with the dragon hat inside, fans mounted in silver, jade stone drinking cups and saucers, gold and silver cups, platters, chopsticks and forks, three English Port wine bottles, and one ditto of Coward's mixed pickles. At various places are suspended an English naval sword, some dragon caps, a couple of Japanese knives, two French plates, and an old engraving of the Holy Well in Flintshire. Lying on the bed is a mass of silver ingots tied up in cloth. Chairs and stools with marble seats are placed round a marble table, and an attendant dressed in spotless white crape, with blue jacket pulls a punkah [fan], and so keeps you beautifully cool. Here the Shield King will give you a pretty dinner and lots of wine. He told me that when the Heavenly King prohibited wine, he applied for a dispensation asserting that unless he drank he could not eat, and that the dispensation was immediately granted.[28]

Surprising though the wine drinking may be in the atmosphere of the Heavenly Capital, the Shield King's openness to foreigners stands in studied contrast to the aloofness or hostility showed to the *Hermes, Cassini,* and *Susquehanna* five years or so before both by the Heavenly King and by Yang Xiuqing. Trying to express his feelings on this matter, Hong Rengan writes in his memorandum to Hong Xiuquan of the most sensible way to handle foreigners:

> Insulting expressions are used in verbal quarrels; they have no real meaning in high-level affairs and are apt to cause disasters. Even when we apply such expressions to nearby small countries, such as Siam, Annam, Japan, and the Ryukyu Islands, they are bound to be resented, because regardless of their low stations, human beings are not willing to be considered inferior; even if they admit their inferiority, they do so because of compulsion, not out of wholehearted submission. If wholehearted submission is to be won, it must be won not by power but by the perfection of government within and the demonstration of faith without, for that is the only way.[29]

In his same memorandum, Hong Rengan seeks to widen the Heavenly King's knowledge of foreign countries through brief vignettes of their major attributes. The British tend to be intelligent, he writes, though "proud by nature," and have attained their reputation as "the most powerful nation" through the stability of their institutions and ruling family. They respond well in conversation to such concepts as "equal status, friendship, harmony, and affection."[30] The United States of America not only has righteousness, wealth, and power but refrains from encroaching upon her neighbors. Surprisingly, if gold or silver is discovered there, foreigners are allowed to come and dig for it. The country has no beggars, proof of its virtue. Men called "chiefs of the country" serve for five years then "retire to live in comfort" while the various component states choose a new leader by putting the names of their choices into large boxes. It is accepted by the American people that those they choose as rulers will be "worthy and capable," and that the "decisions reached by the majority are considered just."[31]

Germans are primitive—they "resemble people of ancient times"—but are devout and conscientious; Scandinavians, "serene" of countenance under their pale hair, are broad-minded and friendly; France, the source of the arts and technologies now adopted by the other foreigners, is itself too steeped in mystical religion to be truly praised; Russia has embarked on great reforms, and given its vast size will soon be a major force. Japan, recently opened to trade with America, has been speedily acquiring new techniques, and "will certainly become skillful in the future."[32]

In case the Heavenly King is worried that the foreigners will use the chance of entrance into China to cheat the Taiping out of their wealth, Hong Rengan suggests that the Taiping follow a self-conscious policy of preferential treatment for their own subjects:

With foreigners, one has to devise ways to hold one's own. For instance, if they and we each open a store, we should not be required to pay rent, whereas the foreigners should be made to pay rent; we should use few workers, while they employ many; we should sell our products at a lower price, while they have to sell at a higher price. Thus we shall be benefited, while they suffer losses. We can prosper indefinitely, whereas they will collapse. How long can they maintain themselves in such a situation?[33]

Following this line of reasoning, Hong Rengan begins to develop the germ of a plan that the Taiping armies should try to make a bold march on the city of Shanghai to the southeast. Once in Shanghai, the Taiping should use one million ounces of the silver stored in their common treasury to buy a fleet of twenty modern steam vessels. With this fleet at their command, they could steam back up the Yangzi, raise the Qing siege around Nanjing, reopen the campaign to the west, and regain control of the key cities along the riverbank that they had been slowly losing to the Qing counterattacks.[34]

As the seeds of this plan develop, the Heavenly King assigns Li Xiucheng to direct the military side of operations. The choice is a shrewd one. A skimpily educated farm worker when he joined the Taiping troops on their 1851 march toward Yongan, Li has risen rapidly through the Taiping ranks because of his natural brilliance as a military commander in their campaigns in west and central China, till in December 1859 he is named Loyal King, equivalent in rank to Hong Rengan.[35] Outspoken and generous—and apparently the only senior Taiping leader who wears spectacles—Li is trusted and admired by his troops and by the foreigners he meets.[36] It is not clear whether it is he or Hong Rengan who formulates the exact details for the eastern campaign of 1860, but whoever plans it, it is Li who carries through the most dazzling part: a swift dash with several thousand troops across the Yangzi delta to seize the great city of Hangzhou, and create a diversion to relieve Nanjing. There follows a forced march back to Nanjing, where the great Qing encampments, fatally weakened by the transfer of the troops sent to relieve Hangzhou, fall into the Taiping hands. And that accomplished, Li leads a renewed push eastward to seize Suzhou, which falls to the Taiping forces on June 2. And finally, his troops are massed before Shanghai, with every expectation of a quick and easy capture of the Chinese section of the city.[37]

The Loyal King, Li Xiucheng, has an optimistic view of Westerners— which echoes those presented in the memorandum of Hong Rengan— and believes them susceptible to reason. Since the Westerners have expressed their interest in neutrality in the Taiping battles with the demons, and since the Taiping forces have expressed their willingness to trade in all the Western goods save opium, alcohol, and tobacco, there should be no reason for the Westerners to do anything but welcome the Taiping soldiers when they drive the demon Qing from the Chinese city of Shanghai. Li believes that the foreigners in Shanghai will actually welcome him, and that the Chinese citizens will yield up their city with only minimal resistance, just as the citizens of Suzhou have done.[38]

As Li advances on Shanghai in mid-August 1860, with a military force of around three thousand men, he sends letters to the foreign envoys stationed there to clarify his views. All foreign residences, and all foreign merchant buildings, will be left unmolested if they simply post a yellow flag as an identifying mark. Yellow flags should also be hung in all foreign churches—both Protestant and Catholic—so that his troops (who may not recognize the buildings by their architecture) leave them undamaged. As a further proof of his good intentions, Li orders the execution of one of his Taiping soldiers who has killed a foreigner—even though in this case the foreigner was in fact fighting alongside a squad of Qing demon troops. To make doubly sure, however, while the Taiping forces are engaged in storming the Chinese city, all foreigners are advised to stay indoors until the battle is concluded.[39]

Li Xiucheng is shocked and bewildered when Western leaders abandon their stated position of neutrality, and during three days of heavy fighting use the concentrated fire of their artillery and small arms to stop his men from taking the Chinese city of Shanghai. Li's soldiers seem equally unprepared for the fire unleashed on them by the Westerners, and stand motionless at first, "like men of stone, immovable, without returning a single shot," while the bullets shred their ranks.[40] In a letter ringing with bitterness and disappointment, on August 21, 1860, Li addresses the consuls of Great Britain, the United States, and other countries:

> I have, however, taken into consideration that you and we alike worship Jesus, and that after all, there exists between us the relationship of a common basis and common doctrines. Moreover I came to Shanghai to make a treaty in order to see us connected together by trade and commerce; I did not come for the purpose of fighting with you. Had I at once commenced to attack the city and kill the people, that would have been the same as the members of one family fighting among themselves, which would have caused the demons to ridicule us.
>
> Further, amongst the people of foreign nations at Shanghai, there must be varieties in capacity and disposition: there must be men of sense, who

know the principles of right, and are well aware of what is advantageous and what injurious. They cannot all covet the money of the demon's dynasty, and forget the general trading interests in this country.[41]

The setback before Shanghai marks the moment at which the 1860 eastern campaign, hitherto so brilliant in its execution, turns out to be disastrous in its consequences. By seeking to divert their demon enemies, the Taiping end up by fragmenting their own energies and fatally antagonizing the foreign powers. Not only do the British and French commanders now demand that the Taiping keep clear of Shanghai around a radius of thirty miles; they also forbid the foreign merchants to ship any more supplies or arms upriver to the Taiping garrisons. This decision in turn leads to the Taiping loss of their crucial inland river base at Anqing, for as soon as Qing patrol boats assisted by British ships prevent merchants or smugglers from unloading at the Anqing wharves, the ultimate fate of the city is sealed. The well-led and disciplined Xiang army forces, under the command of the former Hunan gentry leader Zeng Guofan and his brother Zeng Guoquan, are able to tighten the siege and starve the city into submission, killing almost every single member of the Taiping garrison forces, more than sixteen thousand in all. With the fall of the river garrison of Anqing in September 1861, the Taiping lines of communication with inland China to the west and north lose their crucial anchor.[42]

But in August 1860 the fate of Anqing is still more than a year away, and Hong Xiuquan himself makes no specific comment on the course of the eastern campaign. He neither praises Hong Rengan and Li Xiucheng for the raising of the Nanjing siege and the capture of Suzhou, nor upbraids them for the setback at Shanghai. Hong does still appear to harbor dreams for a great new "northern campaign," one that perhaps will at last bring down the pillars of the demon's kingdom, for the forces led by Lord Elgin have seized Peking in September 1860, burned the emperor's summer palace to the ground, and forced the emperor himself to flee beyond the wall. But when Li argues that such a northern campaign cannot be undertaken at this time, Hong Xiuquan, though "full of righteous indignation," lets his general have his way.[43]

Neither the problems in Shanghai, the use of force against the Taiping by the Western troops, nor their steady patrolling of the Yangzi River causes the Heavenly King to waver in his absorption with the True Religion. Indeed, Hong has found a new book now to supplement his rewritten Bible, a book that according to the Shield King, Hong Rengan, becomes his favorite reading at just this time. The book is *Pilgrim's Prog-*

Chinese illustrations to Pilgrim's Progress. In the mid-1850s Hong Xiuquan read John Bunyan's *Pilgrim's Progress,* which had just been translated into Chinese by Protestant missionaries. He later declared that the book was his favorite reading. The edition that Hong read contained ten illustrations specially prepared for the Chinese translation, of which the first and the last are shown here. In the first the figure of the book's hero Christian, weighed down by his burden

圖 路 天 就 始

of sin, is seen as he leaves his wife and children and sets out on his pilgrimage to the Heavenly City. He is pursued by two of his neighbors, Obstinate and Pliable, whose long queues of hair are clearly visible. In the second picture, having crossed the last great barrier, the River of Death, Christian and his travelling companion Hopeful enter the gates of God's eternal kingdom, as the angels blow their trumpets and salute them joyfully. *Credit: Library of Congress.*

圖 城 天 進

ress (1678), by John Bunyan.[44] One of Hong Rengan's missionary acquaintances from his Hong Kong days, William Burns, has translated the book into Chinese, and published it in Amoy in 1853. Short summaries of *Pilgrim's Progress* have been printed in Chinese before, but now the Heavenly King can follow Christian's journey to the new Jerusalem in all its solemnizing detail, aided by ten carefully rendered illustrations. Possibly Hong Rengan brings the book with him in 1858 and gives it to his sovereign, but Hong may have obtained a copy earlier, for the book has been circulating widely, and besides the 1853 edition there have been others printed in the mid-1850s in Hong Kong, Shanghai, and Fuzhou.[45]

The man called Christian in the *Pilgrim's Progress* is presented by Bunyan as being the product of a dream, but a dream so vivid we can understand with all our souls how Christian staggers under the weight of his guilt and sin, till freed by faith and the words of the evangelist who watches over him. To make his way toward his New Jerusalem, he gives up all the comforts of home and wife and children, and risks suffering, torture, and death. Many of his closest companions die along the way, and others—feigned companions—turn out to be deceivers, lost in idleness or faithlessness. The illustrations heighten the emotion of various episodes: Christian's baby in his mother's arms, stretching out his hand toward his disappearing father; the burden falling off Christian's back as he prays before the cross of Jesus; and Christian, flanked by the guardian knight and shepherds, gazing through a telescope toward the New Jerusalem.[46]

Narrow is the gate through which Christian must pass before his adventures are well begun, and many are the distractions and false detours before he reaches it.[47] "Earnestly exhort all the people of the world to enter the narrow door," Hong tells his family and his ministers in his proclamation of March 1861, for "this day is the heavenly day of great peace, prophesied long ago in the Gospel, and now proven. The narrow door lies in the Holy Edict of the Father and the Elder Brother."[48] Though Hong Xiuquan now never leaves his palace and the shelter of its double row of yellow walls, every morning new edicts in his own hand, in vermilion ink on yellow silk, are posted at one of the gates of his Heavenly Palace, the gate called "Holy Heavenly Gate of the True God." These texts now deal mainly with religion, including the relationship and nature of God and His Son or Sons.[49]

As Hong explains in an edict he gives to yet another visiting Protestant missionary, asking him to take it back with him to the city of Shanghai and share it with all the foreigners there, it is Hong's son Tiangui, the Young Monarch, who henceforth will "regulate affairs appertaining to this world," while Hong Xiuquan himself will lead the peoples of the earth "to the Heavenly abode." The revelation of 1848 is clear at last: "The Father and the Elder Brother descended into the world in order, through me and the Young Monarch, to establish endless peace," and thus will "heaven, earth, and man, the past, the present, and the future" be as one.[50] These broadenings of Hong's claims are reflected in the preambles to the proclamations of 1860 and 1861. First they are addressed to Hong's inner family and his court officials, but then he begins to address them to "all the western brothers and sisters" so that "Chinese and Westerners, in eternal harmony, shall observe the agreements, and peace and unity shall reign and our territories widen." The last ones are addressed to "all the officials and people of this world, one family."[51]

Hong's comments on the eastern campaigns, and on the Taiping's prospects of eventual victory, are couched exclusively in celestial terms. When Hong goes to Heaven, he tells his people in other proclamations of June 1861, he confers on the progress of the war with the East King and the West King. Together they plan their strategies, together they lead their troops victoriously into battle.[52] On some of these journeys the Young Monarch, Tiangui, now twelve years old, joins his father and the East King. Hong tells his son to fear nothing, for his Heavenly Grandfather will be always by his side. To reinforce this support, Hong changes his son's name to Tiangui Fu, "Heaven's Precious Happiness." The character "Fu" shall henceforth be tabooed for ordinary use, like the characters within the names Jehovah and Jesus, and when writing Fu all people will add an extra stroke at the center of the character.[53]

Though Tiangui is still so young, his dreams begin to intersect with his own father's. He has already predicted the second great relief of the Nanjing siege by the Taiping troops in 1860, by dreaming that two huge serpents surrounded the city, but that with his own sword he was able to slay them. His proud father celebrates the fulfillment of this dream by establishing a full Taiping holiday in its anniversary commemoration.[54] In poetry and prose Hong Xiuquan also celebrates his son's achievements, linking them to his own dream triumphs:

Father and son, Grandfather and grandson, sit in the Heavenly Court;
Peace and unity consume the serpents and the tigers.[55]

"God and Christ guided and directed me, and having decapitated the snake-tiger-dog devils, the Father and the Elder Brother guided me eastward to rule the rivers and mountains. Being of the same family, and the same clan, I returned victoriously."[56]

God also calls to Hong through Hong's wife, the Second Chief Moon.

"Tell your husband," God tells her in a dream, "to ease his heart and breast. Great peace will flow across the world, and immediately it shall be seen that the road to the heavenly hall of great peace is open. One day the southern heavenly door will open. Close your ranks for the great battle and eternal glory."[57]

Sometimes, too, Hong's visions blend with his mother's, as well as with those of his son and wife. Before the great Taiping victory at Suzhou in 1860, Hong tells his followers, his own earthly mother saw all three dead kings, East, West, and South, "depart to exterminate the demons," and as they marched before the Golden Dragon Palace they cheered aloud, "Ten Thousand Years."[58]

At dawn, one day in October 1860, Hong Xiuquan records, he sees in a dream sent to him by his Holy Father "countless heavenly soldiers and generals faithfully placing before me their tributes of sacred articles and treasure, and I smiled happily and silently."[59] Two days later, God comes to Hong again in another dream. Hong is walking with two women down a road. The road ahead is blocked by four yellow tigers. Seeking to save the women, Hong turns back. The tigers pursue him, and he fights them savagely with his bare hands; as they fight, the tigers change into human form, and Hong wakens abruptly, with a start. Between dreaming and waking he writes a poem:

Now the four tigers have been killed and cast away,
And, throughout the world, officials and people rejoice as I return in victory.
The road to Heaven lies open with the demon tigers crushed.
High Heaven arranges the unity of all existence.[60]

Hong sleeps again and returns to the scene of the battle. Now he sees the four tigers sprawled there, dead. But lying with them are new apparitions, two black dogs. One of the dogs is clearly dead as well, but one still shows signs of life. When Hong strikes it with his hands, the dog cries out, in a human voice, "I'm afraid." Hong replies, "I have to kill you," and in his dream beats the dog to death. Hong wakes rejoicing. He knows now, he tells his followers, that he and his son will reign a myriad years.[61]

PRIEST-KING

 Issachar Roberts finally reaches Nanjing on October 13, 1860, while Hong Xiuquan dreams of vanquishing the demon dogs and tigers. With Roberts' arrival, many hopes and thoughts converge. It is now thirteen years since Hong Rengan and Hong Xiuquan together visited Roberts' chapel in Canton.[1] It is over eleven years since Hong Xiuquan, as if puzzled by Roberts' refusal to give him the rites of baptism, asked Jesus through the mouth of Xiao Chaogui, whether "the foreigner Roberts has a truly sincere heart or not" and received the answer from Jesus that "his heart is indeed sincere, you are connected together."[2] It is over seven years since Hong Xiuquan, on first entering into his Heavenly Capital, sent a trusted emissary to Canton in person, to invite Roberts to visit Nanjing and preach there to the Taiping faithful.[3] It is close to two years since Hong Xiuquan, seeking to woo Lord Elgin to his cause, asked if Roberts was with Elgin on the mission, and met with no reply.[4] And it is a little over a year since Hong Rengan, in his elaborate memorandum, mentioned to his Heavenly King that just as newly developed weapons of war can be purchased to strengthen the Heavenly Kingdom, so is it in the best interests of the

Taiping to let certain foreigners into their domains. Instructors from countries that are "advanced in technical skills" and have "elaborate institutions" should be encouraged to enter Taiping areas, along with foreign missionaries, as long as they offer their advice to the kingdom as a whole and do not "slander" the Taiping ways.[5]

Roberts' arrival in Nanjing, in turn, is made possible only by a concatenation of events. One is the result of Lord Elgin's violence in Peking, which has forced the emperor to yield new treaty rights that will let foreigners travel freely in the interior of China, whether to trade or to preach the gospel. Another is the eastern campaign, which, even if failing to seize Shanghai, by making the city of Suzhou a Taiping bastion has made travel from Shanghai comparatively easy.[6] And Roberts himself, though not exactly for the happiest of reasons, is for a time free of the family and financial problems that have dogged his life for years: his wife, weakened by illness and alienated from Roberts, has insisted on living in the United States with their two children; his first Chinese assistant has died and the second, after grave mistreatment, has abandoned him; and years of tenacious legal wrangling have finally led exhausted Qing officials to grant the perennially bankrupt Roberts $5,200 in restitution for his Canton home and chapel, which have twice been looted by Chinese mobs.[7]

Hong Xiuquan initially receives Roberts almost as rapturously as he received Hong Rengan eighteen months before. Shortly after his arrival, Hong grandly promises freedom of worship to all Christians in his domain. He endorses Roberts' appeals for more Protestant missionaries to come to Nanjing, so that there can be eighteen new chapels in the city, and as many as two to three thousand more outside the walls. Seeing himself as *the* pioneer" in this venture, Roberts writes to his friends of the great opportunity now offered to the Baptists to reach out to the thirty million souls who live in the six provinces more or less controlled by the Taiping forces. Success in this "will doubtless prove the surprise and admiration of Christendom."[8]

Hong announces that Roberts will be his minister of foreign policy and of justice in all cases involving foreigners. He gives him free lodgings— two rooms, upstairs, not far from his own palace—and food and a stipend. He offers Roberts three new wives—Roberts declines the offer—but when Hong offers him Taiping clothes, Roberts accepts. A missionary who sees him in Nanjing writes that Roberts looks resplendent, "robed in Taiping costume, a blue satin fur gown, and yellow embroidered jacket over it, with red hood, and satin boots."[9]

Yet the only personal meeting Roberts has with his former baptismal candidate is disconcerting: the pomp of the moment in Hong's palace is undeniable; the honor to a foreign visitor, unique in Taiping history, is patent; and Hong seems imposing to Roberts—"a much finer-looking man than I thought he was. Large, well-made, well-featured, with fine black moustaches which set off considerably, and a fine voice."[10] But the retinue makes it clear to Roberts that he should kneel in Hong's presence, and when he refuses he is tricked into doing so by the sudden shouted command that all present should now kneel in the honor of the Lord— which Roberts follows automatically, till he realizes it is Hong who is being knelt to. Their hour-long conversation is interrupted several times by the assembled Taiping leaders' further kneeling and chanting in Hong's honor. Roberts now stands throughout these genuflections— indeed he is never invited to be seated, the only one besides the Heavenly King so honored being his son Tiangui. And when Hong invites Roberts to dine, he means with the other kings but not with him.[11]

Hong Xiuquan makes it clear that the Christianity he expects Roberts to preach is Taiping Christianity, with its own special revelations; to Roberts, who has come to Nanjing in hopes of purifying Hong's religion of its misconceptions, this is a bitter blow. Roberts' secret hope has been to replace the Gutzlaff version of the King James Bible, used by the Taiping, with the American Baptist Bible of Goddard, which a group of Baptist co-workers have already translated into Chinese. Roberts himself has prepared an annotated version of Luke's Gospel for Hong, while two of his Baptist colleagues have annotated Acts and Romans.[12] Less serious, but also dispiriting, is the curious but intrusive rule that Roberts may have no visiting foreigners to stay with him in his small Nanjing residence. And yet just as Roberts begins to grow most guarded, convinced that Nanjing is run by martial law, with only a glimmering of truth in its so-called Christian teachings, and no clear sense of its future fate, he is struck favorably and afresh by the Taiping's stated need for a church, their desire for true preachers, their determination on the battlefield, their openness, and Hong's willingness to debate his stands.[13]

It is hard for Nanjing visitors not to be moved by the outdoor services on one of the open plots of land in the center of Nanjing, when a great crowd assembles on the Sabbath day, while "a sea of flags and streamers, red, yellow, white and green, floated in the wind over them," to listen to the two Taiping preachers appointed for that day. The Taiping preachers, standing in their glittering yellow coronets on a rostrum that itself is raised upon a great square platform, address the throng in turn, one on the topic of a soldier's duties, love of family and attention to prayer, one on the reason for excluding traders from the city and on the need for charity toward the elderly and destitute. Then, as each preacher himself kneels on the rostrum, the congregation also kneels, and prays together as a group, in perfect silence. Once the Taiping service is over, Roberts is free to preach his own sermons, on what he considers "the central truths of Christianity," either in the Cantonese dialect that he already knows or in the Nanjing dialect he is studying daily to acquire. Clearly much work still lies ahead, for when a soldier, chosen at random, is asked, "Who is the Holy Spirit?" he replies, "The Eastern King."[14]

Roberts begins to doubt that he can convert Hong to the truest meanings of his faith, but Hong never despairs of converting Roberts, writing in a letter to the American Baptist:

> Add to your faith. Do not suppose that I am deceived. I am the one saviour of the chosen people. Why do you feel uncertain of the fact of divine communications to me? When Joshua formerly destroyed the enemies of God, the sun and moon stood still. When Abraham sat under the oak, three men stood by him. Carefully think of all this. Do you become conscious of it? Do you believe? I am grieved at heart, having written very many edicts on these matters, and all men being with me as one family. When the Shield King came to the capital, he also had a revelation. To recognise these divine communications is better than being baptized ten thousand times. Blessed are they that watch. Your Father, your Lord, comes to you as a thief, and at a time when you know not. He that believeth shall be saved. You will see greater things than these. Respect this.[15]

The British missionary Joseph Edkins, a scholar of fluid dynamics and Milton's *Paradise Lost* as well as of biblical theology, and friend to the Shield King ever since they met in Shanghai in 1854, also visits the Heavenly Capital, in the spring of 1861.[16] While there he presents to Hong Xiuquan a copy of an essay he has published in Chinese, "That God Is without a Body Is True," and several other shorter theological pieces. Having learned from friends that Hong Xiuquan is having great trouble with his eyesight, and refuses to read materials that are written out in too-small characters—unlike Loyal King Li Xiucheng, Hong has not adjusted to wearing spectacles—Edkins sends essays that have been printed in big clear characters and writes out his own remarks "in a large hand."[17] The arguments advanced by Edkins speak to the immateriality of God's nature, leaning heavily on chapter 1, verse 18, of John's Gospel: "No man hath seen God at any time; the only begotten Son, which is in the bosom of the Father, he hath declared him." Edkins also argues strongly for the divinity of Jesus Christ, and sends Hong translations of both the Nicene and the Athanasian Creeds, to warn him that he must not fall into the heresy of Arius, who was condemned for denying the divinity of Jesus.[18]

Edkins' strategy of writing in large characters is successful. Hong responds with a stream of his own commentary, so that Edkins, even if not convinced, is still gratified to find his own letter "covered with vermilion corrections and notes," all of which have clearly been "dashed off roughly" with a "very thick-pointed" writing brush. In the passage from John 1:18, Hong has erased the word "only" from the phrase "only begotten Son," so that his own Sonship is not denied: "Christ is in God's form," Hong adds, since "the Son is as the Father." In his letter to Hong, Edkins has also quoted a passage from the "Revelation of John the Divine," explaining to Hong Xiuquan that the description of God contained within it must be read as strictly "figurative."

> After this I looked and, behold, a door was opened in heaven; and the first voice which I heard was, as it were, of a trumpet talking with me; which said, Come up hither, and I will show thee things which must be hereafter. And immediately I was in the Spirit; and, behold, a throne was set in heaven, and one sat on the throne. And he that sat was to look upon like a jasper and a sardius stone; and there was a rainbow round about the throne, in sight like unto an emerald. (Revelation 4:1–3)

In his reply, Hong erases the word "figurative" with his blunt-nosed brush, and writes in the word "real."[19]

Showing himself to be fully aware of the purport of Edkins' remarks on Arius, and of how the views of Arius had been fully revoked by Athanasius and a council of the church, Hong comments briefly that in that case the council was wrong, Arius right.[20] Hong not only deigns to read all of Edkins' arguments; he sends his own handwritten poem in rebuttal:

God is vexed most by idols and images,
So human beings are not allowed to see the Father's likeness.
But Christ and myself were begotten by the Father,
And because we were in the Father's bosom, therefore we saw God.
The Father created Adam and Pangu in his own image—
If you acknowledge the truth of this, you can still be pardoned.
The Elder Brother and I have personally seen the Father's heavenly face;
Father and Sons, Elder and Younger Brother, nothing is indistinct.
The Father and the Elder Brother have brought me to sit in the Heavenly Court;
Those who believe this truth will enjoy eternal bliss.[21]

Branching out from this private correspondence with the Western missionary to his own followers at large, Hong explains in a proclamation of May 1861 that the problem is partly one of numbers of participants as well as of belief, of history as well as present reality. If over twenty people suddenly said God was their Father, the world would justly doubt the claim, and believe it violated human relationships. If two hundred all claimed kin with the Elder Brother, one would justly believe God was being slighted. Because "since ancient times, no man has seen God," there has been a justifiable fear—too often realized—that men in their ignorance would "make false images and consequently go to hell." But such strictures do not apply to Hong himself, *can*not apply: "Only the divine Son can recognize the divine Father. It is well known that the Elder Brother and I know the Father." Thus it is that in high Heaven the Father, the Elder Brother, and Hong the "Shining Sun" pour their light "brightly upon the earthly world. The Father, the Elder Brother in Heaven, and I, the true Sun, together shall establish peace for myriads of years. This day is the heavenly day of great peace, prophesied long ago in the Gospel, and now proven."[22]

Hong feels that certain aspects of these divine relationships are still not clearly understood. The fact that he and his brother naturally see their Father does not mean they in any way claim parity with Him: "I now proclaim clearly," says Hong, "that in Heaven, upon earth, and among mankind, the Heavenly Father, God, is alone the most revered. Since the Creation, this has been the greatest principle." To emphasize this point, Hong orders that the "Taiping Heavenly Kingdom" be renamed "God's Heavenly Kingdom." All state seals must be recut to reflect this new reality. All honorific titles held by his officials, and all future grants bestowed, shall reflect the same change, from Taiping to God.[23]

Edkins and Roberts should not be surprised that they do not see Hong in person, and that he reaches them by commentary, poems, and proclamations. Virtually nobody gets to see the Heavenly King any more, save for a tiny circle of his family and his closest confidants. With the exception granted on one occasion only to Issachar Roberts, foreign missionaries, even if promised a personal audience and brought to the palace in a glittering retinue under yellow banners, sit in vain for hours before his empty throne, listening to the chanted hymns, and watching the smoke curl lazily from the sacrificial fire, above which are laid out offerings of rice and meat.[24] And Western consular officials, demanding their new treaty rights, can even angrily force their way through the seven miles of wide streets of the capital and sit in Hong Xiuquan's own antechamber, hour

after hour, among baskets of charcoal, pails of steaming water, and stacks
of firewood, peered at by crowds of boys, or the bolder palace women,
listening to the booming of the gongs, and watching the royal proclamations carried by on rolls of yellow silk, but Hong himself never appears.[25]

Seen from outside by other foreign visitors, the gates through the huge
walls of Hong's palace open at intervals to allow the palace women and
attendants to pass through with special gifts of food, while in a kind of
shed outside the gates, beached now, lies the great gilded dragon boat in
which the Heavenly King first glided down the river to his capital.[26] In
the outer courtyard—under gleaming lanterns hanging from silken cords,
one all of glass, brought from the Qing governor's mansion in Suzhou—
sits an old servant who has known the Heavenly King since his young
days in Canton. He lets no one pass. Above the gilded columns is the
inscription "Of the True God, the Sacred Heavenly Door," reflecting
Hong's changing of his kingdom's name from peaceful to divine. Spiritual
matters are now the focus of Hong Xiuquan's own life, he tells his followers. Henceforth it is his son Tiangui Fu who will handle "common
things."[27]

The challenges posed by Issachar Roberts and Joseph Edkins have
intermeshed perfectly with the current "spiritual matters" that occupy the
time of the Heavenly King. For months, perhaps for years, he has been
writing his own commentaries in the ample margins of the Bible—both
Old and New Testaments—that he has already corrected. These commentaries link him to the text by verse or chapter, but apart from that limita-
tion his thoughts are free to wander. For whereas in revising the Bible's
text, Hong felt constrained to fit his thoughts to the exact space available
in the altered sections, in his own commentary he writes what he feels, at
any length he chooses.[28] This freedom to browse and reflect, coming so
soon after his careful revisions of the aspects of the Bible that disturbed
him, means that though he has never been trained as a preacher Hong
can often respond to Edkins and Roberts with chapter and verse.

Most of the seventy surviving comments by Hong written in the margins of his revised New Testament—and perhaps in scores of others, as
in the case of John's Gospel, that now are lost—show his concern with the
dual themes of family relationships and the uniqueness of God as Father.
Again and again, Hong emphasizes that Jesus cannot be God, is not God,
just as he Hong is not God, can never be, and will never claim to be. The
role of Yang Xiuqing, the East King, the Comforter, and carrier of Divine
Breath or Holy Spirit, is often invoked as well, to prove that there is no
parity in what others call the Trinity, for God is the Holy Spirit, but Yang

as breath of God cannot himself be God. Hong reminds his followers that "God the Father knew that the New Testament contains mistakes; therefore he sent down the East King to testify the truth that the Holy Spirit is the same as God, but that His breath is the East King." By the same token, writes Hong, "since God knew that some people on earth erroneously believed that Christ is God," therefore "Christ himself sent down the West King to make it clear that he was [merely] the Heir Apparent. For the Father is the Father, a son is a son, the Elder Brother is the Elder Brother, and a younger brother is a younger brother." If there is such a concept as a "three in one," then it refers to God's three children, Jesus, Hong, and Yang, three brothers born together: for "the East King is [also] God's beloved son, born of the same mother as his Eldest Brother and myself; before Heaven and earth existed, we three were all sons of the same Father."[29]

Hong constantly reemphasizes the nature of the family bonds. The passage of Mark's Gospel, chapter 12, verses 35 to 37, where Jesus talks with the scribes in the temple at Jerusalem, before the Passover, debating the proposition that the Messiah would be the "Son of David," prompts Hong to a counterargument. As Hong puts it, "If Christ were God, and ascended to Heaven where he and God became as one, . . . then how could it be that when I myself ascended to Heaven I saw that in Heaven there was God the Father, there was the Heavenly Mother, and there was also the Elder Brother Christ and the Heavenly Elder Sister-in-law? And that now I am come down to earth there are still the Heavenly Father, Heavenly Mother, Heavenly Elder Brother, and Heavenly Elder Sister-in-law?"[30] And Hong gladly accepts the words of Stephen, just before his martyrdom, as recorded in the Acts of the Apostles, to be a support of Hong's own interpretation. When Stephen calls out to the crowd, "Behold, I see the heavens opened, and the Son of Man standing at the right hand of God," Hong points out, this "clearly proves one is Father and one is Son."[31] Surely, as Hong writes in another comment, "whether ascending to Heaven or descending to earth, it is always the same: hearing with one's ears is not as good as seeing with one's own eyes."[32]

In other comments, Hong shows that he has in no way forgotten the earlier debates, held between Yang Xiuqing and Mellersh and the "synod" aboard the *Rattler* on the materiality or immateriality of God. Whenever the New Testament reports that Jesus physically touches someone, Hong makes sure to emphasize by his comments that God, while not *being* Jesus, is separately and yet physically at the scene, and that Jesus gains his powers from God's literal presence. In Matthew's Gospel, for example, when Jesus heals the mother of Peter's wife by touching her hand with His, Hong writes, "God being present in the Elder Brother, when He spoke and reached forth His hand, thus was she healed."[33] Or also as described by Matthew, when Jesus "touched the eyes" of two blind men to cure them, Hong comments, "God being present in the Elder Brother, therefore when He touched their eyes they were able to see."[34] God is present "above" Jesus when he cures the man sick of palsy, and when Jesus cures a leper by touching him, it is because God is at the scene, even more literally, "upon the head" of Jesus.[35] Even when Hong does not place God in person at the site of an apparent miracle, as when Jesus raises the only son of a widow from the dead by "touching the bier," Hong is careful to explain in his commentary that Jesus acts here only as a "prophet" sent by God, not in any sense as God Himself.[36]

The New Testament offers, Hong tells his followers, signs or answers to many of the enigmas that attended the founding of the Taiping Heavenly Kingdom. Thus the "Earthly Paradise," the "Xiao tiantang" of which he spoke on Thistle Mountain and again in the dark days in Yongan, can be explained in the light of Paul's First Epistle to the Corinthians, chapter 15, which states that "as we have borne the image of the earthy, we shall also bear the image of the heavenly." In this sense, the "Little Heaven" or Earthly Paradise, the current "Heavenly Court" of Nanjing, is God's kingdom for men's physical bodies on this earth, whereas His "Greater Heaven" is where their souls will ascend in glory.[37] In Acts 15:14–16, also, the prophecy of the rebuilding of the tabernacle fits well with current Taiping goals. In the words of the Bible:

> Symeon hath declared how God first did visit the nations, to take out of them a people for his name. And to this agree the words of the prophets, as it is written: After this I will return, and will build again the tabernacle of David, which is fallen down; and I will build again its ruins, and I will set it up. . . .

As Hong comments, this passage prefigures the way in which "God and Christ have come down to earth to rebuild God's tabernacle in the Heavenly Capital at the Heavenly Court."[38]

What Hong Xiuquan does not tell either Edkins or Roberts is that he has grown convinced he speaks with the voice of Melchizedek, at once God's highest priest and king. Hong has found the two Bible passages that discuss Melchizedek most clearly. The first is in Genesis, chapter 14. It is only a fleeting reference to Melchizedek, but it is enough for Hong to build on. As Genesis 14:18 explains, when Abraham returned victorious from his battles, "Melchizedek, King of Salem, brought forth bread and wine; and he was the priest of the Most High God." Hong has already made three revisions to this single verse, so that in the Taiping Bible it now reads, "Melchizedek, King of the Heavenly Realm, brought forth bread and cakes; and he was the highest priest of the Most High God." In his commentary, Hong explains the newly rewritten text as follows: "This Melchizedek is I myself. In former times, when I was in Heaven, I came down to earth to make these traces plain, and to provide the proof that I would descend to earth at the present time to be your King. For with everything that is carried out by Heaven, there must [first] be a sign."[39]

Hong continues this train of thought in his commentary on Genesis, chapter 15, where God offers his own promise of blessings and a rich posterity to Abraham. Hong writes:

> When God came down to earth to rescue Israel from out of Egypt, it was the sign that in our present age God would come to earth to direct the founding of the Heavenly Kingdom. When the Elder Brother [Jesus] descended to be born in the country of Judea and redeem the sins of the world, it was the sign that in our present age the Elder Brother would come to earth to help us with our heavy burdens. When I myself came down to earth to give solace and blessing to Abraham, it was the aptest sign that in our present age I myself would come down to earth to direct the salvation of mankind. Thus does each of God's sacred decrees have plentiful modes of expression, evidence and proof. Respect these words.[40]

The second passage, or rather cluster of passages, on Melchizedek occurs in Paul's Epistle to the Hebrews. There Paul writes of the "hope we have as an author of the Soul, both sure and steadfast, . . . even Jesus, made an high priest for ever after the order of Melchizedek."[41] Paul sees Melchizedek as "without father, without mother, without descent, having neither beginning of days, nor end of life; but made like unto the Son of God; abideth a priest continually" (Hebrews 7:3). And even Levi, from whom the later high priests claim their authority, "was yet in the loins of his father, when Melchizedek met him" (Hebrews 7:10). In the margin above these verses, Hong has written:

> This Melchizedek is none other than myself. Formerly in Heaven our Old Mother bore the Elder Brother and also all those of my generation. At that time I knew the Father was going to have my Elder Brother born of Abraham's descendants. Therefore I comforted the officers and troops, and con-

gratulated and blessed Abraham, for Abraham was a good man. The Father's sacred proclamation says, "Hong shall be ruler and save the virtuous man." This was said to serve as a sign that at the present time I would come down to earth to be the ruler. Respect these words.[42]

"The time I spent in Heaven, during the days of Abraham," Hong has written elsewhere in the margin of his Bible, "is still quite clear within my memory. I knew that God was going to send the Elder Brother to be born of Abraham's descendants; therefore I went down to earth to save Abraham and to bless Abraham."[43]

Edkins has also challenged Hong Xiuquan to respond to the Protestant view that the depiction of God in the fourth chapter of the Book of Revelation is figurative, and been bluntly rejected by Hong with the words that the depiction is "real." Hong's commentary shows that he knows the context of Edkins' example in considerable detail. For instance, next to the passage in the Book of Revelation, chapter 3, verse 12, that "the name of the city of my God . . . is New Jerusalem, which cometh down out of Heaven from my God," Hong has written in the margin:

> Now the Elder Brother is come. In the Heavenly Court is the temple of the Heavenly Father, God, the True Deity; there also is the Elder Brother Christ's temple, wherein are already inscribed the names of God and Christ. The New Jerusalem sent down from Heaven by God the Heavenly Father is our present Heavenly Capital [Tianjing]. It is fulfilled. Respect these words.[44]

Hong too has read in Revelation how the seven seals are opened and how each one has its signs: the white horse, whose rider goes forth to conquer; the red horse, whose rider has the power to take peace from the earth; the black horse, whose rider carries the scales; and the pale horse, which bears Death upon his back. But he has given his greatest attention to the moment when the sixth seal is opened. The Bible says:

> And I beheld, when he had opened the sixth seal and, lo, there was a great earthquake, and the sun became black as sackcloth of hair, and the moon became like blood; and the stars of heaven fell unto the earth, even as a fig tree casteth her untimely figs, when she is shaken of a mighty wind. And the heaven departed as a scroll when it is rolled together; and every mountain and island were moved out of their places. And the kings of the earth, and the great men, and the rich men, and the chief captains, and the mighty men, and every slave, and every free man, hid themselves in the dens and in

the rocks of the mountains, and said to the mountains and rocks, Fall on us, and hide us from the face of him that sitteth on the throne, and from the wrath of the Lamb; for the great day of his wrath is come, and who shall be able to stand? (Revelation 6:12–17)

All along the margins above this passage Hong has written his own judgment and elaborated on the ancient words so as to enlighten his embattled followers:

I am the sun; my wife is the moon. "[The sun] became black, [the moon] became like blood" is a hidden message that we would descend to earth to be human beings. The heavenly generals and heavenly soldiers are the stars of heaven. "Fell unto the earth" is a hidden message that they would descend to earth to kill the demons. "Heaven departed as a scroll when it is rolled together; and every mountain and island were moved out of their places" is a hidden message that the old would be cast out and replaced by the new, and in the Taiping unification all regions would change to the new. "The chiefs of the earth hide in the dens and in the rocks of the mountains" is a hidden message that at this very time the snakes and beasts will be set upon and killed and the evil demons will be exterminated. Now it is fulfilled. Respect these words.[45]

In a final bold attempt to draw all these themes together, Hong takes the opening of the twelfth chapter of Revelation and shares it with his followers:

There appeared a great wonder in heaven—a woman clothed with the sun, and the moon under her feet, and upon her head a crown of twelve stars. And she, being with child, cried, travailing in birth, and pained to be delivered. And there appeared another wonder in heaven; and, behold, a great red dragon, having seven heads and ten horns, and seven crowns upon his heads. And his tail drew the third part of the stars of heaven and did cast them to the earth; and the dragon stood before the woman who was ready to be delivered, to devour her child as soon as it was born. And she brought forth a male child, who was to rule all nations with a rod of iron; and her child was caught up unto God, and to his throne. (Revelation 12:1–5)

And as he has done with the earlier chapter, Hong fills the available open space above this passage with his own commentary, to show how this woman is his mother, and how Hong as her son is also Melchizedek, priest and king:

I still remember that when I entered the womb of this woman, the Father made a sign, which was that she should be clothed with the sun, thereby to evidence that the fetus within her body was the sun. But who would have known that the serpent devil, the demon Yan Luo, also knew that this woman's fetus was I? God had specially dispatched me to be born into the world to kill and eradicate this serpent. Thus it was that the serpent wanted to devour me, hoping thereby to usurp God's great works. Little did he know that God is omnipotent; the son which was born could not be harmed by the serpent. I myself now earnestly give proof that the Melchizedek of former times was I. After the Elder Brother ascended into Heaven, his body was clothed with the sun. The son born to this woman also is I. Therefore the Father and the Elder Brother now have descended into the world, bringing me to be the sovereign, especially to eradicate this serpent. Now the serpents and the beasts have been set upon and killed, and the realm is in peace. It is fulfilled. Respect these words.[46]

21

SNOWFALL

 Issachar Roberts leaves Nanjing on January 20, 1862, and seeks shelter on a British ship moored in the Yangzi River. In indignant letters to the press, he claims he has been greatly wronged by the Shield King, Hong Rengan, and that Hong Xiuquan is "a crazy man, entirely unfit to rule [and] without any organized government."[1] Reporting Roberts' safe arrival at Shanghai in early February, the *North China Herald* shows little sympathy for the preacher it has already sarcastically dubbed "His Grace the Archbishop of Nanking" and a "sham Diogenes of former days, and would-be Plato among missionaries."[2] Roberts' flight, to the paper's editors, is merely poetic justice for the man who had misled the public for years about the Taipings. "Even he who first lighted the match which has led to such a wide-spread conflagration of blasphemy and murder has at last fled from the monster he has conjured up—like Faust fleeing from the demon Mephistopheles."[3]

Roberts' flight from the Heavenly Capital comes just as General Li Xiucheng, determined this time to face down the foreigners and make up for the disastrous losses at Anqing, has massed new Taiping armies outside Shanghai. Confirmation of the nearness of the Taiping troops, their strength, and their readiness for combat comes to the Western community from two of their own, one drunk, one sober, but both experienced in the ways of war. The first of them, Charles Goverston, is a seaman on a British vessel, the *British Empire,* moored in Shanghai harbor. Given a forty-eight-hour "liberty" to explore Shanghai in early January 1862, as he explains subsequently to the British vice-consul, he overstayed his leave "through intoxication." Not yet "perfectly sober," he sets out "with a Chinaman who could talk English," to take a look at the vaunted Taiping, and finds them all too quickly. Suddenly surrounded by a squad of Taiping troops, only two or three miles from the shelter of the city, Goverston is terrified, indeed "the fright quite sobered him," though he swiftly returns to his former state when a Taiping officer gives him more "liquor to drink which quite capsized him." But thereafter, the terror gone, and no more drink provided, Goverston is held by the Taiping and questioned for four days through his Chinese companion-interpreter. The questions focus on whether there are French and English troops in Shanghai, where and how many, whether they are also in the Chinese city, and whether they have heavy guns. The interrogation finished, the Taiping give Goverston a message to take back to the foreigners: the Taiping request the French and British to withdraw from the city, which the Taiping are determined on taking. They undertake not to damage any European property, and not to plunder.

Neither too drunk nor too terrified to keep his eyes open, Goverston estimates the Taiping troops just in his area of confinement to number about fifteen thousand men: "The villages all around are full of them: every house crammed." Many of the Taiping are armed with foreign muskets, some with "the Tower-mark," others German-made. There are several Europeans with the Taiping forces, and one English-speaking "Arab" who acts as "servant" to a Taiping officer. The Arab tells Goverston there are other Taiping armed with the latest Enfield rifles. Goverston notes that the Taiping troops seem well fed and fit, "very fine-looking men" with "plenty to eat." But they treat their conscripted Chinese coolie laborers with great cruelty, killing those who cannot manage their loads; nor do they pay their foreign helpers, but promise that when Shanghai is taken they will "get lots."[4]

On January 20, 1862, another Englishman, Joseph Lambert, gives an even more detailed description of Taiping plans and troop strengths to the British officials. Lambert has been one of the supervisors, with a European "mate," on a fleet of forty-two boats sent by Chinese merchants under the

French flag to buy silk up-country. Arrested by the Taiping, held for three days, and interrogated through an English-speaking Cantonese in the Taiping force, the foreigners are threatened with death, but are spared when their employer offers their captors two thousand dollars. Lambert is then ordered to return to Shanghai and buy muskets and powder for the Taiping forces, and to deliver four letters, to the English, French, American, and Dutch consuls. If he tries to evade the Taiping order, they will behead him when they enter Shanghai, for they will be sure to recognize him. The message for Lambert to deliver is blunt:

> They said that if the French or English attempted to resist them when they attacked Shanghae, they would cut off the heads of all foreigners they could get hold of, and stop all the tea and silk trade; that if French and English did not interfere with them, all white men might go over all the country, and trade.

Lambert estimates the Taiping troops in the area where he was held captive at around forty thousand. They seem poorly armed—perhaps one in ten has a musket—but they have established "a regular iron-foundry," where they are casting the barrels for large guns.[5]

The information acts as a catalyst for the already nervous foreign community. The Shanghai land defenses are further strengthened by "zigzag redoubts" and gun emplacements that ring the foreign concession areas, manned by a force of four thousand troops, and with eight British warships now anchored off the Shanghai Bund. In the gun emplacements—twelve feet high, built with eight-by-eight-inch beams of Singapore hardwood, to be replaced by hewn stone at a later date when time allows—the allied troops mount swivel guns capable of firing 32-pounder shells. To prevent accidental explosions, all spare munitions are to be stored in an old hulk, moored out in the river. For these and the other necessary defensive measures, the foreign community pledges eighty-six thousand taels of its own money.[6]

The British "Shanghai Land-renters Association" meetings that assemble at the British consulate are attended by from thirty to forty-five wealthy merchants. Even on the eve of possible annihilation their plans for defending the city are intermeshed with shrewd schemes to make their investments pay. The defensive ditches, for instance, can serve double duty as drainage canals, so that the Chinese owners of the land will be happy to help defray the costs. Making their concession area a "city of refuge" for the wealthier of the fleeing Chinese has not only led to satisfactorily high rents but encouraged the Chinese "better class" to "subscribe freely

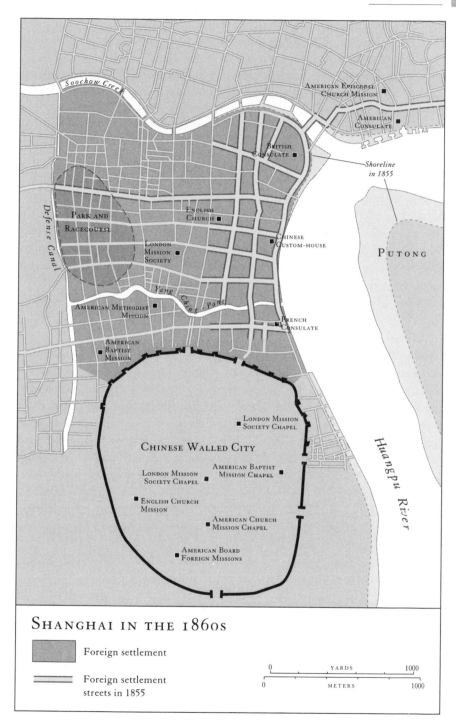

Shanghai in the 1860s

Foreign settlement

Foreign settlement
streets in 1855

towards the expense of the blockhouses." The blockhouses in turn will have excellent value as long-range investments, for they can always be used "in case of a riot, [to] keep the mob in check."[7]

One man at the meeting of January 15, 1862, Mr. J. C. Sillar, suggests that the British "enter into friendly communication with the Tae-ping leaders," and hand over the Chinese city to them, thus enabling "men who printed the Bible" to take over "the idolatrous native city," and "the city to change rulers amicably." Thus would the British not only purge themselves of a "national sin" but be able to prevent panic and terror among the Chinese refugees now in the foreign settlements—Mr. Sillar dramatically estimates the total of refugees to be 700,000—who would otherwise "rush down the streets in hundreds and thousands, and drown themselves in the river ... while the streets would be choked up with the bodies of those trampled under foot." But Mr. Sillar can get no one to second his motion, and a missionary's response that now is the time "for prompt and decisive action against the Tae-pings" is "received with acclamation."[8]

What nobody, Chinese or foreign, has figured into the careful calculations is the weather. The snow starts to fall on January 26, 1862, and it continues, steadily and unrelentingly, for fifty-eight hours, leaving at least thirty inches on the ground and on the rooftops, and drifts of infinitely greater depth wherever the wind can carry them. As the snow ceases, the hard frosts begin, and the thermometer slowly drops. By January 30, the temperature is down to ten degrees on the Fahrenheit scale. For three weeks the countryside remains buried in what the Shanghai weather report in the *North China Herald* calls a weather pattern "unprecedented in the meteorological annals of Shanghai for its severity and the low range of the thermometer."[9]

The snow is a disaster for the Taiping forces, which lack adequate winter clothing, and can neither force their way across country nor break the ice that blocks the river. "We could not move," General Li later laconically explains.[10]

With their momentum checked by the weather in the crucial early months of 1862, the Taiping forces fail to break through the strengthened defenses of Shanghai, whether to occupy the Chinese city or to subdue the foreigners themselves. And seizing the opportunity offered by the absent Taiping armies, in the late spring of 1862 Qing troops advance downriver from Anqing, led by the brother of Zeng Guofan, and capture a strategic base at the foot of Yuhua Hill between the Yangzi River shore and the south gate of Nanjing city itself. Abandoning the attempt to take Shanghai, Li Xiucheng and his troops exhaust their strength throughout the autumn of 1862 in assaults against the new Qing stockades and earth-works in their own backyard, but despite numerous sorties, and attempts to undermine the fortifications, all are unsuccessful.[11]

Grim as conditions are for the Taiping troops, their sufferings hardly compare with those of the masses of refugees and homeless villagers who wander in the area, displaced again and again by fighting that seems to have no end. These farmers and small-town dwellers of the Yangzi delta have now to contend with at least eight different kinds of troops who march and countermarch around their former homes. There are the Taiping field armies themselves, secret-society or other irregular armies loosely affiliated with the Taiping, independent gangs of river pirates or land-based marauders, the local militias and peasant defenders of rural communities, the large Qing armies recruited by provincial leaders like Zeng Guofan and his brothers, Qing regular forces commanded by the officials of Jiangsu province, Western mercenaries hired by the Qing authorities and currently commanded by the American Frederick Ward, and regular military or naval forces commanded by the British, led by Admiral Hope and Brigadier General Staveley.

For more than a year now, foreigners and Chinese traveling the roads and creeks from Shanghai through Suzhou toward the Yangzi, or even to the walls of Nanjing itself, have grown almost accustomed to a range of somber sights. Across a fifty-mile swath of land one might see almost every house destroyed, wantonly burned by one side or the other, or stripped of its doors and roof beams. That wood then serves either as fuel for the troops, or as makeshift supports for temporary bridges across the myriad canals and creeks, or to shore up the defensive ramparts of some short-lived garrison stockade, erected around villages where every man and boy has been pressed into service by one army or another, and the women carried off, where "human bones lie bleaching among cannon balls" and only the elderly are left to pick among the debris.[12] In what is left of these communities, "the houses are in ruins; streets are filled with filth; human bodies are left to decay in the open places or thrown into pools and cisterns there to rot." On many riverbanks, sometimes for tens of miles, every hut or house is gutted and the people sleep as best they may under rough shelters of mats or reeds.[13]

Anything that can be used for fuel, whether wood or straw, cotton stalks or reeds, has doubled or tripled in price. Villagers stand along the banks of the creeks, holding out small baskets of produce—eggs, or oranges, or bits of pork—but they are "principally old people, with coun-tenances showing their suffering and despair."[14] Other villagers, encountered on the way, have the four characters "Heavenly Kingdom of Great Peace" tattooed deeply into their faces, proof that they have fled from combat and been recaptured by some Taiping general, and thus been warned not to stray again. Some have scarred and pitted cheeks, where they have tried to cut the same words out with a knife.[15]

Refugees pass by the travelers, some in small groups, others in crowds of as many as 350 people, men and women, old and young, children and the lame, some carrying their possessions, some flags or spears, some empty-handed. Western missionaries traveling by road or track walk through deserted villages where only animals pick among the ruins and the bodies lie scattered by the road. Those traveling by water find at times that their boats have to push their way slowly through the bodies of the dead, which float, decomposing, in the channels.[16] For one missionary traveling in the country near Suzhou, worn by the sight of human bodies "till my heart was sick," the image that he knows will haunt his brain the longest is that of the "wasted form" of "a little child which had been starved to death, as it sat propped up in a kind of chair or crib, such as the Chinese use for children who are unable to walk."[17]

Even veteran British army officers, used to the sufferings caused by wars around the world, of which they have seen so many, and initially sarcastic about the sentimental China missionaries who they feel are prone to exaggerate the suffering they see around them, end up with very similar views. "In all such places as we had an opportunity of visiting," writes Garnet Wolseley, quartermaster general on the British expeditionary force, "the distress and misery of the inhabitants were beyond description. Large families were crowded together into low, small, tent-shaped wig-wams, constructed of reeds, through the thin sides of which the cold wind whistled at every blast from the biting north. The denizens were clothed in rags of the most loathsome kind, and huddled together for the sake of warmth. The old looked cast down and unable to work from weakness, whilst that eager expression peculiar to starvation, never to be forgotten by those who have once witnessed it, was visible upon the emaciated features of the little children."[18]

Yet life goes on as people make their adjustments to the reality around them. One Western observer, out with a scouting party in the countryside a day or two after the snow has stopped, steps carefully around the corpse of a Chinese man with a spear driven clear through his skull, and finds himself on a path worn by villagers' feet through the deep drifts of snow. At the end of the track, a group of villagers have gathered, and are brewing tea amidst the ruins of their still smoldering homes. They are celebrating the dawning of the Chinese New Year, which falls the following day, according to the lunar calendar.[19]

Many of the Chinese refugees gravitate toward the city of Shanghai, their pace dictated by the prevalence of rumors concerning the nearness of Taiping or other troops: sometimes they "rushed pell-mell along the roads and through the streets like a herd of stricken deer," at other times "trudging along with their scanty bundles of food and apparel, fear depicted in their countenances."[20] Alarmed at the possibilities of infiltration by squads of disguised Taiping troops among the refugees—a technique used by the Taiping in their recent capture of Hangzhou and many other towns—the Chinese authorities order the gates of the Chinese city closed against them. The promenade, or "bund," in the foreign areas is crammed, and, the danger of famine and disease rising, the foreigners take steps to quarantine their areas of control. The sepoy troops on the canals receive orders to raise the drawbridges, and the foreign police enforce a curfew forbidding all Chinese to be on the streets after eight in the evening.[21] Foreigners have a password they must use if stopped by patrols, and Chinese with a proven right to residence are issued "pass tickets." All Chinese found at night without these tickets are arrested and evicted from the foreign-controlled areas.[22]

Captain Charles Gordon of the Royal Engineers, assigned to see to the defenses of Shanghai by the commanding British officer, General Staveley, is under no illusions about the volatility of the situation. He plans his defensive emplacements, redoubts, and ditches so that the British may be protected as well from attack by the Taiping outside the fortifications as from the Chinese residents or refugees within—"a contingency not unlikely to occur considering the disaffected state of some of the inhabitants."[23] British scouting parties can see the flames of burning villages and the flags and troops in the Taiping camps. Surprising a Taiping looting party after the snow has melted, they are struck by the mundane needs of the Taiping troops, marching under their heavy loads of rice, peas and barley, cooking pots, beds and clothing, and driving pigs and goats ahead of them with their spears.[24]

Even by the summer of 1862 things have grown no better. The British consul reports, "We are once more overrun with refugees, and this time in greater numbers than ever. They are actually camping out on the bund in front of the house, and on the roads near the stone bridge. It is frightful to see the numbers of women, aged and children, lying and living out in the open air, and not over abundantly supplied with food."[25] Those country dwellers rendered destitute by the endless raids live in abject misery

in Shanghai, if they ever manage to reach its walls. One shocked Westerner, signing himself simply "Humanitas," writes of stumbling into one
such camp of Chinese refugees in the summer of 1862, after Li Xiucheng's
latest assault on the city has been repulsed. The refugees are crammed
into half a dozen bamboo huts off Hanbury's Road, all "emaciated and
wretched in appearance" and some "dying of starvation and disease," lying
on mud floors that flood with every rise in the tidal flow of the river. The
living are mixed in with corpses "in all stages of decay," sometimes blending life and death in one family scene, as in the case of one still living
mother, lying on the floor too weak to rise, her two dead and naked
children "covered with slush and mud" lying by her side. Such living
skeletons are fed only by an erratic system of donated "rice tickets," to
buy more of which "Humanitas" appeals to the Shanghai residents to
donate $500, of which he promises to provide one-third.[26] As the cold at
the end of 1862 ushers in a new winter, all foreigners going to watch the
plays at the Chinese theater are asked to give the equivalent of their
admission money "to provide food for the Chinese starving poor."[27]

It is just after the great snowfall of 1862 that the Westerners' dogs start
disappearing. A black retriever is the first to go, in February, taken from
the hospital area.[28] "Teazer" is next, a light-brown long-legged bull mas-
tiff with a stumpy tail and black muzzle.[29] Then "Smut" vanishes, a black-
and-tan bull terrier from the HMS *Urgent,* followed by two dogs
together—both bitches—one a small white-and-black "Japanese," one a
white long-haired "Pekinese" with black ears, called Chin-Chin, almost
ready to bear her puppies.[30] General Staveley's dog, a "liver and white
pointer" with his name in Chinese characters on the chain collar around
his neck, is lost on August 8.[31] The brass-collared "Goc," large and white,
with black spots, disappears on August 15, the day "Humanitas" stumbles
upon the dead and dying refugees, and shortly thereafter the first New-
foundland to go, "Sailor," recently cropped, is taken from the London
Missionary Society compound.[32] Then, as winter returns again at the close
of 1862, it is hard to list them all, the other Newfoundlands and setters,
the bulldogs, pointers, spaniels, scotties: "Bull" and "Die," "Bounce" and
"Tie," "Punch" and "Rover," "Beechy," "Toby," "Mus," and "Griffin,"
"Towzer," "Nero," "Bill."[33]

The very number of the vanished pets acts as a kind of index to the
miseries of the countryside at large. In these endlessly fought-over areas
along the Yangzi River, the once vaunted land system of the Taiping
Heavenly Kingdom has now become a matter of extracting what grain
one can, through levies, gifts, or confiscations. In some of the fertile delta

lands to the east, the Taiping are still viewed as liberators by disgruntled peasants, who are glad to see their landlords flee, and willingly pay the Taiping from their resources in lieu of rent.[34] But in many areas, after 1861, it is the peasants themselves who form defensive militias to drive the Taiping out, invoking their own gods and fostering their own military champions to keep the "long-hairs" at bay.[35] Taiping officers on campaign suffer major losses when bridges they relied on for escape routes are secretly cut by local peasants, leaving their soldiers cornered on some riverbank or creek as the Qing advance. Furious crowds of local villagers, armed with primitive weapons, surround the Taiping troops and make them fear for their lives. Local villagers also stop Taiping convoys of supplies and cash, outnumbering the transporters, and making off with vital resources needed in the bitterly fought campaigns.[36]

To the Western troops and merchants in Shanghai, on the other hand, the snowstorm, though uncomfortable, is seen as an act of "providence," and the blow to the Taiping forces is accepted as a blessing, even if the patrolling Western vessels along the smaller creeks are hindered in their work by the ice and snow. For those Westerners with experience of traveling in the last few years through Taiping terrain, much that once seemed colorful or bold has lost its luster and allure. Taiping clothes appear now not as dramatic and original but as "tawdry harlequin garb," a "burlesque costume."[37] The newly enfeoffed Taiping kings present "a drowsy dissipated appearance," in their "mountebank yellow dresses and tinsel crowns."[38] The streets of Nanjing are crammed with "a wonderful number of good-looking young women" in gorgeous silks, but these are the captured women from Suzhou, prisoners of war who often try to run away; and though huge new palaces are rising in the city they "stand conspicuous among the ruins," each strip of cleared land surrounded by evicted families.[39] Similarly, the playful Taiping boys who once seemed charming to the Westerners are seen now as sinister, or as starvelings. The very silence of the city, once a harbinger of peace, seems now heavy with the menace of impending doom.[40] And the vaunted Taiping warriors, on closer glance, are "dirty and diseased," displaying, underneath their glittering silks, arms jingling with golden bracelets that cannot hide the scabs of running sores.[41]

Even Joseph Edkins, intrigued by his religious arguments with the Heavenly King and eager to be one of those missionaries sought to bring new life to Taiping religion, slowly and reluctantly gives up his dream of settling in the town of Nanjing that once had seemed to him so beautiful. For Edkins has a young wife of twenty-three, and he worries over her safety in the insurgents' city should he be away preaching. He grieves too over the Taiping's practice of forbidding day laborers from entering the city, the low-quality housing offered to him and his wife, and the terrible unhealthiness of the climate and foulness of the water. He notices that even the Chinese who have lived in the city for years still choose to mix large doses of medicinal drugs into their water before they dare to drink it. Ultimately, for the young couple, "duty calls to Nankin, while inclination says the north," and inclination wins.[42]

After the departures of Roberts and Edkins, there are no Westerners left in the Heavenly Capital except for a few mercenaries still held to the Taiping cause by love or money. One last Protestant missionary travels there in the late spring of 1863, and he is wary rather than hostile in the brief report he gives to the Hong Kong press. Nanjing seems to him still fairly prosperous; some crops are growing within the walls. He is granted an interview with the Shield King, Hong Rengan, whom he finds baffled by the foreigners' unfriendly behavior, and threatening to wreck all foreign trade if they send armed forces against Nanjing.[43] As to Hong Rengan himself, for several years the courteous mediator with the Westerners, he claims merely that Roberts' flight from Nanjing is due to "some slight misunderstanding."[44] But either that misunderstanding or something else unexplained is sufficient for Hong Rengan to forfeit the high office and trust that Hong Xiuquan has given him since he first arrived. Instead of being confirmed in his position as the modernizer of the Heavenly Kingdom, and joint director of the Taiping armies, he is told to supervise the education of the Young Monarch, Tiangui, an assignment that leaves him so "filled with anxiety" that he gives "way to tears."[45]

The constant fighting in the area around Shanghai and the growing isolation of Nanjing do not mean that trade has fallen off for the foreigners. Indeed since the revised commercial and diplomatic treaty settlements of 1860 with the Qing, and the reopening of trade by riverboat and steamer with the inland Yangzi city of Hankou, Shanghai is the booming center of the trade in silk and opium, munitions, food and tea. So many ships are moored along the bund and in the lower reaches of the Huangpu River that a special daily broadsheet—the *Daily Shipping and Commercial News*—is published to supplement the weekly *North China Herald*.[46] By September 1862, another supplement begins, published in Chinese to cover Chinese trade, "The Chinese Shipping List and Advertiser," to appear on Tuesdays, Thursdays, and Saturdays.[47]

It is true that the American presence in Shanghai has somewhat fallen off, for the "East India Squadron" of the United States has been dissolved in 1861, as news of the Civil War at home reaches the ships of the China station. Though the commanding officer, Flag Officer Cornelius Stribling, refuses to accept the resignations offered by those of his officers who support the Confederacy until he receives confirmation from the Navy Department, he himself is abruptly relieved of his command on orders from Washington because his native state is South Carolina. The serviceable American vessels are ordered to steam or sail at once for home. Thereafter, for three years, the only major sign of the American naval presence comes from the largely imagined threats of Confederate "privateers."[48] But as if in compensation, in June 1862 the first Japanese ship to dock in Shanghai, the *Zen Sai Maroo*—formerly the British ship *Armistice,* bought by the Japanese government for $34,000—arrives "with a cargo of sundries," and bringing with her to Shanghai "a sort of Commission charged with the duty of acquiring all kinds of information, commercial, statistical, and geographical."[49]

The foreigners now pouring into Shanghai span the whole range from affluence to desperation, and the city adapts swiftly to receive them. For the wealthiest, there is the Hôtel de l'Europe, open now for "tiffin," and the French concession offers fine rooms in the new Hôtel des Messageries Impériales.[50] A new luxury hotel, the Clarendon, opens in July 1863, to supplement the old Imperial Hotel, where as a legacy from the departed Americans, there is now a brand-new tenpin bowling alley.[51] A recently departed visitor is honored in the newly named Elgin Arms, headquarters for the weekly assemblies of the North China Pigeon Club.[52] The Astor has a new billiard room, and it is perhaps a sign of the changing values in the town that the Oriental Billiard Saloon has taken over the former Shanghai library on the corner of Church Street and Mission Road, where it also sells wines and spirits.[53] Miller's Hotel, going everyone else one better, offers both a bowling alley and a billiard room. While for those who want a calmer life, just off the Yang-king-pang Creek that separates the British from the Chinese city, the old brig *Sea Horse* has been converted into the Sea Horse Floating Hotel, and offers a "quiet and comfortable home" for permanent or transient boarders, at decent rates of sixty dollars a month, with one dollar extra for breakfast or dinner, though all board must be paid "invariably in advance."[54]

The city's amenities expand to respond to these newest needs and tastes. Fogg and Co. is offering for sale six sets of tenpins and bowling balls, and six sets of billiard balls and cues, complete with extra tips and chalk. Two "photographic portrait rooms" are established in the town, which as well as taking pictures of the locals offer "sceneograms" of troops in the recent battles.[55] "Professor Risley and the most Numerous and Talented Company of Artistes with Ten unrivalled Horses" performs in the town, while not only has the racecourse been expanded, but a consignment of twenty Arab racehorses arrives from Sydney in Australia, along with mares and geldings to serve as carriage horses.[56]

From the ships that cram the harbor come, as well, a steady stream of deserters, ne'er-do-wells, and drifters. The police station logbooks are full of the harassments, the delinquencies, and the random violent acts of those they list as "distressed subjects," or as "vagrants." Some of the crimes are often pathetic in their smallness, hinting at the real misery of the offenders: at various times Westerners are booked for stealing a loaf of bread, a piece of meat, some peaches, or some pairs of socks, all from Chinese vendors.[57] But others show different levels of violence, from drunken assaults and attempted rape of both Chinese and Western women in the town to the abduction of Chinese boys.[58] There are stabbings and murders in the run-down rooming houses where the derelicts congregate, such as those run for the "Manilamen" in Bamboo Town, or in Mr. Harvey's Grog Shop in Hong-que, in the "low public house in the French Concession" known as the Liverpool Arms, or in Allen's Mariner's Home, across the river on the Putong side, effectively beyond the range of either Western or Chinese law.[59]

The British consul attempts to control both the pleasures and the violence by issuing annual licenses to the "Houses of Entertainment" in the Hong-que district, but there are constant setbacks and deceptions: Police Sergeant Mason, for example, turns out to be a secret partner in a hotel in Hong-que where many of the crimes occur, and Police Constable Hayden has for months been "receiving money from keepers of gambling houses without authority."[60] Indeed around a quarter of the cases prosecuted in Shanghai during 1863 concern the police constables themselves, charged with being absent from duty, asleep at their posts, drunk and incapable, disorderly, or with committing assault and battery on the populace they are meant to be protecting. In many cases the constables are repeat offenders: there is a seventh arrest for drunkenness for Police Constable 4, a ninth for PC 118, and a fourteenth for PC 32.[61] As the chief inspector of police points out plaintively to the Shanghai Municipal Council in early 1863, he has only enough reliable men to patrol the north–south streets effectively. Fully aware of this, the local rowdies and criminals concentrate their robberies on the streets that run from east to west.[62]

Most difficult to control are the cases of those who deal in weapons with the Taiping. The numbers of cases grow steadily in 1863: "P. Lodie, aged 31, Scotland, resident Shanghai, selling arms to rebels." "W. Hardy and others, having charge of a cargo boat with arms and rebel passes." "H. Stokes, alias Beechy, and others, Breach of Neutrality."[63] The materials of war are everywhere in the city, and there is apparently no way to contain them. Some of the arms travel huge distances, from Hong Kong and even from Singapore, where at least three thousand cannon a year enter the international arms market, and the marine stores all sell both artillery and small arms.[64] The municipal council itself contributes to some of the spread, despite its protestations, by selling off all its old muskets and percussion caps to raise money when a new batch of Enfield rifles is shipped in for the volunteer forces.[65] The British army also contributes through General Staveley, who sells off the "arms and accoutrements" of the Twenty-second Punjab Native Infantry and the Fifth Bengal Native Infantry to ease the logistics of their passage when they are posted home to India.[66]

The Westerners in Shanghai carry arms as a matter of course; the inventories of their possessions often show shotguns, rifles, and revolvers, along with the brandy and cigars, the furniture, crockery, dogs, and bedding.[67] The British interpreter Thomas Taylor Meadows, an adventurous but pacific soul who remains one of the Taiping's most forceful backers long after most other Westerners have turned against them, casually describes the personal armory he takes on his trips upriver as consisting of "a Jacob's single-barrelled 32 gauge rifle; two long single-barrelled shoulder wild-fowl guns (Colonel Hawker's kind); two double-barrelled shot guns with longish barrels; two double-barrelled shot guns of the usual length; and, lastly, a pair of holster and a pair of belt revolvers of the London Armory Company (Adam's patent)."[68]

Gunrunners and arms dealers operate on an ever-larger scale, as shown by the register of arms sold to the Taiping in April 1862 by an American firm "well known for their dealings with the rebels": 2,783 muskets, 66 carbines, 4 rifles, 895 field pieces of artillery, 484 powder kegs, 10,947 pounds of gunpowder, 18,000 cartridges, and 3,113,500 percussion caps. The dealers—in this case four Americans, their linguist, and eleven coolies, operating two boats—carry passports valid "by land or water" anywhere in Taiping territory, signed by an officer of the Loyal King, Li Xiucheng, and dated "12th year of 4th moon, and 2nd day, of the Kingdom of Universal Peace of God the Father, God the Son, and God the Heavenly King."[69] Less than two months later, in a double raid, British police seize a boat, manned partly by Europeans, that is conveying an additional 1,550,000 percussion caps and forty-eight cases of muskets to the Taiping, while the French stop another boat that has around 5,000 "stands of arms." Significantly, the French also impound "the implements for manufacturing them," and a Shanghai newspaper notes that many of these arms are manufactured "under our very eyes, on the opposite bank of the Wong-poo River."[70]

Such sales of equipment are important to the Taiping. A Western observer in Nanjing in the summer of 1862 notes that "the city possesses some men of ingenuity," and the guns made there—including heavy cannon—are far better than those manufactured by the Qing.[71] Boxes of percussion caps are used instead of currency by foreign traders dealing with the Taiping.[72] Other arms shipments intercepted include 300 pounds of gunpowder marked as "kegs of salted butter," while percussion caps are shipped as "screws" or even as "religious tracts," and rifles as "umbrellas."[73] The bulk of these foreign gunrunners and illicit traders are British or American, but some are Belgian, Swedish, Prussian, or Italian.[74] The Taiping also capture Western arms in combat, including gunpowder, muskets, and even a 12-pounder howitzer, and add these windfalls to their own stockpiles at Nanjing and elsewhere.[75]

It is in early 1863 that Li Xiucheng attempts to launch a new campaign to the west, on the north bank of the Yangzi, in Anhui province, to distract Zeng Guofan and his brother from the Nanjing siege. Within a few weeks Li's troops, which have set out so boldly, are bogged down in mud and driving rain. The areas on the north bank of the Yangzi they campaign in have been fought over so often that no grain supplies are left, and the new crops have not yet had a chance to ripen. Many of Li's troops fall sick; some of them eat grass; others die of hunger. The Qing garrisons in Anhui, made canny by past experience, simply sit tight behind their defenses and refuse to be lured out in combat.[76] Like Li's Shanghai ventures, the new campaign is a brave but costly failure, which deflects tens of thousands of Taiping troops and new recruits from either relieving the siege of Nanjing directly or strengthening the cities between Suzhou and Shanghai. These fall one by one to the inexorable and well-armed British and French military and naval forces stationed in Shanghai, working in conjunction with Qing troops and the Ever-Victorious Army, led first by Frederick Ward of Salem, Massachusetts, and then by Charles Gordon.[77]

In May 1863 Li abandons the Western campaign as a failure, and hurries back down the north bank of the Yangzi River to Nanjing on the urgent orders of the Heavenly King. He is met, as he attempts to cross the river, by the Qing forces, now much strengthened and armed with Western implements of war. In Li Xiucheng's own words, "It was just at

In 1860 the Taiping threat to Shanghai prompted the formation of a foreign mercenary defense force, which evolved into the Western-officered force of Chinese troops called the Ever-Victorious Army. Trained in Western drill and tactics, well-armed and neatly uniformed, the force was led in turn by the American Frederick Ward and the British officers John Holland and Charles Gordon. A similar type of force, commanded by French officers, was named the Ever-Triumphant Army. These armies, though at times erratic in performance, played a significant role in establishing a defensive perimeter around Shanghai, and later in helping the Qing suppress the Taiping in East China. The first photographs of combat troops in China were made during Lord Elgin's assaults on the north in 1860. These two photographs of the Sino-foreign forces in the Shanghai region probably date from 1863 or 1864.

the time when the Yangzi was in spate; the roads had been destroyed by the floods, and there was no means of advancing. . . . The army was in disorder. Combat officers and troops, and the horses, were first taken across the river in boats. The crossing was almost completed, but some old and very young, and horses which refused to embark, were left on the river bank. Jiufu zhou was flooded and the soldiers had nowhere to lodge. Even if they had rice, there was no fuel to cook with, and a great many died of hunger. Just at this time, Zeng Guoquan sent river troops to attack."[78] The resulting battle, as described by a Western mercenary still loyal to the Taiping cause, is catastrophic:

> Even when [the Taiping] had arrived within sight of their capital, the sufferings of the unfortunate people were not completed until they had endured much more loss by the assaults of the enemy. Upon the arrival of the famished and emaciated troops at the brink of the river, they were saluted with one continuous cannonade from the gunboats that now found ample opportunities of slaughtering them as they crowded the bank for a distance of nearly two miles. With incredible fortitude they maintained their position, and did not flinch backward by the least perceptible movement; and, in the face of the terrible fire poured into their dense masses at point-blank range (mostly from *English* guns), proceeded to the work of embarkation as steadily as their weakened condition would permit. . . .
>
> The fearful sights that met my gaze upon every part of the shore I shall never forget. Very many of the weakest men, totally unable to assist themselves further, were left to die within sight of the goal for which they had striven so hard and suffered so greatly, their number being so large that their comrades were not sufficient to help, or get them over the river in the presence of the enemy. The horrible "thud" of the cannon shot crashing continuously among the living skeletons, so densely packed at places that they were swept off by the river, into which they were forced by the pressure from behind; the perfect immobility with which they confronted the death hurled upon them from more than a thousand gunboats; and the slow effort the exhausted survivors made to extricate themselves from the mangled bodies of their stricken comrades, were scenes awful to contemplate. It was dreadful to watch day after day during the time occupied in getting the remnant of that once splendid army across the river, with but little means to succour them, the lanes cut through the helpless multitude on the beach by the merciless fire of the enemy; all so passively endured.[79]

Once again, Hong Xiuquan has no specific words for General Li, neither of solace nor of encouragement. Nor has Hong himself received such words for some time now, not from his Heavenly Father, nor from his

Elder Brother. And if his earthly wife, his mother, or his eldest son have told him of their dreams, Hong has not shared them with his Taiping faithful followers. In the last of the books that he has written, and published in Nanjing, Hong has passed in review all the visits down to earth that Jesus made, and all the messages he conveyed through Xiao Chaogui in the days at Thistle Mountain; he has lived again through the diatribes and promises of God the Father, relayed to Yang Xiuqing and his attendants in the early days in which the city of Nanjing became the Heavenly Capital. He has written out the somber words of Xiao Chaogui, after his wounding in Yongan, that the greater the suffering the more a man can grow, and transcribed with his blunt-nosed brush the final cry of Yang Xiuqing: "The city of your God is set aflame. There is no way to save it."[80] How often the voices from Heaven spoke in those far-off days! Now Heaven has fallen silent.

PARTINGS

During the same week of mid-June 1863 in which Li Xiu-cheng helplessly watches so many of his men slaughtered on the north bank of the Yangzi, a thousand miles away in the province of Sichuan, Shi Dakai—the Wing King—surrenders to the Qing. Since leaving Nanjing in 1857, Shi has conducted a ceaseless and exhausting campaign, across fifteen different provinces over a distance of more than six thousand miles, seeking first a permanent base, and then mere survival, while the number of his loyal troops slowly shrinks due to illness, death, or desertion. On June 13, cornered, helpless, and exhausted, Shi Dakai simply walks into the camp of the commanding Qing general and gives himself up, in the hopes that with his own life he can ransom the pardon of the two thousand veterans who have been with him all those years. He has prepared for this step by having his five wives commit suicide, and his infant children drowned, to save them from the inevitable shame and agony at the hands of the Qing troops. After six weeks of interrogation by the newly appointed governor-general, Luo Bingzhang—who so long before directed the defense of Changsha at which the West King lost his life—Shi is executed by slow dismemberment. His two thousand followers, who have been held under guard in a local temple complex, are massacred.[1]

News of Shi Dakai's surrender has not yet reached Nanjing by July 1863, when the Heavenly King orders Li Xiucheng into battle once again, this time to shore up the defenses of Suzhou. Li has had a month to size up the situation in the Heavenly Capital, and before he leaves he offers to Hong Xiuquan what seems to him now the only feasible plan: to stockpile all available grain in Nanjing, along with weapons, ammunition, and gunpowder, so that it remains the Heavenly Capital in word and deed, and becomes a truly impregnable fortress, impervious to siege. Such a base might wear down the morale of Zeng Guofan, who is proving invincible to the west, and of Zeng's rising protégé Li Hongzhang, whose troops have been cooperating with the Westerners and performing ably in recapturing the area around Shanghai.[2] But this plan, according to Li Xiucheng, is also ruined, this time by the greed of Hong Xiuquan's relatives, who forbid any residents of Nanjing to buy grain until they have first bought permits, or to use the permits until they have bought passports—the money for all of which paperwork goes into the pockets of Hong's staff—and even if people go through these procedures, and manage to find grain to buy, they are taxed according to its value when they return to Nanjing.[3]

The situation grows even graver in October 1863, when Qing troops, moving inexorably closer to the Heavenly Capital, seize hundreds of tons of stockpiled Taiping grain supplies, along with a thousand Taiping soldiers, their horses, and their mules.[4] In November, the Qing commander orders a moat over ten miles in length dug around the southern perimeter of Nanjing, running from the Yangzi River past the city's southern wall and curving up toward the east. Suzhou falls to the Qing in early December, just after Li Xiucheng has left it to campaign nearby. The city's fall is marked by the Qing commander's treacherous murder of all the surrendering Taiping generals, to whom he had promised amnesty, and the massacre of the civilian population. In mid-December, by which time Li Xiucheng has returned to supervise the capital's defense, the Qing make their first assault on the walls of Nanjing, using deep tunnels filled with gunpowder that shatter a major section of the city walls, though Taiping troops are able to repel the Qing troops that try to force their way through the breach.[5]

By December 1863 Li Xiucheng, having surveyed all the options, can see no way of defending the city. Gathering his courage to address the ruler who still overawes him, Li reports, "The supply routes are cut and the gates blocked. In the capital the morale of the people is not steady.

Four scenes of Qing victories over the Taiping. These paintings, honoring the victories of Zeng Guofan and his armies, are from a set of twelve made soon after the suppression of the Taiping. The four chosen here each illustrate different campaigns: the Qing victory at Yozhou on Dongting lake in Hunan, on July 25, 1854, which saved Changsha; the battle of Tongcheng in October 1855, which checked the last Taiping attempt to seize Hunan; the Qing recapture of Wuchang on December 19, 1856; and lastly, the Qing troops who captured Hong Xiuquan's eldest son Tiangui Fu in October, 1864, bringing an end to the short-lived Hong dynasty. *Credit: National Palace Museum, Taipei, Taiwan, Republic of China.*

There are many old people and children but no fighting troops. There are many court officials and civil officials, many people who expend food and supplies. . . . The capital cannot be defended. It is closely besieged by General Zeng's troops, with deep moats and strong forts. There is no grain or fodder in the city, and no relief comes from outside. We should give up the city and go elsewhere."[6]

Hong's answer to General Li is at once evasive and sublimely confident:

> I have received the sacred command of God, the sacred command of the Heavenly Brother Jesus, to come down into the world to become the only true Sovereign of the myriad countries under Heaven. Why should I fear anything? There is no need for you to petition and no need for you to take charge of the administration. You can do as you like; remain in the capital or go away. If you do not serve in [my] invincible Kingdom there are those who will. You say that there are no troops; but my Heavenly soldiers are as limitless as water. Why should I fear the demon Zeng? You are afraid of death and so you may well die. State matters are nothing to do with you.[7]

General Li, though he remains loyal to the Heavenly King, has grown suspicious of this kind of language. It seems to him to have disturbing connotations in the military sphere, and to exacerbate a problem that has been growing steadily ever since Hong Xiuquan ordered his troops and followers to drop the name Taiping, and instead to use the one word "Heavenly," to pay proper homage to God the Father. As Li later phrases his unease:

> The Heavenly King always used heavenly words to admonish people. We, his officials, did not dare to challenge him, but let him give what names he wanted. Calling them "Heavenly Dynasty, Heavenly Army, Heavenly Officials, Heavenly People, Heavenly Commanders, Heavenly Soldiers and Royal Troops" made them all into his personal troops and stopped us from calling them our troops. Anyone who spoke of "my troops" or "my soldiers" would be reprimanded thus: "You have treacherous intentions! This is the Heavenly Army; there are Heavenly Officials, Heavenly Troops, and this is the Heavenly Kingdom. How can they be your troops?" If one did not call them "Heavenly Soldiers, Heavenly Kingdom and Heavenly Officials" he was afraid that people were going to take his Kingdom from him.[8]

There are still enormous Taiping armies campaigning south of the Heavenly Capital, but slowly the Qing drive wedges of their own forces between those troops and the Heavenly King. Hong Rengan, the Shield King, is sent out in early 1864 on a mission to the region around Lake Tai, to gather supplies and "urge upon the troops the necessity of hastening to the relief of the capital," but he finds few willing to follow him, despite his kingly rank and fame: "the Heavenly Troops were fearful of the lack of provisions, and the greater part of them would not respond to the call."[9] By spring, the Qing troops are massed around Nanjing in such force that Hong Rengan is unable to return to his Heavenly King, and has to make his own base in the city of Huzhou, south of the lake, two hundred miles from Nanjing.[10]

Li Xiucheng makes yet another bold foray out of the Heavenly Capital in January 1864, and tries to reopen a route for supplies by breaking the Qing siege of the grain distribution center at Changzhou.[11] Failing in that design, he develops a new strategic plan, ordering four route armies under separate Taiping commanders to move south into Jiangxi province and obtain grain supplies there. Though these armies fight effectively enough to cause a diversion to the Qing, they cannot stop the steady forward advance of Zeng Guoquan, backed by foreign forces with their armored and shallow-draft steamships, from slowly driving the Taiping out of city after city. The last large grain shipment gathered by the Taiping foragers—more than thirty thousand pounds in weight—is seized by Qing forces within sight of the Heavenly Capital's walls in late February 1864, and in the next three months the remaining supply depots that might have been able to help Nanjing are lost in turn.[12]

One by one, the Qing armies have captured every strategic hill around Nanjing, and despite fiercely fought sorties by Li and other Taiping generals, the hills cannot be recaptured. The Qing have also completely surrounded Nanjing with a double line of breastworks, which snake across the country, three hundred yards apart. The breastworks are bolstered by about 120 forts, spaced at quarter- to half-mile intervals, each fort garrisoned with its own force of Qing troops.[13] No one can now leave Nanjing, save for occasional Taiping soldiers scavenging for edible weeds, who are let down from the city walls on ropes to make their meager harvest, often under the indifferent eyes of the Qing besiegers, or small groups of fugitives from the city, who risk their lives to flee across the no-man's land to the shelter that—as a propaganda gesture—has been promised by Zeng Guoquan to women and children who manage to escape. With the desperation of the poor who tyrannize the poor, gangs inside the city watch at the city's gates, not to stop but to rob those who are trying to flee of their possessions, before releasing them to their uncertain fate.[14] The women who make it through the lines are placed in special stockades by the Qing commanders, where, Gordon observes, the "country people ... take as wives any who so desired."[15]

No one can come or go by river either, for not only are the flats between the city walls and the river patrolled and guarded, but all foreign merchants have been forbidden by their governments to send supplies by boat to the beleaguered city, and only a handful of the most reckless foreigners risk the heavily armed Qing patrols to bring in supplies of food. Running in loads of rice, cooking oil, and charcoal to Nanjing from either Hankou or Shanghai is now as profitable as selling guns and ammunition for the latest generation of Western drifters. A foreign ship that is known to have made such runs successfully becomes in turn a sure mark for other water-borne Western desperadoes, who might board the vessel, kill the crew, and take the accumulated piles of silver.[16]

Edging ever closer to the capital's huge walls, much of the war moves underground, as the Qing commander orders his men to dig tunnel after tunnel, while the Taiping countertunnel in their turn, filling the Qing tunnels with water and sewage, or battling hand to hand, only to be driven out in turn by clouds of poisonous smoke forced into the tunnels' openings by Qing troops with bellows. By the late spring of 1864, over thirty tunnels have been started or are near completion. Some are on a truly massive scale, as observed by Charles Gordon on a visit to the Qing defensive perimeter:

> We went down to the mines and found a gallery driven a hundred and fifty yards fifteen feet below the ground, four to five feet wide and about seven feet high; it then divided into branches twenty yards from the wall, and had small shafts at intervals for ventilation. The gallery was framed with wooden supports and brushwood, some fifteen feet being driven each day.[17]

The longer tunnels can be easily seen by Taiping observers on the city walls, either because the vegetation above them dies, or because there is no way for the Qing to hide the excavated earth. But the Qing drive their encircling earthworks ever nearer to the walls, closing in to a distance of less than thirty yards in some places, from where they can direct a murderous fire from massed cannon at any Taiping defenders who try to interrupt the tunnelers' work.[18]

In the spring of 1864 General Li Xiucheng, according to his own account, tells Hong Xiuquan, "There is no food in the whole city and many men and women are dying. I request a directive as to what should be done to put the people's mind at ease." But starvation stirs no fears in the Heavenly King. He has read the sixteenth chapter of Exodus with care, and knows God will preserve the Taiping faithful, just as He preserved the children of Israel for forty years in the wilderness of Sinai, by scattering manna on the ground amidst the dew each morning. Since at least 1862, Hong has been ordering his subjects to emulate the children of Israel and store ten bushels of manna every year to see them through their times of trouble. Though it is not exactly clear what manna is—the Bible says it is small and white, with a scent of coriander and a taste like honey (Exodus 16:31)—the two phrases used in the Chinese Taiping Bible to describe it are *Tianlu* and *Ganlu,* one of which means simply "sweetened dew" and the other a kind of medicinal herb.[19] Hong Xiuquan replies to Li, "Everyone in the city should eat manna. This will keep them alive," and issues the order: "Bring some here, and after preparing it I shall partake of some first." When no one knows how to respond to this command, "the Sovereign himself," in the words of General Li, "in the open spaces of his palace, collected all sorts of weeds, which he made into a lump and sent out of the palace, demanding that everyone do likewise, without defaulting. He issued an edict ordering the people to act accordingly and everyone would have enough to eat."[20] Thereupon the Heavenly King begins to eat the clotted weeds within his palace.

Hong Xiuquan falls ill in April 1864, a few months after his fiftieth birthday. He rallies in May, but soon is sick again. The nature of the sickness is not clear. General Li Xiucheng, not surprisingly, says it comes from "eating manna" and because "when this man was ill he would not take remedies." His cousin Hong Rengan says it was "a lingering illness of twenty days." His son Tiangui Fu merely says his father "succumbed to sickness."[21] In a decree of May 30, Hong Xiuquan—or someone in his name—announces that the time has come for him to visit Heaven and request that his Heavenly Father and Heavenly Elder Brother send a celestial army to defend the capital.[22]

There is no great fanfare at Hong's death, which comes quietly on June 1, 1864. He is wrapped in a simple shroud of yellow silk by one of the palace women and buried in the bare ground, as he has taught the Taiping to do with their dead. No coffins are needed when one will rise so soon to Heaven. Hong indeed has long before ordered that coffins be abandoned and that the word for "death" be tabooed amongst his followers, who should use instead the phrase "ascend to Heaven" or "find one's happiness."[23]

Five days after his father's death Hong's son, the Young Monarch, Tiangui Fu, takes his seat upon his father's throne; his Taiping ministers, having first prayed to God, then pay homage to him as their new king. While the Qing carefully plan their final assault, the Young Monarch has his six-week reign. As he recalls, "Court matters were under the control of the Shield King, and military affairs in the hands of the Loyal King. All decrees which were issued were drawn up by [these two], and I was directed to subscribe my name to them."[24] Yet given Shield King Hong Rengan's continuing absence in Huzhou, to the south, the Young Monarch is essentially in the hands of his Loyal King, Li Xiucheng. "After the Young Sovereign came to the throne," says Li, "there was no grain for the soldiers, and there was chaos in the armies. . . . The Sovereign was young and had no ability to make decisions," and as a result "no one, civil or military, in the capital, could think of a solution."[25]

It is noon on July 19, 1864, when the Qing general Zeng Guoquan gives the signal to fire the explosives in the tunnels under a section of the eastern wall of Nanjing. The force of the colossal explosion hurls sixty yards of the massive fabric into the air. The Qing troops pouring through the breach are checked briefly by the Taiping, but soon all is chaos, retreat, and slaughter. At first the Young Monarch stands bewildered in his palace, while his four young wives cling to him to stop him from fleeing. But breaking away from them he runs through the crowds with his two young brothers to the Loyal King's palace. With what horses they can muster, and bodyguards clustered around them, the four try to escape the city through different gates in turn, but are always turned back. Hiding out for a time in an abandoned temple on the western side of the city, perched on a hill from which they can see the movements of the Qing forces within the town, the members of the Taiping royal party don Qing army uniforms prepared for this emergency; and seizing a moment in the gathering darkness when the Qing forces are fully occupied with rape and looting, or with setting fires to cover up the looting that has already taken place, they break through a gap in the wall near the eastern gate and race for safety. In the chaos the two young brothers of Tiangui Fu are left behind, and meet their deaths among the ten to twenty thousand victims of the night.[26]

As the rest of the group rides rapidly to the south, away from the burning city, the horse of the Loyal King, Li Xiucheng, collapses, and the others gallop on without him. Exhausted and bewildered, Li climbs a hill at dawn and shelters in an abandoned temple, where he falls asleep. He wakes to find that peasants from a nearby village have robbed him of his hidden valuables; soon after, others, angry at his inability to buy them off, turn him over to the Qing. He is interrogated, writes a lengthy confession, and is executed. Before he dies, he begs the senior Qing officials to stop the slaughter in Nanjing, and to spare the old Taiping veterans from

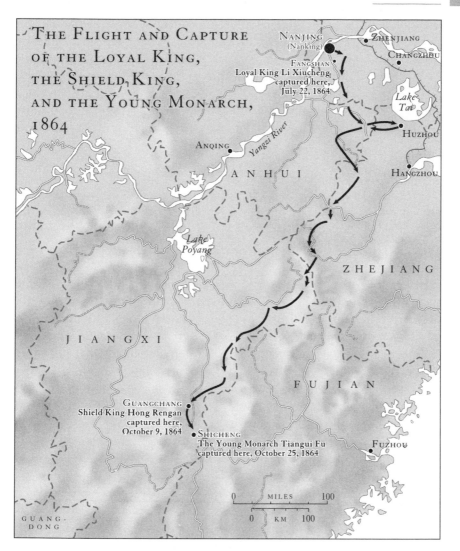

THE FLIGHT AND CAPTURE
OF THE LOYAL KING,
THE SHIELD KING,
AND THE YOUNG MONARCH,
1864

NANJING
(Nanking)
ZHENJIANG
CHANGZHOU
FANGSHAN
Loyal King Li Xiucheng
captured here,
July 22, 1864
Lake
Tai
ANQING
Yangzi River
Huzhou
ANHUI
Hangzhou
Lake
Poyang
ZHEJIANG
JIANGXI
FUJIAN
GUANGCHANG
Shield King Hong Rengan
captured here,
October 9, 1864
SHICHENG
The Young Monarch Tiangui Fu
captured here, October 25, 1864
Fuzhou

0   MILES   100
0   KM   100

GUANG-
DONG

Guangxi and Guangdong, to give them permission to return home and
"engage in some trade." "If you are willing to spare them," Li points out
to his interrogators, "everyone will hear of it, and everyone will be willing
to submit."[27]

Li Xiucheng also has advice for his captors: buy the best cannon from
the foreigners, and the most efficient type of gun carriages—for one is
useless without the other—and then find the finest Chinese craftsmen and
have them make exact replicas, while teaching others how to do the same.

Thus "one craftsman can teach ten, ten can teach a hundred and everyone in our country will know.... To fight with the foreign devils the first thing is to buy cannon and get prepared early. It is certain that there will be a war with them."[28] As to the Taiping's role in the future, it is over: "Our Heavenly Kingdom is finished ... and this is because the former Heavenly King's span was ended. The fate of the people was hard, such a hard fate!" How then could he himself, Li asks rhetorically, have helped his Heavenly King so long, and so tenaciously? His confession breaks off in the middle of his answer: "It is really because I did not understand. If I had understood ..."[29]

Li Xiucheng, upon his capture, thinks the Young Monarch must be already dead. But in fact Tiangui Fu is safe, and still accompanied by around a hundred followers. Circling around the west shore of Lake Tai, they reach Huzhou, where the Shield King, Hong Rengan, commands a large but isolated Taiping garrison.[30] Huzhou is almost ringed by hostile troops, those of the Qing army commanded by Li Hongzhang, and a strong force known as the Ever-Triumphant Army, a mixed band of Chinese and Filipino mercenaries, commanded by French officers. This force has been so named in deliberate emulation of and rivalry to the Ever-Victorious Army, commanded in the region of Shanghai first by the American mercenary Frederick Ward, and after his death in combat in 1862 by the British officer Charles Gordon. Side by side with the French and Qing combatants, some former Taiping generals are also fighting. They are defectors, having chosen to support at last the dynasty they so long opposed, and thus gain official titles, a chance to keep their accumulated loot, play at cards, and smoke their opium in peace. To the surprise of the French officers, the most able of these defected Taiping generals still holds it to be an "incontestable truth" that Hong Xiuquan was "raised to heaven for forty days and that he had received there the instructions necessary to begin his mission."[31]

The atmosphere in Huzhou is harsh and uneasy. The handful of foreign mercenaries still there fighting—with various degrees of willingness—for the Taiping see scores of executions every day, often for the most trivial causes, while Chinese suspected of treason are tied to piles of brushwood and set afire. The roads leading to the city have been strewn with the bodies of dismembered dead, to warn the Qing, the French, and the Taiping renegades of their fate if they are caught. Two of the French commanders have already died, though not at Taiping hands—one blown to pieces by a faulty cannon seized from a captured Taiping town, and another shot in the back of the head by his own troops, whether on pur-

pose or by accident none can say. Other French officers, calling their
assembled troops to charge the Taiping entrenchments, and rushing out
ahead with sabers drawn to set a fine example, realize too late that none
of their men have followed them, and are seized and cut to pieces by the
Taiping troops.[32]

One of the mercenaries inside Huzhou is an Englishman called Patrick
Nellis, who commands a small band of Westerners—Irish and English,
Greek and Austrian, French and German. After listening with half an ear
to an hour-long sermon by the Shield King, Hong Rengan, of which he
hardly understands a word, Nellis is startled after the service to be
addressed by Hong Rengan himself. Hong, speaking "in English, very
slow," asks Nellis his nationality. When Nellis replies that he is English,
Hong Rengan, reflecting the years of disappointment since he left Hong
Kong, says that "he had never met a good foreigner." Yet Hong nevertheless tells Nellis that he will soon be leaving Huzhou for the south, and
asks him to come along, since Nellis is skilled at both artillery and rifle
fire. In the event, they do not travel together, nor does Nellis ever see the
Young Monarch, Tiangui Fu. No one dares talk of the kingdom's new
ruler, nor of what has just happened in the Heavenly Capital: as Nellis
explains, "The Rebels said nothing about Nanking; and in fact all conversation of that sort was most dangerous, for the small boys in the service of
the Wangs [Taiping kings] were nothing but spies, and any talk of the
sort was certain death."[33]

Apart from such mercenaries as Nellis, the British are less involved in
the war than once they were. Though for a time they abandoned their
neutrality and unabashedly fought beside the Qing, in the spring of 1864
their government decides that British officers should not, after all, fight in
the lines on behalf of China, and the Ever-Victorious Army, which had
effectively come under their command, is ordered disbanded.[34] Relieved
of their most urgent duties, the British troops, as they await the news of
the final destruction of the Taiping forces, while away their time with
games. They sprint, they jump, they put the thirty-two pound shot, they
leap the hurdles, they throw the cricket ball for distance, they hop with
sacks around their legs, they run three-legged races, and try to cross the
city moat on tightropes. Most popular of all, to the spectators, is the wheelbarrow race, run blindfold over a seventy-five-yard course. The collisions,
spills, and falls are always fun to watch, but the onlookers' joy is greatest
when one man with his barrow turns clear around and races off alone
across the field.[35]

The French forces, however, are still actively in the fray, and eager to best their foreign rivals. They fight their way forward in the blinding heat, as the siege is tightened around the fugitive kings in the city of Huzhou. Even the veterans of China service have known no heat like this in their past experience, and deaths by sunstroke fell some, while others succumb to the cholera that spreads among all armies from the piles of unburied corpses along the lanes of towns and on the country roads.[36] The French officers swiftly learn that the cholera victims treated in the Western way, with brandy and camphor, often die; whereas when they use Chinese doctors, who treat the sufferers with acupuncture needles inserted into nose and lips, stomach and forehead, under the fingernails and in the leg joints, the illness is overcome.[37]

To keep their spirits up, the Frenchmen sing their songs from home, and drink champagne, which they chill in shaded pits filled with cold water brought from nearby wells and mountain springs.[38] One dons his bathing clothes and swims in the warm canal, spanning the stream with a rough plank bridge when a Chinese woman refugee, abandoned on the farther bank, shows willingness to join him. Noting this shared moment, the French commander, on his next trip to a recently recaptured village, brings a whole group of women back to serve his troops.[39] Some of the officers arrange to have a billiard table brought up to the front lines, and place it under the shaded awnings that shelter their redoubts, so they can play together while waiting for the battle.[40] And those who wish to escape more deeply make their way at dusk to drink their absinthe in the spot they have named—using the slang picked up from the Arabs by the troops in North African campaigns—their "fountain of Maboul," their fountain of craziness, their fountain of forgetting.[41]

The Qing, the French, and the Taiping renegades, with their modern arms and growing numbers, are too much for the Taiping defenders of Huzhou, and at the end of August 1864 Hong Rengan and the Young Monarch flee the city. They move ever farther down toward the south, drawn, it seems, back to the regions of Guangdong where their movement started. They survive another month on the run until October, when a sudden Qing raid on their camp forces them to separate. Hong Rengan is captured first, on October 9.[42] In his interrogation by the local Qing officials, Hong Rengan reiterates his belief in the extraordinary powers of the Heavenly King. Hong Xiuquan "was nine years older than I," he tells them, "and gifted with extraordinary powers of intelligence. A glance at anything was all that was required to impress the subject on his memory."[43] The rising at Thistle Mountain, says Hong Rengan, gives "undoubted evidence of the display of divine power throughout those years," and despite the ultimate collapse of the Taiping movement, "among those who have enjoyed the smiles of fortune for the longest time the Heavenly King stands pre-eminently forward," for he survived every one of the colleagues with whom he started out from Thistle Mountain. Hong Rengan is executed in the Jiangxi capital of Nanchang on November 23.[44]

When the Qing troops raid the camp and capture Hong Rengan, the Young Monarch, Tiangui Fu, manages to slip away with about ten followers. Crossing a small bridge, they climb a nearby hill and hide in a pit. The Young Monarch's entourage is discovered by Qing soldiers and taken away, but somehow Tiangui Fu evades the searchers. For four days he hides out in the hills, frightened and alone, finally so paralyzed by hunger that he longs for death. Suddenly, either in vision or in reality, "a great tall man, his whole body white as snow," gives him a piece of flat bread to eat, and vanishes. Restored to strength, Tiangui Fu shaves off his long Taiping tresses, and finds work for a few days with a local farmer, pretending that his name is Zhang and that he is from Hubei. When the harvest is all gathered in, he travels onward, until he is robbed of his remaining clothes by one man, and forced to carry loads of bamboo for another.[45]

Tiangui Fu is arrested at last by Qing patrols on October 25, 1864. He throws himself on the mercy of the state, and makes a brief confession. What he remembers of his father is briefly said: "The old Heavenly King told me to study religious books, and would not allow me to study ancient books, which he said were all demonic. I managed, however, to read secretly thirty or more volumes, and still retain some recollection of their subjects and contents."[46] Of the entire long war, and all its hopes, he tells his captors merely, "The conquest of the empire was the ambition of the old Heavenly King, and I had no part in it." His own greatest ambition, he tells his interrogators, if they release him, is to study quietly at the Confucian classics and try to gain the lowest degree, that of licentiate.[47] It would have taken judges with a true sardonic wit to reprieve the Young Monarch, and set him on the road to pass the examinations that his father always failed. There are none bold enough to take the chance, and on November 18, 1864, the Young Monarch is executed, a week before his fifteenth birthday.[48]

So by the year's end of 1864, not only the Heavenly King is gone, but all the inner core of kings he built around himself have left this life: the Kings of the North and East, the South and West, the Wing King, Shield King, Loyal King, and Hong's own son, the Young Monarch, Tiangui

Fu. But if God, the Heavenly Father, is saddened at Hong's passing, He gives no sign. Hong's Elder Brother, Jesus, too, is mute. And even his Heavenly Mother, who cried out with such anguish at his birth, and fought to keep her infant from the seven-headed dragon's jaws, stays silent in her realm.

In the boom towns they are creating, where the masts and smokestacks of the merchant ships now cluster thickly at the water's edge, the Westerners proceed in whatever ways they choose. Some walk on tightropes. Some tie themselves to partners and lurch, three-legged, down the track. Some grip the handles of their barrows and—eyelashes pressed against the cloth of unfamiliar blindfolds—race through the cheering throngs in search of a finish line that they cannot see. And out beyond the walls, shielded by awnings from the sweltering sun, stand other men who chalk their cues and calculate the angles, waiting for the enemy to make his move. While their companions, wearied by the omnipresent smell of death, leave the encampment and walk to the beckoning fountain of Maboul. There, clasping the well-cooled glasses in their hands, they watch the glimmering of the Heavenly Army's nighttime fires; and with ears lulled by the sounds of signal gongs and drums, they glide their way toward oblivion.

Notes

ABBREVIATIONS

BPP / Elgin   *British Parliamentary Papers, Correspondence Relative to the Earl of Elgin's Special Missions to China and Japan, 1857–1859* (London, 1859)

BPP / IUP   *British Parliamentary Papers,* Irish University Press Area Studies Series, China, 32, *Correspondence, Memorials, Orders in Council, and Other Papers Respecting the Taiping Rebellion in China, 1852–1864*

CR   *The Chinese Repository,* 20 vols. (Canton and Macao, 1831–51)

DSCN   *Daily Shipping and Commercial News*

NCH   *The North China Herald*

LMS   London Missionary Society

NA-DD   National Archives, Diplomatic Despatches from United States Ministers to China, 1843–1867

PRO / FO   Public Records Office / Foreign Office Archives

TR   Franz Michael and Chung-li Chang, *The Taiping Rebellion: History and Documents,* vols. 2–3

FOREWORD

1. Some aspects of Taiping growth and communitarian sense in a time of radical change and foreign impact fit well with the analysis in Benedict Anderson's *Imagined Communities;* see esp. 20, 22, on "sacred" and "truth" languages; 40, on "the privileged access" and "high center"; and 55, on pilgrimages and "centres of sacred geographies."

2. Cohn, *Cosmos,* 19–20.

3. Ibid., 55.

4. Ibid., 77, 95, on dating of millenarian ideas; quoted 56, 99, for phrases. Cohn (96) hypothesizes that these millenarian beliefs sprang from the "suffering" caused to Zoroaster and other thinkers by the destruction of their "ancient way of life, with its familiar certainties and safeguards."

5. Wilhelm, *I Ching,* 9, 29, 121, hexagrams "ch'ien," "sung," and "li."

6. *Lao Tzu, Tao Te Ching,* tr. D. C. Lau, 101, 103.

7. See Seidel, "Image," 216, 223, and quotations on 225 from the "Sutra of the Transformations of Lao Tzu."

8. Zürcher, "Prince Moonlight," 2–5, 12–18, 21, 53. Boardman, "Millenary Aspects," 70–71, 79, discusses the Taiping in relation to Norman Cohn's categories of millenarian thought.

9. Ter Haar, *White Lotus,* 212, 260. On 120 Ter Haar specifically rejects the idea that Manichaean elements influenced the Chinese case.

10. A good introduction to the European tradition is McGinn, *Visions.* On Hussites, Taborites, and Anabaptists, see Cohn, *Pursuit of the Millennium;* on the Puritan "Diggers" and "Levellers," see Woodhouse, *Puritanism and Liberty;* and on the ethos of John Bunyan's world, Hill, *Tinker.* For the American experience, see Holstun, *Rational Millennium,* esp. 103–65, on John Eliot and his "empirical millennialism," and Bloch, *Visionary Republic,* 25, 120, 205. Rubinstein, *Origins,* gives an erudite analysis of the work of the early nineteenth-century Protestant missionaries in China.

11. The English edition of Jen Yu-wen's work was brought to completion after Mary Wright's death by Adrienne Suddard, and published as *The Taiping Revolutionary Movement* (New Haven: Yale University Press, 1973).

12. These texts are entitled the *Tianfu Shengzhi* and the *Tianxiong Shengzhi.* For Wang Qingcheng's latest analysis of their importance, see his essay " 'Tianfu Shengzhi,' 'Tianxiong Shengzhi' he Taiping Tianguo Lishi," in his *Taiping Tianguo de wenxian he lishi* (Beijing, 1993), 197–244.

13. A forceful exposition of this view is given by Esherick, *Origins,* esp. 326, where he argues that like other peasant societies China was replete with "teachers, prophets, or just plain madmen preaching a variety of new cults and doctrines" and that therefore it is "far less important to know where they got their ideas than to understand how their ideas attracted an audience." See Wills, *Mountain of Fame,* 259–73, for a recent biographical summary of Hong.

14. A recent exploration of this important area of Bible translation and missionary endeavor is that by Smalley, *Translation as Mission.*

15. The best surveys in English of Taiping history remain Jen, *Revolutionary Movement,* and TR. On Taiping religion the subtlest coverage is in Bohr, "Eschatology," and Wagner, *Heavenly Vision.* On suppresion, the key works remain Wright, *Last Stand,* Kuhn, *Rebellion,* and Smith, *Mercenaries.*

CHAPTER 1: WALLS

1. *Chinese Repository* (hereafter *CR*), 2:196; *CR,* 4:536, on top of walls; *Canton Register,* Jan. 26, 1836, on perimeter walk; *Canton Press,* Nov. 28, 1835, on fire; Downing, *Fan-qui,* 3:74, on factory roofs. S. Wells Williams discussed the 1835 fire in a letter to his brother Fred, Canton, Nov. 24, 1835. See Williams Papers, MS no. 547.

2. Hillard, *Journal,* 78–82; Hunter, *Fan Kwae,* 74. A detailed plan of the factories, drawn in 1840, is in Morse, *East India Company,* 3:1.

3. Hodges, *Peacock,* 347 n. 20, on opium sales; Morrison, *Commercial Guide,* 11, on mail, passim on trade; King and Clarke, *Research Guide; Canton Register,* Aug. 26, 1834; Hunter, *Fan Kwae,* 50–51, on the milking cows; Hutcheon, *Chinnery,* 65, 78, 109, for illustrations of the buildings; Downing, *Fan-qui,* 1:259–67, on the hotels.

4. Hunter, *Fan Kwae*, 12–15, 18–19, 78; Hutcheon *Chinnery*, 65, 78, 109. A vivid description of the fire by Robert Morrison is in *CR*, 4:34–36. For successive panoramas of the factories and waterfront between 1730 and 1832, see Morse, *East India Company*, 1:192, 256, 2:144, 3:218, 368, 4:64, 336.

5. Hunter, *Fan Kwae*, 54–55.

6. Ibid., 64.

7. *CR*, 4:437.

8. Hodges, *Peacock*, 158–59, 343–44; Hillard, *Journal*, 153–54.

9. Stifler, "Language Students," 62–67.

10. Ibid., for detailed coverage; Hunter, *Fan Kwae*, 19, 27; Stevens, "Gospel," 432; Barrett, *Singular Listlessness*.

11. *CR*, 4:535; Morrison, *Commercial Guide*, 46.

12. Hunter, *Fan Kwae*, 27, 37–39; *CR*, 4:428–35; "Jargon spoken at Canton," *Canton Press*, Feb. 6, 1836; Morrison, *Commercial Guide*, glossary following p. xii; Fairbank, *Trade*, 13; Downing, *Fan-qui*, 2:124.

13. *CR*, 4:432–33.

14. Adapted from Hunter, *Fan Kwae*, 22.

15. Ibid., 8–9.

16. *CR*, 4:189; Hodges, *Peacock*, 180–81.

17. *CR*, 4:44, 342.

18. *CR*, 4:192–93.

19. Hunter, *Fan Kwae*, 21–24, 31–32; *CR*, 5:432.

20. *CR*, 4:464–71; compare with Hoo Loo, who died at Guy's Hospital, 1831; *CR*, 3:489–96.

21. *CR*, 4:462–64, and tables, 472; Gulick, *Parker*.

22. *CR*, 4:244.

23. *CR*, 4:190.

24. *CR*, 4:342, 535.

25. *CR*, 4:38–39, 43–44, 191.

26. Hodges, *Peacock*, 179.

27. *CR*, 4:44–45, 101–2, 245.

28. Hodges, *Peacock*, 171–72; Morrison, *Commercial Guide*, 13; *CR*, 4:291–92, for paintings, including *Battle of the Bogue*.

29. *CR*, 4:102, "An Outcast," dated Sat., June 6, 1835.

CHAPTER 2: THE WORD

1. Bridgman, "Obituary," 314–15; Wylie, *Memorials*, 84; *CR*, 4:436–37, on robberies; Morrison, *Commercial Guide*, 12, on the journey. For the detailed background of the Canton Protestant community, see Rubinstein, *Origins*, chaps. 5–8.

2. *CR*, 4:45.

3. Stevens, "Seamen," 423–24; Morrison, *Commercial Guide*, 13.

4. *CR*, 1:292, estimate; Downing, *Fan-qui*, 1:239–44; *Canton Register*, Oct. 4, 1836, on Portsmouth Point, and Nov. 15, 1836; Shen Fu, *Six Records*, 118–19, for a Chinese view.

5. Dialogue from Downing, *Fan-qui*, 1:84, also cited with variants in Hutcheon, *Chinnery*, 88–89, and Collis, *Foreign Mud*, 33; on Tanka dress and morals, see Bingham, *Narrative*, 2:272.

6. Morrison, *Commercial Guide*, 12; Downing, *Fan-qui*, 200–201.

7. Bridgman, "Obituary," 516.

8. Ibid., 515–16.

9. Liang, *Quanshi,* 291, 96; Bohr, "Liang Fa's Quest," 36–38; Stevens, "Milne," 322; Milne, *Memorials,* 22–30.

10. Liang, *Quanshi,* 302; Wylie, *Memorials,* 21; Gutzlaff, *Journal,* lxxi–lxxvii; Bays, "Christian Tracts," 22–25.

11. Liang, *Quanshi,* 306; Wylie, *Memorials,* 22; Robert Morrison, letter of Nov. 26, 1819, LMS, "South China," Box 2, folder 1.

12. Liang, *Quanshi;* McNeur, *Liang A-fa;* Bohr, "Liang Fa's Quest," 40–46.

13. Liang discusses his methodology in his diaries, which are extracted by Robert Morrison in various letters between 1830 and 1833. See LMS, "South China," esp. Box 3, folders 1 and 2.

14. Wylie, *Memorials,* 11–12, on Kew Agong.

15. Ibid., 22.

16. Stevens, "Gospel," 434.

17. Ibid., 436; Schlyter, *Gutzlaff als Missionar,* 92–93, 294–95. Gutzlaff's strong influence in the United States is explored in Lutz, "Grand Illusion."

18. Stevens, "Bohea," 92–93. Letters to Peter Parker, Canton, Aug. 27, 1835, Williams Papers.

19. Ibid., 87–88, 93; Stevens, "Huron," 330–33; Medhurst, "Huron," 408, was less excited, claiming only 3,500 books distributed in Shandong.

20. Stevens, "Morrison," 180–81. For a detailed study of Morrison and the missionary background, see Rubinstein, *Origins,* chaps. 1–4.

21. Hunter, *Fan Kwae,* 43; Lutz, "Karl Gutzlaff," 68–69; Gutzlaff, *Journal,* 103; Stevens, "Bohea," 85, 89; Hutcheon, *Chinnery,* 102, for an illustration of Gutzlaff in Chinese dress; see also Stifler, "Language Students," 64, 74, 79, for earlier cases of Thomas Manning and Lee / Plumb.

22. Stevens, "Bohea," 93. In a letter to his brother dated Canton, Feb. 19, 1835, S. Wells Williams noted Stevens' presence, Gutzlaff's present work, and Liang Afa's recent departure. See Williams Papers, MS no. 547.

23. *CR,* 4:343, citing edict of Daoguang 15/8/24.

24. *Canton Register,* April 15, 1834; Milne's original edition is summarized in Wylie, *Memorials,* 19–20. Drake, "Protestant Geography," 95–100, is skeptical of the effectiveness of Gutzlaff's journal.

25. *Canton Register,* June 14, 1836, mentioning that the printer "Keuhachaou" "is still in prison where he has lain for some months past."

26. Stevens, "Bohea," 94; Stevens, "Huron," 317–19.

27. Stevens, "Bohea," 95–96.

CHAPTER 3: HOME GROUND

1. Jen, *Revolutionary Movement,* 12–14. Snowfall: *Canton Register,* Feb. 9, 1836, and *CR,* 5:581. Exam timing is based on calculations in *Canton Register,* April 14, 1835, and *CR,* 1:483 n. For a summary of the earlier possible dates, see Boardman, *Christian Influence,* 98–99 n. 124.

2. Earlier discrepancies on Hong's family are cleared up by Chen Zhoutang, *Hongshi zongpu,* 54, which proves Hong's mother's name was Wang, correcting Hamberg, *Visions,*

2, which gives her name as Choo; by Wang Qingcheng, "Zupu"; and Luo Ergang, *Taiping Tianguo shi,* 1697–99. On Hong's first arranged marriage to the sister of Su Si'an, see Chen Zhoutang, ed., *Guangdong dichu,* 46–47. Hamberg, *Visions,* 6, on the stipends. My thanks to Xia Chuntao for much help in clarifying these relationships.

3. *Canton Register,* Sept. 8, 1835.

4. *Huaxian zhi,* prefaces; juan 1, 12–18, and chap. 4, 1–26, on founding; juan 3, 1–7, on staff and garrisons; juan 2, 25–26, on acreage and population.

5. Hamberg, *Visions,* 3; Wang Qingcheng, "Zupu," 493–94.

6. Hashimoto, *Hakka Dialect,* 1. The background of Hakka history is thoroughly presented in Bohr, "Eschatology," 14–19, 285–86. He discusses the Hakka quotas in 296 n. 67.

7. *CR,* 4:494.

8. The fullest historical overview of Hakka culture is Luo Xianglin, *Kejia.* Contemporary Hakka remnants of former customs in Taiwan are fully analyzed by Gao, *Kejia.* On Tanka, see Davis, *Chinese,* 2:27.

9. Hashimoto, *Hakka Dialect,* 16, referring to Chang Shou-p'eng and Lu Fei's work of 1783, and the *Hsing-ning hsien-chih* of 1811.

10. Chen Zhoutang, *Hongshi zongpu,* 6, 15, 22–23; Cohen, "Hakka," 242, expresses skepticism on the pre-Song data.

11. Chen Zhoutang, *Hongshi zongpu,* 40–44.

12. *Huaxian zhi,* 3:37–46.

13. Cohen, "Hakka," 249–54, 271–73; Luo Xianglin, *Kejia,* 336–45, illustrations 20–24.

14. Hamberg, *Visions,* 4.

15. *Huaxian zhi,* 1:38–45.

16. Wieger, *Moral Tenets,* 133–34; Mair, "Language and Ideology," 335–40, 349–56.

17. *Huaxian zhi,* 1:46b, 51b–52.

18. Ibid., 58–59.

19. Ibid., 61.

20. *Canton Register,* April 28, May 5, May 12, 1835.

21. Ibid., June 2, 1835.

22. Ibid., Sept. 6, 1836.

23. Hamberg, *Visions,* 8.

24. Ibid., 8–9. *Guangzhou fuzhi,* juan 8, has detailed maps and a plan of the examination halls. Jen, *Revolutionary Movement,* 14 n.

25. Wylie, *Memorials,* 84; Bridgman, "Obituary of Stevens," 515.

26. Stevens, "Gospel," 432.

27. Bridgman, "Obituary," 514.

28. As in *CR,* 5:169. Shen Fu, *Six Records,* 124, confirms ease of Canton gate bribes.

29. Stevens, "Huron," 326.

30. Wylie, *Memorials,* 12, 22.

31. J. R. Morrison, letter to Rev. Ellis, Canton, May 15, 1836, LMS, "South China," Box 3, folder 2, jacket C.

32. Bridgman, "Obituary," 517; Wylie, *Memorials,* 84. S. Wells Williams refers to Stevens' death in three letters written from Macao, Feb. 22, May 15, and Dec. 26, 1837. See Williams Papers, MS no. 547.

33. Hamberg, *Visions,* 9.

34. Liang, *Quanshi,* reprint 3, line 7, for Hong and destruction; 213, line 4, for Jehovah. On earlier Chinese deluge themes see Zürcher, "Prince Moonlight," 21–22, 29.

35. Liang, *Quanshi,* 213–20, for translation of Genesis chap. 6 and chap. 7, up to verse 23.

36. Ibid., index 6, line; on 271–74 Liang paraphrases the destruction of Sodom and Gomorrah.

Chapter 4: Sky War

1. *Huaxian zhi,* 1:32–33; *Canton Register,* April 14, 1835, Feb. 23, 1836. Tragedy sometimes mixed with local belief, as in the case of the racing crew from a village near Canton. Ignoring the custom that all dragon boats be buried under the ground between the annual festivals, they had kept theirs above ground all year. Practicing in 1836 on the river near a rival's village, they sank suddenly, and twenty of their village men were drowned, including one military licentiate from the recent exams. See *Canton Register,* June 28, 1836.

2. *Huaxian zhi,* 1:31–33; *Canton Register,* Sept. 1, 1835; these descriptions from Hua can be compared with the detailed coverage in Wieger, *Moral Tenets,* 405–39.

3. *Canton Register,* Sept. 29, 1835, July 19, Oct. 25, 1836. At other times, the mishaps are merely comic, though close to tragedy, as when two small boys, climbing a tree to watch the festival plays outside the west gate, fall in their excitement on the head of an old man underneath; they could have killed him, but fortunately all survived. Ibid., Nov. 3, 1835.

4. *Huaxian zhi,* 1:30–33.

5. Ibid., 1:32; *Canton Register,* Feb. 16, 1836.

6. *Huaxian zhi,* 1:32b.

7. Ibid., 1:32b–33, 35.

8. Ibid., 1:32, 33b, 34; *Canton Register,* Oct. 13, 1835; for contemporary Hakka following of such practices, see Gao, *Kejia,* chap. 6 and passim.

9. Kaltenmark, "Ideology," 39; Wilhelm, *I Ching* (book of changes), first hexagram; Wieger, *Moral Tenets,* 399–400.

10. De Groot, *Religious System,* 6:953–55.

11. Ibid., 963.

12. Hou, "Baleful Stars," 209–19.

13. De Groot, *Religious System,* 6:957.

14. Ibid., 967–68.

15. *Yuli zhibaochao,* 39–40; G. W. Clarke, "Yu-li," 233–44. On possible links between this text and Taiping doctrine, see Wagner, *Heavenly Vision,* 50–51.

16. The British Library 1839 copy of the *Jade Record, Yulichao chuan jingshi* (Blackfriars Road, cat. no. 15103.C35), has a supplement listing the sums contributed and the copies distributed by the faithful.

17. *Yuli zhibaochao,* 33b–34, for illustration; 38b for Tiandi's transmission; 55 for monks' reception; 68 for Li Zongmin's historical reconstruction.

18. Wieger, *Moral Tenets,* 119; Rong, "Yan Luo he Yuli," for the range of editions, and the provocative suggestion that the texts in fact *support* aspects of Confucian statism.

19. *Yuli zhibaochao,* 43–44; Wieger, *Moral Tenets,* 363–67; G. W. Clarke, "Yu-li," 324–27.

20. Wieger, *Moral Tenets,* 367; *Yuli zhibaochao,* 44.

21. The term for Jade Emperor the Highest God was Yuhuang datiandi. See Wagner, *Heavenly Vision,* 34–35, 49–50; G. W. Clarke, "Yu-Li," 238–39; Shuck, "Sketch of Yuhwang Shangte."

22. *Yuli zhibaochao* 39; Wieger, *Moral Tenets,* 347–49; G. W. Clarke, "Yu-Li," 251–54.

23. G. W. Clarke, "Yu-Li," 272.

24. Ibid., 289.

25. Ibid., *Yuli zhibaochao,* and Wieger, *Moral Tenets,* passim.

26. For annual executions in the hundreds, and totals of up to seventeen a day, see *CR,* 1:291, 4:385.

27. *Canton Register,* Aug. 25, 1835.

28. *CR,* 4:376, 384.

29. *Canton Register,* Oct. 27, 1835, and *CR,* 4:536, on the prevalence of child kidnapping; *Canton Register,* Aug. 23, 1836; on similar "diabolical arts," see G. W. Clarke, "Yu-li," 360–67.

30. *Yuli zhibaochao,* 50b–51b, 58b; G. W. Clarke, "Yu-li," 398–400; Wieger, *Moral Tenets,* 391, has variants of these themes.

31. *Yuli zhibaochao,* 50; G. W. Clarke, "Yu-Li," 394; Wieger, *Moral Tenets,* 385.

32. *Canton Register,* Aug. 30, 1836. From the late summer date, we know this was for licentiates who had passed the lower two stages of the exam.

33. *Yuli zhibaochao,* 78b, 79, for the Huang and Xu family exam successes, and G. W. Clarke, "Yu-li," examples passim. On the printers' shortage, see *Canton Register,* June 28, 1836.

34. Hamberg, *Visions,* 9; *Yuli zhibaochao,* 58.

35. Hamberg, *Visions,* 9.

36. Franz Michael, *The Taiping Rebellion: History and Documents,* vols. 2–3 (hereafter cited as *TR*), 53, slightly modified following Chin, *Shiliao,* 6, and Xiang, *Ziliao,* 2:632.

37. Hamberg, *Visions,* 9; *TR,* 53. The two texts intersect at numerous points, but are not identical, even though both are ascribed to Hong Rengan. For a subtle analysis of the dream, see Wagner, *Heavenly Vision,* 18–19, 34. The dream is presented as the "delirium fable" or a "twilight state" in the pioneering essay by Yap, "Mental Illness," 298. A comparative context for Hong's dream is provided in Wagner, "Imperial Dreams."

38. See the transcript of *Taiping tianri,* as reproduced in *Taiping Tianguo yinshu,* vol. 1, item 3, p. 4; *TR,* 54, 1516; Hamberg, *Visions,* 10.

39. *Taiping tianri,* in *Yinshu,* 4b; *TR,* 54.

40. *Taiping tianri,* in *Yinshu,* 5b; *TR,* 54.

41. *Taiping tianri,* in *Yinshu,* 6; *TR,* 55.

42. *Taiping tianri,* in *Yinshu,* 6b–7b; *TR,* 55–56.

43. M., 54–59. *Taiping tianri,* in *Yinshu,* 10b, for the sword and seal; 11b for the sparing of Yan Luo.

44. *TR,* 59–60. *Taiping tianri,* in *Yinshu,* 13, on palace and family.

45. On the names, see *Taiping tianri,* in *Yinshu,* 13; *TR,* 59–60.

46. *Taiping tianri,* in *Yinshu,* 16b; *TR,* 62.

47. Hamberg, *Visions,* 12. Compare Zürcher, "Prince Moonlight," 38, where the Mara kings, wielding "diamond clubs," also shout *sha,* "kill."

48. Adapted from the Chinese version of Hamberg, *Visions,* 12, and the translation in *TR,* 1517.

49. *TR,* 20 [C. L. Chang]; Xiang, *Ziliao,* 2:848. Kuhn, "Origins," 357–58, sees the poems as foretelling a "vague but immense personal mission."

50. Hamberg, *Visions,* 12, on the brothers' watchfulness; Ng, *Madness,* explains the legal implications of insanity.

51. Wagner, *Heavenly Vision,* 21–25, gives an insightful analysis of the idea of corroboration and categories in this dream. Yap, "Mental Illness," 295, discusses the overlays of inflexibility and "submission to dominating ideas" shown by Hong, and on 299 sees him as "hysterical," not schizophrenic.

Chapter 5: The Key

1. Hamberg, *Visions,* 19; *TR,* 63–64.

2. Among the scholars who have worked most carefully on Liang's tracts and their theology in the context of Hong's thought are Jen Yu-wen, *T'ung-k'ao,* 1665–93 (chap. 18, sec. 6); Bohr, "Eschatology"; and Xia, *Zongjiao.* See also works listed under Wagner, Shih, Boardman, Barnett, Kuhn, and Doezema. My especial thanks to Liu Chiu-ti for helping me enormously in my attempt to understand the whole of Liang's nine tracts.

3. Hunter, *Fan Kwae,* 87–89; Fairbank, *Trade,* 64–65.

4. Hunter, *Fan Kwae,* 88.

5. On this looting see Bernard, *Nemesis,* 2:13, and *CR,* 10:295.

6. Wakeman, *Strangers,* 12; Fairbank, *Trade,* 81; Bernard, *Nemesis,* 2:11–12, for false queues, and 37–39; Rait, *Gough,* 2:181–91.

7. Wakeman, *Strangers,* 16–17; *CR,* 10:530, on the stolen foot.

8. Wakeman, *Strangers,* 17–19; Bernard, *Nemesis,* 2:54–55; Bingham, *Narrative,* vol. 2, chap. 5; *CR,* 10:399–400.

9. Wakeman, *Strangers,* 19–21, 40–41; Bernard, *Nemesis,* 2:57; *CR,* 10:519–22.

10. Wakeman, *Strangers,* 73; *CR,* 10:527–528; *Yapian zhanzheng,* 3:15–16.

11. Wakeman, *Strangers,* 48–50; *CR,* 10:292, for sticks in ears.

12. Wakeman, *Strangers,* 50.

13. Bernard, *Nemesis,* 2:331; Fairbank, *Trade,* 87–89; Elliott, "Bannerman."

14. Isaiah 1:5–7, changing "head" to "heart" in verse 5, following Liang; Liang, *Quanshi,* 47–48 (1/16). Bohr, "Eschatology," chap. 2, gives a different but intense reading of Liang's text.

15. Bernard, *Nemesis,* 1:271, on the Jan. 7, 1841, battle in Anson's Bay.

16. Ibid., 264–65, 272–73.

17. On this ship, briefly renamed the *Chesapeake,* originally the *Cambridge,* see Bingham, *Narrative,* 1:167, 2:153; Bernard, *Nemesis,* 1:357–60; also Hunter, *Fan Kwae,* 90–91, though Hunter appears to conflate the Anson's Bay battle with the sinking of the *Cambridge,* events over a month apart.

18. Isaiah 1:28–31; Liang, *Quanshi,* 51 (1/18), subsituting Liang's "hemp fibers" for the Bible's "tow."

19. Liang, *Quanshi,* 17 (1/1). The strange being(s) is / are termed Ge-lu-bi-mai, Liang's version of "Cherubims."

20. Ibid., 158–59 (3/13–14), 69 (2/1), 281 (6/1).

21. Ibid., 158 (3/13b), 23 (1/3b–4).

22. "Out of a state of nothingness" is *zi wuwu zhong,* ibid., 80–81 (2/6b–7).

23. Ibid., 163 (3/16).

24. Ibid., 163 (3/16), 156 (3/12b).

25. Ibid., 72–74 (2/2b–3b).

26. Ibid., 163–64 (3/16).

27. Ibid., 87 (2/10).

28. Matthew 5:10–12; Liang, *Quanshi,* 52 (1/18b).

29. Matthew 6:9–13; Liang, *Quanshi,* 59 (1/22).

30. Matthew 7:15–20; Liang, *Quanshi,* 64 (1/24b).

31. Liang, *Quanshi,* 25–26 (1/5–6). My thanks to Liu Chiu-ti for her rendering of this passage.

32. Ibid., 82 (2/7b).

33. Ibid., 25 (1/4b–5).

34. Ibid., 31 (1/8).

35. Ibid., 32 (1/8b).

36. Ibid., 33 (1/9).

37. Ibid., 35 (1/10).

38. Ibid., 34 (1/9b).

39. Ibid., 29–30 (1/7).

40. Ibid., 27 (1/6).

41. Ibid., 359 (7/17).

42. Ibid., 362–63 (7/17b–18).

43. Pruden, "Roberts," 35–45, 66 n. 56, for Hakka speech; Coughlin, "Strangers," 113–18; Schlyter, *Gutzlaff als Missionar,* 129–30.

44. Liang, *Quanshi,* 401 (8/3).

45. Ibid., 88 (2/10b); Matthew 19:18–19; Liang, *Quanshi,* 96 (2/14b), on opium, *yang yan.* The "Collection of Missionary Works in Chinese," folder 14, contains several anti-opium tracts, including one vividly illustrated Rake's Progress of an opium addict, and one on "the six evils of opium."

46. Liang, *Quanshi,* 402–4 (8/3b–4b).

47. Ibid., 407 (8/6b).

48. Ibid., 409 (8/7).

49. Ibid., 430–31 (8/17b–18).

50. Acts 19:1–8; Liang, *Quanshi,* 461 (9/1).

51. Liang, *Quanshi,* 298–99 (6/9b–10).

52. Ibid., 302 (6/11b), 307 (6/14), 308 (6/14b).

53. Ibid., 456 (8/30b).

54. Ibid., 496 (9/18b), 498 (9/19b).

55. Ibid., 500–501 (9/20b–21).

CHAPTER 6: WANDERING

1. Hamberg, *Visions,* 20; *TR,* 4, 21, 65, retranslated; Liang, *Quanshi,* 144 (3/6b).

2. Hamberg, *Visions,* 24–25, modified according to his Chinese text. The characters were "Zhan yao jian."

3. Ibid., 19–22; Guo Yisheng, *Ditu,* 17; Liang, *Quanshi,* 306–7; in this work Liang does not, as far as I can discover, translate any of the clearest baptismal texts, such as those in Matthew 3, Mark 1, Luke 3, or John 1.

4. Hamberg, *Visions,* 21–22. The puritan essence of Hong's new belief is explored by Zurcher, "Purity."

5. Psalms 19:3–4; Liang, *Quanshi,* 166 (3/17b); Hamberg, *Visions,* 22, which confuses verses 3 and 4.

6. Psalms 19:9–10; Liang, *Quanshi,* 167 (3/18); Hamberg, *Visions,* 22–23.

7. Psalms 19:12; Liang, *Quanshi,* 167 (3/18); Hamberg, *Visions,* 23.

8. Hamberg, *Visions,* 27.

9. *Huaxian zhi,* 2:8.

10. Ibid., 2:8b–17. Wilson, *Genealogy,* 23–71, gives a full history of the process of "canonization" of Confucius' followers. A complete list is given ibid., appendix A.

11. Hamberg, *Visions,* 22; the significance of this incident is discussed in Weller, *Resistance,* 39. Hamberg, *Visions,* 23–24, seems to suggest it is Hong Rengan who converts Hong Xiuquan's family, but his wording is ambiguous.

12. Hamberg, *Visions,* 25, reworked.

13. Ibid., 26, reworked.

14. Ibid., 26; Weller, *Resistance,* 39.

15. *TR,* 66; *Taiping tianri,* in *Yinshu,* 22.

16. *Taiping tianri,* in *Yinshu,* 22; lunar calendar Daoguang 24/2/15, solar April 2; Jen, *Revolutionary Movement,* 24, suggests they were "disguised" as peddlers, which seems a rather strained interpretation.

17. *Taiping Tianri,* in *Yinshu,* 22b; lunar 3/18, solar May 5. Guo Yisheng, *Ditu,* 19–20; Jen, *Quanshi,* 1:67–68.

18. *TR,* 66; *Taiping Tianri,* in *Yinshu,* 22b.

19. See route map in Guo Yisheng, *Ditu,* 19.

20. *Taiping Tianri,* in *Yinshu* 23; *TR,* 66, lunar 4/5. For the general situation in Guiping, see Weller, *Resistance,* 40–43.

21. *Taiping Tianri,* in *Yinshu,* 23b; *TR,* 67; Hamburg, *Visions,* 27. A thorough evaluation of these early writings is given by Bohr, "Eschatology," 105–35. The chronology of Hong Xiuquan's own writings becomes an important part of the story at this point, but is not easy to disentangle. Before leaving for Guangxi in 1844, Hong had written only short poems. During the seven months of his 1844 sojourn in Sigu in Guangxi, according to an early brief account by his cousin Hong Rengan, Xiuquan wrote "more than fifty items" (*gong you wushi yu zhi*). See *TR,* 4; Xiang, *Ziliao,* 2:689. The word I translate here as "items" (*zhi*) could refer to pamphlets, chapters, volumes, or even loose sheets. Hong Rengan specifies four of these alleged fifty: *Quanshi zhenwen* (True words to exhort the age); *Baizheng Ge* (Ode on the hundred correct things); *Gaixie quizheng* (Eschewing heterodoxy and returning to the true); and a four-word title of which two characters are now missing, Yuan . . . jing (Classic of the original . . .). Hamberg, in *Visions,* 29 however, who used mainly Hong Rengan as his source, writes that *after* returning from Guangxi to Guanlubu, (i.e., after Dec. 1844, or in 1845–47), Hong Xiuquan wrote "An Ode on the Hundred Correct Things," "An Essay on the Origin of Virtue for the Awakening of the Age," "Further Exhortations for Awakening the Age," and "Alter the Corrupt and Turn to the Correct," adding that "most of which are contained in the 'Imperial Declaration of Thai-p'hing,'" afterwards printed at Nanking"—a clear reference to the *Taiping zhaoshu.*

A median version is presented in the often month-by-month account of Hong's period in Guangxi later published by the Taiping themselves, the *Taiping tianri* (Taiping heavenly chronicle). This states clearly (*Yinshu* version, 27a; *TR,* 70) that only *after* Hong Xiuquan returned to Guangdong from Guangxi, during the *yisi* year (i.e., 1845), when he was thirty-three *sui* old, did he write the *Yuandao jiushi zhao* and the *Yuandao jiushi xun,* which surely refer to the two longest titles subsequently included in the four-piece *Taiping zhaoshu.* But while Hong Xiuquan was in Guangxi in the *jiachen* year (1844), the *Taiping tianri* also says, Hong Xiuquan "wrote proclamations (*zhao*) exhorting (*quan*) the people to worship the Heavenly Father, the Supreme Lord and Great God, and distributed them among the people." (*Taiping tianri,* in *Yinshu,* 23a and b, somewhat modifying *TR,* 67.) The *Taiping tianri* does not specify what these proclamations were, but since it explicitly says three pages later they were *not* either the *Yuandao jiushi zhao* or the *Yuandao jiushi xun,* we can conclude that if they were not works now totally lost, then they included the two other titles later collected in the official Taiping collection the *Taiping zhaoshu*—namely, the *Yuandao jiushi ge* (Ode on the origin of the way and our salvation) and the *Baizheng ge* (ode on the hundred correct things). The *Baizheng ge* seems incomplete, perhaps an abandoned draft, later rescued and published. But the "Ode on the Origin of the Way and Our Salvation," originally with a different title (probably one of the first two mentioned by Hong Rengan in his list of four in his earliest account) seems to fit the Guangxi circumstances perfectly. Hong still knew only the six commandments, which he was trying to refine to his Guangxi world. He was still genuinely full of praise for Confucius' moral virtue. He did not use too many scholarly analogies, and those he did use were close to his basic memorized readings, and would have needed no textual checking. Jen, *Quanshi,* 1:84–85, dates the *Baizheng ge* in 1844 and the *Yuandao jiushi ge* to 1845, citing the *Taiping tianri* as his evidence. But this seems to be a slip, since the *Taiping tianri* in fact says the *Yuandao jiushi zhao* and *xun* were written in 1845 or later. It does not mention the *ge*.

It also seems to me probable that the earliest prayers used in Guangxi would have been the simplest ones, echoing in part those Hong had just read in Matthew's Gospel via Liang Afa's translation of the Sermon on the Mount; these simple prayers contain no anachronistic references to the Ten Commandments or other theological matters of which Hong Xiuquan knew nothing until later (as, for example, does the prayer on *TR,* 119). Hence I place them here.

22. The various Confucian elements in Hong's early thought are carefully examined in Shih, *Taiping Ideology,* chap. 8. If Hong did need help with a quotation or a detail, it is almost certain that one of the families with whom he lodged would have had at least one of the scores of simplified cribs and outlines that circulated in China at the time, and could be bought in local bookshops, perhaps even from roving peddlers in town or country. See Bai, "Primers and Paradigms," chap. 2.

23. *Taiping zhaoshu,* in *Yinshu,* 1; *TR,* 25.

24. The six can be clearly seen in *Taiping zhaoshu,* in *Yinshu,* 2–5; *TR,* 26–30.

25. Legge, *The She King (shijing),* 19.

26. *Taiping zhaoshu,* in *Yinshu,* 2b, echoing Legge, *Analects,* 250, *feili siwu.*

27. The exact characters used by Hong for this episode in *Taiping zhaoshu,* in *Yinshu* 3, are in the *Shujing.* See Legge, *Shoo-king,* 2/3/21, 66. With variants, the passage is also glossed in Mencius—see Legge, *Mencius,* 5/1/1, 342–43. Hong seems to have conflated this with a *Zuozhuan* passage on the elephants' and birds' actions at the time of Shun's death—see *Yinshu,* 3, and Murohashi, *Daikanwa,* 11105 (10:663), top line.

Again, Hong turns to an allusion from the *Book of Poetry* that he learned by heart in school, an allegorical poem in which a grieving son expresses his sorrow and remorse that he could not have served his parents better while they lived.

> Fatherless, who is there to rely on?
> Motherless, who is there to depend on?
> When I go abroad, I carry my grief with me;
> When I come home, I have no one to go to.

> Cold and bleak is the Southern Hill,
> The rushing wind is very fierce.
> Other people all are happy—
> Why am I alone so miserable?
>
> The Southern Hill is very steep,
> The rushing wind is blustering.
> Other people all are happy—
> I alone have left my tasks unfinished.

TR, 237, and *Yinshu,* 3b; Legge, *She-King,* 2/5/8, verses 3, 5, 6, with minor changes, 350–51.

28. *Taiping zhaoshu,* in *Yinshu,* 3b–4; *TR,* 29.

29. *TR,* 29; *Taiping zhaoshu,* in *Yinshu,* 4; Watson, *Meng Ch'iu,* 118.

30. *TR,* 29; Watson, *Meng Ch'iu,* 57.

31. *TR,* 29, *Taiping zhaoshu,* in *Yinshu,* 5; see passages in Liang, *Quanshi,* 101–2, 490. Hong may well be echoing the philosopher Xunzi here.

32. *TR,* 30–31; *Taiping zhaoshu,* in *Yinshu,* 6.

33. *Taiping zhaoshu,* in *Yinshu,* 6, modifying *TR,* 31.

34. *Taiping tianri,* in *Yinshu,* 23b, amending *TR,* 67; Hamberg, *Visions,* 38.

35. *Taiping tianri,* in *Yinshu,* 24, modifying *TR,* 67.

36. Hamberg, *Visions,* 35–36. For the hymns, see Isabel Wong, "Geming Gequ," 113–14.

37. *TR,* 115–16 and n. 13, slightly modified following *Tiantiao shu,* in *Yinshu,* 3. On dating the prayers, see *TR,* 111, and discussion in Bohr, "Eschatology," 161.

38. Hamberg, *Visions,* 28. This ritual is startlingly like the Taoist ritual of "the Sacrifice of the Writings," as described in Schipper, *Taoist Body,* 89, though there the documents are burned "outside the ritual area" and the presiding masters "mime drunkenness."

39. Hamberg, *Visions,* 28, 35–36, and *TR,* 116, both slightly modified following *Tiantiao shu,* in *Yinshu,* 3b.

40. Hamberg, *Visions,* 27–28. *Taiping tianri,* in *Yinshu,* 24–25 (*TR,* 68), gives a rather different time span, with the young man's release being on 8/15. There is a misprint in the son Huang Weizheng's name in *Yinshu,* 25.

41. *TR,* 68; *Taiping tianri,* in *Yinshu,* 25–26.

42. *TR,* 69; *Taiping tianri,* in *Yinshu,* 25b–26.

CHAPTER 7: THE BASE

1. *Taiping tianri,* in *Yinshu,* 25b–26b; *TR,* 69; Hamberg, *Visions,* 29.

2. Hamberg, *Visions,* 29.

3. See *Taiping tianri,* in *Yinshu,* 26b; *TR,* 69; and the detailed map in Guo Yisheng, *Ditu,* 21.

4. *Taiping tianri,* in *Yinshu,* 26b–27; *TR,* 69–70; Guo Yisheng, *Ditu,* 21.

5. Laai, "Pirates," 167, drawing on later Nanjing God-worshipers' registers.

6. Curwen, *Deposition,* 83, 88.

7. Laai, "Pirates," 169.

8. Murray, *Pirates,* 57–59.

9. Ibid., 25, 67–68.

10. Ibid., 71–73, 149–50. Shi Yang was also often known simply as Zheng Yi Sao, "Zheng Yi's wife."

11. Fox, *Admirals,* 89–91, 96–97.

12. Ibid., 93–95.

13. Laai, "Pirates," 109.

14. Ibid., 30, 182; Fox, *Admirals,* 92, and Scott, *Destruction, 7.*

15. Scott, *Destruction,* 47.

16. Ibid., 100 n, 141; Laai, "Pirates," 27, 78.

17. Scott, *Destruction,* 97–98, 248–50.

18. Laai, "Pirates," 68–70, 112; Bingham, *Narrative,* 2:264, emphasizes the number of these mixed liaisons in Macao.

19. Scott, *Destruction,* 209–10, 217, 234; Laai, "Pirates," 79–80.

20. Scott, *Destruction,* 224, on children and rent; 218 on guns; 235 on spoiled opium; 226, 232, for her possessions.

21. Ibid., 229, 235; Laai, "Pirates," 83.

22. Laai, "Pirates," 62, 90, 109, 110.

23. Ibid., 108, 118–19. There were eleven such "companies"—*mifanzhu tang*—in Nanning alone by 1850.

24. Murray and Qin, *Tiandihui,* 16–19, 143–44; ibid., 18, translates the phrase *jushi* as "carry out a rebellion," which seems too precise in the context. The Heaven-and-Earth Society was just one of dozens of informal and clandestine groups and federations that spread in China at this time, as vastly growing populations brought new pressures on the land, compounded by bureaucratic inefficiencies, unfair taxation patterns, natural disasters, erosion of uplands, and other environmental damage to lakes, hills, and waterways. But unlike many others, it survived and spread, sparking more than fifty-five local uprisings or attacks on cities in the southeast coastal provinces and in Guangxi between 1800 and 1840, prompting massive government reprisals, and thus a deepened sense of injustice. See ibid., 231–35, appendix C. This number also included occasional risings in Yunnan, Guizhou, Hunan, and Jiangxi.

25. Ibid., 189, omitting the Chinese transcriptions; see also Murray, "Migration," 180; David Ownby, introduction to *Secret Societies Reconsidered,* 18. An excellent overview of the intersection of demographic problems with the growth of the secret societies is Jones and Kuhn, "Dynastic Decline," 108–13, 134–44.

26. Murray and Qin, *Tiandihui,* 183–84; Ter Haar, "Messianism," 169.

27. Murray and Qin, *Tiandihui,* 45, 185.

28. Ibid., 44, 48.

29. Ibid., 30, 290, and other references as listed ibid., index, 344.

30. Ter Haar, "Messianism," 159, 165, 169.

31. Ibid., 156; Murray and Qin, *Tiandihui,* 75, 189, 192.

32. Murray and Qin, *Tiandihui,* 69–76; Laai, "Pirates," 13–14, 31–32, 179.

33. Scott, *Destruction,* 248; Laai, "Pirates," 15; Scott, *Destruction,* 219, 233, testimony of the Chinese interpreter Tom Achik.

34. Laai, "Pirates," 31–32, 36, 112, 173.

35. Ibid., 185–87.

36. Ibid., 92–93; 95 n. 18, for the phrase *Chou ke fensheng.*

37. Ibid., 96, 101–2.

38. Ibid., 150, 176.

39. Curwen, *Deposition,* 88, with minor changes. The sense of the passage seems much clearer if we drop, as I do here, the extra phrase "if they were God-worshipers."

40. P. Clarke, "Coming," 148–49; Schlyter, *Gutzlaff als Missionar,* chap. 5.

41. P. Clarke, "Coming," 153, correcting the misprint of "effectuatelly."

42. Ibid., 152, 154, 158, 166 n. 55, 176 n. 80, 161, 163–64. However, Clarke's attempt to include Feng Yunshan among the Hong Kong converts to the Chinese Union (the Hanhui) is firmly rebutted by Mao, "Guanyu Guo Shili," 269, 271. For more details on the Chinese Union see Schlyter, *Gutzlaff als Missionar,* chap. 6, and 266–99.

43. P. Clarke, "Coming," 149, 179–80.

44. Variants of these formats can be seen in the New York Public Library, the British Library, and the Library of Congress. The base of Gutzlaff's European support is studied in Schlyter, *Heimatbasis,* chap. 4, for the growth period of the 1840s.

45. Romans 1:14–15. Twenty-six numbered Chinese Union tracts are listed with titles and summaries in Robert Douglas' 1877 *Catalogue of the British Museum,* 3–5, 37. The serial numbers cited there range from Tract 10, the lowest, to Tract 52. In the same chapter, Paul gives his own list of prohibitions that far exceeds in comprehensiveness either the six prohibitions of Hong Xiuquan or the Ten Commandments handed to Moses by God at Sinai. Though, like Hong's, Paul's list (Romans 1:26–31) includes murder, lust, and disobedience to parents, it adds almost twenty further sins, including envy, whispering and backbiting, pride and malignity, and the practice of male homosexuality.

46. *TR,* 35–36; Legge, *Li-Ki.*

47. *TR,* 36, Wilhelm/Baynes, *I Ching,* 56–57, hexagram *tongren*; *Taiping zhaoshu,* in *Yinshu,* 10.

48. *TR,* 34, modified following *Taiping zhaoshu,* in *Yinshu,* 8.

49. *TR,* 36, slightly modified following *Taiping zhaoshu,* in *Yinshu,* 10.

50. *TR,* 38.

51. *TR,* 38–39, 44. On the Yuliji see *Taiping zhaoshu,* in *Yinshu,* 12.

52. See *TR,* 39, 41, 46–47.

53. See detailed accounts in Coughlin, "Strangers," and Pruden, "Roberts."

54. A full description of such a baptism is given by Roberts in two letters to Gutzlaff of July 21 and July 29, 1844. See "Chun's Doings in Canton," #19 (July 21, 1844) 3, plate 1927, fiche 17; and #20 (July 29, 1844) 1 and 2, plates 1917 and 1918, fiche 17. My thanks to Laura McDaniel for furnishing me transcripts of "Chun's Doings."

55. P. Clarke, "Coming," 171, on the assistant Zhou Daoxing and Gutzlaff's union connection; *TR,* 70; Hamberg, *Visions,* 31.

56. Hamberg, *Visions,* 32; Coughlin, "Strangers," 256–61.

57. Hamberg, *Visions,* 32; *TR,* 70–71; *Taiping tianri,* in *Yinshu,* 28.

58. *Canton Register,* Sept. 1, 1835. See also *Shilu, Daoguang,* 269/3b.

59. Laai, "Pirates," 36, 66–67.

60. Ibid., 113, 144.

61. *Taiping tianri,* in *Yinshu,* 28b; *TR,* 71. For earlier esoteric use of cryptic utterances and finger codes see Zürcher, "Prince Moonlight," 37.

62. Hamberg, *Visions,* 33.

63. *Taiping tianri,* in *Yinshu,* 30b; *TR,* 72. The characters *jiusui,* translated as "according to the old calendar" in *TR,* 72, must surely in fact mean "the previous year"; otherwise the chronology makes no sense. Guo Tingyi, *Shishi,* 47, amends the text in this sense.

64. *TR*, 72, modified; *Taiping tianri*, in *Yinshu*, 30b–31; compare the use of "Wu" in the opening line of the poem ibid., 20b.

65. Dates in *Taiping tianri*, in *Yinshu*, 30b, 31; *TR*, 72; Hamberg, *Visions*, 34.

CHAPTER 8: JUDGMENTS

1. *Taiping tianri*, in *Yinshu*, 31, for "their writings are distributed" *(xieshu songren)*, even though the nature of these *shu*, or "writings," is not specified; the translation in *TR*, 72, "wrote letters to be sent to people," seems somewhat too limited. See also Wang, *Tianfu*, 159, 191, and Bohr, "Eschatology," 136–76, for their work at this time.

2. Liang, *Quanshi*, 359 (7/17); *TR*, 41, modified; *Taiping zhaoshu*, in *Yinshu*, 14. Hong here combines Exodus 20:4–5 and 31:18.

3. Psalms 115:1–8; *TR*, 43; and *Taiping zhaoshu*, in *Yinshu*, 16. Hong uses this fuller passage of Psalms 115:1–8, rather than the briefer list in Psalms 135:16–17.

4. *TR*, 45, retranslated from *Taiping zhaoshu*, in *Yinshu*, 17b.

5. *TR*, 57, modified after *Taiping tianri*, in *Yinshu*, 10, and abbreviating repetitions of God's full name.

6. *TR*, 61; *Taiping tianri*, in *Yinshu*, 15b.

7. *TR*, 62, modified; *Taiping tianri*, in *Yinshu*, 16.

8. *Taiping tianri*, in *Yinshu*, 27, 31b; *TR*, 69–70, 73; Guo Yisheng, *Ditu*, 21.

9. Hamberg, *Visions*, 36; *TR*, 73; Weller, *Resistance*, 57–58, on shrine numbers and reputation.

10. Hamberg, *Visions*, 36; *TR*, 73; I interpret *Taiping tianri*, in *Yinshu*, 31b–32, as showing it was the worshipers, not "temple guardians," who took these preventive measures.

11. *Taiping tianri*, in *Yinshu*, 32; *TR*, 73.

12. *TR*, 73–76; *Taiping tianri*, in *Yinshu*, 32–35b; Hamberg, *Visions*, 37; Hong Rengan variants in *TR*, 1518–19; Weller, *Resistance*, 62–63.

13. Jen, *Quanshi*, 1:120–23; Jen, *Revolutionary Movement*, 38–39; Li, *Zhongxing bieji*, 1:6.

14. Li, *Zhongxing bieji*, 1:6a; Xia, *Zongjiao*, 33.

15. Li, *Zhongxing bieji*.

16. For the general Guangxi background, see Kuhn, "Taiping Rebellion," 264–66. See also Xia, *Zongjiao*, 29, on the Guiping area militias *(tuanlian)* and God-worshipers.

17. Kikuchi, "Taihei tengoku," 7, for the Lan and Luo families in Jintian; Inada, "Taihei tengoku," 61–64, on "Hakka" as a term. My special thanks to Wen-wen Liu for help with these articles.

18. Kikuchi, "Taihei tengoku," 4, on the Xus, originally from Tongcheng, Anhui, and their long reign as Guiping magistrates.

19. Ibid., 7, on the "Yaoming huiguan."

20. Ibid., 8.

21. Ibid., 9–11.

22. Ibid., 12–15, 16, on the *Anliang yue*.

23. Ibid., 17; *Anliang yue*, 347–48.

24. Kikuchi, "Taihei tengoku," 19–20, on the Huang family, which was not related to Hong's friends, the Sigu village Huangs.

25. Ibid., 24, 26–27.

26. Inada, "Taihei tengoku," 71.

27. Ibid., 74; *Anliang yue*, 345.

28. Inada, "Taihei tengoku," 76–77, citing *Anliang yue.*

29. Ibid., 78–79, on *gongbao* registry.

30. This is especially significant for Wei Changhui—later the Taiping "North King"—and his father's and uncle's landholdings, as discussed ibid., 75; see ibid., 82, for the Wei family's token payment of 4 *qian* to the local shrine. On p. 78 Inada argues that "perhaps" Wei's Hakka identity was a factor here.

31. See Laai, "Pirates," 167 n. 36, 168 n. 37.

32. Li, *Zhongxing bieji,* 1:6b; Wang, *Tianfu,* 192; Jen, *Revolutionary Movement,* 38–40; Naquin, *Millenarian Rebellion,* and Kuhn, *Soulstealers,* both offer vivid examples of such treatment of suspects under investigation.

33. Wang, *Tianfu,* 192; Jen, *Revolutionary Movement,* 40.

34. As analyzed in Weller, *Resistance,* 70–75.

35. Xia, *Zongjiao,* 30–31; Hamberg, *Visions,* 34, cites Xiao's wife, Yang Yunjiao, as also having visions. See also *TR,* 69, on Hong Rengan; for Xiao's hour-long trances see *Tianxiong shengzhi,* 1:4b–5. Bohr, "Eschatology," 177, argues that during this period of Hong's and Feng's absence from Guangxi, Yang and Xiao, by their "shamanic leadership," were "unleashing the revolutionary implications" of Hong's theology.

36. *Tianxiong shengzhi,* 1:1, 2, 8; Wang, *Tianfu,* 4, 9.

37. *Tianxiong shengzhi,* 1:9; Wang, *Tianfu,* 10.

38. *Tianxiong shengzhi,* 1:6; Wang, *Tianfu,* 7–8; Weller, *Resistance,* 82–83, suggests this as a prototype for women's power and possession.

39. *Tianxiong shengzhi,* 1:7–8, 9b; Wang, *Tianfu,* 8–11; Zhong Wendian on Hakka idioms, interview with author in Guilin, summer 1992; Xia, *Zongjiao,* 34, discusses the importance of this consanguinity in local religious terms.

40. Weller, *Resistance,* discusses this rich mix at length—see esp. p. 56, on the Jintian area as "thick with extraordinary possibilities," and p. 84, on the final "saturation." For these examples see *Tianxiong shengzhi,* 1:3, 10, 12; Wang, *Tianfu,* 5, 11, 13. The two accounts of the same incident in the text have a variant reading, Siwang and Shiwang, for the name of the village. For its location, see Guo Yisheng, *Ditu,* 24.

41. Hamberg, *Visions,* 45.

42. *Tianxiong shengzhi,* 1:2b, 5, first description by Jesus, second by Xiao Chaogui.

43. *Tianxiong shengzhi,* 1:3b; Wang, *Tianfu,* 5.

44. *Tianxiong shengzhi,* 1:5b, "*shouzhi ... yu wo kan,*" "pointed out with His hand, for me to see."

45. Genesis 32:24; *Tianxiong shengzhi,* 1:5b, "*gangshou chiao.*" That the phrase refers to a Hakka wrestling grip was explained to me by Zhong Wendian in 1992.

46. Kutcher, "Death and Mourning"; Kuhn, *Soulstealers,* 58–59, 102–3. The "three years" of mourning was usually interpreted as twenty-seven months.

47. Hamberg, *Vision,* 40; Jen, *Revolutionary Movement,* 40. Wang, *Tianfu,* 192. Hong's son was born in Daoguang 29/10/9 (Nov. 23, 1849), a little more than nine months after Hong's return to Guanlubu.

CHAPTER 9: ASSEMBLING

1. Guo Yisheng, *Ditu,* 23, 25, 27.

2. Many are listed in Guo Tingyi, *Shishi,* 65–70.

3. Graham, *China Station,* chap. 9; Hay, *Suppression,* 27–44; Laai, "Pirates," 66–72; Guo Tingyi, *Shishi,* 68–69.

4. *Tianxiong shengzhi,* 1:16b.

5. Ibid., 1:17; Wang, *Tianfu,* 17.

6. Hamberg, *Visions,* 46.

7. Ibid., 46–47; Weller, *Resistance.*

8. *Tianxiong shengzhi,* 1:21, for Daoguang 29/10/23; Wang, *Tianfu,* 22, which accidentally omits the leaders' uneasy reply.

9. The two are Huang Weizheng and Ji Nengshan. *Tianxiong shengzhi,* 1:18b, Daoguang 29/9/11; this is clearly earlier than the early part of 1850 suggested for these events by Jen, *Revolutionary Movement,* 54.

10. *Tianxiong shengzhi,* 1:19a, dated 29/9/14.

11. Ibid., 1:20b, dated 29/9/28, where God is called "Gao Lao" for the first time in this text. For the term "Gao Lao" see Luo Ergang, "Jingji kao" 28; *TR,* 99.

12. *Tianxiong shengzhi,* 1:20b, dated 29/10/4, and 1:35a, 30/1/4; Hamberg, *Visions,* 51. Bohr, "Eschatology," 194–96, on militia and Taiping organizations.

13. Jen, *Revolutionary Movement,* 42–44; *TR,* 378–79; Curwen, *Desposition,* 80–81.

14. *Tianxiong shengzhi,* 1:33b, Daoguang 30/1/4 (Feb. 15, 1850); Wang, *Tianfu,* 33–34.

15. Hamberg, *Visions,* 42.

16. Retranslated from the Chinese ibid., 43.

17. *Tianxiong shengzhi,* 1:41b–42, dated 30/2/23.

18. Hamberg, *Visions,* 43.

19. Ibid., 55–56, modernizing romanization of Chinese names.

20. Ibid., 50, Chinese text, modifying his translation and that in *TR,* 77.

21. The key passages are in *Tianxiong shengzhi,* 1:28b–31b, Daoguang 29/12/27 and 29/12/29; Hong's leg injury is mentioned ibid., 1:21b, under Daoguang 29/10/23; Wang, *Tianfu,* 29–31.

22. *Tianxiong shengzhi,* 2:20b–21, Daoguang 30/8/13; Guo Tingyi, *Shishi,* 84, has other details on Shi Dakai's involvement at Baisha.

23. *Tianxiong shengzhi,* 1:31b–32b, Daoguang 30/1/2.

24. Ibid., 1:34a, Daoguang 30/1/4, and 1:36–37, Daoguang 30/1/16; Wang, *Tianfu,* 36 n, explains the codes. There was a similar ceremony on 30/1/17.

25. *Tianxiong shengzhi,* 1:38b, Daoguang 30/1/17.

26. Ibid., 1:41b, Daoguang 30/2/23.

27. Ibid., 1:42–44b, for initiation, 1:46b, for baptism, Daoguang 30/2/27 and 28; Wang, *Tianfu,* 41–43, 45.

28. *Tianxiong shengzhi,* 1:25b, Daoguang 29/12/1; Wang, *Tianfu,* 27; Hamberg, *Visions,* 34, however, suggests it was Xiao's first wife, Yang-yun-kiau, who was the women's model.

29. *Tianxiong shengzhi,* 1:26.

30. Ibid., 1:20b, Daoguang 29/10/4, describes the woman as being *guai dai,* "kidnapped" or "decoyed."

31. Ibid., 1:26b, where Jesus calls her his *baomei.* On the true identity of Xiao's wife, née Huang, who later used the name of Yang, see Luo Ergang, "Chongkao," 134, 136.

32. *Tianxiong shengzhi,* 1:26b. This "second sister Chen" was possibly older sister to "third sister Chen," prominent among Hong's court women in 1860, as shown in *TR,* 931.

33. *TR,* 390, translation of *Tianqing daolishu,* in *Yinshu,* 29b.

34. Hamberg, *Visions,* 45, says Hong Rengan sent the message. Hong's son was born in Daoguang 29/10/9. Jen, *Quanshi,* 1:128.

35. The three were Huang Shengjue, Hou Changbo, and Jiang Longchang. See Jen,

Quanshi, 1:191; Hamberg, *Visions,* 47, 53; *TR,* 811, on "Hou Ch'ang-po and Huang Sheng-chueh," probably also refers to their role on this trip. See also Wang, *Tianfu,* 81 and n. 1, on Hou Changbo; Jen, *Revolutionary Movement,* 352–53, on Jiang Longchang's death in 1852.

36. Jen, *Revolutionary Movement,* 55; Jen, *Quanshi,* 1:192.

37. *Tianxiong shengzhi,* 1:24b, Daoguang 29/11/27.

38. Hamberg, *Visions,* 47–48.

39. *TR,* 374; Hamberg, *Visions,* 46; Jen, *Revolutionary Movement,* 56.

40. *TR,* 374–75, modified from *Tianqing daolishu,* in *Yinshu,* 11b; Wang Qingcheng, in *Tianfu,* 195 n. 1, explains why he believes Yang had recovered by Sept., as opposed to the Nov. date given in *Tianqing daolishu.*

41. On the ulcers *(chuangdu)* see *Tianxiong shengzhi,* 2:13b, Daoguang 30/8/1; Wang, *Tianfu,* 66.

42. *Tianxiong shengzhi,* 1:46b–47, Daoguang 30/3/4.

43. Ibid., 1:47b, Daoguang 30/4/22.

44. Ibid., 2:8, Daoguang 30/7/26.

45. Ibid., 1:52b, Daoguang 30/6/20; Wang, *Tianfu,* 50; Jen, *Revolutionary Movement,* 43–44, for Chen and Qin.

46. *Tianxiong shengzhi,* 1:54b–55.

47. Ibid., 1:53.

48. Ibid., 1:53b–54.

49. Ibid., 1:54.

50. The logistics, quarrels, and final success can be reconstructed from several messages in *Tianxiong shengzhi,* 2:1–3b, those dated Daoguang 30/7/5, 30/7/16, 30/7/18, 30/7/19, and 30/7/21; Wang, *Tianfu,* 55–57.

CHAPTER 10: EARTH WAR

1. *Tianxiong shengzhi,* 1:48, Daoguang 30/6/19 (27 July 1850); Jiang, "Dengji," suggests April 3, 1850, as Hong's throne day.

2. Zhuang, "Ling Shiba," 102, gives a full list.

3. *Tianxiong shengzhi,* 2:25, Daoguang 30/9/10.

4. Ibid., 2:26b, Daoguang 30/9/25; Wang, *Tianfu,* 77; Wang, "Jintian qiyi," 72–88, fully analyzes the uprising as a process throughout 1850.

5. Jen, *Revolutionary Movement,* 49, and Zhuang, "Ling Shiba," 101.

6. *TR,* 133, *Taiping junmu,* in *Yinshu,* 1–2.

7. *TR,* 137–38, *Taiping junmu,* in *Yinshu,* 32; *TR,* 419–20.

8. See Shih, *Taiping Ideology,* 259–64, for a meticulous analysis; and Biot, trans., *Le Tcheou-li,* vol. 2, bk. 28.

9. E.g., *Tianxiong shengzhi,* 2:23, Daoguang 30/8/20, for "face" in the context of Yang's illness.

10. See ibid., 2:11b–12, Daoguang 30/7/29, literally "Those two men don't recognize much of characters written in ink" and "accomplish things by natural talent." See also the mockery of geographical and astronomical scholarship ibid., 2:18b, Daoguang 30/8/9, and of classical poetry in 2:33b, Taiping 1/3/18.

11. Ibid., 2:22, where Yang Liu is given a hundred blows on Daoguang 30/8/19 although he had apparently already reached the eighth commandment without an error.

12. *TR*, 123, modified following *Tian tiaoshu*, in *Yinshu*, 11b–12.

13. Jen, *Revolutionary Movement*, 58–60; Hamberg, *Visions*, 48–49; Guo Tingyi, *Shishi*, 92.

14. Jen, *Revolutionary Movement*, 67–68; Laai, "Pirates," 95, 199–204; Jen, *Quanshi*, 1:214–20, valiantly tries to unravel all the overlapping and contradictory accounts of these conflicts.

15. Jen, *Revolutionary Movement*, 62–63; Jen, *Quanshi*, 1:218–19, on Zhang Yong; Wang, "Jintian qiyi," 64–71, dismisses much prior discussion of this battle as unreliable.

16. *Tianxiong shengzhi*, 2:27, Daoguang 30/11/first ten days of month.

17. Guo Yisheng, *Ditu*, 33–34.

18. *TR*, 425.

19. *TR*, 425–26.

20. The Chinese date of the battle was Daoguang 30/11/29. Guo Yisheng, *Ditu*, 33–34; Jen, *Revolutionary Movement*, 64–65; Jen, *Quanshi*, 1:221–23; Guo Tingyi, *Shishi*, 97. Jen somewhat garbles Ikedanbu's name.

21. *Tianming zhaozhi shu*, in *Yinshu*, 6, modifying *TR*, 103; Guo Tingyi, *Shishi*, 98. Kuhn, "Taiping Rebellion," 273–74, sees Hong's Jan. 11, 1851, birthday as marking the time "a political regime had at last emerged from Hung's messianic vision."

22. Laai, "Pirates," 204–5; Jen, *Revolutionary Movement*, 68; Hamberg, *Visions*, 55–56; Guo Tingyi, *Shishi*, 98, 100.

23. Guo Tingyi, *Shishi*, 104–7; Hamberg, *Visions*, 53–55; Jen, *Revolutionary Movement*, 71–72.

24. *Tianxiong shengzhi*, 2:40, for this *zaibing* of Hong, Taiping 1/3/20; Guo Tingyi, *Shishi*, 108–15; Wang, "Jintian qiyi," 84–87; Jiang, "Dengji," suggests a formal earlier date of April 3, 1850.

25. *Tianxiong shengzhi*, 2:30, Taiping 1/2/28.

26. Ibid., 2:30–32b, Taiping 1/2/28.

27. *TR*, 99.

28. *Tianxiong shengzhi*, 2:35.

29. Ibid., 2:37b–38, Taiping 1/3/18, modifying *TR*, 99–100; this is one of the only *Tianxiong shengzhi* passages chosen for inclusion in the *Tianming zhaozhi shu*; see *Yinshu* ed., 2.

30. *Tianxiong shengzhi*, 2:38b–39, for Lai's failure to attend, and 2:39–40, for Huang's and Wei's lateness, and Chen's hasty responses.

31. Zhuang, "Ling Shiba." Ling never joined Hong and was killed by Qing troops in 1852. Ling's two 1850 approaches to Jintian and the Taiping caution are in *Tianxiong shengzhi*, 2:4a–5b and 2:25b, Daoguang 30/7/22 and 30/9/10; Ling's campaigns are shown in detail in Guo Yisheng, *Ditu*, 28, 31; for a harsh Taiping view of Ling see *TR*, 392–93.

32. *Tianxiong shengzhi*, 2:40b, Taiping 1/5/12.

33. Women in *Tianxiong shengzhi* 2:42, Taiping 1/6/27.

34. *TR*, 427 and n. 2. The Taiping used the phrase "belonging to the third watch"—i.e., the midnight hours—as a euphemism for the deserters.

35. *Tianxiong shengzhi*, 2:42, Taiping 1/6/27.

36. See *TR*, 100, and *Tianxiong shengzhi*, 2:42, both dated 1/7/13.

37. *TR*, 104, Xianfeng 1/7/19, modified according to *Tianming zhaozhi shu*, in *Yinshu*, 6b–7b.

38. Curwen, *Deposition*, 83.

39. Zhong, *Yongan* 11–13; Guo Yisheng, *Ditu* 41–42.

CHAPTER 11: THE FIRST CITY

1. Zhong, *Yongan*, 22–23, on Hong's residence.

2. *TR*, 105–6, modified from *Tianming zhaozhi shu*, in *Yinshu*, 8b–9.

3. Zhong, *Yongan*, 24–26.

4. Ibid., 29–32, 36, 42–43.

5. Shih, *Taiping Ideology*, 158–60, on the treasury and brotherhood; Wagner, *Heavenly Vision*, 48–57, on salvation history and the millennium. Kuhn, "Taiping Rebellion," 276, emphasizes the mix in Yongan of "religious content" and "ethnic nationalism." Bohr, "Eschatology," 198–206, discusses the emergence in Yongan of a new form of "charismatic" leadership, and the identification of the Manchus with the forces of evil.

6. *TR*, 106; *Tianming zhaozhi shu*, 9b, on the *Xiaotiantang*. There has been considerable discussion of this *Xiaotiantang* by scholars: see Laai, "Pirates," 248; Su, " 'Xiaotiantang' xinjie," argues for Beijing, not Nanjing; Fang and Cui, "Taiping Tianguo 'Xiaotiantang,' " also argues against prior identifications of Nanjing. See also Xia, *Zongjiao*, 84–85; Wang, *Lishi he sixiang*, 208–9; Wagner, *Heavenly Vision*, 67–69.

7. *TR*, 323–24, and discussion of sources ibid., 321–23; Jen, *Revolutionary Movement*, 80–81; Zhong, *Yongan*, 94–96.

8. *TR*, 107; *Tianming zhaozhi shu*, in *Yinshu*, 10b.

9. *TR*, 125–28.

10. *TR*, 108, slightly modified following *Tianming zhaozhi shu*, in *Yinshu*, 12; decree formally issued on Dec. 17, 1851, though I assume it was prepared a few days earlier; and *Taiping lizhi*, in *Yinshu*, 5b–6, and *TR*, 129, for one-thousand-year titles.

11. That this character shift was already in place in Yongan can be seen from the 1852 *Sanzijing*, in *Yinshu*, 2b, where the pharaoh of Egypt is referred to as the *kuang* rather than the *wang*, as are all Chinese rulers later in the same text.

12. *TR*, 142–43; *Banxing zhaoshu*, in *Yinshu*, 1–2; *TR*, 143, 144 n. 4.

13. See *Tianxiong shengzhi*, 2:41b–42, for 1/6/27. The most dramatic example, that of Zhou Xineng and 190 others, originated in July 1851 and was discovered in November. The unmasking of the spies was given extensive coverage by the Taiping as an example of Yang Xiuqing's perspicacity. See *TR*, 88–97, 382–84.

14. Zhong, *Yongan*, 53–56. Jen, *Revolutionary Movement*, 78, estimates the Taiping in Yongan at 40,000, of whom half were combatants.

15. Guo Tingyi, *Shishi*, 136–40, lists these numerous attacks, as does Zhong, *Yongan*, 64–75; on p. 61 Zhong gives the 46,000 figure; on pp. 107–10 he discusses illicit trade; Guo Yisheng, *Ditu*, 43–44, has detailed maps.

16. Guo Tingyi, *Shishi*, 141, dated 1/10/18; Laai, "Pirates," 254. This may be the battle described for 1/10/17 in the *Overland Friend of China*, as cited in Clarke and Gregory, *Reports*, 14–15.

17. *Tianxiong shengzhi*, 2:45.

18. Ibid., 2:45b.

19. Ibid., 2:47, and on the pain (*Zhongku*); *TR*, 102, cites the almost identical passage as it is found in *Tianming zhaozhi shu*, in *Yinshu*, 5.

20. The last phrases uttered by Jesus are on 2/3/15 in *Tianxiong shengzhi*, 2:49b, i.e., May 3, 1852, during the Guilin siege.

21. *TR*, 102.

22. *TR*, 108, *Tianming zhaozhi shu*, in *Yinshu*, 12b.

23. *TR*, 139–141, modified from *Taiping tiaogui*, in *Yinshu*.

24. Zhong, *Yongan*, 99–102, on Yongan printing. The tables of contents, from 1851 and 1853, in *Yinshu* editions of *You xue shi* and *Taiping jiushi ge* both show thirteen titles. The New Testament was not included. The misprinting of item 9, *Taiping tiaogui*, in these two volumes as *Taiping guitiao*, was later corrected, and serves as evidence of these texts' early date.

25. *TR*, 153–55, some changes following *Sanzijing*, in *Yinshu*, 1b–6b. Since the biblical term for "manna" was rendered "sweet dew" in Chinese, I use "manna" here.

26. *TR*, 121–22, modified from *Tiantiao shu*, *Yinshu*, 7b–8.

27. *TR*, 109; *Tianming zhaozhi shu*, in *Yinshu*, 12b–13.

28. *TR*, 108, *Tianming zhaozhi shu*, in *Yinshu*, 12b, *guifei*.

29. *Tianxiong shengzhi*, 2:28b.

30. *You xue shi*, in *Yinshu*, 9, modifying *TR*, 166. For the imagery in the third line of the husband's stanza—*Hedong shizi*, "the lion east of the river"—see the lengthy entry in Murohashi, *Daikanwa*, 6:6727. The third line of the wife's stanza, literally "if the hen calls out the dawn," has the sense of the English-language idiom "if the woman wears the trousers."

31. *TR*, 129–30. Jen, *Tongkao*, 2:1251–59, surveys the evidence and provides some names. The man known as Hong Daquan estimated in 1852 that Hong had thirty-six consorts in the city, and took "thirty or so" of them with him when he left. See the confession of Hong Daquan, in *TR*, 191–92. But the exact rank and identity of this man have been long debated and the accuracy of his confession disputed. See *TR*, 187–88; Guo Tingyi, *Shishi*, 153–75; Jen, *Revolutionary Movement*, 84.

32. *TR*, 110, modified according to *Tianming zhaozhi shu*, in *Yinshu*, 14.

33. Zhong, *Yongan*, 106–7.

34. *TR*, 109, modified according to *Tianming zhaozhi shu*, in *Yinshu*, 13.

35. Zhong, *Yongan*, 122, 127.

36. Jen, *Revolutionary Movement*, 83–86; Zhong, *Yongan*, 127; *TR*, 191–92, confession of Hong Daquan; Curwen, *Deposition*, 83–84.

CHAPTER 12: THE HUNT

1. Jen, *Revolutionary Movement*, 85; Curwen, *Deposition*, 187 n. 60.

2. Laai, "Pirates," 205–7.

3. See analysis by Zhong, "Youguan Taiping Jun."

4. Jen, *Revolutionary Movement*, 86; Curwen, *Deposition*, 187 n. 61.

5. Laai, "Pirates," 245, 256.

6. Ibid., 254–56. Ling was killed by Qing troops in July 1852.

7. Guo Yishu, *Ditu*, 47–48; Laai, "Pirates," 208, 257. This bribe led to Big-head Yang's execution by the Qing.

8. Jen, *Revolutionary Movement*, 88–89. When exactly Feng was fatally wounded is still debated by historians. Luo Ergang, *Taiping Tianguo shi*, vol. 3, juan 43, agrees with Jen Yu-wen; but Mao Jiaqi, in *Taiping Tianguo tongshi*, 1:307–12, expresses doubt that Feng was first struck at Quanzhou. My thanks to Xia Chuntao for clarification of this point.

9. Jen, *Revolutionary Movement*, 89–90.

10. Guo Tingyi, *Shishi*, 181.

11. Kuhn, *Rebellion*, 106–7; Cai, "Lei Zaihao he Li Yuanfa," concludes these were not Tiandihui risings.

12. Kuhn, *Rebellion*, 106–11.

13. Ibid., 113–15; *Eminent Chinese*, 136–37.

14. Jen, *Quanshi*, 1:388–89, based on his own survey of the area; Laai, "Pirates," 258.

15. Guo Yisheng, *Ditu*, 49–50; Jen, *Revolutionary Movement*, 90–92; Guo Tingyi, *Shishi*, 182, estimates the date a little later, on June 10; Laai, "Pirates," 258–59.

16. Guo Yisheng, *Ditu*, 53; Curwen, *Deposition*, 188 n. 65.

17. *TR*, 143, 148.

18. *TR*, 144.

19. Zhong, "Taiping jun daqi," 246–47; see also *Taiping Tianguo shige qiantan*, 13–17, 50.

20. *TR*, 146, modified following *Banxing zhaoshu*, in *Yinshu*, 5b.

21. *TR*, 148, modified following *Banxing zhaoshu*, in *Yinshu*, 7b.

22. *TR*, 146–47, modified following *Banxzing zhaoshu*, in *Yinshu*, 6.

23. *TR*, 145–46, modified following *Banxing zhaoshu*, in *Yinshu*, 4b–5.

24. *TR*, 147; *Banxing zhaoshu*, in *Yinshu*, 6b; Wilhelm / Baynes, *I-Ching*, 9. For parallel slogans on early Taiping banners, see Zhong, "Taiping jun daqi," 244–45.

25. *TR*, 151; *Banxing zhaoshu*, in *Yinshu*, 10b.

26. Curwen, *Deposition*, 84; Wang, "Renzi ernian," 166.

27. Curwen, *Deposition*, 84, 188 n. 65; Laai, "Pirates," 261.

28. Wang, "Renzi ernian," 164–69; Guo Tingyi, *Shishi*, 186–92; Jen, *Revolutionary Movement*, 98. With Xiao's death following Feng's, the subordinate kings have been reduced from five to three; though this news is surely known to all inside the Taiping ranks, Hong regularly issues decrees in the dead kings' names. The Qing learn the news when captured Taiping prisoners reveal the location of Xiao's grave to their Qing inquisitors and his corpse is disinterred, dismembered, and defaced. See Cheng, *Taiping Rebellion*, 31.

29. Wang, "Renzi ernian," 170.

30. See ibid., 172, for calculations.

31. *Eminent Chinese*, 537; *Qingshi liezhuan*, 45:24.

32. *Qingshi liezhuan*, 45:25b–26.

33. Laai, "Pirates," 262; Wang, "Renzi ernian," 179–82, on Shi Dakai; Guo Yisheng, *Ditu*, 55.

34. Curwen, *Deposition*, 189, 191, discusses these techniques at various sieges; Wang, "Renzi ernian," 182–83.

35. Curwen, *Deposition*, 189.

36. This seems to be the ex-pirate Luo Dagang's idea coordinated with those of Yang Xiuqing, the East King. Laai, "Pirates," 241–42, 263.

37. *TR*, 421–22.

38. *TR*, 423–24.

39. *TR*, 421, slightly modified from *Xingjun zongyao*, in *Yinshu*, 5.

40. Li Xiucheng in Curwen, *Deposition*, 83, talks of villagers lost one hundred *li* from home.

41. *TR*, 417–18, slightly modified from *Xingjun zongyao*, in *Yinshu*, 1.

42. *TR*, 391–92.

43. Jen, *Revolutionary Movement*, 100–102; Laai, "Pirates," 264–68.

44. Chen Huiyan, *Wuchang jishi*, 587–90.

45. Zhao, "Chengshi zhengce," 49–50; Chen Huiyan, *Wuchang jishi*, 593–96.

46. Cheng, *Taiping Rebellion*, 27–30.

47. Laai, "Pirates," 268–69.

48. Curwen, *Deposition*, 193–94 n. 86.

49. Jen, *Revolutionary Movement*, 108–12.

50. *TR*, 185–86.

51. *TR*, 183–84, slightly modified and titles translated.

52. Rait, *Gough*, 1:278–79; Davis, *China during the War*, 1:289.

53. Jen, *Revolutionary Movement*, 116–18, 124; Zhang Runan, *Jinling*, 692–705; Withers, "Heavenly Capital," 58–62.

CHAPTER 13: THE EARTHLY PARADISE

1. *TR*, 314–15, 320, and *Tianchao tianmou*, in *Yinshu*, 2b–3, 7b. Bohr, "Eschatology," 219–66, discusses the Nanjing early years of the Taiping as a "theocratic millennium." Bohr emphasizes the importance of Hong's biblical commentaries at this time, though I see their composition and influence as coming later in the Taiping, after the death of Yang Xiuqing.

2. *TR*, 314–15; *Tianchao tianmou*, *Yinshu*, 2b–3. Kuhn, "Taiping Rebellion," 279, points out the "perplexing problem" that the land regulations never discuss "the idea of periodic reallocation of land."

3. *TR*, 314–15.

4. *TR*, 320; *Tianchao tianmou*, in *Yinshu*, 8.

5. *TR*, 318–19.

6. Xie, *Jinling guijia*, 651; Zhang Runan, *Jinling*, 695.

7. *TR*, 564–65. The originals of some other household registration sheets are preserved in the Jen Yu-wen Collection.

8. *TR*, 566–69.

9. Withers, "Heavenly Capital," 199–200; Zhao, "Chengshi zhengce," 50–52.

10. Jen, *Revolutionary Movement*, 121–22, on the Hankou merchant Wu Fucheng; Withers, "Heavenly Capital," 76–77, discusses women's dress and makeup.

11. *TR*, 448–50; Chin, *Shiliao*, 130–31; Jen Yu-wen Collection.

12. See Withers, "Heavenly Capital," 87–90.

13. Alexander Wylie, report of 1859, cited in Clarke and Gregory, *Reports*, 220.

14. Report by Xavier Maresca, in Mercier, *Cassini*, 268–69; on disorder, see Withers, "Heavenly Capital" 53–54.

15. Report of Xavier Maresca, in Mercier, *Cassini*, 269–72.

16. By an even more ironic decision, the office of gunpowder manufacture is placed in the former temple to Guandi, Goddess of Mercy. Withers, "Heavenly Capital," 104, 107–8; Jen, *Revolutionary Movement*, 126; Qi, "Taiping Tianguo wenshu," and Wang Qingcheng, "Guanyu zhizhun banxing," discuss problems of printing and dispersion.

17. Despite the appearance of the Old Testament, *Jiuyizhao shengshu*, in some Taiping indexes of 1852, Wang Qingcheng argues firmly for the 1853 date—"Guanyu zhizhun banxing," esp. 190 and 196–97. For variants in the early edition, see Xia, *Zongjiao*, 91 n. 2; *TR*, 221, citing *NCH*, July 16, 1853.

18. See British Museum edition, *Jiuyi jiaoshengshu*, and ibid., *Yinshu*, 24; Xia, *Zongjiao*, 96–97. Though the theological issue is more complex than Hong thought, given the fact that Moab descended from Lot, and Ruth (wife of Boaz) was a Moabite. I am grateful to George Doramajian for this valuable gloss.

19. On numbers of printers, see Fishbourne, *Impressions*, 391, for the 400 figure, and Taylor, *Five Years*, 369–70, for 600 and on Matthew; *TR*, 222–24.

20. Jen, *Revolutionary Movement*, 165–66; Guo Yisheng, *Ditu*, 67, 73.

21. *TR*, 253, slightly modified by *Jian Tianjing yu Jinling lun*, in *Yinshu*, 1; other references are in *TR*, 254–76.

22. *TR*, 296, 307.

23. *TR*, 298–99. Three examples of wooden Taiping seals are preserved in the Jen Yu-wen Collection.

24. *TR*, 305, 307.

25. "*Qianshan sheng.*" *TR*, 277–78; *Bian yaoxue*, in *Yinshu*, 1.

26. *TR*, 289, 291.

27. *TR*, 291; *Bian yaoxue*, in *Yinshu*, 9b; and *TR*, 252, on degree.

28. Shi, "Zaozi yu gaizi," 157, 159.

29. Ibid., 157.

30. Ibid., 158–59.

31. Ibid., 157; on pp. 151–55 Shi analyzes 78 Taiping words in two basic categories: 22 new coinages and 56 substitutions; on p. 160 he adds 9 marginal variants. For Taiping period lists, see Zhang Runan, *Jinling*, 718, 722; Zhang Dejian, *Zeqing*, 242–44; *Qinding jing bi ziyang*; Xie, *Jinling*, 654; also see Luo Ergang, "Jingji kao," 27–28. For British queries in 1854 on the reasoning behind some of these taboos, see Gregory, *Great Britain*, 182.

32. *TR*, 394, 396.

33. *TR*, 458.

34. *TR*, 580; Zhang Dejian, *Zeqing*, 231.

35. *TR*, 457.

36. *TR*, 563, citing Guo Tingyi, *Shishi*, 1:232; Withers, "Heavenly Capital," 105–6, 108.

37. Zhang Runan, *Jinling*, 695.

38. Ibid., 716; Zhao, "Chengshi zhengce," 50, 52–53.

39. *TR*, 474, for poison plot; 473, for planned uprising.

40. *TR*, 451, minor changes.

41. See Jen, *Revolutionary Movement*, 139–40, and the couplets in *TR*, 548–55.

42. *TR*, 452; Zhang Dejian, *Zeqing*, 204.

43. *TR*, 466.

44. 466; Chin, *Shiliao*, 133.

45. As with the three doctors in Clarke and Gregory, *Reports*, 185. See also the discussion and references in Withers, "Heavenly Capital," 108–10.

46. Guo Yisheng, *Ditu*, 59–64; *TR*, 533, and Zhang Runan, *Jinling*, 705–6.

47. For palace information, see *TR*, 459, 487; Zhang Runan, *Jinling*, 705, 706, on Hong and Yang residences; Taiping art is collected in *Taiping Tianguo yishu*; see also the analysis by Audrey Spiro in her "Paintings of the Heavenly Kingdom."

48. Zhang Runan, *Jinling*, 710; Jen, *Revolutionary Movement*, 130; Withers, "Heavenly Capital," 174.

49. Taylor, *Five Years*, 341–42, on Zhenjiang in June 1853; *TR*, 578–79, on stakes; Zhang Dejian, *Zeqing*, 134–36, has vivid illustrations of the spikes and palisades.

50. *TR*, 436, from *Xingjun zongyao*.

51. *Yuzhi qianzi zhao*, in *Yinshu*, 1–2; *TR*, 409.

52. *TR*, 415, modified following *Yuzhi qianzi zhao*, in *Yinshu*, 13b–14.

CHAPTER 14: THREE SHIPS

1. Wong, *Calendar,* 225, item 4; *BPP* / IUP, 12, 13, on the three ships; Mercier, *Cassini,* 228, on Bonham's and *Hermes*'s arrival on March 21; ibid., 229, on *Susquehanna*'s presence there; ibid., 222, on *Cassini*'s anchoring in Shanghai on March 15; ibid., 224, on Chinese requests that *Cassini* go to Nanjing, for March 17 and 19; p. 231 for April 5.

2. Mercier, *Cassini,* 229.

3. Ibid., 231, 233.

4. Ibid., 237.

5. *NCH,* April 2, 1853; Mercier, *Cassini,* 245; *BPP* / IUP, 24.

6. *NCH,* April 9, 1853.

7. Mercier, *Cassini,* 251, 254.

8. Clarke and Gregory, *Reports,* 3–35, has a sampling of these sources.

9. Ibid., 19–20, and Wylie, *Memorials,* 95, both citing the *Chinese and General Missionary Gleaner.*

10. *BPP* / IUP, 23.

11. Ibid., 11, March 28, 1853.

12. Ibid., 12–13; Gregory, *Great Britain,* 15–24, for a summary of the mission; Mercier, *Cassini,* 221, on Portuguese.

13. *BPP* / IUP, 15.

14. Ibid., 26.

15. Ibid., 26, 28.

16. Ibid., 40.

17. Ibid., 34, 38.

18. Ibid., 38.

19. Ibid., 37.

20. Ibid.

21. Fishbourne, *Impressions,* 141–44, 152, 154–55.

22. See Meadows in *BPP* / IUP, 45–54.

23. *BPP* / IUP, 41–42; also cited in *TR,* 515–17.

24. *BPP* / IUP, 42–43.

25. Ibid., 32, 35.

26. Ibid., 32, 54.

27. *NCH,* May 14, 1853.

28. Wong, *Calendar,* 228–29, items 23 and 26.

29. Mercier, *Cassini,* 17, 18.

30. Ibid., 23–24, 29–30, 42–44, 52–53.

31. Ibid., 229–31.

32. *BPP* / IUP, 19–25, on defenses.

33. Mercier, *Cassini,* 320.

34. Ibid., 318, 326, 328. That this continued to be a problem for the French is shown by the 1854 letter of Consul Edan to Alcock, March 19, 1854, stored in PRO/FO 671/2.

35. Mercier, *Cassini,* 222, 325, 366.

36. Ibid., 258, 338–39.

37. Ibid., 340–43.

38. Clavelin, cited in Clarke and Gregory, *Reports,* 94.

39. Ibid., 96.

40. Ibid., 94–96.
41. Ibid., 106–9.
42. Ibid., 97.
43. Ibid.
44. Ibid., 100; Jen, *Revolutionary Movement,* 273–74.
45. Clarke and Gregory, *Reports,* 101.
46. Mercier, *Cassini,* 356.
47. Cited from French Foreign Ministry archives by Clarke and Gregory, *Reports,* 90.
48. Translated by the author from Mercier, *Cassini,* 363–65.
49. Ibid., 372–73.
50. Ibid., 229.
51. Tong, *Diplomacy,* 122 n. 8, 126; Mercier, *Cassini,* 246, 251.
52. Mercier, *Cassini,* 257, 294, 370; on Marshall and Perry see R. E. Johnson, *China Station,* 63–66; Tong, *Diplomacy,* 121–25.
53. *TR,* 125.
54. Teng Yuan Chung, "Roberts" 60; Wylie, *Memorials,* 95.
55. Teng Yuan Chung, "Roberts," 60.
56. Ibid., 61.
57. NA-DD, Microcopy 92, roll 10, Macao, April 8, 1854; and Shanghai, June 14, 1854; Teng Yuan Chung, "Roberts," 61; Tong, *Diplomacy,* 148–49.
58. NA-DD, 92:10, Capt. Buchanan letter of May 26, 1854, enclosed with McLane of June 14 and marked "Exhibit A"; also cited in *TR,* 521–22.
59. Clarke and Gregory, *Reports,* 109; *TR,* 525.
60. *TR,* 526.
61. As recalled by Lewin Bowring, in Clarke and Gregory, *Reports,* 168.
62. *TR,* 528–29.
63. *TR,* 529–30, citing NA-DD, 92:10, enclosed with McLane of June 14, but reworking it in light of the Chinese original.
64. *TR,* 527.
65. NA-DD, memorandum of June 1, 1854, enclosed with McLane of June 14 as Exhibit C, Dispatch no. 6, by Charles F. Forbes, Assistant Surgeon.
66. See the Irish mercenary quoted in Clarke and Gregory, *Reports,* 199.
67. NA-DD, June 1, 1854, Exhibit C.
68. *TR,* 531.
69. Clarke and Gregory, *Reports,* 131.
70. McLane June 14, cited ibid., 133.
71. Ibid., 135.
72. Ibid., 136–37.

CHAPTER 15: THE SPLIT

1. Jen, *Revolutionary Movement,* 171, 175.
2. Ibid., 185–88.
3. Ibid., 182–83.
4. Ibid., 193–94; Guo Yisheng, *Ditu,* 67–68.
5. Wright, *Last Stand,* chap. 9; Kuhn, *Rebellion,* chap. 4.
6. Jen, *Revolutionary Movement,* 237–38. Chen was the nephew of Chen Chengyong.

7. Ibid., 202–3, 210–12; Guo Yisheng, *Ditu,* 73–74, 77.

8. Jen, *Revolutionary Movement,* 196–98, 254–56; Wakeman, *Strangers,* chaps. 14 and 15; Guo Yisheng, *Ditu,* 97.

9. Jen, *Revolutionary Movement,* 131–32; Withers, "Heavenly Capital," 178–80.

10. Guo Tingyi, *Shishi,* appendix, 41–44.

11. Jen, *Revolutionary Movement,* 206–7, on communications, and 209.

12. *TR,* 199–200, 203.

13. *TR,* 200, 204, 213.

14. *TR,* 205, 215, 217. An early warning of Hong's violence to his wife was given by Jesus through Xiao Chaogui in 1849; see *Tianxiong shengzhi,* 1:13b.

15. *TR,* 205–7, one change.

16. *TR,* 214–15.

17. *TR,* 217; *Tianfu xiafan zhaoshu,* no. 2, in *Yinshu,* 19.

18. See reprises in *Tianxiong shengzhi,* 1:5, Daoguang 28 (1848) middle of 11th month.

19. Ibid., 1:13, Daoguang 29/1/18.

20. Ibid., 2:14b, Daoguang 30/8/1.

21. *TR,* 217; *Tianfu xiafan zhaoshu,* no. 2, in *Yinshu,* 19.

22. *Tianxiong shengzhi,* 1:3b–4, Daoguang 28/10/24.

23. W. H. Medhurst, the original author of this Chinese text, translated it back into English with meticulous notations on the additions and deletions, the whole Hong version appearing in *NCH,* Sept. 22, Sept. 29, Oct. 6, 1855. See also *TR,* 344–64.

24. *TR,* 201–3, 219; *Tianfu xiafan zhaoshu,* no. 2, in *Yinshu,* 20b; 1 John 5:7; *TR,* 234, for Hong's familiarity with the verse; and Jen, *Revolutionary Movement,* 159–60.

25. *TR,* 204; *Tianfu xiafan zhaoshu,* no. 2, in *Yinshu,* 7, where Qin (the "Ting-t'ien-hou") has to *fu*(a), or "carry on the back," the East King, while Wei *fu*(b), "escorts," Hong to his palace.

26. *TR,* 218, modified following *Tianfu xiafan zhaoshu,* no. 2, in *Yinshu,* 20.

27. *TR,* 214, *Tianfu xiafan zhaoshu,* no. 2, *Yinshu,* 17.

28. Fishbourne, *Impressions,* 239 n, for Tiangui as the third brother; *TR,* 202 n, citing Xie Jiehe, a Nanjing resident under the Taiping, for Feng.

29. *TR,* 377–78.

30. *TR,* 379, 391; Xia, *Zongjiao,* 93.

31. *Tianfu shengzhi,* 5–9, dated Taiping 4/1/27. Manacled were Chen Chengyong, Meng De'en, and Shi Dakai's father-in-law, Huang Yukun; accused and pardoned, Lu Xianba; see Jen, *Revolutionary Movement,* 161, for Lu's Ten Commandments work; executed was Chen Zongyang.

32. In *Tianfu shengzhi,* 7, God / Yang specifically reminds the audience of the earlier Huang Yizhen and Zhou Xineng cases. For Zhou, see also *TR,* 89–97; for Huang, *TR,* 102, 443.

33. *Tianfu shengzhi,* 3–4; see also Wagner, "Operating," 133–34, for a somewhat different translation and analysis.

34. *Tianxiong shengzhi,* 1:5b–6; Wang, *Tianfu,* 7; Wagner, "Operating," 131.

35. *TR,* 200–16, identifies four different passages quoted by Yang from the *Analects* and one from the *Great Learning.*

36. Jen, *Revolutionary Movement,* 230–31, original translation by Jen Yu-wen, slightly modified following Chinese text in Jen's *Quanshi,* 2:1084.

37. Jen, *Revolutionary Movement,* 266–67, and *Quanshi,* 2:1271–76.

38. Gregory, *Great Britain,* 173; most of this report by Lewin Bowring and W. H. Medhurst Jr. is included in Clarke and Gregory, *Reports,* 157–71. Their entire longhand draft, with deletions and corrections, is preserved in PRO / FO 671/2.

39. PRO / FO 17/214, folio pp. 198v–99, also cited in full in Gregory, *Great Britain,* 180–86, quotations on 181; Clarke and Gregory, *Reports,* 170, on the envelope.

40. PRO / FO 17/214, folio pp. 203r and v; Gregory, *Great Britain,* 186. Two key discussions of this passage are Wagner, *Heavenly Vision,* 44–46, 65, and Xia, *Zongjiao,* 103–8.

41. Gregory, *Great Britain,* 187–88.

42. Ibid., 190–91.

43. PRO / FO 17/214, folio p. 207v; Gregory, *Great Britain,* 189–90; Lewin Bowring in Clarke and Gregory, *Reports,* 171, on the "synod."

44. Gregory, *Great Britain,* 193.

45. Clarke and Gregory, *Reports,* 165, 168.

46. *Tianfu shengzhi,* 12b–13, dated Taiping 4/6/1; Xia, *Zongjiao,* 98–100; Wagner, "Operating," 136–37.

47. *Tianfu shengzhi,* 12b–13b, dated Taiping 4/6/1.

CHAPTER 16: THE KILLING

1. *Tianfu shengzhi,* 15, dated Taiping 5/3/19; Clarke and Gregory, *Reports,* 187.

2. *TR,* 442, modified following Xiang, *Ziliao,* 3:191; *Tianfu shengzhi,* 16, dated 5/6/17.

3. See seven examples in *Tianfu shengzhi,* dated 4/8/24, 4/12/13, 5/2/13, 5/6/7, 5/6/17, 5/8/17, and 5/11/2.

4. All these procedures can be seen in *Tianfu shengzhi,* 20–24b, dated 5/7/19, and 32b–33, dated 6/3/5.

5. I.e., *Tianfu shengzhi,* 25b–27b, dated 5/8/26; Clarke and Gregory, *Reports,* 196, shows a case of Hong going to Yang's palace.

6. *Tianfu shengzhi,* 26b, dated 5/8/26.

7. Ibid., 31b, dated 5/9/5.

8. Ibid., 29b, dated 5/8/27, calling God "Tian Agong."

9. See Guo Tingyi, *Shishi,* appendix, 21, for their 1854 kingships as Yanwang and Yuwang; *Tianfu shengzhi,* 14, dated 4/12/13; Jen, *Revolutionary Movement,* 292, for cancellation.

10. *Tianfu shengzhi,* 14b–15, dated 5/2/13.

11. *TR,* 385–86, case of Li Yusong; for this punishment, see Zhang Runan, *Jinling,* 716.

12. *TR,* 393–94, case of Li Fengxian.

13. *Tianfu shengzhi,* 16b–19b, dated 5/6/28, for four such cases.

14. Ibid., 19b–20, dated 5/6/30.

15. Jen, *Revolutionary Movement,* 278–86; Clarke and Gregory, *Reports,* 181–85.

16. Jen, *Revolutionary Movement,* 290–91; Curwen, *Deposition,* 86.

17. Curwen, *Deposition,* 198; Clarke and Gregory, *Reports,* 180; Dr. J. MacGowan, in an article for *NCH,* April 25, 1857, nicknames the man "Canny," but does not query the accuracy of his account. E. C. Bridgman, in an earlier letter to *NCH,* Jan. 2, 1857, also sees "no reason to question the accuracy" of the Irishman's story. The entire account is printed in three consecutive issues of the *Overland Friend of China,* 1857: Jan. 15, issue 1, p. 2; Jan. 21, issue 2, p. 10; Jan. 30, issue 3, supplement. These will be cited as #1, #2, and #3. My special thanks to Nicholas Spence for procuring the copies of this text for me.

18. Wong, *Calendar*, 228–29, item 26.

19. Gregory, *Great Britain*, 208, citing Captain Mellersh, June 24, 1854; another "negro" who joined the Taiping in 1853 is mentioned in Clarke and Gregory, *Reports*, 182.

20. Gregory, *Great Britain*, 34.

21. Clarke and Gregory, *Reports*, 82, quoting Mr. Williams, June 30, 1853.

22. Gregory, *Great Britain*, 35; Wakeman, *Strangers*, 147.

23. Bowring to Clarendon, Jan. 25, 1855, cited in Gregory, *Great Britain*, 215 n. 12.

24. Mercier, *Cassini*, 225, 284.

25. Clarke and Gregory, *Reports*, 181, 186.

26. Clarke and Gregory, *Reports*, 182.

27. *Overland Friend*, #1; Clarke and Gregory, *Reports*, 181.

28. *Overland Friend*, #1; Clarke and Gregory, *Reports*, 182.

29. Clarke and Gregory, *Reports*, 183, 185, 198.

30. Ibid., 184–85.

31. Ibid., 186–87.

32. *Overland Friend*, #2; Clarke and Gregory, *Reports*, 187.

33. *Overland Friend*, #3; Clarke and Gregory, *Reports*, 196.

34. Clarke and Gregory, *Reports*, 187–88, 199.

35. Ibid., 195, 199.

36. Ibid., 196; *Overland Friend*, #3.

37. Clarke and Gregory, *Reports*, 193.

38. *Tianfu shengzhi*, 34, dated 6/7/9.

39. *Overland Friend*, #2; Clarke and Gregory, *Reports*, 188.

40. Jen, *Revolutionary Movement*, 294–95; Curwen, *Deposition*, 86, 196–98. I follow Jen Yuwen and Li Xiucheng in placing Qin at the scene, rather than the version in Guo Tingyi; see Curwen, *Deposition*, 89, 209 n. 19.

41. Clarke and Gregory, *Reports*, 189.

42. *Overland Friend*, #2; Clarke and Gregory, *Reports*, 190–91.

43. *Overland Friend*, #2 and #3, records that 500 of Yang's former palace women were beheaded, and gives a dramatic but unlikely figure of 40,000 for the total of Yang's followers killed; Clarke and Gregory, *Reports*, 190–92, 196.

44. Jen, *Revolutionary Movement*, 299–300; Clarke and Gregory, *Reports*, 191; Curwen, *Deposition*, 86–87, 198.

45. Clarke and Gregory, *Reports*, 193, describes his departure from the Yangzi force.

46. *Overland Friend*, #2; Clarke and Gregory, *Reports*, 195.

47. *Overland Friend*, #3; Clarke and Gregory, *Reports*, 195.

CHAPTER 17: FAMILY CIRCLES

1. *TR*, 931 n. 1.

2. *TR*, 989–91; Jen, *Revolutionary Movement*, 158 n. 52.

3. Guo Tingyi, *Shishi*, 755, and appendix, 20; *TR*, 931.

4. Jen, *Revolutionary Movement*, 301–2; Guo Tingyi, *Shishi*, appendix, 20 and 22.

5. Clarke and Gregory, *Reports*, 194.

6. Curwen, *Deposition*, 87, 91; *TR*, 1401, follows the *NCH* version of 1865.

7. *TR*, 697, modified following Xiang, *Ziliao*, 2:694.

8. Curwen, *Deposition*, 92.

9. Kuhn, *Rebellion,* pt. 4; Wright, *Last Stand,* 73–77.

10. *Qingdai dangan,* 1:2, 7, 10, 14, 20, 29.

11. Ibid., 57–58, Xianfeng 7/3/23 and 7/8/5; ibid., 62–63, 8/6/24, shows that in 1858 the annual Manchu winter hunts were canceled as a further economy measure.

12. As argued by Li Xiucheng, cited in Curwen, *Deposition,* 92.

13. Guo Tingyi, *Shishi,* appendix, 19 and 23; *TR,* 981–82.

14. Jen, *Revolutionary Movement,* 352–53; Guo Tingyi, *Shishi,* appendix, 23, 24, 38, for the "guozong" and the 1856 and 1857 dates. The "guozong" category also contained relatives of the other kings.

15. *BPP* / IUP, 153; also cited in *TR,* 985.

16. See his confession, in *TR,* 1530. Other contemporaries suggested a total of 148 consorts or more—see *TR,* 585, and Zhang Dejian, *Zeqing,* 310. All of these consorts were entitled to the honorable term of *niangniang,* or Senior Queen, and were not divided into a hierarchy of concubines by rank, as in the imperial model prevalent in Peking. See Jen, *Revolutionary Movement,* 138.

17. Confession, in *TR,* 1531.

18. *TR,* 898–900, *Youzhu zhaoshu;* memorization, *TR,* 1531.

19. *Tianfu shi,* in *Yinshu,* vol. 14, dated 1857, *TR,* 585–666, cited by stanza numbers, which are identical in the English and the Chinese versions.

20. Stanzas 139, 157, 358.

21. Stanzas 134–37, 243–45.

22. Stanzas 218, 304, 151, 230.

23. Stanzas 148, 394, 470, 212; 189 for organ, *fengqin.*

24. Stanzas 170, 260, 416.

25. Trash, stanza 129; leprosy, 446, 490; spittoons, 152, 154, 296; insects, 158, 159, 241; fans, 177, 263.

26. Stanzas 192, 303.

27. Stanzas 179–80, 188, 297, 224, 281.

28. Body, stanza, 283; face, 485, 200, 393; feet, 174; navel, 485.

29. Stanzas 216, 197, 237.

30. Stanzas 267, 337, 338, 310.

31. Stanzas 46, 107, 153, 281.

32. Stanzas 284, 393, 286, 410–11, 9, 282.

33. Stanza 412.

34. Stanzas 217, 247, 414, 415, 422, 423, 426.

35. *TR,* 1531, Young Monarch's confession.

36. Stanzas 265, 427.

37. Stanzas 275, 30.

38. Stanzas 392, 364, 390, 375.

39. *Tianfu shi,* in *Yinshu,* 28, stanza 313. A different rendering is in *TR,* 636.

40. Stanzas 55, 312. The same message seems implicit in stanzas 187 and 354.

41. Stanzas 378, 389.

42. Stanzas 164, 264.

43. Stanzas 264, 328.

44. Mistakes, stanza 327; good cheer, 212, 343, 362; beating, 17, 18, 111, 189; death, 340; women bathed, 429, 432.

45. Stanza 21.

46. The British Library, Oriental and India Office Collections, Blackfriars Road, London, contains two versions of the early Taiping Bible: the slightly modified Gutzlaff version, *Jiuyizhao shengshu* (comprising Genesis 1–28, call number 15116.b.9), and the only known surviving copy of *Qinding Jiuyizhao shengshu* (Genesis through Joshua) containing Hong's full range of revisions (call number 15117.e.20) For brevity, these will be cited here as Bibles A and B. A virtually complete listing of all variants is given by Wu Liangzuo and Luo Wenqi in their invaluable essay "Taiping Tianguo yinshu jiaokan ji," 267–73.

47. *Tianfu shi,* stanza 448; *TR,* 657.

48. Wu and Luo, "Yinshu," 267.

49. Ibid., 268; a similar insertion is made in Genesis 18:16 and 22, and 48:16.

50. As Hong does in Genesis 38:12 and 43:29.

51. Wu and Luo, "Yinshu," 274.

52. See Bibles A and B, 1:11b; Wu and Luo, "Yinshu," 267.

53. *Genesis,* 20:2–13, *Yinshu,* 24b–25; Wu and Luo, "Yinshu," 268–69. The parallel story of Abimelech seeing Isaac "sporting" with Rebekah, in Genesis 26:7–9, uses almost identical words to clear Isaac of deceit; Wu and Luo, "Yinshu," 269.

54. Divide is "fen." Genesis 25:31–34, Bibles A and B, 1:34b; Wu and Luo, "Yinshu," 269.

55. Bibles A and B, 1:36–37b; Wu and Luo, "Yinshu," 270–71. Hong purges other references to wine as an offering—for instance, from Leviticus 23:13 and Numbers 6:20 and 18:27.

56. Wu and Luo, "Yinshu," 281.

57. For all these corrections see Wu and Luo, "Yinshu," 272–73.

58. Ibid., 275. To make space for his own rewriting, Hong cuts Exodus 22:18 altogether.

CHAPTER 18: THE WRONG MAN

1. Arrival, in *BPP / Elgin,* 19; armaments, Walrond, *Elgin,* 190, 192, 195, 198, and *BPP / Elgin,* 35, 40.

2. Earl of Clarendon to Elgin, April 20, 1857, *BPP / Elgin,* 2–3, 5. For an analysis of the "Arrow War" that sparked his mission see Fairbank, *Trade,* and Wong, *Arrow War.*

3. For the Elgins, father and son, see *DNB,* 104–6, 130–31.

4. Oliphant, *Narrative,* 1:292–350; Walrond, *Elgin,* 210–57.

5. *Tianxiong shengzhi,* 1:3, dated Daoguang, 28/10/24.

6. Ibid., 1:12b, dated Daoguang, 29/1/16.

7. *BPP / Elgin,* 444; Walrond, *Elgin,* 285.

8. *BPP / Elgin,* 444.

9. Walrond, *Elgin,* 285.

10. Oliphant, *Narrative,* 2:311.

11. Quotations from ibid., 313–14; see also Walrond, *Elgin,* 285; *BPP / Elgin,* 455.

12. *BPP / Elgin,* 454; *TR,* 713.

13. *BPP / Elgin,* 471–72, Wade's translation with romanization modified; *TR,* 717.

14. *TR,* 718–19; *BPP / Elgin,* 472–73; Chin, *Shiliao,* 95–97.

15. Chinese text in Chin, *Shiliao,* 97–98; partly following translations by Thomas Wade in *BPP / Elgin,* 473, and *TR,* 720.

16. Oliphant, *Narrative,* 2:461.

17. Ibid., 454.

18. Chin *Shiliao,* 138–39; *BPP / Elgin,* 470; *TR,* 721–22.

19. Walrond, *Elgin,* 301–2; on the trip, see *BPP / Elgin,* 470; Oliphant, *Narrative,* 2:447–48.

20. *BPP / Elgin,* 451, Wade's account.

Chapter 19: New Worlds

1. Jen, *Revolutionary Movement,* 356–57; Guo Tingyi, *Shishi,* appendix, 23.

2. Jen, *Revolutionary Movement,* 351–56.

3. Xiang, *Ziliao,* 2:846, modifying *TR,* 1511.

4. *TR,* 759 n. 7, 760–61 nn. 8–10; see also Wylie, *Memorials,* 159–60, for Hamberg; 175–76 for Burns; 117–22 for Legge; 125–28 for Hobson; Yung, *My Life,* 108. Yung had been in the Yale College class of 1854.

5. Pfister, "Legge," pt. 2, p. 34.

6. Legge, "Colony," 169.

7. Pfister, "Legge," pt. 1, p. 44; Legge, "Colony," 172.

8. Legge, "Colony," 171–72.

9. Wylie, *Memorials,* 118; Pfister, "Legge," pt. 1, p. 45. Other missionaries had also championed the use of Shangdi, though it remained a controversial choice to many. A full summary of the various arguments is given in Medhurst, *Dissertation.*

10. Legge's view as summarized by Pfister, in "Legge," pt. 1, pp. 48–49.

11. Ibid., pt. 2, pp. 35–36.

12. Welsh, *Hong Kong,* 169; Legge, "Colony," 165–66, 171.

13. Legge, "Colony," 167–68; Welsh, *Hong Kong,* 164–66, 218.

14. Legge, "Colony," 165; Welsh, *Hong Kong,* 212, on Caldwell, and 152, on entrepreneurs.

15. Legge, "Colony," 171.

16. Pfister, "Legge," pt. 1, p. 44; Jen, *Revolutionary Movement,* 356.

17. *TR,* 1512; Jen, *Revolutionary Movement,* 357, citing Lin-le, *Ti-ping,* 1:226; Wylie, *Memorials,* 217–18, on Chalmers, who received the letter, Legge being away at the time.

18. *TR,* 765, 767; Hong Rengan, *Zizheng xinbian,* in *Yinshu,* 14, 16.

19. On insurance, *TR,* 769; houses, 771; banks, 765–66; roads, 764, 765; patents, 766.

20. *TR,* 768–69.

21. *TR,* 767; a rather similar comment of Hong's is on p. 764.

22. *TR,* 772, slight changes from *Zizheng xinbian,* in *Yinshu,* 21.

23. Yung, *My Life,* 110.

24. J. S. Burdon, in Clarke and Gregory, *Reports,* 240; Forrest, "Taipings at Home," *NCH,* Oct. 19, 1861, also cited ibid., 360.

25. "Questions Recently Addressed to the Kan Wang," *NCH,* Aug. 11, 1860, also cited in Clarke and Gregory, *Reports,* 241.

26. *NCH,* Aug. 11, 1860.

27. Ibid.

28. Forrest, "Taipings at Home," translating "Kan Wang" and "T'ien Wang." This passage is also printed in Blakiston, *Five Months,* 51.

29. *TR,* 758, some changes following *Zizheng xinbian,* in *Yinshu,* 8b.

30. *TR,* 758.

31. *TR,* 759; *Zizheng xinbian,* in *Yinshu,* 9.

32. For Japan, *TR,* 763; for Germans, 760; Scandinavians and France, 761; Russia, 762.

33. *TR,* 773, modified following *Zizheng xinbian,* in *Yinshu,* 22.

34. Curwen, *Deposition,* 234 n. 77; *TR,* 1525.

35. Curwen, *Deposition,* passim; Guo Tingyi, *Shishi,* appendix, 21.

36. Clarke and Gregory, *Reports,* 233, on Li's "small keen features" and glasses.

37. Curwen, *Deposition,* 109–15, 230–33; *TR,* 1524–25.

38. Curwen, *Deposition,* 117–19.

39. Brine, *Taeping,* 253–54; *TR,* 923–24, on the Catholics, and 1119–20.

40. As cited in Lin-le, *Ti-ping,* 1:298; this "scenario" is discussed in Wagner, *Heavenly Vision,* 113.

41. Brine, *Taeping,* 258–59, changing Shanghae to Shanghai and "imps" to "demons"; *TR,* 1124.

42. Jen, *Revolutionary Movement,* 403–28, has a brilliant analysis of the Anqing (Anking) campaign; Li Xiucheng is rather casual about the loss—Curwen, *Deposition,* 130, and 260–64, citing piercing testimony from Zhao Liewen's diary; Hong Rengan blames Li for the loss, *TR,* 1513, 1525–26.

43. Curwen, *Deposition,* 121, 244 n. 42.

44. *NCH,* Aug. 11, 1860, also cited in Clarke and Gregory, *Reports,* 243, echoed by Griffith John as quoted in Lin-le, *Ti-ping,* 1:294; Wagner, *Heavenly Vision,* 59–60.

45. The 1853 illustrated Amoy edition, *Tianlu licheng,* is in the Library of Congress, Washington, D.C., and an 1855 illustrated Hong Kong edition is in the British Library, Oriental Collection. A summary in thirteen leaves was published by Muirhead in 1851, according to Wylie, *Memorials,* 168. On other editions, see ibid., 175–76, and ibid., 282, for Burns' translation of Bunyan's follow-up volume on the journey of Christian's wife, Christiana, published in Peking in 1866.

46. See Bunyan text, *Tianlu licheng,* and illustrations 1, 3, and 8, and the interpretation in Rudolf Wagner, *Heavenly Vision,* 59. Wagner suggests early influence through Milne's summary of 1816; but Hong Rengan to Edkins, *NCH,* Aug. 11, 1860, also cited in Clarke and Gregory *Reports,* 243, specifies it was Burns' translation, which first appeared in 1853, that Hong liked to read.

47. Bunyan, *Tianlu licheng,* 9, and 21; see comment by Wagner, *Heavenly Vision,* 59; Xia, *Zongjiao,* 151–52, also discusses this "narrow gate," *zhuimen,* and its relationship to *Pilgrim's Progress.*

48. *TR,* 939.

49. Joseph Edkins, "Narrative," 279.

50. Much of the rest of this edict, as translated by the missionary J. L. Holmes, is too garbled to make sense. It is reproduced in *TR,* 1126–27, from Brine, *Taeping,* 266–67. I substitute Young Monarch for Junior Lord.

51. *TR,* 939, 941, 943, 945.

52. *TR,* 944, 945.

53. *TR,* 945, 946.

54. *NCH,* March 2, 1861, as observed and reported by a "Native Christian" and translated by the Reverend William G. E. Cunnyngham on a Nanjing visit.

55. *TR,* 936.

56. *TR,* 940, proclamation of April 4, 1861.

57. *TR,* 945–46.

58. *TR,* 931.

59. *TR,* 931.

60. *TR,* 933, modified following Chin, *Shiliao,* 106.

61. Chin, *Shiliao,* 107; *TR,* 934.

CHAPTER 20: PRIEST-KING

1. Hamberg, *Visions,* 31–32.

2. *Tianxiong shengzhi,* 1:14, dated Daoguang 29/1/21. I translate *qianlian* as "connected together." See also Joseph Edkins' remark, in "Narrative," 265, that Hong Xiuquan had been "divinely informed, so he believed," of Roberts' goodness.

3. *TR,* 573–75, for testimony of the courier Yeh. A. Happer's record of the courier's visit is given in Clarke and Gregory, *Reports,* 75–80. One letter, claimed for a time to be Hong's actual invitation, is now regarded as probably a later fabrication. See *TR,* 509–10.

4. *BPP / Elgin,* 473.

5. *TR,* 758.

6. See Roberts' letter of Sept. 29, 1860, in *NCH,* Oct. 27, 1860, and his letter to the *Overland China Mail* cited in Clarke and Gregory, *Reports,* 253.

7. Pruden, "Roberts," 215, 284, and Y. C. Teng, "Roberts," 61, on the illness of his wife; Pruden, "Roberts," 164, on the case of the second assistant A-Chun, and 108–18 and 284 on the legal battles. The death of Chun, his first helper, in 1845 is movingly described by Roberts in a letter of April 6, 1845, Southern Baptist Foreign Mission Board, Richmond, Va., Roberts files, "Chun's Doings in Canton," Fiche 15, plate 1760, no. 49. For Virginia Young Roberts' disgust with her husband, see her letter of Oct. 6, 1867, ibid., correspondence, Fiche 1. My thanks to Laura McDaniel for this and other references to this collection and that of the American Baptist Foreign Mission Society.

8. American Baptist Foreign Mission Society, Archives, Valley Forge, Pa., Issachar Roberts, Folder 75-5, dated Nanking, Nov. 8, 1860, and Dec. 1, 1860, enclosures to Bro[ther] Lord; Pruden, "Roberts," 289–90.

9. Coughlin, "Strangers," 274; Pruden, "Roberts," 290–91; Edkins, "Narrative," 265, 267; *NCH,* Sept. 7, 1861. Roberts' former colleague T. P. Crawford, however, visited Nanjing in spring 1861 and wrote to a friend of seeing Roberts "in the old cast-off robes of the chiefs," "the dirtiest, greasiest white man I ever saw," cited in Coughlin, "Strangers," 276; for the Reverend Hobson it was "a dirty yellow Chinese robe—a miserable spectacle of dirt and slovenliness"—cited in Clarke and Gregory, *Reports,* 298. Yung Wing, who had met Roberts long before in Mrs. Gutzlaff's Macao school, found him looking old, though moving "leisurely in his clumsy Chinese shoes" (*My Life,* 107).

10. Roberts letter, cited in Clarke and Gregory, *Reports,* 254.

11. Ibid., 255.

12. *NCH,* Sept. 7, 1861; Wylie, *Memorials,* 97, item 5. For Roberts' collaborators Charles Washington Gaillard and Rosewell Hobart Graves, see Wylie, *Memorials,* 230, 240–41, and Pruden, "Roberts," 205, 285. Roberts' own inscribed copy of the Goddard Bible is preserved in the library of Brown University, Providence, R.I.

13. Josiah Cox, cited in Clarke and Gregory, *Reports,* 313, on the restriction. Roberts letter to *NCH,* March 30, 1861, also cited in Clarke and Gregory, *Reports,* 262–64.

14. Edkins, "Narrative," 276–77.

15. As translated by Edkins in "Narrative," 274, and translating Kan-wang as Shield King. The idea that "the day of the Lord so cometh as a thief in the night" (1 Thessalonians

5:2) had been read by Hong first in Liang Afa's version; see *Quanshi,* 469–71. Hong also used the passage to refer to himself in his commentary on Revelation 22:17–20; see *TR,* 237.

16. Wylie, *Memorials,* 187–91; Milton and science, ibid., 189.

17. Edkins, "Narrative," 294–96, includes two of Hong's own comments on his eye troubles. The eye problem is corroborated by Griffith John, letter to his brother, in Clarke and Gregory, *Reports,* 297. See also Wagner, *Heavenly Vision,* 99.

18. Edkins, "Narrative," 295; Forrest, "Nanking," also notes Hong's knowledge of Athanasius and other church fathers.

19. Edkins, "Narrative," 295; Xiao, *Zhaoyu,* item 2 (plate 6), includes a photograph of Edkins' Chinese text with Hong's comments and marks of emphasis. The original is in the British Library as Or. 8143 bound into the volume 5896(J). It is written very clearly in black ink on pale blue pages.

20. Edkins, "Narrative," 272 n, mentions that Hong saw Edkins' writing of 1857 on this topic in a "Chinese monthly magazine." This is presumably Edkins' essay "On the Oneness of Jesus with God," mentioned by Wylie, *Memorials,* 189, no. 8, as appearing in the *Huayang hehe tongshu* (Chinese and foreign concord almanac) for that year.

21. This original poem in Hong's calligraphy is written in red ink on the last sheet of Edkins' essay (see n. 19 above). It can be authenticated by the massive square Taiping seal on the back of the document, of which about half is legible. Jen Yu-wen has reconstructed most of the characters in his Collection, p. 33, photographs of seals. The poem is photographically reproduced in Xiao, *Zhaoyu,* item 2, second page, plate 7, and a transcript is printed in Xiang, *Ziliao,* 2:672. A rendering rather different from mine is given in *TR,* 1205.

22. *TR,* 939.

23. *TR,* 938.

24. J. L. Holmes, in *NCH,* Sept. 1, 1860, cited in Clarke and Gregory, *Reports,* 250.

25. Parkes 1861, April 2, *BPP* / IUP, 122, Inclosure 2 in no. 5, Admiralty to Hammond of June 15, 1861.

26. Forrest, "Nanking."

27. Ibid., and *BPP* / IUP, 100.

28. The commentaries are preserved in the British Library edition of the revised Taiping Bible, *Qinding Jiuyizhao shengshu* and *Qinding Qianyizhao shengshu.* Though it is not possible to date Hong's commentaries precisely, the evidence of R. J. Forrest in his "Christianity of Hung Tsiu Tsuen," 190, 200, shows that those we have now cannot be later than Oct. 1861, when Forrest obtained his copy of this Bible. Xia, *Zongjiao,* 142, argues for 1860.

29. Chin, *Shiliao,* 85, somewhat modifying *TR,* 234.

30. Chin, *Shiliao,* 80, *TR,* 230.

31. Acts 7:56; Chin, *Shiliao,* 81; *TR,* 231; Bohr, "Eschatology," 362 n.

32. Chin, *Shiliao,* 85; *TR,* 235.

33. Matthew 8:15; Chin, *Shiliao,* 77; *TR,* 227.

34. Matthew 9:29; Chin, *Shiliao,* 77; *TR,* 228.

35. Mark 2:3–5; Chin, *Shiliao,* 79; *TR,* 229; and Matthew 8:3; Chin, *Shiliao,* 77, "upon the head" being *toushang; TR,* 227.

36. Luke 7:14–15; Chin, *Shiliao,* 80; *TR,* 230.

37. 1 Corinthians 15:49–53; *TR,* 232; Chin, *Shiliao,* 83.

38. Acts 15:14–16; *TR,* 231; Chin, *Shiliao,* 81.

39. Chin, *Shiliao,* 75, partly following *TR,* 225; Wu and Luo, "Yinshu," 283, point out the misprint in the original printing of *wang* (king) for *ju* (lord), and note that Chin Yü-fu mistakenly puts this passage under chap. 15 of Genesis.

40. Chin, *Shiliao,* 75–76, partly following *TR,* 225.

41. Hebrews 6:19–20. There is also a reference in Psalms 110:4, but Psalms was not printed in the Taiping Old Testament, which ended with Joshua.

42. *TR,* 233, modified following Chin, *Shiliao,* 84, and rendering "Hewang" as "Hong."

43. *TR,* 236, slightly modified following Chin, *Shiliao,* 86.

44. *TR,* 235, modified following Chin, *Shiliao,* 86.

45. *TR,* 235, slightly modified following Chin, *Shiliao,* 86.

46. *TR,* 236; Chin, *Shiliao,* 87. I understand Hong to be using the word *tai* in its two different senses here, first as "womb" and then as "fetus."

CHAPTER 21: SNOWFALL

1. *BPP* / IUP, 250, Roberts letter of Jan. 22, 1862, Inclosure 6 in no. 44, Medhurst to Russell, Feb. 7, 1862; also printed in Clarke and Gregory, *Reports,* 314–15.

2. *NCH,* Sept. 7, 1861.

3. *NCH,* Feb. 8, 1862; *DSCN,* Feb. 3, 1862, lists Roberts among passengers arriving in Shanghai on Feb. 2, aboard the *Willamette.* Roberts' follow-up letters and partial retractions of the charges against Hong Rengan are in *NCH,* March 6, 1862, and *BPP* / IUP, 370–71. Lindley in *Ti-ping,* 2:566–568 n, gives a blistering attack on Roberts' activities in Nanjing.

4. *BPP* / IUP, 235–36, C. Goverston statement to Vice-Consul Markham, Jan. 18, 1862, Shanghai, Inclosure 11 in no. 41, Medhurst to Russell, Jan. 23, 1862. Consul Medhurst had warned British subjects against such "ventures" on Jan. 14, 1862. *BPP* / IUP, 227.

5. *BPP* / IUP, 232–37, Joseph Lambert statement to Vice-Consul Markham, Jan. 20, 1862, Inclosure 12 in no. 41, Medhurst to Russell, Jan. 23, 1862.

6. *BPP* / IUP, 231–32, Minutes of Special Meeting of Jan. 15, 1862, Shanghai, Inclosure 9 in no. 41; *NCH,* Feb. 1, 1862; *BPP* / IUP 256.

7. *BPP* / IUP 229, Minutes of Jan. 3, 1862, Inclosure 7 in no. 41.

8. *BPP* / IUP, 233–34, Inclosure 9 in no. 41. The same meeting is covered in *NCH,* Jan. 25, 1862.

9. *NCH,* Feb. 1, 15, 1862. *BPP* / IUP, 256, Medhurst to Bruce, Feb. 4, 1862.

10. Curwen, *Deposition,* 130, on ice and snow; ibid., 138, 273, shows the lack of winter clothing later in 1862.

11. Jen, *Revolutionary Movement,* 518–21.

12. *NCH,* March 2, 1861, by "A Native Christian," trans. Rev. W. G. E. Cunnyngham; and J. S. Burdon in Clarke and Gregory, *Reports,* 237–39.

13. "Native Christian," in *NCH;* "H" [Hughes], in *NCH,* March 2, March 23, April 6, 1861.

14. *BPP* / IUP, 261; Yung, *My Life,* 101. Yung Wing dates this sight to Nov. 1859, but since it is after the fall of Suzhou, and from other internal evidence, we can tell he means Nov. 1860.

15. "Native Christian," in *NCH.*

16. Ibid.; Griffith John, in Clarke and Gregory, *Reports,* 231–32.

17. J. L. Holmes, ibid., 230.

18. Wolseley, *Narrative,* 350, also printed ibid., 335. A comprehensive analysis of the loss of life during this stage of the Taiping rebellion is in Ho, *Population,* 236–42. Ibid., 274, gives the bleak analysis made by the scholar and Taiping captive Wang Shiduo.

19. *DSCN,* Feb. 3, 1862.

20. *BPP / IUP,* 239.

21. Ibid., 238–41, Inclosure 2 in no. 42.

22. *DSCN,* Jan. 27, Feb. 24, 1862.

23. PRO / FO 671/2, Gordon to Staveley, June 1862.

24. *DSCN,* March 27, 1862.

25. *BPP / IUP,* 392, Medhurst to Bruce, Shanghai, June 9, 1862.

26. *DSCN,* Aug. 15, 1862.

27. *DSCN,* Dec. 1, 1862.

28. *DSCN,* Feb. 21, 1862.

29. *DSCN,* March 11, 1862.

30. *DSCN,* May 30, July 7, 1862.

31. *DSCN,* Aug. 8, 1862.

32. *DSCN,* Aug. 15, Sept. 26, 1862.

33. All these lost dogs are sought by their owners in advertisements placed in *DSCN* between Oct. 2, 1862, and May 27, 1863.

34. Katherine Bernhardt, *Rents, Taxes,* chap. 3, esp. pp. 106–9; Curwen, *Deposition,* 133, 243 nn. 31–32.

35. Cole, *Bao Lisheng,* esp. 26–29, 41–43.

36. Curwen, *Deposition,* 118, 124–25.

37. *BPP / IUP,* 288–89.

38. Ibid., 116.

39. Ibid., 115, 370.

40. Forrest, "Ming Tombs," *NCH,* July 6, 1861.

41. *BPP / IUP,* 170.

42. Edkins, "Narrative," 291; Jane Edkins, *Chinese Scenes,* 201, 204. Her letters show the decision as much more debated by them and difficult than her husband suggests in his "Narrative."

43. W. Lobschied, whose visit and letter to the Hong Kong "Daily Press" are given in Lin-le, *Ti-ping,* 2:598–603.

44. *TR,* 1527.

45. *TR,* 1513.

46. Growing out of the *Daily Shipping News,* the *DSCN* was first published in 1862. See King and Clarke, *Guide,* 77, 177.

47. *The Shanghai xinbao,* as announced in *DSCN,* Sept. 26, 1862. Shanghai's earlier commercial history and periods of prosperity are well described in Linda Cooke Johnson, "Shanghai."

48. R. E. Johnson, *China Station,* 109–13.

49. *BPP / IUP* 392, Medhurst to Bruce, Shanghai, June 9, 1862.

50. *DSCN,* Dec. 1, 1862, April 10, 1863.

51. *DSCN,* June 3, 1863; *NCH,* July 4, 1863.

52. *DSCN,* Nov. 22, 1862.

53. *DSCN,* May 26, 1863, Sept. 26, 1862.

54. *DSCN,* Dec. 1, 1862.

55. Fogg in *DSCN,* Jan. 8, 1863, and photo stores in *DSCN,* Jan. 27, 1862, Feb. 21, 1862, June 3, 1862. The shops were J. Newman and C. & W. Saunders.

56. Risley, *DSCN,* Sept. 26, 1862; racehorses, *DSCN,* Feb. 14, May 29, 1863.

57. PRO / FO 97/111, cases 252, 327, 120, and 328.

58. PRO / FO 17/405, cases 30, 63, and 106, and PRO / FO 97/111, case 346, for the assault on Susan Cheshire.

59. *DSCN,* Feb. 28, 1862; *NCH,* March 15, 1862, June 23, 1864.

60. Licenses, *DSCN,* Dec. 1, 1862; Mason, *DSCN,* May 30, 1863; Hayden, PRO / FO 17/405, case 112.

61. PRO / FO 97/111, passim, and cases 314, 321, and 344, for the dramatic repeat offenders. For an astonishing case of police abuse to some Shanghai "gentlemen" who are beaten and rolled in the mud see *DSCN,* May 20, May 21, 1863.

62. *DSCN,* Feb. 18, 1863.

63. PRO / FO 97/111, cases 17, 55, and 202.

64. *BPP /* IUP, 424, Bruce to Russell, July 14, 1862.

65. *DSCN,* Feb. 23, 1863.

66. *BPP /* IUP, 521, Staveley to Bruce, Shanghai, Nov. 13, 1862, Inclosure 3 in no. 103.

67. As in *DSCN,* July 7, 1862, where the gentleman concerned owns "five Colt revolvers" as well as a bloodhound.

68. *NCH,* Oct. 27, 1860.

69. *BPP /* IUP 469, Admiral Hope to Admiralty, Oct. 1862, Inclosure 1 in no. 74.

70. *DSCN,* May 30, 1862.

71. *NCH,* June 28, 1862; Curwen, *Deposition,* 161–62.

72. *BPP /* IUP, 442–43.

73. *DSCN,* Sept. 26, 1862, for butter; *NCH,* Feb. 1, 1862. This latter is a sardonic piece, dated to "1962" and signed "C'est moi."

74. Belgian, *BPP /* IUP, 458; Swedish, *NCH,* June 15, 1861; Prussian, *NCH,* June 16, 1864; Italian, *BPP /* IUP, 489.

75. Curwen, *Deposition,* 118, 135, 136; Jen, *Revolutionary Movement,* 458; *BPP /* IUP, 101, 247, 259, 383, for the howitzer.

76. Curwen, *Deposition,* 138–39.

77. Jen, *Revolutionary Movement,* 452–60; Smith, *Mercenaries,* passim; Curwen, *Deposition,* 238–42 nn. 15–23. The most recent study of Ward is Carr, *Devil Soldier.*

78. Curwen, *Deposition,* 139–40, changing romanization.

79. Lin-le, *Ti-ping,* 2:623–24.

80. See *Tianxiong shengzhi,* 2:49b, and *Tianfu shengzhi,* 34a. Hong's work on these two texts seems to fit well with the fine exposition in Wagner, *Heavenly Vision,* 110, that after 1853 "the vision did not provide any further guidance," and consequently there was a "foreshortening" of the "scenario." For Hong Rengan on the same texts, see Xia, *Zongjiao,* 180–81. The unique surviving copy of the *Tianxiong* and *Tianfu shengzhi,* now in the British Library, is undated. In the list of Taiping publications printed in vol. 1, the character *qian,* "former," in the title of the revised New Testament, *Qianyizhao shengshu,* has clearly been inserted to replace the earlier *xin,* "new." Thus the book was probably prepared *before* and circulated *after* the revised New Testament. Xia, *Zongjiao,* 142, 148, concludes from this that the book was printed *after* the 29th Taiping book, Hong's elder brothers' account of their younger brother's revelations, which still has the *xin* in the title of the New Testament, and before the Taiping calendar for 1861, where *qian* appears in

the contents as a regular-sized character. This is shrewd. But it remains unclear why the *Tianxiong shengzhi,* if published later, was not numbered as no. 30, and why it is in a style of print quite different from that of the other Taiping volumes, both the vol. 29 and the 1861 calendar. Since R. J. Forrest did not obtain this text in 1861 or 1862 when he got all the others, including the revised Old and New Testaments, it apparently was not in general circulation at that time.

CHAPTER 22: PARTINGS

1. Jen, *Revolutionary Movement,* 318–19. For Shi's immense trail of campaigns see ibid., 304–17, and Guo Yisheng, *Ditu,* 115–20.

2. Curwen, *Deposition,* 136; ibid., 87, suggests Li still did not know of Shi's fate in 1864. On the growth of Li Hongzhang's power see Spector, *Li Hung-chang,* and Cheng, *Taiping Rebellion,* chap. 6.

3. Curwen, *Deposition,* 122, 146.

4. Jen, *Revolutionary Movement,* 524, says the stored grain totaled over 50,000 piculs—a picul being approximately 130 pounds.

5. Jen, *Revolutionary Movement,* 525.

6. Curwen, *Deposition,* 140.

7. Ibid., 141; Xia, *Zongjiao,* 273, gives the religious contexts of this confrontation.

8. Curwen, *Deposition,* 147–48.

9. *TR,* 1513.

10. Prosper Giquel cites deserters' testimony to place Hong in Huzhou in May 1864, though he was probably there some months earlier; Hong Rengan in his confession is vague on the dates; see Giquel, *Journal,* 80, 87; *TR,* 1513–14.

11. Curwen, *Deposition,* 289 n. 83; Jen, *Revolutionary Movement,* 526.

12. Curwen, *Deposition,* 145; Jen, *Revolutionary Movement,* 527.

13. Gordon report in Curwen, *Deposition,* 298 n. 42.

14. Ibid., on the scavengers; ibid., 151, 294–95 nn. 24–26, on the fugitives.

15. Cited in Curwen, *Deposition,* 298 n. 42.

16. Jen, *Revolutionary Movement,* 525. See the testimony of David Williams, alias Thomas Sayers, Charlie, Charles, *NCH,* Oct. 3, 1863.

17. Curwen, *Deposition,* 295 n. 27; quotation from ibid., 299 n. 42.

18. Ibid., 297 n. 41.

19. Ibid., 291; *Jiuyizhao shengshu,* Exodus, in *Yinshu,* 26b.

20. Curwen, *Deposition,* 145–46; *TR,* 1474–75, with variant of Hong's wording.

21. Li in Curwen, *Deposition,* 153; Hong Rengan in *TR,* 1513; Tiangui in *TR,* 1531.

22. Guo Tingyi, *Shishi,* 2:1072; Jen, *Revolutionary Movement,* 528.

23. See the annotated prayer for the dead in *TR,* 118, as contrasted with *Tiantiao shu,* in *Yinshu,* 8. Zeng Guofan reported to the emperor that Hong's body, wrapped in yellow satin "embroidered with dragons," was discovered and exhumed on July 30. The corpse was then beheaded and burned. Zeng added that the head was hairless, but with a gray mustache. See Lay, *Autobiography,* 82, 95. On the burial of Hong see also Xia, *Zongjiao,* 299–302.

24. *TR,* 1531.

25. Curwen, *Deposition,* 153.

26. Jen, *Revolutionary Movement,* 530–31; *TR,* 1531, Young Monarch's confession; Cur-

wen, *Deposition,* 154, 299–300 nn. 45 and 46, citing Zhao Liewen's diary on details of the capture.

27. Curwen, *Deposition,* 157–58.

28. Ibid., 161–62.

29. Ibid., 182; also ibid., 305 n. 84. Curwen's appendixes 1 and 2 also have further conversations by Li with his captors, including Zhao Liewen. Appendix 3 contains a comprehensive analysis of the variant editions of Li's confession.

30. Curwen, *Deposition,* 155; Guo Yisheng, *Ditu,* 143, for exact route and dates.

31. See Giquel, *Journal,* 72, 75, on the former Gui Wang, Deng Guangming. Ibid., 101, mentions the Young Monarch's presence in the area in Aug. On the origins of the Ever-Triumphant Army see Leibo, *Transferring Technology,* 26–31, 36–38.

32. Giquel, *Journal,* 32, 78, on bodies; ibid., 35, 36, on commanders and officers killed.

33. "Account given by Patrick Nellis," *NCH,* Nov. 12, 1864. See also "the Statement of Mark Conroy" in the same issue.

34. Richard Smith, *Mercenaries,* 131–32, 155–56.

35. *NCH,* May 21, 1864. Such blindfold wheelbarrow races, using real barrows over long courses, were common in England from the 1830s; other variants of wheelbarrow races are discussed in the eccentric and charming volume *Causeries brouettiques,* 212–20; ibid., 236–40, discusses Chinese wheelbarrows.

36. Giquel, *Journal,* 77, 83, 88–89. For an overview of the Huzhou campaign, see Leibo, *Transferring Technology,* 51–60.

37. Giquel, *Journal,* 88–89.

38. Ibid., 77, 84, 98.

39. Ibid., 99, 102.

40. Ibid., 84.

41. Ibid., 85, 152 n. 46.

42. *TR,* 1507.

43. *TR,* 1514.

44. *TR,* 1521, 1529; Jen, *Revolutionary Movement,* 536.

45. *TR,* 1532, slightly modified following Xiang, *Ziliao,* 2:856.

46. *TR,* 1531.

47. *TR,* 1532.

48. Jen, *Revolutionary Movement,* 536. For some time after the deaths of these Taiping leaders remnants of the various Taiping field armies that had been out foraging for supplies at the time Nanjing fell fought on in Fujian and in northern Guangdong; the last of these Taiping forces was destroyed by Qing troops in early Feb. 1866. See ibid., 537–44. Jen notes ibid., 535 n. 63 and 536 n. 65, that one son of Hong Rengan and one son of Li Xiucheng managed to survive, and grow to maturity. Jen's further assertion (536 n. 65) that Hong Xiuquan's two youngest sons also managed to survive is not generally accepted by Taiping scholars.

Bibliography of Works Cited

American Baptist Foreign Mission Society Archives. Valley Forge, Pa. Issachar Jacox Roberts Papers and Correspondence.

Anderson, Benedict. *Imagined Communities: Reflections on the Origin and Spread of Nationalism.* London, 1985.

Anliang yue (Local pacification agreement). Compiled in 1845 for Jintian villages, Guiping county. Reprinted in *Taiping Tianguo wenxian shiliao ji,* 345–48.

Bai Limin. "Primers and Paradigms: A Comparative Approach to Understanding Elementary Education as a Pre-condition for Industrialization in Late Imperial China." Ph.D. diss., La Trobe University, 1993.

Bak, Janos M., and Gerhard Benecke, eds. *Religion and Rural Revolt.* Manchester, 1984.

Banxing zhaoshu (Imperially sanctioned proclamations). 1851. In *Taiping Tianguo yinshu,* vol. 3, item 2.

Barnett, Suzanne Wilson, and John King Fairbank, eds. *Christianity in China: Early Protestant Missionary Writings.* Cambridge, Mass., 1985.

Barrett, T. H. *Singular Listlessness: A Short History of Chinese Books and British Scholars.* London, 1989.

Bays, Daniel H. "Christian Tracts: The Two Friends." In Barnett and Fairbank, eds., *Christianity in China,* 19–34.

Bernard, W. D., and W. H. Hall. *Narrative of the Voyages and Services of the Nemesis, from 1840 to 1843. . . .* 2 vols. London, 1844.

Bernhardt, Kathryn. *Rents, Taxes, and Peasant Resistance: The Lower Yangzi Region, 1840–1950.* Stanford, Calif., 1992.

Bian yaoxue wei zuili lun (Essays on renaming the demon's den and the criminals' province). 1853–54. In *Taiping Tianguo yinshu,* vol. 10, item 2.

Bingham, J. Elliot. *Narrative of the Expedition to China, from the Commencement of the War to the Present Period.* . . . 2 vols. London, 1842.

Biot, Edouard, tr. *Le Tcheou-li ou rites des Tcheou* (The rites of Zhou). 2 vols. Paris, 1851.

Blakiston, Thomas W. *Five Months on the Yang-tsze.* London, 1862.

Bloch, Ruth H. *Visionary Republic: Millennial Themes in American Thought, 1756–1800.* Cambridge, 1985.

Boardman, Eugene Powers. *Christian Influence upon the Ideology of the Taiping Rebellion, 1851–1864.* Madison, Wis., 1952.

————. "Millenary Aspects of the Taiping Rebellion (1851–1864)." In Sylvia Thrupp, ed., *Millennial Dreams in Action: Studies in Revolutionary Religious Movements.* New York, 1970, 70–79.

Bohr, P. Richard. "Liang Fa's Quest for Moral Power." In Barnett and Fairbank, eds., *Christianity in China,* 35–46.

————. "The Politics of Eschatology: Hung Hsiu-ch'uan and the Rise of the Taipings, 1837–1853." Ph.D. diss., University of California, Davis, 1978.

BPP / Elgin: British Parliamentary Papers. Correspondence Relative to the Earl of Elgin's Special Missions to China and Japan, 1857–1859. London, 1859.

BPP / IUP: British Parliamentary Papers. Irish University Press Area Studies Series, China, 32. *Correspondence, Memorials, Orders in Council, and Other Papers respecting the Taiping Rebellion in China, 1852–1864.* Shannon, 1971.

Bridgman, Elijah. "Obituary of the *[sic]* Edwin Stevens, Late Seamen's Chaplain in the Port of Canton." *Chinese Repository* 5 (March 1837): 513–18.

Brine, Lindesay. *The Taeping Rebellion in China: A Narrative of Its Rise and Progress.* London, 1862.

Broman, Sven. *Studies on the Chou Li.* Stockholm, 1961.

Brown, Carolyn T., ed. *Psycho-Sinology: The Universe of Dreams in Chinese Culture.* Washington, D.C., 1988.

Bunyan, John. See *Tianlu licheng.*

Cai Shaoqing. "Taiping Tianguo geming qianxi Lei Zaihao he Li Yuanfa qiyi de jige wenti" (Aspects of the Lei and Li uprisings on the eve of the Taiping revolution). In *Taiping Tianguo xuekan* 2 (1985): 350–62.

Callery, Joseph M., and M. Yvan. *History of the Insurrection in China; with Notices of the Christianity, Creed, and Proclamations of the Insurgents,* trans. John Oxenford. New York, 1853.

Cambridge History of China, The. Vol. 10, pt. 1. *Late Ch'ing, 1800–1911.* Edited by John K. Fairbank. Cambridge, 1978.

Canton Press, The. Sept. 1835–Dec. 1837. British Library, Colindale, London.

Canton Register, The. Jan. 1834–Dec. 1836. Beinecke Library, Yale University. January–December 1837. British Library, Colindale, London.

Carr, Caleb. *The Devil Soldier.* New York, 1991.

Causeries brouettiques (Wheelbarrow talk). Madrid, 1925.

Chen Huiyan. *Wuchang jishi* (Record of the events in Wuchang). In Xiang Da et al., eds. *Taiping Tianguo ziliao congkan,* 4:577–606.

Chen Zhoutang. *Hongshi zongpu* (Genealogy of the Hong lineage). Hangzhou, 1982.

————, ed. *Guangdong dichu Taiping Tianguo shiliao xuanbian* (Selected Guangdong local history materials on the Taiping). Guangzhou, 1986.

Cheng, J. C. *Chinese Sources for the Taiping Rebellion, 1850–1864.* Hong Kong, 1963.

Chin Yü-fu. *Taiping Tianguo shiliao* (Historical materials on the Taiping). Beijing, 1955.

Chinese Repository, The. 20 vols. Canton and Macao, 1831–51.

Clarke, G. W. "The Yu-li or Precious Records." *Journal of the China Branch of the Royal Asiatic Society* 28 (1893–94): 233–400.

Clarke, P[rescott]. "The Coming of God to Kwangsi: . . . Karl Gutzlaff and the Chinese Union. . . ." *Papers on Far Eastern History* (ANU, Canberra), 7 (March 1973): 145–81.

Clarke, Prescott, and J. S. Gregory. *Western Reports on the Taiping: A Selection of Documents.* Canberra, 1982.

Cohen, Myron L. "The Hakka or 'Guest People': Dialect as a Socio-cultural Variable in Southeastern China," *Ethnohistory* 15 (1968): 237–92.

Cohn, Norman. *Cosmos, Chaos, and the World to Come: The Ancient Roots of Apocalyptic Faith.* New Haven, Conn., 1993.

————. *The Pursuit of the Millennium.* London, 1957.

Cole, James H. *The People versus the Taipings: Bao Lisheng's "Righteous Army of Dongan."* Berkeley, Calif., 1981.

Collection of Missionary Works in Chinese. Yale University, Sterling Memorial Library, Room 207. (This also contains tracts in Korean.)

Collis, Maurice. *Foreign Mud: Being an Account of the Opium Imbroglio at Canton in the 1830's.* New York, 1947.

Coughlin, Margaret Morgan. "Strangers in the House: J. Lewis Shuck and Issachar Roberts, First American Baptist Missionaries to China." Ph.D. diss., University of Virginia, 1972.

CR: See *Chinese Repository.*

Curwen, C. A. *Taiping Rebel: The Deposition of Li Hsiu-ch'eng.* Cambridge, 1977.

Daily Shipping and Commercial News (Shanghai, China). Various issues spanning the period from Jan. 27, 1862 (vol. 7, no. 2214), to June 3, 1863 (vol. 8, no. 2633). British Library, Colindale, London.

Davis, John Francis. *The Chinese: A General Description of the Empire of China and Its Inhabitants.* 2 vols. London, 1836.

———. *China, during the War and since the Peace.* 2 vols. London, 1852.

De Groot, J. J. M. *The Religious System of China.* 6 vols. 1892. Reprint, Taipei, 1989.

DNB: The Dictionary of National Biography.

Doezema, William R. "Western Seeds of Eastern Heterodoxy: The Impact of Protestant Revivalism on . . . Hung Hsiu-ch'uan, 1836–1864." *Fides et Historia* 25, no. 1 (1993): 73–98.

Douglas, Robert K. *Catalogue of Chinese Printed Books, Manuscripts and Drawings in the Library of the British Museum.* London, 1877.

Downing, C. Toogood. *The Fan-qui in China in 1836–7.* 3 vols. London, 1838.

Drake, Fred W. "Protestant Geography in China: E. C. Bridgman's Portrayal of the West." In Barnett and Fairbank, eds., *Christianity in China,* 89–106.

DSCN: See *Daily Shipping and Commercial News.*

Eberhard, Wolfram. *Studies in Hakka Folktales.* Taipei, 1974.

Edkins, Jane R. *Chinese Scenes and People.* London, 1863.

Edkins, Joseph. "Narrative of a Visit to Nanking." Included as a supplement to Jane Edkins, *Chinese Scenes and People,* 239–307.

Elliott, Mark C. "Bannerman and Townsman: Ethnic Tension in Nineteenth-Century Jiangnan." *Late Imperial China* 11, no. 1 (June 1990): 36–74.

Eminent Chinese of the Ch'ing Period. Ed. Arthur W. Hummel. 2 vols. Washington, D.C., 1943.

Esherick, Joseph W. *The Origins of the Boxer Uprising.* Berkeley, Calif., 1987.

Fairbank, John King. *Trade and Diplomacy on the China Coast: The Opening of the Treaty Ports, 1842–1854.* Stanford, Calif., 1969.

Fang Zhiguang and Cui Zhiqing. "Taiping Tianguo 'Xiaotiantang' nei hanyan biankao" (Alternative explanations of the meaning of the Taiping 'Xiaotiantang' [Earthly Paradise]). In *Taiping Tianguo xuekan* 1 (1983): 209–23.

Fishbourne, E. G. *Impressions of China and the Present Revolution, Its Progress and Prospects.* London, 1855.

Forrest, Robert James. "The Christianity of Hung Tsiu Tsuen: A Review of Taeping Books." *Journal of the North China Branch of the Royal Asiatic Society,* n.s., 4 (Dec. 1867): 187–208.

[Forrest, Robert James]. "The Ming Tombs." *North China Herald,* no. 571 (July 6, 1861).

[Forrest, Robert James]. "Nanking and the Inhabitants Thereof." *North China Herald,* no. 570 (June 29, 1861).

[Forrest, Robert James]. "Soochow to Nanking." *North China Herald,* no. 564 (May 18, 1861), no. 567 (June 8, 1861).

[Forrest, Robert James] ("Rusticus Expectans"). "The Taipings at Home." *North China Herald,* no. 586 (Oct. 19, 1861).

Fox, Grace. *British Admirals and Chinese Pirates, 1832–1869.* (London, 1940).

Gao Xianzhi. *Kejia jiulixu* (The old Hakka rituals and customs). Taipei, 1986.

Giquel, Prosper. *A Journal of the Chinese Civil War, 1864,* ed. Steven A. Leibo. Honolulu, 1985.

Goddard, Francis Wayland. *Called to Cathay.* New York, 1948.

Graham, Gerald S. *The China Station: War and Diplomacy, 1830–1860.* Oxford, 1978.

Gregory, J. S. *Great Britain and the Taipings.* London, 1969.

Guangzhou fuzhi (Gazetteer of Canton prefecture). 163 juan, 1879.

Gulick, Edward V. *Peter Parker and the Opening of China.* Cambridge, Mass., 1973.

Guo Tingyi. *Taiping Tianguo shishi rizhi* (Daily record of events in the Taiping). 2 vols. 1946. Reprint, Taipei, 1976.

Guo Yisheng, *Taiping Tianguo lishi ditu ji* (Historical atlas of the Taiping Heavenly Kingdom). Beijing, 1989.

Gutzlaff, Charles [Karl]. *Journal of Three Voyages along the Coast of China, in 1831, 1832, and 1833.* London, 1834.

Hamberg, Theodore. *The Visions of Hung-siu-tshuen, and [the] Origin of the Kwang-si Insurrection.* Hong Kong, 1854. Reprint, with Chinese translation by Jen Yu-wen, Peiping, 1935.

Hashimoto, Mantaro J. *The Hakka Dialect: A Linguistic Study of its Phonology, Syntax and Lexicon.* Cambridge, 1973.

Hay, John C. Dalrymple. *The Suppression of Piracy in the China Sea, 1849.* London, 1889.

Hill, Christopher. *A Tinker and a Poor Man: John Bunyan and His Church, 1628–1688.* New York, 1989.

Hillard, Katharine, ed. *My Mother's Journal [Harriet Low]: A Young Lady's Diary of Five Years Spent in Manila, Macao, and the Cape of Good Hope, from 1829–1834.* Boston, 1900.

Ho Ping-ti. *Studies on the Population of China, 1368–1953.* Cambridge, Mass., 1959.

Hodges, Nan Powell, ed. *The Voyage of the* Peacock: *A Journal by Benajah Ticknor, Naval Surgeon.* Ann Arbor, Mich., 1991.

Holstun, James. *A Rational Millennium: Puritan Utopias of Seventeenth-Century England and America.* Oxford, 1987.

Hou Ching-lang. "The Chinese Belief in Baleful Stars." In Welch and Seidel, eds., *Facets of Taoism,* 193–228.

Huang Chun-chieh and Erik Zürcher, eds. *Norms and the State in China.* Leiden, 1993.

Huaxian zhi (Gazetteer of Hua county), 4 juan, 1687 and 1890 eds. Reprint, Taipei, 1967.

Hunter, William C. *Bits of Old China.* Shanghai, 1911.

———. The "Fan Kwae," at Canton, before Treaty Days, 1825–1844 1882. Reprint, Shanghai, 1938.

Hutcheon, Robin, Chinnery: The Man and the Legend. Hong Kong, 1975.

Inada Seiichi. "Taihei tengoku zenya no Kyakumin ni tsuite" (The guest people (Hakkas) before the founding of the Taiping Kingdom). In Toyoshi kenkyu hokoku (Journal of oriental history, Nagoya University) 11 (1986): 60–91.

Jen Yu-wen. The Taiping Revolutionary Movement. New Haven, Conn., 1973.

———. Taiping Tianguo dianzhi tongkao (Studies on the institutions of the Taiping Heavenly Kingdom). 3 vols. Hong Kong, 1958.

———. Taiping Tianguo quanshi (Complete history of the Taiping). 3 vols. Hong Kong, 1962.

Jen Yu-wen Collection on the Taiping Revolutionary Movement. Yale University, Sterling Memorial Library.

Jian Tianjing yu Jinling lun (Essays on the establishment of the Heavenly Capital in Nanjing). 1853–54. In Taiping Tianguo yinshu, vol. 10, item 1.

Jiang Tao. "Hong Xiuquan 'dengji' shishi bianzheng" (The true date of Hong Xiuquan's ascending the throne). In Lishi yanjiu (1993), no. 1, pp. 146–47.

Jiuyizhao shengshu (The Old Testament). 1852–53. In Taiping Tianguo yinshu, vols. 5–8. (For Taiping early edition of Genesis, see also British Library, 15116.b.9.)

Johnson, David, Andrew J. Nathan, and Evelyn S. Rawski, eds., Popular Culture in Late Imperial China. Berkeley, Calif., 1985).

Johnson, Linda Cooke. "Shanghai: An Emerging Jiangnan Port, 1683–1840." In Linda Cooke Johnson, ed., Cities of Jiangnan in Late Imperial China. Albany, N.Y., 1993.

Johnson, Robert Erwin. Far China Station: The U.S. Navy in Asian Waters, 1800–1898. Annapolis, 1979.

Jones, Susan Mann, and Philip Kuhn. "Dynastic Decline and the Roots of Rebellion." In The Cambridge History of China, vol. 10, pt, 1, pp. 107–62.

Kaltenmark, Max. "The Ideology of the T'ai-p'ing Ching." In Welch and Seidel, eds., Facets of Taoism, 19–45.

Karlgren, Bernhard. The Early History of the Chou Li and Tso Chuan Texts. Stockholm, 1931.

Kikuchi Hideaki. "Taihei tengoku zenya no kosei ni okeru iju to 'Kyaku seki' erito" (The migration and growth of the Hakka elites in Guangxi province before the Taiping Kingdom). Shigaku zasshi 101, no. 9 (1992): 1–36.

King, Frank H. H., and Prescott Clarke. A Research Guide to China-Coast Newspapers, 1822–1911. Cambridge, Mass., 1965.

Kuhn, Philip. "Origins of the Taiping Vision: Cross-cultural Dimensions of a Chinese Rebellion." Comparative Studies in Society and History 19 (1977): 350–66.

————. *Rebellion and Its Enemies in Late Imperial China: Militarization and Its Social Structure, 1796–1864.* Cambridge, Mass., 1970.

————. *Soulstealers: The Chinese Sorcery Scare of 1768.* Cambridge, Mass., 1990.

————. "The Taiping Rebellion." In *The Cambridge History of China,* vol. 10, pt. 1, pp. 264–317.

Kutcher, Norman Alan. "Death and Mourning in China, 1550–1800." Ph.D. diss., Yale University, 1991.

Laai Yi-faai. "The Part Played by the Pirates of Kwangtung and Kwangsi Provinces in the Taiping Insurrection." Ph.D. diss., University of California, 1950.

Lao Tzu: Tao Te Ching. Trans. D. C. Lau. New York, 1963.

Lay, W. T. *The Autobiography of the Chung-wang.* Shanghai, 1865.

Legge, James, trans. *The Chinese Classics.* 2nd rev. ed. 7 vols. 1892. Reprint, Taipei, 1963.

————."The Colony of Hong Kong." *China Review* 1 (1872): 163–76.

Leibo, Steven. *Transferring Technology to China: Prosper Giquel and the Self-Strengthening Movement.* Berkeley, Calif., 1985.

Leung, Angela Ki Che. "To Chasten Society: The Development of Widow Homes in the Qing, 1773–1911." *Late Imperial China* 14, no. 2 (1993): 1–32.

Li Bin. *Zhongxing bieji* (Records of the Restoration), 1910.

Liang Afa. *Quanshi liangyan* (Good words for exhorting the age). Canton, 1832. Reprint, Taiwan, 1965.

Lin-le [Augustus Lindley]. *Ti-ping Tien-Kwoh: The History of the Ti-ping Revolution.* 2 vols. London, 1866.

LMS: London Missionary Society Archives. "South China and Ultra Ganges, 1807–1874." Held at London University, School of Oriental and African Studies, Council for World Missions Collection.

Low, Harriet. See Katharine Hillard.

Luo Ergang. "Chongkao 'Hong Xuanjiao' conghe er lai" (An examination of the origins of "Hong Xuanjiao"). In *Lishi yanjiu* (1987), no. 5, pp. 132–37.

————. "Taiping Tianguo jingji kao" and "houji" (A Study of the Taiping publications, and further thoughts on the same topic) in *Xueyuan (Campus Scientiae)* 2, no. 1 (1948): 13–28, and no. 3, 66.

————. *Taiping Tianguo shi* (History of the Taiping). 4 vols. Beijing, 1991.

Luo Xianglin, *Kejia shiliao huipian* (Historical sources on the Hakkas). Hong Kong, 1965.

Lutz, Jessie Gregory. "The Grand Illusion: Karl Gutzlaff and Popularization of China Missions in the United States during the 1830's." In Patricia Neils, ed., *United States Attitudes,* 46–77.

————. "Karl F. A. Gutzlaff: Missionary Entrepreneur." In Barnett and Fairbank, eds., *Christianity in China,* 61–87.

MacIver, D. *A Chinese-English Dictionary, Hakka-Dialect.* Revised by M. C. Mackenzie. Shanghai, 1926.

————. *A Hakka Index to the Chinese-English Dictionary of Herbert A. Giles . . . and S. Wells Williams.* Shanghai, 1904.

Mair, Victor H. "Language and Ideology in the Written Popularizations of the Sacred Edict." In David Johnson et al., eds., *Popular Culture,* 325–59.

Malan, S. C. *The three-fold San-tsze-king or the Triliteral Classic of China.* London, 1856.

Mao Jiaqi. "Guanyu Guo Shili he Feng Yunshan de guanxi wenti" (On the problem of Gutzlaff's contact with Feng Yunshan). In *Taiping Tianguo xuekan* 1 (1983), 267–71.

————. *Taiping Tianguo tongshi* (History of the Taiping). 3 vols. Nanjing, 1991.

Marty, Martin E., and R. Scott Appleby, eds. *Fundamentalisms Observed.* Chicago, 1991.

McAleavy, H. *Wang T'ao: The Life and Writings of a Displaced Person.* London, 1953.

McGinn, Bernard. *Visions of the End: Apocalyptic Traditions in the Middle Ages.* New York, 1979.

McNeur, George Hunter. *China's First Preacher, Liang A-fa, 1789–1855.* Shanghai, 1934.

Meadows, Thomas Taylor. *The Chinese and Their Rebellions. . . .* London, 1856.

Medhurst, W. H. *A Dissertation on the Theology of the Chinese.* Shanghai, 1847.

————. "Extract from the Manuscript Journal of the Reverend W. H. Medhurst in the Huron [in] 1835." *Chinese Repository* 4 (Jan. 1836): 406–11.

Memoir of Rev. William Milne, D. D., Late Missionary at Malacca [anon]. Dublin, 1825.

Mercier, V. *Campagne du "Cassini" dans les mers de Chine, 1851–1854.* Paris, 1889.

Michael, Franz, and Chung-li Chang. *The Taiping Rebellion: History and Documents.* Vol. 1, *History.* Seattle, 1966. Vols. 2 and 3, *Documents and Comments.* Seattle, 1971. Vols. 2 and 3, with continuous pagination, are abbreviated as *TR.*

Morrison, John Robert. *A Chinese Commercial Guide, Consisting of a Collection of Details Respecting Foreign Trade in China.* Canton, 1834.

Morse, Hosea Ballou. *The Chronicles of the East India Company Trading to China, 1635–1834.* 5 vols. Oxford, 1926–29.

————. *The International Relations of the Chinese Empire, 1834–1911.* Vol. 1, Shanghai, 1910. Vols 2 and 3, London, 1918.

Moule, Archdeacon. *Personal Recollections of the T'ai-p'ing Rebellion, 1861–1863.* Shanghai, 1898.

Murohashi Tetsuji. *Daikanwa jiten* (Chinese Dictionary). 12 vols. N.p., 1961–69.

Murray, Dian. "Migration, Protection, and Racketeering: The Spread of the Tiandihui within China." In Ownby and Heidhues, eds., *"Secret Societies" Reconsidered*, 177–89.

———. *Pirates of the South China Coast, 1790–1810*. Stanford, Calif., 1987.

Murray, Dian, and Qin Baoqi. *The Origins of the Tiandihui: The Chinese Triads in Legend and History*. Stanford, Calif., 1994.

NA-DD: National Archives. Diplomatic Despatches from United States Ministers to China, 1843–1906. Records of the Department of State. Microfilm series 92. Washington, D.C.

NA-DI: National Archives. Diplomatic Instructions, China, vol. 1, 1843–1867. Records of the Department of State. Microfilm series 77. Washington, D.C.

Naquin, Susan. *Millenarian Rebellion in China: The Eight Trigrams Uprising of 1813*. New Haven, Conn., 1976.

"Native Christian, A." "Journey from Shanghai to Nanking, January 15, 1861," trans. Rev. W. G. E. Cunnyngham. *NCH*, no. 553 (March 2, 1861).

NCH. See North China Herald.

Neils, Patricia, ed. *United States Attitudes and Policies toward China: The Impact of American Missionaries*. Armonk, N.Y., 1990.

Ng, Vivien W. *Madness in Late Imperial China: From Illness to Deviance*. Norman, Okla., 1990.

North China Herald, The. Printed in Shanghai. Issues for 1851–65.

Oliphant, Laurence. *Narrative of the Earl of Elgin's Mission to China and Japan in the Years 1857, '58, '59*. 2 vols. Edinburgh and London, 1859.

Overland Friend of China, The. Hong Kong, 1857. The British Library, Colindale, London.

Ownby, David, and Mary Somers Heidhues, eds. *"Secret Societies" Reconsidered: Perspectives on the Social History of Early Modern South China and Southeast Asia*. Armonk, N.Y., 1993.

Perry, Elizabeth J. *Rebels and Revolutionaries in North China, 1845–1945*. Stanford, Calif., 1980.

———. "Taipings and Triads: The Role of Religion in Inter-rebel Relations." In Bak and Benecke, eds., *Religion and Rural Revolt*, 342–53.

Pfister, Lauren F. "Some New Dimensions in the Study of the Works of James Legge (1815–1897)" (in two parts). *Sino-Western Cultural Relations Journal* 12 (1990): 29–50, and 13 (1991): 33–48.

PRO / FO: Public Record Office, Foreign Office Archives. Kew Gardens, London.

PRO / FO 17/214: "Despatch no. 78 of Sir John Bowring to the Earl of Clarendon, July 1854."

PRO / FO 17/405: "Shanghai Police Sheets for 1862." Enclosure in Sir F. Bruce's no. 136, Aug. 1863.

PRO / FO 97/108: "Shanghae Consulate Police Sheet, Year Ending 31st December, 1860."

PRO / FO 97/109: "Shanghae Consulate Police Sheet, Year Ending Dec. 31st. 1861."

PRO / FO 97/111: "Shanghae Consulate Police Sheet for Year Ending 31 December, 1863."

PRO / FO 97/113: "Shanghai Consulate Police Sheets for Year Ending 31 Dec. 1864."

PRO / FO 671/2: "China: 1854–1864. Correspondence, General." Includes Lewin Bowring and W. H. Medhurst, Jr., draft report of 1858 to Elgin, and Gordon report on Shanghai defenses to General Staveley.

PRO / FO 672/2: "Shanghai Registers—Deaths—7 March 1851 to 3 Dec. 1864."

Pruden, George Blackburn, Jr. "Issachar Jacox Roberts and American Diplomacy in China during the Taiping Rebellion." Ph.D. diss., American University, 1977.

Qi Longwei. "Taiping Tianguo wenshu shilue" (Brief history of Taiping printed books). In *Taiping Tianguo xuekan* 5 (1987): 224–29.

Qinding jing bi ziyang (List of honorific and tabooed characters compiled by Taiping imperial order). In *Taiping Tianguo yinshu,* vol. 20, item 3, no page, no date.

Qinding Jiuyizhao shengshu (Bible B) (Taiping Revision of the Old Testament—Genesis through Joshua). British Library, Oriental and India Office collection, Blackfriars, #15117.e.20.

Qinding Qianyizhao Shengshu (Taiping Revision of the New Testament, lacking John's Gospel). British Library, Oriental and India Office collection, Blackfriars, #15117.e.19.

Qingdai dangan shiliao congbian (Collected historical materials from Qing archives). Beijing, 1978. Vol. 1, 1–81.

Qingshi liejuan (Biographies of Qing dynasty notables). 80 juan in 10 vols. Reprint, Taipei, n.d.

Rait, Robert S. *The Life and Campaigns of Hugh First Viscount Gough, Field-Marshal.* 2 vols. London, 1903.

Roberts, Issachar Jacox. "Chun's Doings in Canton." Southern Baptist Foreign Mission Board, Archives. Richmond, Va.

Rong Mengyuan. "Yan Luo he Yuli" (King Yan Luo and the Jade Record). In *Taiping Tianguo xuekan* 1 (1983): 189–200.

Rubinstein, Murray. *The Origins of the Anglo-American Missionary Enterprise in China: The Canton Years, 1807–1840.* Forthcoming from American Theological Library Association.

Sanzijing (The Taiping three-character classic). 1852. In *Taiping Tianguo yinshu,* vol. 4, item 2.

Schipper, Kristofer. *The Taoist Body,* trans. Karen Duval. Berkeley, Calif., 1993.

Schlyter, Herman. *Der China-missionar Karl Gutzlaff und seine Heimatbasis.* Lund, 1976.

———. *Karl Gutzlaff als Missionar in China.* Lund, 1946.

Scott, Beresford. *An Account of the Destruction of the Fleets of the Celebrated Pirate Chieftains Chui-Apoo and Shap-Ng-tsai.* . . . Gillingham, Kent, 1851.

Seidel, Anna. "The Image of the Perfect Ruler in Early Taoist Messianism: Lao-tzu and Li Hung." *History of Religions* 9 (1969–70): 216–47.

Shen Fu. *Six Records of a Floating Life,* trans. Leonard Pratt and Chiang Su-hui. London, 1983.

Shi Shi. "Taiping Tianguo de zaozi yu gaizi" (Newly formed characters and altered characters in the Taiping). In *Taiping Tianguo xuekan* 4 (1987): 148–64.

Shih, Vincent C. Y. *The Taiping Ideology: Its Sources, Interpretations, and Influences.* Seattle, 1967.

Shilu: Daqing lichao shilu, Daoguang (Veritable records of the Qing dynasty, Daoguang reign, 1820–1850). Reprint, Taipei, n.d.

Shuck, Jehu Lewis. "Sketch of Yuhwang Shangte, One of the Highest Deities of the Chinese Mythology." *Chinese Repository* 10 (1841): 305–9.

Smalley, William A. *Translation as Mission: Bible Translation in the Modern Missionary Movement.* Macon, Ga., 1991.

Smith, Richard J. "Divination in Ch'ing Dynasty China." In Richard Smith and D. W. Y. Kwok, eds. *Cosmology, Ontology, and Human Efficacy: Essays in Chinese Thought.* Honolulu, 1993, 141–78.

———. *Mercenaries and Mandarins: The Ever-Victorious Army of Nineteenth Century China.* Millwood, N.Y., 1978.

Southern Baptist Foreign Mission Board (SBFMB), Archives. Richmond, Va.

Spector, Stanley. *Li Hung-chang and the Huai Army: A Study in Nineteenth Century Chinese Regionalism.* Seattle, 1964.

Spiro, Audrey. "Paintings of the Heavenly Kingdom: Rebellion and Its Conservative Art." Unpublished paper, 1992.

Stevens, Edwin. "A Brief Sketch of the Life and Labors of the Late Rev. William Milne, D.D." *Chinese Repository* 1 (1832): 316–25.

———. "Expedition to the Bohea (Wooe) Hills." *Chinese Repository* 4 (1835): 82–96.

———. "Obituary Notice of the Reverend Robert Morrison, D.D., with a Brief View of His Life and Labors." *Chinese Repository* 3 (1834): 177–84.

———. "Promulgation of the Gospel in China." *Chinese Repository* 3 (1835): 428–38.

———. "Seamen in the Port of Canton." *Chinese Repository* 2 (1834): 422–25.

———. "Voyage of the Huron." *Chinese Repository* 4 (1835): 308–35.

Stifler, Susan Reed. "The Language Students of the East India Company's Canton Factory." *Journal of the North China Branch of the Royal Asiatic Society* 69 (1938): 46–82.

Su Kaihua. " 'Xiaotiantang' xinjie" (A new discussion of the term "Xiaotiantang" [Earthly Paradise, Lesser Heaven]). In *Taiping Tianguo xuekan* 4 (1987): 290–94.

Taiping jiushi ge (Song of the Taiping's world salvation), attr. to Yang Xiuqing. 1853. In *Taiping Tianguo yinshu,* vol. 4, item 3.

Taiping junmu (Table of Taiping military organization). In *Taiping Tianguo yinshu,* vol. 2, item 4.

Taiping lizhi (Taiping ceremonial regulations, first rendition). 1851–1852. In *Taiping Tianguo yinshu,* vol. 15, item 3.

Taiping Tianguo geming shiqi Guangxi nongmin qiyi ziliao (Historical materials on peasant risings in Guangxi during the Taiping revolution). 2 vols. Beijing, 1978.

Taiping Tianguo shige qiantan (Taiping popular songs). Compiled by the Tianjin Municipality Historical Institute. Beijing, 1978.

Taiping Tianguo wenxian shiliao ji (Collected source materials on the Taiping). Compiled by the Chinese Academy of Social Sciences. Beijing, 1982.

Taiping Tianguo yinshu (Facsimile reproductions of Taiping texts). Compiled by the Taiping Historical Museum. 20 vols. Nanjing, 1961.

Taiping Tianguo yishu (The Arts of the Taiping). Nanjing, 1959.

Taiping tianri (Narrative of the Taiping earliest years). Compiled in 1848. In *Taiping Tianguo yinshu,* vol. 1, item 3.

Taiping tiaogui (Taiping army regulations). 1852. In *Taiping Tianguo yinshu,* vol. 2, item 3.

Taiping zhaoshu (The Taiping proclamation). ?1844–46. In *Taiping Tianguo yinshu,* vol. 1, item 1.

Taylor, Charles. *Five Years in China, with Some Account of the Great Rebellion.* Nashville, Tenn., 1860.

Teng Ssu-yü. *Historiography of the Taiping Rebellion.* Cambridge, Mass., 1962.

———. "Hung Jen-kan, Prime Minister of the Taiping Kingdom and His Modernization Plans." *United College Journal* (Hong Kong), 8 (1970–71): 87–95.

———. *New Light on the History of the Taiping Rebellion.* Cambridge, Mass., 1950.

Teng Yuan Chung. "Reverend Issachar Jacox Roberts and the Taiping Rebellion." *Journal of Asian Studies* 23, no. 1 (1963): 55–67.

Ter Haar, Barend J. "Messianism and the Heaven and Earth Society: Approaches to Heaven and Earth Society Texts." In Ownby and Heidhues, eds., *"Secret Societies" Reconsidered,* 153–76.

———. *The White Lotus Teachings in Chinese Religious History.* Leiden, 1992.

Tianchao tianmou zhidu (The land system of the Heavenly Dynasty). 1853. In *Taiping Tianguo yinshu,* vol. 9, item 3.

Tianfu shengzhi (Sacred declarations of the Heavenly Father). 1 juan. ?1860–61. Bound together with two juan of *Tianxiong shengzhi,* British Library, Oriental Collection, #15293.e.29.

Tianfu shi (Poems by the Heavenly Father). 1857. In *Taiping Tianguo yinshu,* vol. 14.

Tianfu xiafan zhaoshu (Declarations made during the Heavenly Father's descents to earth). No. 1, 1852, in *Taiping Tianguo yinshu,* vol. 3, item 1; no. 2, 1853–54, ibid., vol. 11, item 1.

Tianli yaolun (Basic discussion of the heavenly principles). Original by W. H. Medhurst, Batavia, 1834, modified and reprinted as a Taiping text, 1854. In *Taiping Tianguo yinshu,* vol. 12, item 1.

Tianlu licheng (The Pilgrim's Progress, by John Bunyan). Trans. William Burns. Editions of 1853 (Amoy), 1855 (Hong Kong), 1856 (Shanghai).

Tianming zhaozhi shu (Book of heavenly decrees and proclamations). ?1852. In *Taiping Tianguo yinshu,* vol. 3, item 3.

Tianqing daoli shu (Book on the true principles of the heavenly nature). 1854, rev. 1858. In *Taiping Tianguo yinshu,* vol. 12, item 2.

Tiantiao shu (Book of heavenly commandments). ?1847. In *Taiping Tianguo yinshu,* vol. 1, item 2.

Tianxiong shengzhi (Sacred declarations of the Heavenly Elder Brother). 2 juan, ?1860–61, bound together with *Tianfu shengzhi.* British Library, Oriental Collection, #15293.e.29.

Tong Te-kong. *United States Diplomacy in China, 1844–1860.* Seattle, 1964.

TR: See Michael, Franz. *Taiping Rebellion.*

Van Beek, Walter E. A., ed. *The Quest for Purity: Dynamics of Puritan Movements.* Berlin, 1988.

Wagner, Rudolf G. "God's Country in the Family of Nations: The Logic of Modernism in the Taiping Doctrine of International Relations." In Bak and Benecke, eds., *Religion and Rural Revolt,* 354–72.

———. "Imperial Dreams in China." In Brown, ed., *Psycho-Sinology,* 11–24.

———. "Operating in the Chinese Public Sphere: Theology and Technique of Taiping Propaganda." In Huang and Zürcher, eds., *Norms and the State in China,* 104–38.

———. *Reenacting the Heavenly Vision: The Role of Religion in the Taiping Rebellion.* Berkeley, Calif., 1982.

Wakeman, Frederic, Jr. *Strangers at the Gate: Social Disorder in South China, 1839–1861.* Berkeley, Calif., 1966.

Walrond, Theodore, ed. *Letters and Journals of James, Eighth Earl of Elgin.* London, 1873.

Wang Ermin. "Yiba wusi nian Shanghai 'Nicheng zhi zhan' yuan tu" [An original map from the Shanghai 'Battle of Muddy Flat' in 1854). *Bulletin of the Institute of Modern History, Academia Sinica, Taiwan* 14 (1985): 371–75.

Wang Qingcheng. "Guanyu Hong Xiuquan zupu" (On the genealogy of Hong Xiuquan). In Wang Qingcheng, *Taiping Tianguo de lishi he sixiang,* 487–99.

———. "Guanyu 'zhizhun banxing zhaoshu zongmu' he Taiping Tianguo yinshu zhu wenti" (On the official index of authorized books and other questions concerning Taiping printed books). In *Taiping Tianguo xuekan* 5 (1987): 178–23.

———. "Jintian qiyi de zhunbei, shishi he riqi zhu wenti shishuo" (Preparing for the Jintian uprising: an examination of the data and the date). In *Taiping Tianguo xuekan* 1 (1983): 41–88.

———. "Renzi ernian Taiping jun jingong Changsha zhi yi" (The Taiping army's attack on Changsha in 1852). In Wang Qingcheng, *Taiping Tianguo de lishi he sixiang,* 164–92.

———. *Taiping Tianguo de lishi he sixiang* (History and thought of the Taiping). Beijing, 1985.

———. *Taiping Tianguo de wenxian he lishi* (The sources and history of the Taiping). Beijing, 1993.

———. *Tianfu Tianxiong shengzhi (The sacred declarations of the Heavenly Father and Elder Brother). Liaoning, 1986.*

Watson, Burton, ed. and trans. *Meng Ch'iu, Famous Episodes from Chinese History and Legend.* Tokyo and New York, 1979.

Welch, Holmes, and Anna Seidel, eds. *Facets of Taoism: Essays in Chinese Religion.* New Haven, Conn., 1979.

Weller, Robert P. *Resistance, Chaos and Control in China: Taiping Rebels, Taiwanese Ghosts and Tiananmen.* Seattle, 1994.

Welsh, Frank. *A Borrowed Place: The History of Hong Kong.* New York, 1993.

Wieger, Léon. *Moral Tenets and Customs in China,* trans. L. Davrout. Ho-kien-fu, 1913.

———, trans. *Yu Li Ch'ao Ch'uan: The Precious Regulations.* In Wieger, *Moral Tenets,* 332–402.

Wilhelm, Richard, trans. *The I Ching or Book of Changes.* Translated into English by Cary Baynes. Princeton, N.J., 1967.

Williams, Samuel Wells. Correspondence. In Williams Family Papers. Yale University, Sterling Memorial Library, Manuscripts and Archives. MS no. 547.

Wills, John E. Jr. *Mountain of Fame: Portraits in Chinese History.* Princeton, N.J., 1994.

Wilson, Thomas A. *Genealogy of the Way: The Construction and Uses of the Confucian Tradition in Late Imperial China.* Stanford, Calif., 1995.

Withers, John L. II. "The Heavenly Capital: Nanjing under the Taiping, 1853–1864." Ph.D. diss., Yale University, 1983.

Wolseley, G. J. *Narrative of the War with China in 1860.* London, 1862.

Wong, Isabel K. F. "*Geming Gequ:* Songs for the Education of the Masses." In Bonnie S. McDougall, ed., *Popular Chinese Literature and Performing Arts in the People's Republic of China, 1949–1979.* Berkeley, Calif., 1984.

Wong, J. Y. *Anglo-Chinese Relations, 1839–1860: A Calendar of Chinese Documents in the British Foreign Office Records.* Oxford, 1983.

———. "Deadly Dreams; Opium, Imperialism and the 'Arrow' War (1856–60) in China." Unpublished MS.

Woodhouse, A. S. P. *Puritanism and Liberty.* London, 1961.

Wright, Mary Clabaugh. *The Last Stand of Chinese Conservatism: The T'ung-chih Restoration, 1862–1874.* Stanford, Calif., 1957.

Wu Liangzuo. "Luelun Taiping Tianguo bihui de yanjiu he liyong" (A summary of the research and usage of the Taiping's taboo characters). In *Taiping Tianguo xuekan* 5 (1987): 248–74.

Wu Liangzuo and Luo Wenqi. "Taiping Tianguo yinshu jiaokan ji" (A list of the emendations in the Taiping's printed books). In *Taiping Tianguo xuekan* 3 (1987): 266–300.

Wylie, Alexander. *Memorials of Protestant Missionaries to the Chinese* . . . Shanghae [*sic*], 1867.

Xia Chuntao. "Taiping Tianguo dui 'Shengjing' taidu de yanbian" (The evolution of the Taiping attitudes toward the Bible). *Lishi yanjiu* ((1992), no. 1, pp. 139–54.

———. *Taiping Tianguo zongjiao* (The Taiping religion). Nanjing, 1992.

Xiang Da et al., eds. *Taiping Tianguo ziliao congkan* (Collected historical materials on the Taiping). 8 vols. Shanghai, 1952.

Xiao Yishan. *Taiping Tianguo zhaoyu ji shuhan* (Imperial pronouncements and documents of the Taiping Heavenly Kingdom). Preface signed Peiping 1935. Printed Taipei, 1961.

Xie Jiehe. *Jinling guijia jishilue* (A record of Nanjing during 1853 and 1854). In Xiang Da et al., eds., *Taiping Tianguo ziliao congkan,* 4:649–82.

Xingjun zongyao (General rules for military operations). 1855. In *Taiping Tianguo yinshu,* vol. 13, item 2.

Yap, P. M. "The Mental Illness of Hung Hsiu ch'uan, Leader of the Taiping Rebellion," *Far Eastern Quarterly* 13 (1954): 287–304.

Yapian zhanzheng (The Opium War). Edited by Ji Sihe et al. 6 vols. Shanghai, 1954.

You xue shi (Ode for youth). 1851. In *Taiping Tianguo yinshu,* vol. 2, item 2.

Youzhu zhaoshu (The Young Monarch's proclamation). ?1860. In *Taiping Tianguo yinshu,* vol. 20, item 2.

Yulichao chuan jingshi (Amplified edition of the Jade Record). 1839. Held in the British Library, London.

Yuli zhibaochao (The precious Jade Record). Compiled by Li Wei-shu et al. Beijing, 1890. (See also under Clarke and Wieger.)

Yung Wing. *My Life in China and America.* New York, 1909.

Yuzhi qianzi zhao (Imperially composed one thousand character declaration). 1854. In *Taiping Tianguo yinshu,* vol. 13, item 1.

Zhang Dejian. *Zeqing huizuan* (Report on the Taiping rebels). In Xiang Da et al., eds., *Taiping Tianguo ziliao congkan,* 3:25–348.

Zhang Runan. *Jinling shengnan jilue* (An account of the tribulations in Nanjing). In Xiang Da et al., eds., *Taiping Tianguo ziliao congkan,* 4:683–722.

Zhao Dexing. "Lun Taiping Tianguo de chengshi zhengce" (The urban policies of the Taiping). *Lishi yanjiu* (1993), no. 2, pp. 49–62.

Zhong Wendian. "Taiping jun daqi lianyu yu geyao kouhao" (The banner inscriptions and popular ballads of the Taiping army). In *Taiping Tianguo xuekan* 5 (1987): 244–47.

———. *Taiping jun zai Yongan* (The Taiping army in Yongan). Beijing, 1962.

———. "Youguan Taiping jun Yongan tuweihou jinjun luxian de jige wenti" (Some questions on the line of march taken by the Taiping army after breaking the siege at Yongan). *Lishi dang'an* (1988), no. 3, pp. 95–97.

Zhuang Jianping. "Ling Shiba qiyi ji qi lishi zuoyong" (The Ling Shiba uprising and its historical significance). In *Lishi dang'an* (1993), no. 1, pp. 100–107.

Zizheng xinbian (New treatise on administration). Hong Rengan, 1859. In *Taiping Tianguo yinshu,* vol. 16, item 1.

Zürcher, E[rik]. " 'Prince Moonlight': Messianism and Eschatology in Early Medieval Chinese Buddhism." *T'oung Pao* 68 (1982): 1–59.

———. "Purity in the Taiping Rebellion." In van Beek, ed., *The Quest for Purity,* 201–15.

Index

上、

弟係本偽進埋盟、不折磨家為

可係、夢眠教見新雀散

父子兄弟五情牲牲

吾今世常眠化天軸、信家

若亦福来樣弘